Juvenile Justice
A Guide to Practice and Theory

Third Edition

Juvenile Justice
A Guide to Practice and Theory

Steven M. Cox
Western Illinois University

John J. Conrad
Western Illinois University

Wm. C. Brown Publishers

Book Team

Editor *Edgar J. Laube*
Developmental Editor *Sue Pulvermacher-Alt*
Production Coordinator *Jayne Klein*

WCB **Wm. C. Brown Publishers**

President *G. Franklin Lewis*
Vice President, Publisher *George Wm. Bergquist*
Vice President, Publisher *Thomas E. Doran*
Vice President, Operations and Production *Beverly Kolz*
National Sales Manager *Virginia S. Moffat*
Advertising Manager *Ann M. Knepper*
Managing Editor, Production *Colleen A. Yonda*
Production Editorial Manager *Julie A. Kennedy*
Production Editorial Manager *Ann Fuerste*
Publishing Services Manager *Karen J. Slaght*
Manager of Visuals and Design *Faye M. Schilling*

Cover design by Jeanne Marie Regan

Cover image by COMSTOCK, INC./R. Michael Stuckey

Library of Congress Catalog Card Number: 89–82468

ISBN 0–697–10864–3

Printed in the United States of America by Wm. C. Brown Publishers,
2460 Kerper Boulevard, Dubuque, IA 52001

10 9 8 7 6 5 4 3

Contents

Preface

As both practitioners in the juvenile justice system and instructors in sociology and criminal justice courses, we have become painfully aware of the often-repeated plea, "That's great in theory, but what about in practice?" In addition, we have become convinced that a basic understanding of the interrelationships among philosophy, notions of causation, and procedural requirements is a must, if one is to be a more or less successful practitioner in the juvenile justice network. In this text, we have attempted to integrate juvenile law, so-called theories of causation, and procedural requirements while examining their interrelationships. We have attempted to make our treatment of these issues both relevant and comprehensible to those actively employed in the juvenile justice network, to those who desire to become so employed, and to those whose interest in juvenile justice is more or less academic.

We have attempted to present a comprehensive view of juvenile justice philosophy and procedure in a straightforward way, without utilizing unnecessary social scientific or legal jargon. In addition, we discuss the relationships among theory, philosophy, and procedure so the student may better understand these relationships. As a result, we believe the book will be of value to those already practicing in the juvenile justice system, as well as to students who aspire to learn more about that system.

In order to accomplish these goals, chapter 1 briefly discusses the historical antecedents of our current juvenile justice system, with an emphasis on the relevance of such antecedents to recent developments in the field.

In chapter 2, some of the difficulties in defining and measuring delinquency and the consequences of such difficulties for practitioners are discussed.

Chapter 3 deals with social characteristics of juvenile offenders and the implications of family ties, social class, education, and so forth, for practitioners.

Chapter 4 discusses some of the so-called theories of causation which have been advanced and explains the relationships between these theories and philosophy and procedure in juvenile justice.

In chapter 5, the purpose and scope of juvenile court acts are discussed using comparisons between the Uniform Juvenile Court Act and juvenile codes enacted by a number of states (for example, Iowa, Illinois, California, and New York).

Chapter 6 discusses in considerable detail the procedures required by these statutes and the importance of these procedures to practitioners.

Chapters 7 and 8 deal with different components of the juvenile justice system, from police through probation officers and from prosecutors to juvenile court judges. Assessments are made of the training, competence, and discretionary powers of personnel at each level in the system.

In chapter 9, a variety of agencies that relate functionally to the juvenile justice system are discussed, and material on prevention, treatment, and correction of delinquent activity is presented. Examples of attempts at each are presented along with critiques that relate success or failure to theories of causation and the philosophy of the juvenile justice system.

In chapter 11, violence by and against youth is discussed and some of the myths associated with such violence are explored. Programs aimed at reducing the incidence of violence involving youth are also discussed.

Chapter 12 contains material on street gangs and their involvement with drugs and violence.

The final chapter summarizes briefly the interrelationships among philosophy, procedure, and theory and comments on both the current state of affairs and future trends in juvenile justice.

In the appendices we present the Uniform Juvenile Court Act and some of the landmark cases decided by the United States Supreme Court which have had tremendous impact on our juvenile justice system.

In organizing this text, we have provided the student with an understanding of the historical antecedents and conceptual bases of contemporary juvenile justice. This background information should prepare the student to better understand the current dilemmas in defining and measuring delinquency, the difficulties involved in relying upon official statistics as accurate reflections of delinquent behavior, and the various attempts to explain the origins of delinquency.

Having discussed the development of the system and a number of explanatory schemes, we provide the student with a detailed overview of the processes involved in creating official delinquents. This is accomplished by comparing and contrasting selected juvenile court acts.

Next, we focus on each of the component parts of the juvenile justice system as they are typically encountered by the juvenile. In addition to discussing official procedures employed by the police and the courts that lead to labeling a juvenile "delinquent," we discuss attempts by these agencies and a number of related agencies to prevent official labeling.

In spite of attempts to prevent juveniles from becoming delinquent and efforts to divert youth from the official system, some of these youth are adjudicated delinquent and are officially placed on probation or in detention facilities. Since these are possible outcomes of official proceedings, the advantages and disadvantages of each are discussed in terms of juvenile court philosophy and in terms of theoretical relevance.

Fear of violence by youth and evidence of considerable violence against youth have been important factors in shaping a great deal of legislation in recent years. Evidence relating to both concerns is presented and analyzed here, emphasizing the reality of the latter and the overstatement of the former.

In conclusion, we discuss the current state of juvenile justice and possible future trends.

Although the chapters are organized in what we consider to be a logical order, they may be rearranged to suit the needs of students or instructors.

Throughout the text we have taken a critical approach to the juvenile justice system, pointing out major problem areas. It is our belief that improvement in the system depends upon a better understanding of and greater emphasis on these problem areas.

At the end of each chapter a summary and a number of discussion questions highlight the key issues raised in the chapter. Where appropriate, sample cases illustrate problems frequently encountered in juvenile justice proceedings. Additionally, relevant sample documents arc included so the student can become familiar with these basic documents. A number of selected readings are also included at the end of each chapter for those wishing to pursue the subject matter of the chapter further.

For those who use this text in the classroom, we have prepared an accompanying instructor's manual. This manual includes brief chapter summaries to help prepare lectures or for review purposes. In addition, a number of true-false and multiple-choice items are included that may be of value in test preparation.

Acknowledgments

We wish to express our thanks to a number of individuals who helped make this book possible. For kindling an academic interest in juvenile justice, we would like to express our thanks to Professors John P. Clark, Daniel Glaser, Clarence Kraft, Arthur Kline, and Mr. William H. Clark, Jr.

For making it possible to observe firsthand the inner workings of the juvenile justice system, we would like to thank Judge Daniel Roberts, James Grundel, Courtney Cox, James Frakes, Jerry Friend, William Ellsbury, Robert Heyne, Randy Storm, and O. J. Clark.

For continuing support and substantive comments we wish to thank Professors Giri Raj Gupta, John E. Wade, and Jack Fitzgerald. A special note of thanks goes to Professor Dennis C. Bliss, who provided a great deal of material for and invaluable comments on the chapter on gangs.

Our appreciation to the staff of Wm. C. Brown Publishers for providing us the opportunity to improve upon the second edition of this book.

For any mistakes, inaccuracies, or weaknesses in the book, we would once again like to thank each other.

For understanding and encouragement, thanks to Nalda Fava Conrad. This book is dedicated to our children, Craig and Curt Conrad and Matthew and Melissa Cox.

JJC/SMC

The children now love luxury. They have bad manners, contempt for authority, they show disrespect for adults and love to talk rather than work or exercise. They no longer rise when adults enter the room. They contradict their parents, chatter in front of company, gobble down food at the table, and intimidate their teachers. . . .

Socrates (469-399 B.C.)

1 Introduction

The juvenile justice network in the United States grew out of, and remains embroiled in, controversy. Almost a century after the creation of the first family court in Illinois (1899), the debate continues as to the goals to be pursued and the procedures to be employed within the network, and a considerable gap between theory and practice remains. As Lisa Richette pointed out some time ago, "It seems paradoxical that a nation otherwise obsessed with childrearing techniques should treat so casually the official machinery it set up to deal with children who get into trouble or need protection."[1] Meanwhile, delinquency rates remain high and the various components of the juvenile justice network continue to operate largely independently, with little confidence in, and often little interaction with, each other. Due process for juveniles, protection of society, and rehabilitation of youthful offenders remain elusive goals. Frustration and dissatisfaction among those who work with juveniles in trouble remain the reality. How and why did this state of affairs come to exist? Can the reality and the ideal of the juvenile justice network be made more consistent? A brief look at the history of juvenile justice should help to answer the first question. The answer to the second will require a detailed look at the network as it now operates.

Juvenile Justice Historically

The distinction between youthful and adult offenders is not new. Some four thousand years ago, the Code of Hammurabi (2270 B.C.) discussed runaways and children who disowned their parents.[2] Approximately two thousand years ago, both Roman civil law and later canon

1. Lisa Aversa Richette, *The Throwaway Children* (New York: Dell Publishing Co., 1969), 5.
2. Martin R. Haskell and Lewis Yablonsky, *Juvenile Delinquency,* 2d ed. (Chicago: Rand McNally & Co., 1978), 2.

(church) law made distinctions between juveniles and adults based upon the notion of the "age of responsibility." In the fifth century B.C., codification of Roman law resulted in the "Twelve Tables," which made it clear that children were criminally responsible for violations of law and were to be dealt with by the criminal justice system.[3] Punishment for some offenses, however, was less severe for young people than for adults. Thus, theft of crops by night was a capital offense for adults, but offenders under the age of puberty were to be flogged. Adults caught in the act of theft were subject to flogging and enslavement to the victim, but youths received corporal punishment at the discretion of a magistrate and were required to make restitution.[4]

This approach to the treatment of children held criminally responsible for law violations remained in force throughout Roman history, although in the later stages of the empire the law reflected an increasing recognition of the stages of life. Children came to be classified as *infans, proximus infantiae,* and *proximus pubertati.* In general, *infans* were not held criminally responsible, but those approaching puberty who knew the difference between right and wrong were held accountable. For much of Roman history, *infantia* meant the incapacity to speak, but in the fifth century A.D. this age was fixed at seven years and children under that age were exempt from criminal liability. The legal age of puberty was fixed at fourteen for boys and twelve for girls, and youth above these ages were held criminally liable. For children between the ages of seven and puberty, liability was based upon capacity to understand the difference between right and wrong.[5] These two types of law undoubtedly influenced early Anglo-Saxon common law (law based on custom or usage), which emerged in England during the eleventh and twelfth centuries. For our purposes, the distinctions made between adult and juvenile offenders in England at this time are most significant. Under common law, children under the age of seven were presumed incapable of forming criminal intent and therefore were not subject to criminal sanctions.[6]

3. O. Nyquist, *Juvenile Justice: A Comparative Study with Special Reference to the Swedish Welfare Board and the California Juvenile Court System* (London: Macmillan, 1960).

4. F. J. Ludwig, *Youth and the Law: Handbook on Laws Affecting Youth* (Brooklyn: Foundation Press, 1955).

5. H. I. Jolowicz, *Roman Foundations of Modern Law* (London: Oxford University Press, 1957); and W. W. Buckland, *A Textbook of Roman Law from Augustus to Justinian,* 3d ed., rev. by P. Stein (Cambridge, Eng.: Cambridge University Press, 1963).

6. William Blackstone, *Commentaries on the Laws of England,* 12th ed., vol. 4 (London: Strahan, 1803), 22–24.

Children between seven and fourteen were not subject to criminal sanctions unless it could be demonstrated that they had formed criminal intent, understood the consequences of their actions, and could distinguish right from wrong.[7] Children over fourteen were treated much the same as adults. The question of when and under what circumstances children are capable of forming criminal intent (*mens rea*) remains a point of contention in juvenile justice proceedings today. In order for an adult to commit criminal homicide, for instance, it must be shown not only that the adult took the life of another human being without justification, but that he or she intended to take the life of that individual. One may take the life of another accidentally (without intending to) and such an act is not regarded as criminal homicide. In other words, it takes more than the commission of an illegal act to produce a crime. Intent is also required. At what age is a child capable of understanding the difference between right and wrong, or of comprehending the consequences of his or her acts before they occur? For example, most of us would not regard a four-year-old who pocketed some money found at a neighbor's house as a criminal, since we are confident that the child cannot understand the consequences of this act. But what about an eight- or nine- or twelve-year-old?

During the fifteenth century, chancery or equity courts were created by the king of England. Chancery courts, under the guidance of the king's chancellor, were created to grant relief to needy parties and to consider petitions of those who were in need of special aid or intervention, such as women and children left in need of protection and aid by death, abandonment, or divorce. Through the chancery courts the king exercised the right of *parens patriae* (parent of his country) by enabling these courts to act *in loco parentis* (in the place of parents) to provide necessary services for the benefit of women and children.[8] In other words, the king, as ruler of his country, assumed responsibility for all those under his rule and acted to provide parental care for children who had no parents and to assist women who needed aid due to divorce, desertion, separation, or the death of a husband. Although these courts did not normally deal with youthful offenders, they did deal with dependent or neglected youth as do juvenile courts in the United States today.

---

7. Ibid.
8. Haskell and Yablonsky, *Juvenile Delinquency,* 25–26.

In 1562, Parliament passed the Statute of Artificers, which stated that children of paupers could be involuntarily separated from their parents and apprenticed to others.[9] Similarly, the Poor Law Act of 1601 provided for involuntary separation of children from their impoverished parents, and these children were then placed in bondage to local residents as apprentices.[10] Both statutes were based upon the beliefs that the state has a primary interest in the welfare of children and the right to insure such welfare.

At the same time, a system known as the "City Custom of Apprentices" operated in London. This system was established to settle disputes involving apprentices who were unruly or abused by their masters, in an attempt to punish the appropriate parties. When an apprentice was found to be at fault and required confinement, he or she was segregated from adult offenders. Those in charge of the City Custom of Apprentices attempted to settle disputes in a confidential fashion so the juveniles involved were not subjected to public shame or stigma.[11]

In English common law, which became the law in the American colonies, youthful offenders could receive lenient treatment, but for those over the age of seven it was not guaranteed. Except for apprenticeships, there were no distinct policies or separate facilities for juveniles.

Throughout the 1600s and most of the 1700s, juvenile offenders in England were sent to adult prisons, although they were at times kept separate from adult offenders. The first private, separate institution for youthful offenders in England was established by Robert Young in 1788. The goal of this institution was "to educate and instruct in some useful trade or occupation the children of convicts or such other infant poor as are engaged in a vagrant and criminal course of life."[12]

In the early 1800s, changes in the criminal code that would have allowed English magistrates to hear the cases of youthful offenders without the necessity of a long delay were recommended. In addition, dependent or neglected children were to be appointed legal guardians, who were to aid the children through care and education.[13] These changes

9. Douglas R. Rendleman, "Parens Patriae: From Chancery to the Juvenile Court," in *Juvenile Justice Philosophy,* ed. Frederic L. Faust and Paul J. Brantingham (St. Paul, Minn.: West Publishing Company, 1974), 77.

10. Ibid.

11. Wiley B. Sanders, "Some Early Beginnings of the Children's Court Movement in England," in *Juvenile Justice Philosophy,* 46–47.

12. Ibid., 48.

13. Ibid., 49.

were rejected by the House of Lords due to opposition to the magistrates becoming "judges, juries, and executioners," and due to the suspicion concerning the recommended confidentiality of the proceedings, which would have excluded the public and the press.[14]

Meanwhile in the United States, dissatisfaction with the way young offenders were being handled was increasing. Many juveniles were being imprisoned, but few appeared to benefit from the experience. Others simply appealed to the sympathy of jurors and escaped the consequences of their actions entirely.[15] As a result, several institutions for delinquents were established in the East between 1824 and 1828. These institutions were oriented toward education and treatment rather than punishment.[16] Under the concept of *in loco parentis,* institutional custodians were to act as parental substitutes with far-reaching powers over their charges. For example, the staff of the New York House of Refuge, established in 1824, was able to bind its wards out as apprentices, although the consent of the child involved was required.

> *By the mid-1800s, houses of refuge were enthusiastically declared a great success. Managers even advertised their houses in magazines for youth such as the* Youths Casket *(1851). Managers took great pride in seemingly turning total misfits into productive, hard-working members of society.*[17]

However, these claims of success were not undisputed and by 1850 it was widely recognized that houses of refuge were largely failures when it came to reforming or rehabilitating delinquents. As Simonsen and Gordon indicate: "In 1849, George Matsell, the New York City police chief, publicly warned that the numbers of vicious and vagrant youth were increasing and that something must be done. And done it was. America moved from a time of houses of refuge into a time of preventive agencies and reform schools."[18]

In Illinois, in 1855, the Chicago Reform School Act was passed, followed in 1879 by the establishment of Industrial Schools for dependent youth. These schools were not unanimously approved, as indicated

14. Ibid., 50–51.

15. Robert M. Mennel, "Origins of the Juvenile Court: Changing Perspectives on the Legal Rights of Juvenile Delinquents," *Crime and Delinquency* (January 1972): 70.

16. Ibid., 72–74.

17. Clifford E. Simonsen and Marshall S. Gordon III, *Juvenile Justice in America,* 2d ed. (New York: Macmillan Co., 1982), 23.

18. Ibid., 23.

by the fact that in 1870 the Illinois Supreme Court declared unconstitutional the commitment of a child to the Chicago Reform School and commented on the law in these terms:

> *a restraint upon natural liberty is tyranny and oppression. If without crime, without the conviction for an offense, the children of this State are to be thus confined for the 'good of society', then society had better be reduced to its original elements, and free government acknowledged as a failure.*[19]

In 1888, the provisions of the Illinois Industrial School Act were also found to be unconstitutional, although the courts had previously (1882) ruled that the state had the right, under *parens patriae,* to "divest a child of liberty" by sending him or her to an Industrial School if no other "lawful protector" could be found.[20]

In spite of good intentions the new reform schools, existing in both England and the United States by the 1850s, were not effective in reducing the incidence of delinquency. Despite early enthusiasm among reformers, there was little evidence that rehabilitation was being accomplished. Piscotta's investigation of the effects of the *parens patriae* doctrine in the nineteenth century led him to conclude:

> *It would certainly be an oversimplification and distortion of history to suggest that all reformatory managers were cruel xenophobics whose primary concern was the proselytization of innocent Catholic children, that inmates never benefited from their incarceration, or that reformatories were complete failures in achieving their objectives (whatever those were). However, the available investigations and records of nineteenth century juvenile institutions offer compelling evidence that the state was not a benevolent parent. In short, there was significant disparity between the promise and practice of* parens patriae. *Discipline was seldom 'parental' in nature, inmate workers were exploited under the contract labor system, religious instruction was often disguised proselytization, and the indenture system generally failed to provide inmates with a home in the country. The frequency of escapes, assaults, incendiary incidents, and homosexual relations suggests that the children were not, as Pennsylvania court presumed in 1838, 'separated from the corrupting influence of improper associates.'*[21]

The failures of reform schools increased interest in the legality of the proceedings that allowed youths to be placed in such institutions. Court decisions in the last half of the nineteenth century conflicted over the legality of failure to provide due process for youthful offenders. Some

19. *People ex rel. O'Connell* v. *Turner* 55 Ill. 280, 286(1870).

20. *Petition of Ferrier* 103 Ill. 367, 371(1882).

21. Alexander W. Piscotta, "Saving the Children: The Promise and Practice of Parens Patriae, 1838–98," *Crime and Delinquency* 28, no. 3 (July 1982): 424–25.

indicated that due process was required before incarceration (imprisonment) could occur and others argued that due process was unnecessary, since the intent of the proceedings was not punishment but treatment.[22]

One of the outcomes of the *Zeitgeist* (spirit of the times) of the nineteenth century was the development of the first juvenile court in the United States. During the 1870s, several states had passed laws providing for separate trials for juveniles, but the first juvenile or "family" court did not appear until 1899, in Cook County, Illinois. "The delinquent child had ceased to be a criminal and had the status of a child in need of care, protection, and discipline directed toward rehabilitation."[23] By incorporating the doctrine of *parens patriae,* the juvenile court was to act in the best interests of children through the use of noncriminal proceedings. The basic philosophy contained in the first juvenile court act reinforced the right of the state to act *in loco parentis* in cases involving children who have violated the law or are neglected, dependent, or otherwise in need of supervision or intervention. By 1945, all states had passed legislation creating separate juvenile courts.

The period between 1899 and 1967 has been referred to as the era of "socialized juvenile justice" in the United States.[24] Emphasis upon the legal rights of the juvenile declined and emphasis on determining how and why the juvenile came to the attention of authorities and how best to treat and rehabilitate the juvenile became primary. Prevention and removal of the juvenile from undesirable social situations were the major concerns of the court. As Faust and Brantingham note:

> The blindfold was, therefore, purposefully removed from the eyes of 'justice' so that the total picture of the child's past experiences and existing circumstances could be judicially perceived and weighed against the projected outcomes of alternative courses of legal intervention.[25]

It seems likely that the developers of the juvenile justice system in this country intended legal intervention to be provided under the rules of civil rather than criminal law. Clearly, they intended legal proceedings to be as informal as possible, since only through suspending the prohibition against hearsay and relying upon the preponderance of evidence

---

22. Mennel, "Origins of the Juvenile Court," 74–78.

23. Ruth Shonle Cavan, *Juvenile Delinquency: Development, Treatment, Control,* 2d ed. (Philadelphia: J. B. Lippincott Co., 1969), 362.

24. Frederic L. Faust and Paul J. Brantingham, "The Era of the 'Socialized Juvenile Court'—1899 to 1967," in *Juvenile Justice Philosophy,* 145.

25. Ibid.

could the "total picture" of the juvenile be developed. The juvenile court moved farther and farther from the ideas of legality, correction, and punishment towards the ideas of prevention, treatment, and rehabilitation. This movement was, however, not unopposed. There were those who felt that the notion of informality was greatly abused and that any semblance of legality had been lost. The trial-and-error methods often employed during this era made guinea pigs out of juveniles who were placed in rehabilitation programs, which were often based upon inadequately tested sociological and psychological theories.[26] Nonetheless, in 1955, the United States Supreme Court reaffirmed the desirability of the informal procedures employed in juvenile courts. In deciding not to hear the *Holmes* case, the Court stated that since juvenile courts are not criminal courts, the constitutional rights guaranteed to accused adults do not apply to juveniles.[27]

However, twelve years later, forces opposing the extreme informality and license of the juvenile court won a major victory when the Supreme Court handed down a decision in the case of Gerald Gault, a juvenile from Arizona. The extreme license taken by members of the juvenile justice system became abundantly clear in the *Gault* case. Neither Gault nor his parents were notified properly of the charges against him. They were not made aware of their right to counsel, of their right to confront and cross-examine witnesses, of their right to remain silent, of their right to a transcript of the proceedings, or of their right to appeal.[28] The Supreme Court decision in this case left little doubt that juvenile offenders are as entitled to the protection of constitutional guarantees as their adult counterparts, with the exception of participation in a public jury trial. The free reign of "socialized juvenile justice" had come to an end, at least in theory.

Three important points need to be made concerning the juvenile justice system. First, all of the issues that led to the debates over juvenile justice had been evident by the 1850s. The issue of protection and treatment rather than punishment had been clearly raised under the fifteenth-century chancery court system in England. The issues of criminal responsibility and separate facilities for youthful offenders were apparent in the City Custom of Apprentices in seventeenth-century England and again in the development of reform schools in England and the United

26. Ibid., 149.

27. In re *Holmes,* 379 Pa. 599, 109 A. 2d 523 (1954), *cert. denied,* 348 U.S. 973, 75 S. Ct. 535 (1955).

28. In re *Gault,* 387 U.S. 1, 49–50, 87 S. Ct. 1428, 1455 (1967).

States in the nineteenth century. Second, attempts were made to develop and reform the juvenile justice system along with other changes that occurred in the eighteenth and nineteenth centuries. Treatment of the mentally ill underwent humanitarian reforms as the result of efforts by Phillipe Pinel in France and Dorothea Dix in the United States. Campaigns for the rights of women and blacks were becoming common in the United States. The Poor Law Amendment Act had been passed in England in 1834, providing relief and medical services for the poor and needy. Later in the same century, Jane Addams sought reform for the poor in the United States. Thus, the latter part of the eighteenth and all of the nineteenth century may be viewed as a period of transition toward humanitarianism in many areas of social life, including the reform of the juvenile justice system. Third, the bases for most of the accepted attempts at explaining causes of delinquency and treating delinquents had been apparent by the end of the nineteenth century. We will discuss these attempts at explanation and treatment in later chapters. At this point it is important to note that those concerned with juvenile offenders had clearly indicated the potentially harmful effects of public exposure and were aware that association with adult offenders in prisons and jails could lead juveniles to careers in crime.

A Continuing Dilemma in Juvenile Justice

The *Gault* decision obviated the existence of two major, more or less competing, groups of juvenile justice practitioners and scholars. One group favors the informal, unofficial, treatment-oriented approach, referred to as a "casework" or "therapeutic" approach; whereas the other group favors a more formal, more official, more constitutional approach, referred to as a "legalistic" or "formalistic" approach. The *Gault* decision made it clear that the legalists were on firm ground, but it did not deny the legitimacy of the casework approach. Rather, it indicated that the casework approach may be employed, but only within a constitutional framework.

The issues, over which these two groups are divided, are very much alive today. Caseworkers continue to argue that more formal proceedings result in greater stigmatization of juveniles, possibly resulting in more negative self-concepts and eventually careers as adult offenders. Legalists contend that if formal procedures are not followed, innocent juveniles may be found delinquent, and that ensuring constitutional rights does not necessarily result in greater stigmatization, even if the juvenile is found to be delinquent. Edwin Lemert describes this dispute in the following terms:

> In historical retrospect the juvenile court has the look of an agency of social control directed to raising and maintaining standards of child care, protection, and family morals, a purpose currently reinforced by its close association with social welfare organizations. At the same time the juvenile court by virtue of its inescapable identity as a court of law is an agency of law enforcement seeking to reduce and prevent crime, but also protecting legal rights.[29]

Implications for Practitioners

There are a number of practical implications in the legalist-caseworker dispute for practitioners in the juvenile justice system. Many of these implications will be discussed in later chapters, but a few should be noted here. First, the existence of the dispute insures that practitioners who deal with juveniles will have a difficult time with legalists if they operate in a highly informal fashion and with caseworkers if they adhere strictly to legalities. Second, juvenile codes in most states are ambiguous as the result of attempts to satisfy both camps simultaneously. Third, since these codes are ambiguous, a wide discrepancy between ideals (theory) and practices (reality) in the juvenile justice system may be expected. Each of these issues will be discussed in greater detail later.

Summary

The belief that juveniles should be dealt with in the justice system in a different way from adults is not new. The belief that the state has both the right and the responsibility to act on behalf of juveniles in trouble was the key element in juvenile justice in twelfth-century England and remains central to the juvenile justice system in the United States today.

29. Edwin M. Lemert, "The Juvenile Court—Quest and Realities," in President's Commission on Law Enforcement and Administration of Justice, *Task Force Report: Juvenile Delinquency and Youth Crime* (Washington, D.C.: U.S. Government Printing Office, 1967), 91–100.

Age of responsibility and the ability to form criminal intent have also been important issues in juvenile justice and the concepts of *parens patriae* and *in loco parentis* remain basic to juvenile justice philosophy. The dispute between legalists and therapists remains unresolved after a century or more of debate and continues to be problematic for practitioners.

Discussion Questions

1. What do the terms *parens patriae, in loco parentis,* and chancery court mean? Why are these terms important to an understanding of the current juvenile justice system?
2. What is one basic dilemma of the juvenile justice system today and what are its implications for practitioners?
3. What were some of the major issues that led reformers to develop a separate system of juvenile justice?

Selected Readings

Binder, A., G. Geis, and B. Dickson. *Juvenile Delinquency: Historical, Cultural, Legal Perspectives.* New York: Macmillan, 1988.

Dunham, H. Warren. "The Juvenile Court: Contradictory Orientations in Processing Offenders." *Law and Contemporary Problems* 23, no. 3 (Summer 1958): 508–27.

Emerson, Robert M. *Judging Delinquents: Context and Process in Juvenile Court.* Chicago: Aldine, 1969.

Hutzler, John L. "Canon to the Left, Canon to the Right: Can the Juvenile Court Survive?" *Today's Delinquent* 1 (1982): 25–38.

Neigher, Alan. "The Gault Decision: Due Process and the Juvenile Courts." *Federal Probation* 31 (December 1967): 8–18.

Piscotta, Alexander W. "Saving the Children: The Promise and Practice of Parens Patriae, 1838–98." *Crime and Delinquency* 28, no. 3 (July 1982): 410–25.

Platt, Anthony. *The Child Savers: The Invention of Delinquency.* Chicago: University of Chicago Press, 1969.

2 Defining and Measuring Delinquency

One of the major problems confronting those interested in learning more about delinquency involves defining the phenomenon. Without a clear definition, accurate measurement is impossible, making development of programs to prevent and control delinquency extremely difficult.

There are two major types of definitions of delinquency. Strict legal definitions hold that only those juveniles who have been officially labeled by the courts are considered delinquent. Behavioral definitions hold that those juveniles whose behavior violates statutes applicable to them are delinquent whether or not they are officially labeled by the courts. Each of these definitions has its own problems and implications for practitioners and leads to a different conclusion about the nature and extent of delinquency.

Legal Definitions of Delinquency

A basic difficulty with legal definitions of delinquency is that they differ from time to time and place to place. An act that is delinquent at one time and in one place may not be delinquent at another time or in another place. For example, associating with "immoral companions" might be a delinquent act in Arkansas, but not in Illinois. Or the law may change in New York so an act is considered delinquent this year, but not next year. Legal definitions are limited in their applicability to a given time and place because of these inconsistencies. For instance, the Illinois Juvenile Court Act of 1899 defined as delinquent any child under the age of sixteen who violated a state law or city or village ordinance. By 1907, the definition of delinquency had changed considerably to include incorrigibility, knowingly associating with vicious or immoral persons, absenting oneself from the home without just cause, patronizing poolrooms, wandering about the streets at night, wandering in railroad yards, and engaging in indecent conduct. The current Juvenile Court Act in Illinois more closely resembles the 1899 version except that the age for delinquency has been changed to seventeen and attempts to violate laws are also covered.

Another major difficulty with legal definitions of delinquency results from the broad scope of behaviors included. Some states include noncriminal acts in their definitions of delinquency. For example, such acts as being "a minor who is beyond the control of his parents," or "who is habitually truant from school," or "who is habitually disobedient, uncontrolled, wayward, incorrigible, indecent or deports himself as to injure or endanger the morals or health of himself or others" are activities included in the legal definition of delinquency in some states. Over the past two decades, most states have eliminated incorrigible juveniles from the delinquent category and included them under the general category of minors requiring intervention, where they are referred to as "status offenders." The behaviors covered by this category would not be criminal if engaged in by adults, but the state maintains the authority to intervene in these behaviors when they are engaged in by juveniles.

In states using a broad definition of delinquency, there is often no standard definition for "habitual," "incorrigible," or "indecent" conduct. As a result, a wide variety of interpretations is possible and the task of interpretation falls upon practitioners at all levels of the juvenile justice system. Another result of these ambiguous definitions has been that juveniles labeled "incorrigible," "beyond control of parents," "neglected," "truant," "runaways," or "in need of supervision" have come before juvenile courts needing attention and guidance, only to be institutionalized as if they had committed a serious crime. Some juvenile offenders clearly pose a threat to society and institutionalization may be a necessity. However, as important as it is to identify those who may need to be isolated from the community, it is even more important to identify those juveniles who should remain in the community. Unfortunately, we sometimes find in juvenile correctional facilities juveniles who have never been charged with a serious offense, but who may well learn to commit such an offense as a result of institutionalization. In one sense, broad interpretations of delinquency may lead us to "create" delinquents from juveniles with problems of other types. There is a trend today toward accepting the recommendation included in the Uniform Juvenile Court Act, which limits the term delinquency to violations of state or federal criminal law, municipal ordinances, or violations of previous lawful juvenile court orders.[1]

Another problem with legal definitions of delinquency is the ambiguity reflected with respect to age. The juvenile court acts of most states say nothing about lower age limits, which makes it theoretically possible for a child of any age to be considered delinquent. However, Sanford Fox indicates that common law still appears to have some force in juvenile courts due to the lack of cases of juveniles being adjudicated delinquent under the age of seven.[2]

Some states have made it clear that there is a minimum age below which the juvenile court will not hold a child accountable for criminal conduct. For example, Massachusetts' law defines a child as one under the age of seventeen and over the age of seven.[3] Likewise, Texas and Colorado define a child as a person at least ten years of age for purposes of criminal-conduct accountability.[4] At one time, some states provided for lower jurisdictional age limits in urban than rural areas, but this statutory scheme was declared unconstitutional.[5] Similarly, some states formerly established different jurisdictional ages for males and females. These statutes, too, have been declared unconstitutional.[6]

If there is any uniformity among the states regarding age limits, it rests only in the establishment of an upper limit. There is, however, considerable diversity about the specific upper limit. The most frequently cited upper limit for delinquency is eighteen (three-fourths of the states and the District of Columbia), but in four states it is as low as sixteen, and in one as high as nineteen.[7]

Much of this ambiguity results from including the categories of dependent, neglected, and minor in need of supervision under juvenile

1. National Conference of Commissioners on Uniform State Laws, *Uniform Juvenile Court Act* (August 1968). A copy of this act is included in appendix A.

2. Sanford J. Fox, *Juvenile Courts in a Nutshell*, 2d ed. (St. Paul, Minn.: West Publishing Company, 1984), 18.

3. *Massachusetts General Laws Annotated,* Ch. 119, Sec. 52, 1969.

4. *Texas Family Code Annotated,* Sec. 51.02(1)(A), 1986; *Colorado Revised Statutes Annotated,* Sec. 19–1–103(3), (9)(a), 1978.

5. *Long* v. *Robinson,* 316 F. Supp. 22 (D. Md. 1970), aff'd 436 F. 2d 1116 (4th Cir. 1971).

6. *Lamb* v. *Brown,* 456 F. 2d 18, 20 (10th Cir. 1972).

7. Samuel M. Davis, *Rights of Juveniles* (New York: Clark Boardman, 1988), app. B.

statutes. As a result, it is difficult to specify a lower age limit since children of any age can obviously be abused, neglected, or dependent, even though they may not be responsible for illegal acts in a criminal sense. Additionally, some states set higher upper limits for abused, neglected, dependent, and in need of supervision juveniles than for delinquents, hoping to provide treatment and care for juveniles who are still minors even though they are no longer subject to findings of delinquency. An example of the confusion resulting from all of these considerations may be taken from the Illinois Juvenile Court Act.[8] This act establishes no lower age limit, establishes the seventeenth birthday as the upper limit at which an adjudication of delinquency may be made, makes it possible to automatically transfer juveniles over the age of fifteen to adult court for certain types of violent offenses, and sets the eighteenth birthday as the upper age limit for findings of abuse, dependency, neglect, or minor requiring authoritative intervention. Adding to this confusion is the distinction made in the Illinois Juvenile Court Act between minors (those under twenty-one years) and adults (those twenty-one years and over). This leads to considerable confusion about the status of an individual over eighteen, but under twenty-one. For example, a nineteen-year-old in Illinois is still a minor (although he or she may vote), but cannot be found delinquent, dependent, neglected, or requiring authoritative intervention. These age ambiguities make any attempt to compare rates of delinquency across jurisdictions difficult.

The final difficulty with legal definitions of delinquency is that they may lead to a totally unrealistic picture of the nature and extent of delinquent behavior in the United States. Since these definitions require a juvenile to be officially adjudicated before he or she is considered a delinquent, they lead us to concentrate on only a small portion of those who actually commit delinquent acts. This means that most juveniles who commit delinquent acts never come to the attention of juvenile court authorities. A strict legal approach is of little value, if we are interested in determining the nature and extent of delinquency that actually occurs and not just that resulting in adjudication. Some legal definitions require only a police arrest record as an indicator of delinquency, instead of a court adjudication. They are generally inadequate to an accurate understanding of delinquent behavior, since only a relatively small proportion of those who commit delinquent acts come to the attention of the police, and only some of those become a part of official arrest statistics.

8. *Illinois Revised Statutes,* ch. 37, art. 2, 702–2 to 702–7, 1988.

Behavioral Definitions of Delinquency

In contrast to legal definitions, behavioral definitions focus on juveniles whose behavior violates statutes pertaining to them, even if that behavior does not lead to an official label. Using a behavioral definition, a juvenile who shoplifts but is not apprehended is considered delinquent, whereas that juvenile would not be considered delinquent using a legal interpretation. If we concentrate on juveniles who are officially labeled delinquent, we get a much different picture of delinquency than if we include all those who are apprehended, or those who violate pertinent statutes regardless of whether they are adjudicated delinquent in court. For example, estimates of the extent of delinquency based on legal definitions are far lower than those based on behavioral definitions. In addition, the nature of delinquency appears different depending upon the definition employed. We might expect, for example, that the more serious the offense committed, the greater the likelihood of official labeling. If this assumption is correct, relying upon official delinquency statistics may lead us to believe that the proportion of serious offenses among delinquents is much higher than it actually is (using the behavioral definition). Finally, relying only on statistics resulting from arrests or adjudications may lead us to overestimate the proportion of males, blacks, lower social class members, and so forth, actually involved in delinquency. The reasons for this overestimation will be discussed later.

In general, we prefer a behavioral definition of delinquency since it provides a more accurate picture of the nature and extent of delinquency in society. It may be applied at different times and across jurisdictions since it is broad enough to encompass the age and behavioral categories of different jurisdictions. In addition, it allows us to view delinquent behavior from a broader perspective, which helps in the development of realistic programs to prevent or control delinquency as well as in attempts to rehabilitate those who have already been labeled.

In spite of its advantages, there is a major problem with the behavioral definition of delinquency. This definition includes many juveniles who do not become part of the official statistics. We have to rely upon questionable methods of assessing the extent and nature of unofficial or "hidden" delinquency.

Official Statistics and Delinquency

Official statistics on delinquency are currently available at the national level in *Crime in the United States,* published annually by the Federal Bureau of Investigation (FBI). Since 1964 these reports have contained information on arrests of persons under eighteen. In addition, since 1974 the reports have included information on police disposition of juvenile offenders taken into custody, and urban, suburban, and rural arrest rates.[9] The FBI claims that the 1988 report covers roughly 96 percent of the total national population with the most complete reporting from urban areas (98 percent) and the least complete reporting from rural areas (90 percent).[10] Although the FBI statistics are the most comprehensive official statistics available at the national level, there are a few sources of error which must be noted.

First, since UCR are based upon reports from law enforcement agencies throughout the nation, errors in reporting made by each separate agency become a part of the national statistics. Errors might include mistakes in calculating percentages and placing offenders in appropriate categories. Statistics reported to the FBI are based upon "offenses cleared by arrest" and therefore say nothing about whether the offender was actually adjudicated delinquent for the offense in question. These statistics become even more questionable due to the considerable disagreement among police officers (even those working in the same department) about what constitutes an arrest of a juvenile (booking, detention, recorded street contact).[11] Assuming that more serious offenses lead to arrest (however arrest is defined) more frequently than less serious, and more typically juvenile, offenses, arrest statistics would show a disproportionate number of serious juvenile offenses. These statistics clearly reflect only an extremely small proportion of all delinquent acts that actually occur. Donald Black and Albert Reiss indicate that in urban areas only about 5 percent of police encounters with juveniles involved alleged felonies.[12] Similarly, Lundman et al. in a 1980 replication of the

9. *Crime in the United States, 1987* (Washington, D.C.: U.S. Government Printing Office, 1988).

10. Ibid., 4.

11. Malcolm W. Klein, Susan L. Rosensweig, and Ronald Bates, "The Ambiguous Juvenile Arrest," *Criminology* 13, no. 1 (May 1975): 78–89.

12. Donald J. Black and Albert J. Reiss, Jr., "Police Control of Juveniles," *American Sociological Review* 35, no. 1 (February 1970): 67.

Black and Reiss study also found a 5 percent felony rate.[13] These authors also conclude that only about 15 percent of all police-juvenile contacts result in arrest, leaving 85 percent of these contacts that cannot become a part of official police statistics.[14]

There are a variety of additional difficulties with UCR data. If one wants to know the number of juveniles arrested for specific serious offenses in a given period of time in specific types of locations, UCR data from the FBI are useful. But, if one wants to know something about the actual extent and distribution of delinquency, or about arrests of juveniles for less serious offenses, information provided by the FBI is of little value.[15]

Data at the national level are also available from the National Center for Juvenile Justice which collects and publishes information on the number of delinquency, neglect, and dependency cases processed by juvenile courts nationwide. In addition, the Office of Juvenile Justice and Delinquency Prevention in the U.S. Department of Justice maintains statistics on juveniles.

There are a variety of official statistics available at local, county, and state levels throughout the United States. For example, most police departments keep statistics on "offenses known to the police" (those offenses reported to or observed by the police) and "offenses cleared by arrest." Of all official statistics, "offenses known to the police" probably provide the most complete picture of the nature and extent of illegal activity, although there is considerable evidence from victim survey research that even these statistics include information on less than 50 percent of the offenses actually committed.[16]

If the report by Phillip Ennis is reasonably accurate, the police are able to arrest a suspect for only about one out of five reported offenses,

13. Richard J. Lundman, Richard E. Sykes, and John P. Clark, "Police Control of Juveniles: A Replication," in *Police Behavior: A Sociological Perspective,* ed. Richard J. Lundman (New York: Oxford Press, 1980), 130–51.

14. Black and Reiss, "Police Control of Juveniles," 68.

15. This criticism should not be misconstrued to indicate deliberate deception by the FBI, since that agency regularly indicates many of these same deficiencies in the annual UCR.

16. See Phillip H. Ennis, "Crime, Victims, and the Police," *Trans-action* 4 (June 1967): 36–44. See also U.S. Department of Justice, *Criminal Victimization Surveys in 13 American Cities,* National Criminal Justice Information and Statistics Service, June 1975.

Table 2.1
Some Sources of Error at Specified Levels
in the Juvenile Justice System

Levels at Which Data May Be Collected		Sources of Error in Official Statistics
Police	1. Offenses known to police	All offenses not detected + All offenses not reported to or recorded by the police
	2. Offenses cleared by arrest	Errors from level 1 + All offenses reported which do not lead to arrest
Prosecutor	3. Offenses leading to prosecution	Errors from levels 1 and 2 + All offenses which result in arrest but which do not lead to prosecution
Juvenile Court	4. Offenses leading to an adjudication of delinquency	Errors from levels 1, 2, 3 + All offenses prosecuted which do not lead to adjudication
Juvenile Detention Facilities	5. Offenses leading to incarceration	Errors from levels 1, 2, 3, 4 + All offenses leading to adjudication but not to incarceration

which means that 80 percent of the offenses reported to the police are not included in statistics based upon "offenses cleared by arrest."[17]

While the victim survey findings currently available do not deal directly with delinquent behavior, there is no reason to believe that the proportion of delinquencies reported to the police and leading to arrest should be higher than that for adults. In fact, given the less serious nature of many acts considered to be delinquent, we might expect that an even smaller proportion of delinquent acts would be included in official statistics.

Official statistics may be collected at a number of levels in the juvenile justice system. However, each level includes possible sources of error. Table 2.1 indicates some sources of error that may affect official statistics collected at various levels in the system. Each official source of statistics has appropriate uses, but generally speaking, the sources of error increase as we move up each level in the system.[18]

17. Ennis, "Crime, Victims, and the Police," 40–42. Victim survey research is, of course, not free of methodological difficulties either. Forgetting and under- and over-reporting must be considered. Also, certain types of offenses were not covered by Ennis's study.

18. For an additional discussion of the sources of error in official statistics see Herbert A. Block and Gilbert Geis, *Man, Crime, and Society* (New York: Random House, Inc., 1970), 124–26.

Finally, there are two additional sources of error that may affect all official statistics. First, in our current juvenile justice system (as in the adult system), there is a strong tendency for those who are least able to afford the luxury of private counsel and middle-class standards of living to be overrepresented throughout all levels of the system.[19] Whether official statistics represent actual differences in the nature and extent of delinquent behavior by social class or whether they reflect an inability of lower social class members to avoid the official labeling process as readily as their middle- and upper-class counterparts is not entirely clear, although there is considerable evidence to support the latter explanation.[20] Second, it is important to remember that agencies collect and publish official statistics for a variety of administrative purposes (for example, justifying more personnel and more money). This does not mean that all or even most agencies deliberately manipulate statistics for their own purposes. All statistics are open to interpretation and may be presented in a variety of ways depending upon the intent of the presenters.[21]

Unofficial or "Hidden" Delinquency

There is considerable evidence that using official statistics to assess the extent and nature of delinquency is like looking at the tip of an iceberg; that is, a substantial proportion of delinquency remains hidden beneath the surface, if we rely totally upon official statistics. While much delinquency occurs that is not reported to or recorded by officials, there is no accurate method of determining just how much delinquency remains hidden. Attempts to assess the extent and nature of unreported delinquent acts have focused largely upon self-reports from juveniles and observation of police-juvenile encounters.

19. Block and Geis, *Man, Crime, and Society,* 154–59. See also Richard Quinney, *The Social Reality of Crime* (Boston: Little, Brown & Co., 1970), 217–22.

20. See F. Ivan Nye, James F. Short, Jr., and Virgil J. Olson, "Socioeconomic Status and Delinquent Behavior," *American Journal of Sociology* 63, no. 4 (January 1959): 381–89. See also Ronald I. Akers, "Socioeconomic Status and Delinquent Behavior: A Retest," *Journal of Research in Crime and Delinquency* 10 (January 1964): 38–46.

21. For a more complete discussion of the uses and misuses of statistics see Jack D. Fitzgerald and Steven M. Cox, *Unraveling Social Science: A Primer on Perspectives, Methods, and Statistics* (Chicago: Rand McNally & Co., 1975), especially pp. 140–53.

Self-Report Studies

Recognizing that official statistics provide a "false dichotomy" between delinquents (those who are officially labeled and often institutionalized) and nondelinquents (those who may commit the same acts but are not labeled), James Short and F. Ivan Nye decided to use self-reports of juveniles to compare the extent and nature of delinquent activity between institutionalized (labeled) delinquents and noninstitutionalized (nonlabeled) juveniles.[22] Self-reports of delinquent behavior were obtained by distributing questionnaires to both labeled and nonlabeled juveniles. These questionnaires allowed respondents to indicate what types of delinquent acts they had committed and the frequency with which such acts had been committed. Short and Nye conclude that delinquency among noninstitutionalized juveniles is extensive and that there is little difference in the extent and nature of delinquent acts committed by noninstitutionalized and institutionalized juveniles. In addition, Short and Nye indicate that official statistics lead us to misbelieve that delinquency is largely a lower social class phenomenon, since few significant differences in the incidence of delinquency exist among upper, middle, and lower social class juveniles. The conclusions reached in similar studies by Austin Porterfield,[23] Harwin Voss,[24] and Ronald Akers[25] generally agree with those of Short and Nye. Based upon self-report studies and victim survey research (conducted with respect to adult crime), it would seem that the majority of delinquent acts committed never become part of official statistics.

Self-report studies are subject to criticism on the basis that juveniles who serve as respondents may under- or over-report their delinquent activities, either as a result of peer recall or deliberate deception. Some researchers have included "trap questions" to detect these deceptions. None had systematically examined the nature of response bias until 1966, when John Clark and Larry Tifft used follow-up interviews and

22. See James F. Short, Jr. and F. Ivan Nye, "Extent of Unrecorded Juvenile Delinquency: Some Tentative Conclusions," *Journal of Criminal Law, Criminology, and Police Science* 49, no. 4 (July–August 1958): 296–302.

23. Austin L. Porterfield, *Youth in Trouble* (Fort Worth, Ind.: Potishman Foundation, 1946).

24. Harwin L. Voss, "Socioeconomic Status and Reported Delinquent Behavior," *Social Problems* 13 (Winter 1966): 314–24.

25. Akers, "Socioeconomic Status and Delinquent Behavior," 38–46.

the polygraph to assess the accuracy of self-report inventories.[26] Clark and Tifft administered a thirty-five item self-report questionnaire to a group of forty-five male college students. These respondents were to report the frequency of each delinquent behavior they had committed since entering high school. At a later date, each respondent was asked to reexamine his questionnaire and correct any mistakes, after having been told that he would be asked to take a polygraph test to determine the accuracy of his responses. Clark and Tifft indicate that all respondents made corrections on their original questionnaires (58 percent at the first opportunity, 42 percent during the polygraph examination). Three-fourths of all changes increased the frequency of admitted deviancy, all respondents under-reported the frequency of their misconduct on at least one item, and 50 percent over-reported on at least one item.[27] With respect to self-reported delinquency, Clark and Tifft conclude that "those items most frequently used on delinquency scales were found to be rather inaccurate."[28]

The use of self-report scales as the only means of determining the nature and extent of delinquency is, at best, risky. To some extent, these scales may be cross-checked with police records and other official and unofficial statistics. However, as Hindelang et al. conclude:

> In historical perspective, it can be seen that students of crime have focused their attention on at least three measures of youthful misconduct: the Uniform Crime Reports index offenses, local police and court data, and self-report offenses. Because these data are all taken to be measures of delinquent behavior, it is easy to assume that they should produce similar findings without further adjustment for obvious differences among them. Close examination reveals that this assumption is unfounded. These measures are rarely available on the same subjects and the overlap in their content is often minimal. Wholesale comparisons of results using these three measures are therefore inappropriate and, in themselves, say little or nothing about the extent of criminal justice system biases or the adequacy of the self-report method.[29]

26. John P. Clark and Larry L. Tifft, "Polygraph and Interview Validation of Self-Reported Deviant Behavior," *American Sociological Review* 31, no. 4 (August 1966): 516–23.

27. Ibid., 520.

28. Ibid., 523.

29. Michael J. Hindelang, Travis Hirschi, and Joseph G. Weis, "Correlates of Delinquency: The Illusion of Discrepancy Between Self-Report and Official Measures," *American Sociological Review* 44 (December 1979): 1012.

Police Observation Studies

Another method for determining the nature and extent of delinquent acts not included in official statistics is observation of police-juvenile encounters. Several of these studies, conducted over the years, indicate that a large number of delinquent acts, even when they were known to the police, did not lead to official action or official statistics. For example, Irving Piliavin and Scott Briar observed police-juvenile encounters in a city of 450,000 over a nine-month period and concluded that over 60 percent of all potentially delinquent juveniles encountered by the police in that city were dealt with unofficially, either by informal reprimand or outright release.[30] Robert Terry, in his study of police-juvenile encounters in a midwestern city of approximately 100,000, found that 8,014 or 89 percent of the 9,023 juvenile offenses studied resulted in release without official action by the police.[31] As previously indicated, Donald Black and Albert Reiss in their study of police in Boston, Chicago, and Washington found that 85 percent of the encounters between police and juveniles in these cities did not lead to arrest and were not generally included in official statistics on delinquency.[32]

Carl Werthman and Irving Piliavin's study of police-juvenile gang encounters in Oakland and San Francisco, without giving specific figures on proportions of official and unofficial cases, indicates that the police often overlook or deal informally with juvenile offenders whom they regard as essentially "good boys."[33] The reasons given by police for dealing informally with juveniles are both numerous and critical to a complete understanding of the juvenile justice system and official statistics. These reasons will be discussed in greater detail in chapter 7. The basic point is that the number of juveniles who commit delinquent acts but do not become a part of official statistics seems to be considerably larger than the number of juveniles who become a part of official statistics. Relying only on official statistics to estimate the actual extent and nature of delinquency can be extremely misleading.

30. Irving Piliavin and Scott Briar, "Police Encounters with Juveniles," *American Journal of Sociology* 70 (September 1964): 206–14.

31. Robert M. Terry, "The Screening of Juvenile Offenders," *Journal of Criminal Law, Criminology, and Police Science* 58, no. 2 (June 1967): 177.

32. Black and Reiss, "Police Control of Juveniles," 68.

33. Carl Werthman and Irving Piliavin, "Gang Members and the Police," in *The Police: Six Sociological Essays,* ed. David J. Bordua (New York: John Wiley & Sons, Inc., 1967), 56–98.

Finally, a more recent study by Morash using self-report survey data indicates:

> that youths of certain racial groups and in ganglike peer groups were more often investigated and arrested than other youths. Evidence of the independent influence of subject's race and ganglikeness of peers was not provided by the multivariate analysis, however. Thus, there is some question about whether race and gang qualities have an independent influence on police actions, or whether they are related to police actions because they are correlated with other explanatory variables. The multivariate analysis did provide evidence that the police are prone to arrest males who break the law with peers and who have delinquent peers. Alternatively, they are prone not to investigate females in all-female groups. These tendencies cannot be attributed to the delinquency of the youths or to correlations with other independent variables. There is, then, a convincing demonstration of regular tendencies of the police to investigate and arrest males who have delinquent peers regardless of these youths' involvement in delinquency.[34]

Implications for Practitioners

Although there is a decided trend toward uniformity in definitions of delinquency in the United States, practitioners must be aware of several problems arising from definitional difficulties. First, and perhaps most important, practitioners should realize that defining a juvenile as a delinquent is often interpreted as meaning a "young criminal." While we do not deny that juveniles who commit certain types of offenses may be properly so labeled, it is important to note that many juveniles who commit acts which are offenses solely because of their age are also likely to be labeled "young criminals." These offenses would not have been defined as criminal if the juveniles had been adults (for example, drinking under age and truancy).

Second, rehabilitation and treatment programs may be doomed to failure if they are based solely on information obtained from officially labeled delinquents. Recognition of the wide variety of motives and behaviors that may lead to the label delinquent is essential if such programs are to be useful.

In short, the label delinquent (and, for that matter, the more recent label of "minor in need of supervision") tells the practitioners very little

34. Merry Morash, "Establishment of a Juvenile Police Record: The Influence of Individual and Peer Group Characteristics," *Criminology* 22, no. 1 (February 1984): 108–9.

about any particular juvenile. Both juveniles and practitioners would benefit far more from emphasizing the particular behaviors that led to the label.

There are several important implications for practitioners resulting from the problems in accurately measuring delinquency. First, there is no doubt that more delinquency occurs than is officially noted, although the exact extent is not accurately measurable. There are, in other words, scores of delinquent acts committed by those who are never labeled delinquent. This is an important point for practitioners. It is easy for those working with official delinquents to divide the world into delinquent and nondelinquent juveniles, to polarize the differences between the two, and to treat juveniles who are officially labeled as if they were somehow abnormal. In fact, the only abnormal characteristic of many of these juveniles is that they were apprehended and labeled. In most other respects, they differ little from their nondelinquent peers. There are reasons to be both optimistic and pessimistic based on this view. If most juveniles engage in activities similar to those causing some to be labeled delinquent, there is reason to believe that no serious underlying pathology exists as a distinguishing characteristic. Since, in most respects, the official delinquent's behavior closely resembles that of "nondelinquent" peers, reintegration or maintenance within the community should be facilitated. Prospects are not encouraging for those who are alarmed by high, rising rates of delinquency and who prefer to believe that delinquency is atypical behavior. Some types of delinquent behavior occur as a "normal" part of adolescence. Activities such as underage drinking, curfew violation, and experimentation with sex and marijuana seem to be widespread among adolescents. Those viewing these behaviors as atypical or abnormal are faced with essentially two options. They can either define the majority of juveniles as delinquent, thereby increasing official delinquency rates, or they can reevaluate the legal codes prohibiting such behaviors, thereby removing these behaviors from the category of delinquent. Clearly, many prefer to ignore the second option by continuing to polarize the "good kids" from the "bad kids."

A final difficulty encountered by practitioners at the levels of juvenile court judge and prevention/corrections/rehabilitation staff is that their image of the typical juvenile delinquent and his or her rehabilitation requirements can easily be misleading. Discussions with numerous practitioners at these levels indicate that many view the lower social class black male as the typical delinquent. Unfortunately, most social scientific research perpetuates this mistaken impression by focusing on the labeled, incarcerated juvenile offender. While such juveniles may be typical official delinquents, there is a wealth of evidence indicating that they are not typical of all delinquents. Prevention programs, dispositional decisions made by juvenile court judges, and assignment to correctional or rehabilitation programs are influenced by this misleading view of delinquency.

Summary

Both legal and behavioral definitions of delinquency present problems. Legal definitions assess more or less accurately numbers and characteristics of juveniles who become officially labeled delinquent. However, use of legal definitions can be misleading with respect to the actual extent and nature of delinquent activity in society. Behavioral definitions assess the extent and nature of such activity more accurately, but raise problems in the area of data collection.

Official delinquency statistics reflect only a small proportion of all delinquent behavior and are subject to errors in compilation and interpretation at each level in the juvenile justice system. The use of self-report techniques and police observation studies helps to better assess the extent of unofficial or "hidden" delinquency, although each of these methods has some weaknesses.

Practitioners, then, must be aware that official statistics reflect only a portion of delinquent acts and that they may be misleading in terms of the delinquents' characteristics. Successful programs in prevention and correction must take into consideration the proportion of delinquents who remain hidden in terms of official statistics.

Discussion Questions

1. What are the two major types of definitions of delinquency? Discuss the advantages and disadvantages of each.
2. What is the national source of official delinquency statistics? Discuss some of the important limitations of these statistics.
3. What is the major value of self-reported delinquency studies? Discuss some of their major weaknesses.

4. Compare and contrast the nature and extent of delinquency as seen through official statistics on the one hand and as seen through self-report/police observational studies on the other.

Selected Readings

Cohen, L. E., and K. C. Land. "Discrepancies between Crime Reports and Crime Surveys." *Criminology* 22, no. 4 (November 1984): 499–530.

Elliot, D. S., and S. S. Ageton. "Reconciling Differences in Estimates of Delinquency." *American Sociological Review* 45 (February 1980): 95–110.

Erikson, M. L., and L. T. Empey. "Court Records, Undetected Delinquency and Decision-Making," *Journal of Criminal Law, Criminology, and Police Science* 54, no. 4 (December 1963), 456–69.

Gold, M. "Undetected Delinquent Behavior." *Journal of Research in Crime and Delinquency* 13, no. 1 (January 1966): 27–46.

Hardt, R. H., and S. Peterson-Hardt. "On Determining the Quality of the Delinquency Self-Report Method." *Journal of Research in Crime and Delinquency* 14 (July 1977): 247–61.

Kleinman, P. H., and I. F. Lukoff. "Official Crime Data: Lag in Recording Time as a Threat to Validity." *Criminology* 19, no. 3 (November 1981): 449–54.

Paternoster, R., and R. Triplett. "Disaggregating Self-Reported Delinquency and its Implications for Theory." *Criminology* 26, no. 4 (November 1988): 591–625.

Williams, J. R., and M. Gold. "From Delinquent Behavior to Official Delinquency." *Social Problems* 20, no. 2 (Fall 1972): 209–29.

3 Characteristics of Juvenile Offenders

In any discussion of the general characteristics of juvenile offenders, we must be aware of possible errors in the data and must be cautious concerning the impression presented. In general, profiles of the juvenile offender are drawn from official files based on police contacts, arrests, or incarceration. Although these profiles may accurately reflect the characteristics of juveniles who will be incarcerated or who have a good chance for an encounter with the justice system, they may not accurately reflect the characteristics of all juveniles who commit offenses. Studies have established that the number of youthful offenders who formally enter the justice system is small in comparison to the total number of violations committed by youth. Hidden offender surveys, in which youths are asked to anonymously indicate the offenses they have committed, have repeatedly indicated that far more offenses are committed than are reported in official agency reports. In addition, even those juveniles who commit offenses resulting in official encounters are infrequently officially processed through the entire system. The determination of who will officially enter the system depends upon many variables that are considered by law enforcement and other juvenile justice personnel. It is important to remember that official profiles of youthful offenders may not actually represent those who commit youthful offenses, but only those who enter the system.

Unfortunately it has been fairly common practice to use official profiles of juveniles as a basis for development of delinquency prevention programs. Based upon the characteristics of known offenders, prevention programs have been initiated that ignore the characteristics of the hidden and/or unofficial delinquent. For example, there is official statistical evidence indicating that the major proportion of delinquents come from lower socioeconomic families and neighborhoods. The correlates of poverty and low social status include substandard housing, poor sanitation, poor medical care, unemployment, and so forth. It has been suggested that if these conditions were altered, delinquency might be reduced. The eradication of physical slums does not, by itself, eliminate or even substantially reduce delinquency rates. (Recall our earlier comments on middle-class delinquency.) In March 1987, Kansas City, Missouri officials dynamited five high-rise public housing buildings that had opened in 1960, because they had become "as blighted and crime-ridden as the slums they replaced."[1] Similarly, in Chicago in 1988 a Mayor's Advisory Council recommended that most, if not all, of the city's 168 public housing high-rise buildings be demolished over the next ten years, citing "rapidly deteriorating housing, [and] crowded concentrations of large, poor, primarily single-parent families who exist under a reign of terror as hostages to street gangs/drug dealers."[2]

In general, the factors causing delinquency seem to be numerous and interwoven in complex ways. Multiple factors must be considered if we are to improve our understanding of delinquency. Unfortunately, simplistic explanations are often appealing and sometimes lead to prevention and rehabilitation efforts which prove to be of very little value.

Most modern criminologists contend that a number of different factors combine to produce delinquency. With this in mind, let us now turn our attention to some of the factors which are viewed as important determinants of delinquent behavior. It must be emphasized once again that most of the information we have concerning these factors is based upon official statistics. For a more accurate portrait of the characteristics of actual juvenile offenders, we must also concentrate on the vast majority of youth who commit delinquent acts but are never officially labeled delinquent.

Social Factors

Family

One of the most important factors influencing delinquent behavior is the family setting. It is within the family that the child internalizes those basic beliefs, values, attitudes, and general patterns of behavior that give direction to subsequent behavior. Since the family is the initial transmitter of the culture (through the socialization process) and greatly

1. "Public Housing Project Destroyed," *Peoria Journal Star,* 1 Mar. 1987, p. 8.
2. "Report Backs Razing High-Rises," *Peoria Journal Star,* 16 July 1988, p. 10.

shapes the personality characteristics of children, considerable emphasis has been given to family structure, functions, and processes in delinquency research. While it is not possible to review all such research here, we will concentrate on several areas that have been the focus of attention.

A great deal of research focuses on the crucial influence of the family in the formation of behavioral patterns and personality. Contemporary theories attach great importance to the parental role in determining the personality characteristics of children. The Gluecks, almost half a century ago, focused attention on the relationship between family and delinquency, a relationship that has remained in the spotlight ever since.

To the young child, home and family are the basic sources of information about life. Thus, many researchers and theorists have focused on the types of values, attitudes, and beliefs maintained and passed on by the family over generations. Interest has focused on the types of behavior and attitudes transmitted to children through the socialization process resulting in a predisposition toward delinquent behavior. For example, research indicates a strong relationship between delinquency and the marital happiness of the childrens' parents.[3] Official delinquency seems to occur disproportionately among juveniles in "unhappy homes" marked by marital discord, lack of family communication, unaffectionate parents, high stress and tensions, and a general lack of parental cohesiveness and solidarity. In unhappy familial environments, it is not unusual to find a lack of vicarious pleasure derived by the parents from their children. Genuine concern and interest is seldom expressed except on an erratic and convenient basis at the whim of the parents. Also typical of this familial climate are inconsistent guidance and discipline marked by laxity and a tendency to use children against the other parent. It is not surprising to find poor self-images, personality problems, and conduct problems in children of such families. If there is any validity to the adage "chip-off-the-old-block," it should not be surprising to find children in unpleasant family circumstances internalizing the types of attitudes, values, beliefs, and modes of behavior demonstrated by their parents.

It seems that in contemporary society, the family "home" has in many cases been replaced by a "house" where a related group of individuals reside, change clothes, and occasionally eat. It is somewhat ironic

3. F. I. Nye, *Family Relationships and Delinquent Behavior* (New York: Wiley, 1958).

that we often continue to focus on broken homes as a major cause of delinquency rather than on nonbroken homes marked by familial disharmony and disorganization. There is no doubt that the stability and continuity of a family may be shaken when the home is broken by the loss of a parent through death, desertion, long separation, or divorce. At a minimum, one-half of the potential socializing and control team is separated from the family. The belief that one-parent families produce more delinquents is supported both by official statistics and numerous studies. Canter, for example, indicates that "youths from broken homes reported significantly more delinquent behavior than youths from intact homes. The general finding of greater male involvement in delinquency was unchanged when the focus was restricted to youths from broken homes. Boys from broken homes reported more delinquent behavior than girls from broken homes."[4] The author concludes, "This finding gives credence to the proposition that broken homes reduce parental supervision, which in turn may increase involvement in delinquency, particularly among males."[5] There is also, however, some evidence that there may be more social organization and cohesion, guidance, and control in happy one-parent families than in two-parent families marked by discord. It may be that the broken family is not as important a determinant of delinquency as the events leading to the broken home. Disruption, disorganization, and tension, which may lead to a broken family or prevail in a family staying intact "for the children's sake," may be more important causative factors of delinquency than the actual breakup.[6]

The American family unit has changed considerably in the last fifty years. Large and extended families, composed of various relatives living close together, at one time provided mutual aid, comfort, and protection. Today, the family is smaller and has relinquished many of its socialization functions to specialized organizations and agencies that exert a great amount of influence in the education, training, care, guidance, and protection of children. This often results in normative conflict for youths who find their attitudes differing from the views and standards of their parents. This situation is further complicated by the fact that the father's employment and outside leisure activities often keep him away from the

4. Rachelle J. Canter, "Family Correlates of Male and Female Delinquency," *Criminology* 20, no. 2 (August 1982): 163.

5. Ibid., 164.

6. See Richard S. Sterne, *Delinquent Conduct and Broken Homes* (New Haven, Conn., College and University Press, 1964) 21; and R. E. Emery, "Interparental Conflict and the Children of Discord and Divorce," *Psychological Bulletin* 92 (1982): 310–30.

home for many hours during the week. In addition, an increasingly large number of mothers are joining the work force. This leaves the care and training of children in the hands of baby-sitters and nurseries. These steps have brought more economic wealth to the family, but they may have made it more difficult for parents to give constructive guidance and protection to their children.

Recently there has been considerable interest in children with working parents who have come to be known as "latchkey" children. This term generally decribes school-age children who return home from school to an empty house. Estimates indicate that there may be as many as fifteen million children left unsupervised after school and that the number will increase as more mothers enter the work force.[7] These youth are often left to fend for themselves before going to school in the morning, after school in the afternoon, and on school holidays when parents are working or otherwise occupied. This has resulted in older (but still rather young) children being required to care for younger siblings during these periods and is also a factor in the increasing number of youth found in video arcades, shopping malls, and other areas without adult supervision at a relatively young age. While the vast majority of latchkey children undoubtedly survive relatively unscathed, some become involved in illegal or marginally legal activity without their parents' knowledge.

There is little doubt that family structure is related to delinquency in a variety of ways. However, relying upon official statistics to assess the extent of that relationship may be misleading. It may be that the police, probation officers, and judges are more likely to deal officially with youth from broken homes than they are to deal officially with youth from more "ideal" family backgrounds. In fact, Fenwick concludes that the decision to drop charges against juveniles depends first upon the seriousness of the offense and the juvenile's prior record, and second upon the youth's family ties. "Youths are likely to be released if they are affiliated with a conventional domestic network."[8] Further, the decision to detain youth pending a hearing depends more upon the youth's degree of affiliation or disaffiliation to the family than any other factor. "Alleged juvenile offenders characterized by relatively severe levels of family disaffiliation, in all likelihood, are detained for an immediate court hearing, independent of other criteria. At this dispositional juncture, legalistic

7. S. Chollar, "Latchkey Kids: Who Are They?" *Psychology Today* 21 (December 1987): 12.

8. C. R. Fenwick, "Juvenile Court Intake Decision Making: The Importance of Family Affiliation," *Journal of Criminal Justice* 10 (1982): 450.

factors (including status offenses) and demographic factors have no relation to the outcome in question."[9] It often appears that the difference between placing juveniles in institutions and allowing them to remain in the family setting depends more upon whether the family is intact than upon the quality of life within the family. Concentrating on the broken family as the major or only cause of delinquency fails to take into account the vast number of juveniles from broken homes who do not become delinquent as well as the vast number of juveniles from intact families who do become delinquent.

Education

In our society, education has become recognized as one of the most important paths to success. As a result, the educational system has an important place in our society and has taken over many functions formerly performed by the family. The total social well-being of youth, including health, recreation, morality, and academic advancement, has become a concern of educators. Some of the lofty objectives espoused by various educational commissions have been summarized by W. E. Schafer and Kenneth Polk.

> *All children and youth must be given those skills, attitudes, and values that will enable them to perform adult activities and meet adult obligations. Public education must ensure the maximum development of general knowledge, intellectual competence, psychological stability, social skills, and social awareness so that each new generation will be enlightened, individually strong, yet socially and civically responsible.*[10]

The child is expected by his or her parents and by society to succeed in life, but the child from a poor family, where cultural values differ from those of white, middle-class America, encounters many difficulties early in school. Studies indicate that students from middle-class family backgrounds are more likely to have internalized the values of competitiveness, politeness, and deferred gratification which are likely to lead to success in the public schools.[11] Braun also found that teachers' expectations were influenced by physical attractiveness, socioeconomic status,

---

9. Ibid.

10. W. E. Schafer and Kenneth Polk, "Delinquency and the Schools," in *Task Force Report: Juvenile Delinquency and Youth Crime,* President's Commission on Law Enforcement and Administration of Justice (Washington, D.C.: U.S. Government Printing Office, 1967), 224.

11. C. Braun, "Teacher Expectations: Sociopsychological Dynamics," *Review of Educational Research* 46 (Spring 1976): 185–213.

race, gender, name, and older siblings. Lower expectations existed for children from lower socioeconomic backgrounds, who belonged to minority groups, and who had elder siblings who had been unsuccessful in school.[12] Alwin and Thornton found that the socioeconomic status of the family was related to academic success both in early childhood and in adolescence.[13] These studies show that although some difficulties may be partially attributable to early experience in the family and neighborhood, others are created by the educational system itself. The label of "low achiever" or "slow learner" may be attached shortly after, and sometimes even before, entering the first grade, based on the performance of other family members who preceded the child in school. Expectation levels for the child may be reduced and teachers may expect little academic success as a result. Identification as a slow learner often sets into motion a series of reactions by the student, his or her peers, and the school itself, which may lead to negative attitudes, frustrations, and eventually to a climate where school becomes a highly unsatisfactory and bitter experience. Kelley found that early labeling in the school setting had a lasting impact on the child's educational career, and that such labeling occurred with respect to children both with very great and very limited academic potential.[14]

According to William Kvaraceus, school may not directly cause delinquency, but it may present conditions that will foster delinquent behavior.[15] When aspirations for success in the educational system are blocked, the student's self-assessment, the value of education, and of the school's role in his or her life may progressively deteriorate.

Hawkins and Listiner indicate that low cognitive ability, poor early academic performance, low attachment to school, low commitment to academic pursuits, and association with delinquent peers appear to contribute to delinquency.[16] Unless the youth is old enough to "drop out"

12. Ibid.

13. D. F. Alwin and A. Thornton, "Family Origins and the Schooling Process: Early versus Late Influence of Parental Characteristics," *American Sociological Review* 49 (December 1984): 784–802.

14. D. H. Kelley, "Labeling and the Consequences of Wearing a Delinquent Label in a School Setting," *Education* 97 (Summer 1977): 371–80.

15. William C. Kvaraceus, *Juvenile Delinquency and the School* (New York: World Book Co., 1945), 135.

16. J. D. Hawkins and D. M. Listiner, "Schooling and Delinquency," in *Handbook on Crime and Delinquency Prevention,* ed. E. Johnson (Westport, Conn.: Greenwood Press, 1987), 179–221.

of this highly frustrating experience, the only recourse may be to seek others within the school who find themselves in the same circumstances.

Thornberry noted that dropping out of school was positively related to delinquency and later crime over both the long and short terms.[17] Although the presence of others who share the frustrating experience of the educational system may be a satisfactory alternative to dropping out of school, the collective alienation may lead to delinquent behavior.

Most theorists agree that negative experiences in school act as powerful forces which help project youth into delinquency. Achievement and self-esteem will be satisfied in the peer group or gang. In many ways the school contributes to delinquency by failing to provide a meaningful curriculum to the lower class youth in terms of future employment opportunities. There is a growing recognition by many youths of the fact that satisfying educational requirements is no guarantee of occupational success. Walter Schafer and Kenneth Polk feel that the role of the school is rarely acknowledged as producing these unfavorable conditions. Instead of recognizing and attacking deficiencies in the learning structure of the schools, educational authorities place the blame on "delinquent youth" and thus further alienate them from school.[18] In summarizing, Schafer and Polk list the following as unfavorable experiences:

> (1) lower-class children enter the formal educational process with a competitive disadvantage due to their social backgrounds, (2) the physical condition and educational climate of a school located in working class areas may not be conducive for the learning process, (3) youths may early be labeled and placed in ability groups where expectations have been reduced, (4) curriculum and recognition of achievement revolve around the "college bound youth" and not the youth who intends to culminate his educational pursuit by graduating from high school.[19]

Martin Haskell and Lewis Yablonsky have expanded the list of unfavorable experiences and discuss how these experiences may lead to delinquency. First, if a child experiences failure at school every day, that child not only learns little, but becomes frustrated and unhappy. Curricula that do not promise a reasonable opportunity for every child to

17. T. Thornberry, M. Moore, and R. L. Christenson, "The Effects of Dropping Out of High School on Subsequent Criminal Behavior," *Criminology* 23, no. 1 (1985): 3–18.

18. Kenneth Polk and Walter Schafer, *Schools and Delinquency* (Englewood Cliffs, N.J.: Prentice-Hall, Inc., 1972), 182–238.

19. Ibid.

experience success in some area may therefore contribute to delinquency. Second, teaching without relating the subject matter to the needs
and aspirations of the student leaves him or her with serious questions
regarding the subject matter's relevancy. Third, for many lower-class
children school is a prison or a "baby-sitting" operation where they "pass
time." They find little or no activity designed to give pleasure or indicate
an interest in their abilities. Fourth, the impersonal school atmosphere,
devoid of close relationships, may contribute toward the youth seeking
relationships in peer groups or gangs outside the educational setting.[20]
In a similar vein, Polk contends that the number of marginal youth is
growing, and agrees that this is so not only because less successful students have unpleasant school experiences, but also because their future
occupational aspirations are severely limited.[21]

In 1981, Zimmerman et al. investigated the relationship between
learning disabilities and delinquency. They conclude that "proportion-
ately more adjudicated delinquent children than public school children
were learning disabled," although self-report data indicated no significant differences in the incidence of delinquent activity. They hypothesize
that "the greater proportion of learning-disabled youth among adjudicated juvenile delinquents may be accounted for by differences in the
way such children are treated within the juvenile justice system, rather
than by differences in their delinquent behavior."[22]

In another study, Smykla and Willis found that 62 percent of the
youth under the jurisdiction of the juvenile court they studied were either
learning disabled or mentally retarded. They conclude:

> The findings of this study are in agreement with previous incidence studies which
> have demonstrated a correlation between juvenile delinquency and mental re-
> tardation. . . . These results also forcefully demonstrate the need for special
> education strategies to be included in any program of delinquency prevention
> and control.[23]

The emptiness that some students feel toward school and education
demands our attention. Rebellion, retreatism, and delinquency may be

20. Hasken and Yablonsky, *Juvenile Delinquency,* 125–67.

21. K. Polk, "The New Marginal Youth," *Crime and Delinquency* 30 (July 1984):
462–80.

22. Joel Zimmerman, William D. Rich, Ingo Keilitz, and Paul K. Broder, "Some Observations on the Link Between Learning Disabilities and Juvenile Delinquency," *Journal
of Criminal Justice* 9 (1981): 1.

23. J. O. Smykla and T. W. Willis, "The Incidence of Learning Disabilities and Mental
Retardation in Youth under the Jurisdiction of the Juvenile Court," *Journal of Criminal Justice* 9, no. 3 (1981): 219–25.

a response to the false promises of education or simply a response to being "turned off" again in an environment where this has too frequently occurred. Without question, curriculum and caliber of instruction need to be relevant for all youth. Beyond these primary educational concerns, the school may currently be the only institution where humanism and concern for the individual are expressed in an otherwise bleak environment.

Social Class

In the 1950s and 1960s, a number of studies emerged focusing upon the relationship between social class and delinquency.[24] These studies indicated that socioeconomic status was a major contributing factor in delinquency. According to further research, the actual relationship between social class and delinquency may be that social class is important in determining if a particular juvenile becomes part of the official statistics, not in determining if a juvenile will actually commit a delinquent act.[25] Studies of self-reported delinquency have shown little or no difference by social class in the actual commission of delinquent acts. Research indicates that middle-class youths are involved in delinquency to a far greater extent than previously suspected. Joseph Scott and Edmund Vaz, for example, conclude that the middle-class delinquent adheres to specific patterns of activities, standards of conduct, and values different from his parents.[26] Young people a generation ago had more in common with their parents, such as attitudes and outlook on life. However, today's middle-class youth are securely entrenched in a youth culture that is often apart from, or in conflict with, the dominant adult culture. Within the youth culture, juveniles are open to the influence of their peers and

24. See Robert K. Merton, *Social Theory and Social Structure* (New York: Free Press, 1955), chapters 4–5; Richard A. Cloward and Lloyd E. Ohlin, *Delinquency and Opportunity: A Theory of Delinquent Gangs* (New York: Free Press, 1960); Albert K. Cohen, *Delinquent Boys: The Culture of the Gang* (New York: Free Press, 1955); and Walter B. Miller, "Lower Class Culture as a Generating Milieu of Gang Delinquency," *Journal of Social Issues* 14 (1958): 5–19.

25. James F. Short, Jr. and F. Ivan Nye, "Extent of Unrecorded Juvenile Delinquency: Some Tentative Conclusions," *Journal of Criminal Law, Criminology, and Police Science* 49, no. 4 (July–August 1956): 326–31; and Robert A. Dentler and Lawrence J. Monroe, "Early Adolescent Theft," *American Sociological Review* 26 (October 1961): 733–43.

26. Joseph W. Scott and Edmund W. Vaz, "A Perspective on Middle-Class Delinquency," *Canadian Journal of Economics and Political Science* 29 (August 1963): 324–35.

generally conform to whatever behavior patterns prevail. Scott and Vaz identify partying, joy riding, drinking, gambling, and various types of sexual behavior as dominant forms of conduct within the middle-class youth culture. By participating in and conforming to the youth culture, status and social success are achieved through peer approval. Scott and Vaz argue that the bulk of middle-class delinquency occurs in the course of customary nondelinquent activities but moves to the realm of delinquency as the result of a need to "be different" or to "start something new." Accessibility to social objects for participating in the youth culture is an important part of delinquent behavior. Social objects, such as cars, latest styles, alcoholic beverages, and drugs, are frequently part of middle-class delinquency. Peer recognition for male middle-class youths may be a reason for senseless acts of destruction of property. Acts of vandalism in which one's "bravery" can be displayed for peer approval are somewhat different from the violent behavior often seen in lower-class youths, who may demonstrate their "bravery" by rolling drunks, muggings, robbery, and other crimes against people.

While evidence indicates that youths from all social classes may become delinquent, the subculture theorists maintain that many delinquents grow up in lower social class slum areas. According to Richard Cloward and Lloyd Ohlin,[27] the type of delinquency exhibited depends in part on the type of slum in which juveniles grow up. The slum that produces professional criminals is characterized by the close-knit lives and activities of the people in the community. Constant exposure to delinquent and criminal processes coupled with an admiration of criminals provides the model and impetus for future delinquency and criminality. Cloward and Ohlin describe this subculture as a "criminal subculture" in which youth are encouraged and supported by well-established conventional and criminal institutions. Going one step further, Walter B. Miller in his study of lower-class and middle-class norms, values, and behavioral expectations, concludes that a delinquent subculture is inherent in lower-class standards and goals.[28] The desirability of the achievement of status through toughness and smartness, as well as the concepts of trouble, excitement, fate, and autonomy, are interpreted differently depending on one's socioeconomic status. Miller concludes that by adhering to lower-class norms, pressure toward delinquency is inevitable and is rewarded and respected in the lower-class value system.

27. Cloward and Ohlin, *Delinquency and Opportunity,* chapter 7.

28. W. B. Miller, "Lower Class Culture as a Generating Milieu of Gang Delinquency," 5–19.

Lawbreaking is not in and of itself a deliberate rejection of middle-class values, but it automatically violates certain moral and legal standards of the middle class. Miller concludes that lower-class youth, who become delinquent, are primarily conforming to traditions and values held by their families, peers, and neighbors.

In summarizing the findings with respect to the relationship between social class and delinquency, Johnson concludes that prior conceptualizations of social class may have been inappropriate, and that a more appropriate distinction for the 1980s is that between the "underclass" and the "earning class." His results suggest, however, that even given this distinction, there is no reason to expect that social class will emerge as a "major correlate of delinquent behavior, no matter how it is measured."[29]

Brown, however, found evidence of a weak but consistent inverse relationship between social class and maltreatment of youth in his survey of high school freshman. In addition, he found that neglect and emotional abuse were positively correlated with all forms of self-reported delinquent behavior, although physical abuse was not found to be correlated positively with any form of delinquency. Brown suggests that "delinquency prevention efforts might be enhanced by focusing on the neglect and emotional abuse of children."[30]

Gangs

The influence of juvenile gangs is so important and has received so much attention in the recent past, that we have devoted a separate chapter (chapter 13) to the subject. In this section we will simply provide a brief overview of gangs.

Although there are a number of theoretical attempts to explain why juveniles engage in antisocial conduct, it is well known that many delinquent acts are committed in the company of others. As a result, much attention has been given to the role of the gang. Research has focused basically upon two areas—the factors that direct or encourage a youth to seek gang membership, and the effects of the gang on the behavior of its membership.

Albert Cohen has concluded that much delinquent behavior stems from attempts by lower-class youth to resolve status problems resulting

29. Richard E. Johnson, "Social Class and Delinquent Behavior," *Criminology* 18, no. 1 (May 1980): 86.

30. Stephen E. Brown, "Social Class, Child Maltreatment, and Delinquent Behavior," *Criminology* 22, no. 2 (May 1984): 259–78.

from trying to live up to middle-class norms encountered in the educational system. Youths who determine they cannot achieve in this system often seek out others like themselves and form what Cohen calls a "delinquent subculture."[31] According to Cohen, it is in the company of these "mutually converted" associates that a great deal of delinquency occurs.

According to Malcolm Klein,[32] there are numerous factors that bring youths into gangs. Sociological and physical factors include place of residence, the school attended, location of parks and "hangouts," age, race, and nationality. Psychological factors include dependency needs, family rejection, impulse control, and so forth. Still other factors are related to the structure and cohesiveness of the gang and peer group pressure. In the early appraisals of gangs, causation was tied to the theories of the slum community and its inherent attributes of "social disorganization." During the 1920s and 1930s, a group of sociologists at the University of Chicago—including Frederick Thrasher, Frank Tannenbaum, Henry McKay, Clifford Shaw, and William Whyte—conducted a number of studies of gangs in Chicago. According to Frederick Thrasher, the gang is an important contributing factor facilitating the commission of crime and delinquency. The organization of the gang, and the protection it affords, makes it a superior instrument for execution of criminal enterprises.[33] According to Thrasher, gangs originate naturally during the adolescent years from spontaneous play groups, which eventually find themselves in conflict with other groups. As a result of this conflict, it becomes mutually beneficial for individuals to band together in a gang to protect their rights and to satisfy needs that their environment and family cannot provide. By middle adolescence, the gang has distinctive characteristics including a name, geographical territory, mode of operation, and usually an ethnic or racial distinction. Thrasher not only analyzed gang behavior and activity, but was also concerned about the effect of the local community on the gang. He found that if the environment is permissive and lacks control, gang activity will be facilitated. If there is a high presence of adult crime, then a form of "hero worshipping" occurs with high status given to the adult criminal. This type of environment is conducive to, and supportive of, gang behavior. From Thrasher's postulate that gang behavior is a mode of adaption to

31. Cohen, *Delinquent Boys,* 84–7.

32. Malcolm W. Klein, *Juvenile Gangs in Context* (Englewood Cliffs, N.J.: Prentice-Hall, Inc., 1967), 2.

33. Frederick Thrasher, *The Gang* (Chicago: University of Chicago Press, 1936), 381.

environmental pressures, studies were done by others from the Chicago school, which had a lasting impact on the sociological image of delinquency in general and the gang in particular.

The Chicago school spurred other studies of gangs that generally supported the earlier images of that school. As indicated earlier, Albert Cohen, in his book *Delinquent Boys,* emphasized that gang youths have a negative value system by middle-class standards. This results in a "status frustration" that is acted out in a "nonutilitarian, negativistic" fashion through the vehicle of the gang.

Clifford Shaw and Henry McKay found that most offenses were committed in association with others in gangs and that most boys were socialized into criminal careers by other offenders in the neighborhood.[34]

Lewis Yablonsky had indicated that the violent gang, at least, is not as well organized and highly structured as some theorists have supposed.[35] In addition, Yablonsky indicated that the police, the public, and the press may help to create and to unify the gang by attributing to the gang numerous acts which the gang did not commit. Strong support for Yablonsky's conclusions was found in David Dawley's book, *A Nation of Lords,* which is an autobiography of sorts about the Vice Lords in Chicago.[36] Over the past decade, however, violent gangs have unquestionably become more organized with gangs like EL RUKN, illustrating that such organization extends even into prisons. Other gangs are also demonstrating the ability to organize mobile units and maintain branch units in scattered cities, largely in response to drug markets.

Interest in the relationship between gangs and delinquency waned in the 1960s and 1970s, but has increased in the 1980s with reports of gang activities among minority groups both in and out of correctional facilities. Chicano gang activity on the West Coast[37] and Chinese gang activity in "Chinatowns" have received media attention recently.[38] Some have suggested that the amount of attention gangs receive is directly related to the ideology of the political party in power, to economic concerns of citizens, and to fear of victimization.[39]

34. Shaw and McKay, *Juvenile Delinquency in Urban Areas,* 316–21.

35. Lewis Yablonsky, *The Violent Gang* (New York: Macmillan Co., 1962).

36. David Dawley, *A Nation of Lords* (New York: Doubleday & Co., Inc., 1973).

37. "Combat at Hollywood and Vine," *Time,* 24 August 1981, 27.

38. D. Joe and N. Robinson, "Chinatown's Immigrant Gangs: The New Warrior Class," *Criminology* 18, no. 3 (November 1980): 337.

39. H. Bookin and R. Horowitz, "The End of the Youth Gang: Fad or Fact," *Criminology* 21, no. 4 (November 1983): 585–602.

Physical Factors

In addition to social factors, a number of physical factors are often employed to characterize juvenile delinquents. The physical factors most commonly discussed are age, sex, and race.

Age

For purposes of discussing official statistics concerning persons under the age of eighteen, we should note that little official action is taken with respect to juveniles under the age of ten. Rather than considering the entire range from birth to age eighteen, we are basically reviewing statistics covering an age range from ten to eighteen years. Keep in mind also our earlier observations concerning the problems inherent in the use of official statistics (chapter 2) as we review the data provided by the FBI. As table 3.1 indicates, in 1987, 29 percent of all arrests for Index crimes (murder/nonnegligent manslaughter, forcible rape, robbery, aggravated assault, burglary, larceny/theft, motor vehicle theft, and arson) involved persons under eighteen years of age (the maximum age for delinquency in a number of states). The first four Index crimes are crimes of violence, and about 15 percent of all offenders arrested in 1987 for committing such crimes were under eighteen years old. The last four Index crimes are crimes against property, and about 33 percent of those arrested for these crimes were under eighteen.

Table 3.1 also includes statistics on less serious offenses. These offenses, however, are very important for our purposes because, as we have noted previously, much juvenile misconduct falls into this category. Note, for example, that 41 percent of those arrested for vandalism in 1987 were under eighteen years of age, 26 percent of those arrested for liquor law violations were in this age group, and 25 percent of those apprehended for buying, receiving, or possessing stolen property were in the same age category.

As illustrated in table 3.2, the total number of persons under the age of eighteen arrested for Index crimes decreased 13 percent in the ten-year period 1978 and 1987, while the number arrested for violent crimes decreased 8 percent. Comparable figures for those age eighteen and over *increased* 37 and 34 percent respectively. Looking at specific violent crimes, we find that forcible rape, for example, increased 20 percent among the under-eighteen group for the ten-year period, while all

Table 3.1
Total Arrests of Persons under 15, 18, 21 and 25 Years of Age, 1987
[10,616 agencies; 1987 estimated population 202,337,000]

Offense charged	Total all ages	Number of persons arrested				Percent of total all ages			
		Under 15	Under 18	Under 21	Under 25	Under 15	Under 18	Under 21	Under 25
TOTAL	10,795,867	557,278	1,781,240	3,263,215	5,138,232	5.2	16.5	30.2	47.6
Murder and nonnegligent manslaughter	16,714	203	1,592	4,163	7,320	1.2	9.5	24.9	43.8
Forcible rape	31,276	1,660	4,909	8,662	14,049	5.3	15.7	27.7	44.9
Robbery	123,306	7,188	27,682	49,704	74,661	5.8	22.4	40.3	60.5
Aggravated assault	301,734	11,284	38,646	72,126	123,972	3.7	12.8	23.9	41.1
Burglary	374,963	47,601	132,152	200,950	260,425	12.7	35.2	53.6	69.5
Larceny-theft	1,256,552	162,255	388,758	567,350	735,776	12.9	30.9	45.2	58.6
Motor vehicle theft	146,753	14,055	58,573	85,736	107,431	9.6	39.9	58.4	73.2
Arson	15,169	3,851	6,139	7,703	9,516	25.4	40.5	50.8	62.7
Violent crime[1]	473,030	20,335	72,829	134,655	220,002	4.3	15.4	28.5	46.5
Property crime[2]	1,793,437	227,763	585,662	861,739	1,113,148	12.7	32.7	48.0	62.1
Crime Index total[3]	2,266,467	248,098	658,491	996,394	1,333,150	10.9	29.1	44.0	58.8
Other assaults	671,938	35,113	97,880	170,537	290,214	5.2	14.6	25.4	43.2
Forgery and counterfeiting	78,817	1,026	7,097	19,337	35,743	1.3	9.0	24.5	45.3
Fraud	280,809	7,995	18,389	42,122	93,449	2.8	6.5	15.0	33.3
Embezzlement	10,639	137	908	2,552	4,607	1.3	8.5	24.0	43.3
Stolen property; buying, receiving, possessing	119,048	7,858	29,850	52,695	73,427	6.6	25.1	44.3	61.7
Vandalism	230,088	45,853	94,949	128,038	160,076	19.9	41.3	55.6	69.6
Weapons; carrying, possessing, etc.	165,650	6,578	25,653	50,770	81,377	4.0	15.5	30.6	49.1
Prostitution and commercialized vice	100,950	188	2,135	13,974	40,892	.2	2.1	13.8	40.5
Sex offenses (except forcible rape and prostitution)	85,627	6,391	13,544	21,241	32,899	7.5	15.8	24.8	38.4
Drug abuse violations	811,078	9,708	76,037	200,264	377,945	1.2	9.4	24.7	46.6
Gambling	22,762	124	840	1,830	3,812	.5	3.7	8.0	16.7
Offenses against family and children	48,002	829	2,567	6,603	14,589	1.7	5.3	13.8	30.4
Driving under the influence	1,410,397	365	19,717	137,825	402,479	(4)	1.4	9.8	28.5
Liquor laws	505,021	9,261	132,459	329,466	390,097	1.8	26.2	65.2	77.2
Drunkenness	700,662	2,231	20,354	76,838	185,264	.3	2.9	11.0	26.4
Disorderly conduct	599,622	24,646	88,497	178,045	300,236	4.1	14.8	29.7	50.1
Vagrancy	32,518	539	2,452	6,379	10,938	1.7	7.5	19.6	33.6
All other offenses (except traffic)	2,430,913	73,278	273,671	611,127	1,087,944	3.0	11.3	25.1	44.8
Suspicion	11,670	814	2,559	3,987	5,903	7.0	21.9	34.2	50.6
Curfew and loitering law violations	77,556	20,827	77,556	77,556	77,556	26.9	100.0	100.0	100.0
Runaways	135,635	55,419	135,635	135,635	135,635	40.9	100.0	100.0	100.0

[1]Violent crimes are offenses of murder, forcible rape, robbery, and aggravated assault.
[2]Property crimes are offenses of burglary, larceny-theft, motor vehicle theft, and arson.
[3]Includes arson.
[4]Less than one-tenth of 1 percent.

Source: *Crime in the United States: 1987.* U.S. Department of Justice, Federal Bureau of Investigation (Washington, D.C.: U.S. Government Printing Office, July 1988), 180.

Table 3.2

Total Arrest Trends, 1978–1987 [7,282 agencies; 1987 estimated population 177,340,000]

Offense charged	Number of persons arrested								
	Total all ages			Under 18 years of age			18 years of age and over		
	1978	1987	Percent change	1978	1987	Percent change	1978	1987	Percent change
TOTAL	7,609,360	9,506,620	+24.9	1,716,122	1,580,534	-7.9	5,893,238	7,926,086	+34.5
Murder and nonnegligent manslaughter	14,456	15,064	+4.2	1,491	1,450	-2.7	12,965	13,614	+5.0
Forcible rape	21,548	27,917	+29.3	3,638	4,365	+20.0	17,946	23,552	+31.2
Robbery	108,239	114,439	+5.7	34,938	26,029	-25.5	73,301	88,410	+20.6
Aggravated assault	195,075	267,829	+37.3	31,439	34,034	+8.3	163,636	233,795	+42.9
Burglary	384,962	330,411	-14.2	198,436	115,772	-41.7	186,526	214,639	+15.1
Larceny-theft	862,001	1,122,037	+30.2	336,536	345,617	+2.7	525,465	776,420	+47.8
Motor vehicle theft	118,102	131,703	+11.5	58,229	52,363	-10.1	59,873	79,340	+32.5
Arson	13,649	13,383	-1.9	6,737	5,336	-20.8	6,912	8,047	+16.4
Violent crime[1]	339,354	425,249	+25.3	71,506	65,878	-7.9	267,848	359,371	+34.2
Property crime[2]	1,378,714	1,597,534	+15.9	599,938	519,088	-13.5	778,776	1,078,446	+38.5
Crime Index total[3]	1,718,068	2,022,783	+17.7	671,444	584,966	-12.9	1,046,624	1,437,817	+37.4
Other assaults	349,545	593,049	+69.7	64,528	87,074	+34.9	285,017	505,975	+77.5
Forgery and counterfeiting	56,347	69,566	+23.5	6,550	6,115	-6.6	49,797	63,451	+27.4
Fraud	181,677	257,662	+41.8	6,852	17,934	+161.7	174,825	239,728	+37.1
Embezzlement	6,210	9,707	+56.3	632	864	+36.7	5,578	8,843	+58.5
Stolen property: buying, receiving, possessing	85,231	106,879	+25.4	28,271	26,800	-5.2	56,960	80,079	+40.6
Vandalism	176,496	200,928	+13.8	100,464	82,849	-17.5	76,032	118,079	+55.3
Weapons; carrying, possessing, etc.	118,954	146,920	+23.5	19,925	23,286	+16.9	99,029	123,634	+24.8
Prostitution and commercialized vice	75,650	94,493	+24.9	1,941	1,934	-.4	73,709	92,559	+25.6
Sex offenses (except forcible rape and prostitution)	51,859	75,494	+45.6	9,953	12,064	+21.2	41,906	63,430	+51.4
Drug abuse violations	477,213	737,094	+54.4	103,569	69,702	-32.7	373,644	667,392	+78.6
Gambling	44,672	21,202	-52.5	3,757	799	-78.7	40,915	20,403	-50.1
Offenses against family and children	41,064	43,058	+4.9	2,038	2,278	+11.8	39,026	40,780	+4.5
Driving under the influence	927,316	1,158,540	+24.9	33,880	15,967	-52.9	893,436	1,142,573	+27.9
Liquor laws	260,263	423,293	+62.6	82,129	110,816	+34.9	178,134	312,477	+75.4
Drunkenness	870,798	603,977	-30.6	54,737	16,840	-69.2	816,061	587,137	-28.1
Disorderly conduct	545,222	545,655	+.1	98,522	81,041	-17.7	446,700	464,614	+4.0
Vagrancy	39,634	30,819	-22.2	5,367	2,079	-61.3	34,267	28,740	-16.1
All other offenses (except traffic)	1,407,935	2,174,723	+54.5	246,357	246,348	[4]	1,161,578	1,928,375	+66.0
Suspicion (not included in totals)	15,584	10,367	-33.5	4,284	1,968	-54.1	11,300	8,399	-25.7
Curfew and loitering law violations	59,365	70,314	+18.4	59,365	70,314	+18.4			
Runaways	115,841	120,464	+4.0	115,841	120,464	+4.0			

[1]Violent crimes are offenses of murder, forcible rape, robbery, and aggravated assault.
[2]Property crimes are offenses of burglary, larceny-theft, motor vehicle theft, and arson.
[3]Includes arson.
[4]Less than one-tenth of 1 percent.

Source: Crime in the United States, 168

violent crimes increased in the eighteen-and-over age group. Among offenses other than Index crimes, fraud (162 percent), assaults (37 percent), weapons-related offenses (17 percent), sex offenses (21 percent), and other assaults (35 percent) increased significantly among those under eighteen.

According to the Uniform Crime Report (1987), juveniles under the age of eighteen accounted for an estimated 26 percent of the 1987 U.S. population. Persons in this age group accounted for 15.4 percent of violent crime clearances and 32.7 percent of property crime clearances. Murder shows the lowest percentage of juvenile involvement (9.5 percent) in violent crime, and arson shows the highest (40.5 percent). With respect to other crimes, juveniles appear to be overrepresented in burglaries (35 percent), larceny-theft (31 percent), and motor vehicle theft (40 percent), especially when we consider the fact that we are actually only dealing with youth between the ages of ten and eighteen.

Gender

Historically, we have observed three to four arrests of juvenile males for every arrest of a juvenile female. In the ten-year period from 1978 through 1987, this ratio remained relatively constant (see table 3.3). Considering the Index crimes, we note that among those under eighteen arrests for violent crimes declined about 10 percent for males but increased 18 percent for females. Total arrests for Index crimes decreased about 20 percent for males and increased about 30 percent for females. Considering all crimes, we note significant increases in the number of females arrested for the following offenses: robbery (26 percent), aggravated assault (21 percent), larceny theft (34 percent), motor vehicle theft (48 percent), and, among less serious crimes, other assaults (85 percent), forgery (116 percent), fraud (255 percent), embezzlement (352 percent), stolen property offenses (63 percent), vandalism (23 percent), liquor law violations (231 percent), and curfew violations (131 percent). Increases among males in the under-eighteen category occurred with respect to forcible rape (22 percent), fraud (140 percent), and sex offenses (30 percent). Although a study by Steffensmeier and Steffensmeier concluded that female delinquency had remained generally stable over the decade between 1970 and 1980 and that patterns of female delinquency, "especially as revealed in nonofficial sources," had changed little in that period, some significant changes have clearly occurred in the 80s.[40]

40. D. J. Steffensmeier and R. H. Steffensmeier, "Trends in Female Delinquency: An Examination of Arrest, Juvenile Court, Self-Report, and Field Data," *Criminology* 18, no. 1 (May 1980): 62–85.

Table 3.3
Total Arrest Trends, Sex, 1978–1987 [7,282 agencies; 1987 estimated population 177,340,000]

	Males						Females					
	Total			Under 18			Total			Under 18		
	1978	1987	Percent change	1978	1987	Percent change	1978	1987	Percent change	1978	1987	Percent change
TOTAL	6,330,912	7,808,892	+23.3	1,423,487	1,225,421	−13.9	1,278,448	1,697,728	+32.8	292,635	355,113	+21.4
Murder and nonnegligent manslaughter	12,253	13,193	+7.7	1,256	1,324	+5.4	2,203	1,871	−15.1	235	126	−46.4
Forcible rape	21,289	27,600	+29.6	3,493	4,276	+22.4	295	317	+7.5	145	89	−38.6
Robbery	100,365	105,236	+4.9	33,509	24,231	−27.7	7,874	9,203	+16.9	1,429	1,798	+25.8
Aggravated assault	168,756	232,170	+37.6	27,124	28,807	+6.2	26,319	35,659	+35.5	4,315	5,227	+21.1
Burglary	360,261	304,364	−15.5	189,683	107,256	−43.5	24,701	26,047	+5.4	8,753	8,516	−2.7
Larceny-theft	586,143	771,428	+31.6	265,505	250,476	−5.7	275,858	350,609	+27.1	71,031	95,141	+33.9
Motor vehicle theft	107,896	119,116	+10.4	54,590	46,968	−14.0	10,206	12,587	+23.3	3,639	5,395	+48.3
Arson	11,985	11,489	−4.1	6,181	4,767	−22.9	1,664	1,894	+13.8	556	569	+2.3
Violent crime[1]	302,663	378,199	+25.0	65,382	58,638	−10.3	36,691	47,050	+28.2	6,124	7,240	+18.2
Property crime[2]	1,066,285	1,206,397	+13.1	515,959	409,467	−20.6	312,429	391,137	+25.2	83,979	109,621	+30.5
Crime Index total[3]	1,368,948	1,584,596	+15.8	581,341	468,105	−19.5	349,120	438,187	+25.5	90,103	116,861	+29.7
Other assaults	299,828	503,138	+67.8	53,778	67,239	+25.0	49,717	89,911	+80.8	10,750	19,835	+84.5
Forgery and counterfeiting	39,070	45,644	+16.8	5,605	4,076	−27.3	17,277	23,922	+38.5	945	2,039	+115.8
Fraud	110,768	146,341	+32.1	5,532	13,264	+139.8	70,909	111,321	+57.0	1,320	4,670	+253.8
Embezzlement	4,615	5,956	+29.1	563	552	−2.0	1,595	3,751	+135.2	69	312	+352.2
Stolen property; buying, receiving, possessing	75,686	94,514	+24.9	26,742	24,305	−9.1	9,545	12,365	+29.5	1,529	2,495	+63.2
Vandalism	161,263	179,518	+11.3	94,509	75,508	−20.1	15,233	21,410	+40.6	5,955	7,341	+23.3
Weapons; carrying, possessing, etc.	108,855	135,647	+24.6	18,270	21,644	+18.5	10,099	11,273	+11.6	1,655	1,642	−.8
Prostitution and commercialized vice	23,937	32,283	+34.9	1,226	611	−50.2	51,713	62,210	+20.3	715	1,323	+85.0
Sex offenses (except forcible rape and prostitution)	46,819	69,289	+48.0	8,641	11,256	+30.3	5,040	6,205	+23.1	1,312	808	−38.4
Drug abuse violations	410,062	627,551	+53.0	95,042	60,663	−36.2	67,151	109,543	+63.1	8,527	9,039	+6.0
Gambling	39,094	18,326	−53.1	1,659	768	−53.7	5,578	2,876	−48.4	2,098	31	−98.5
Offenses against family and children	36,958	35,568	−3.8	1,300	1,393	+7.2	4,106	7,490	+82.4	738	885	+19.9
Driving under the influence	838,026	1,022,697	+22.0	18,971	13,775	−27.4	89,290	135,843	+52.1	14,909	2,192	−85.3
Liquor laws	219,572	347,840	+58.4	73,054	80,785	+10.6	40,691	75,453	+85.4	9,075	30,031	+230.9
Drunkenness	785,852	547,862	−30.3	29,069	14,134	−51.4	84,946	56,115	−33.9	25,668	2,706	−89.5
Disorderly conduct	451,759	442,710	−2.0	84,276	65,674	−22.1	93,463	102,945	+10.1	14,246	15,367	+7.9
Vagrancy	26,215	27,348	+4.3	4,484	1,705	−62.0	13,419	3,471	−74.1	883	374	−57.6
All other offenses (except traffic)	1,172,077	1,837,588	+56.8	207,919	195,488	−6.0	235,856	337,135	+42.9	38,438	50,860	+32.3
Suspicion (not included in totals)	13,432	8,835	−34.2	3,848	1,567	−59.3	2,152	1,532	−28.8	436	401	−8.0
Curfew and loitering law violations	51,844	52,949	+2.1	51,844	52,949	+2.1	7,521	17,365	+130.9	7,521	17,365	+130.9
Runaways	59,664	51,527	−13.6	59,662	51,527	−13.6	56,179	68,937	+22.7	56,179	68,937	+22.7

[1] Violent crimes are offenses of murder, forcible rape, robbery, and aggravated assault.
[2] Property crimes are offenses of burglary, larceny-theft, motor vehicle theft, and arson.
[3] Includes arson.

Source: *Crime in the United States*, 169

Ageton used self-report data to examine the dynamics of female delinquency for the years from 1976 through 1980. She concluded that the

> *incidence and prevalence of serious female delinquency appear to decline with age, and the 15–17-year-old females in 1980 are significantly less involved in delinquency than their same-age peers were in 1976.*

Further,

> *One would conclude from these findings that the incidence of female delinquency generally declines or remains stable as females move through adolescence, while the proportion of youth involved declines significantly over this same period. Furthermore, there is a noticeable cohort effect, which suggests that delinquent behavior is not attracting the number of female participants today as it did in the past.*[41]

Finally, Jensen and Eve, also relying upon self-report data, conclude:

> *At any rate, the overall impact of research on sex and crime lends considerable support to sociological positions on sex differences. The nature of relationships with other people, institutions, and belief systems dwarfs the importance of sex as a variable in the explanation of delinquency and accounts for a goodly proportion of its contribution to delinquency.*[42]

Race

Official statistics on race are subject to a number of errors, as pointed out in chapter 2. Any index of black arrests may be inflated as a result of discriminatory practices among criminal justice personnel. For example, the presence of a black under "suspicious circumstances" may result in an official arrest even though the police officer knows the charges will be dismissed. In addition, many blacks live in lower social class neighborhoods in large urban centers in which the greatest concentration of law enforcement officers exists. Since arrest statistics are more complete for large cities, we must take into account the sizable proportion of blacks found in these cities rather than the 12 percent statistic derived from calculating the proportion of blacks in our society.

Analysis of official arrest statistics of persons under the age of eighteen has traditionally shown a disproportionate number of blacks. Data

41. Suzanne S. Ageton, "The Dynamics of Female Delinquency, 1976–1980," *Criminology* 21, no. 4 (November 1983): 555–84.
42. Gary J. Jensen and Raymond Eve, "Sex Differences in Delinquency: An Examination of Popular Sociological Explanations," *Criminology* 13, no. 4 (February 1976): 427–48.

presented in table 3.4 show that blacks accounted for more than half of the arrests for violent crime in the under-eighteen age category, about one-third of the arrests for Index crimes, and about one-fourth of all arrests of those under eighteen in 1987.

As previously indicated, social-environmental factors have an important impact on delinquency rates, and perhaps especially on official delinquency rates. A disproportionate number of blacks are found in the lower socioeconomic class with all of the correlates conducive to high delinquency. Unless the conditions are changed, each generation caught in this environment not only inherits the same conditions that created high crime and delinquency rates for its parents, but also transmits them to the next generation. It is interesting to note that, according to research, when ethnic or racial groups leave high crime and delinquency areas, they tend to take on the crime rate of the specific part of the community to which they move. It should also be noted that there are differential crime and delinquency rates among black neighborhoods which gives further credibility to the influence of the social-environmental approach to explaining high crime and delinquency rates.

It is unlikely that any single factor can be used to explain the disproportionate number of black juveniles involved in crime. The most plausible explanations currently center on environmental and socioeconomic factors characteristic of ghetto areas. Violence and a belief that planning and thrift are not realistic possibilities may be transmitted across generations. This transmission is cultural, not genetic, and may account in part for high rates of violent crime and gambling (luck as an alternative to planning).

Drugs

Our society is characterized by high rates of drug use and abuse, and it should not be surprising to find such use and abuse among juveniles. At least one-third of high school students have used illicit drugs other than marijuana, and roughly 55 percent have used cannabis. Ninety percent of twelfth graders report having used alcohol, 10 percent report being drunk at least weekly, and over one-third regularly smoke cigarettes (see table 3.5).[43] Addiction to alcohol, tobacco, prescription drugs, and illicit drugs frequently occurs before the age of fourteen.

43. L. D. Johnston, P. M. O'Malley, and J. C. Bachman, *Drug Use Among American High School Students, College Students, and Other Young Adults: National Trends Through 1985,* (Washington, D.C.: U.S. Government Printing Office, 1986). Also see S. P. Schinke and L. D. Gilchrist, *Life Counseling Skills with Adolescents* (Baltimore, Md.: University Park Press, 1984).

Table 3.4
Total Arrests, Distribution by Race, 1987

Offense charged	Arrests under 18					Percent distribution				
	Total	White	Black	American Indian or Alaskan Native	Asian or Pacific Islander	Total	White	Black	American Indian or Alaskan Native	Asian or Pacific Islander
TOTAL	1,774,567	1,279,696	457,593	15,286	21,992	100.0	72.1	25.8	.9	1.2
Murder and nonnegligent manslaughter	1,591	671	880	16	24	100.0	42.2	55.3	1.0	1.5
Forcible rape	4,898	2,076	2,776	20	26	100.0	42.4	56.7	.4	.5
Robbery	27,651	8,503	18,766	103	279	100.0	30.8	67.9	.4	1.0
Aggravated assault	38,417	20,628	17,208	292	289	100.0	53.7	44.8	.8	.8
Burglary	131,822	97,693	31,597	1,134	1,398	100.0	74.1	24.0	.9	1.1
Larceny-theft	388,150	275,340	102,680	3,981	6,149	100.0	70.9	26.5	1.0	1.6
Motor vehicle theft	58,456	34,785	22,175	569	927	100.0	59.5	37.9	1.0	1.6
Arson	6,121	5,037	958	52	74	100.0	82.3	15.7	.8	1.2
Violent crime	72,557	31,878	39,630	431	618	100.0	43.9	54.6	.6	.9
Property crime	584,549	412,855	157,410	5,736	8,548	100.0	70.6	26.9	1.0	1.5
Crime Index total	657,106	444,733	197,040	6,167	9,166	100.0	67.7	30.0	.9	1.4
Other assaults	97,550	58,586	37,011	675	1,278	100.0	60.1	37.9	.7	1.3
Forgery and counterfeiting	7,076	5,698	1,269	46	63	100.0	80.5	17.9	.7	.9
Fraud	18,384	8,973	9,015	51	345	100.0	48.8	49.0	.3	1.9
Embezzlement	906	628	270	2	6	100.0	69.3	29.8	.2	.7
Stolen property: buying, receiving, possessing	29,780	18,032	11,359	160	229	100.0	60.6	38.1	.5	.8
Vandalism	94,706	77,271	15,809	670	956	100.0	81.6	16.7	.7	1.0
Weapons; carrying, possessing, etc.	25,626	16,149	9,029	118	330	100.0	63.0	35.2	.5	1.3
Prostitution and commercialized vice	2,134	1,275	823	24	12	100.0	59.7	38.6	1.1	.6
Sex offenses (except forcible rape and prostitution)	13,520	9,625	3,709	91	95	100.0	71.2	27.4	.7	.7
Drug abuse violations	75,186	48,010	26,213	319	644	100.0	63.9	34.9	.4	.9
Gambling	840	177	608		55	100.0	21.1	72.4		6.5
Offenses against family and children	2,401	1,836	534	17	14	100.0	76.5	22.2	.7	.6
Driving under the influence	19,465	18,600	547	218	100	100.0	95.6	2.8	1.1	.5
Liquor laws	132,000	124,892	4,308	2,155	645	100.0	94.6	3.3	1.6	.5
Drunkenness	20,252	18,625	1,241	330	56	100.0	92.0	6.1	1.6	.3
Disorderly conduct	88,352	60,365	27,137	501	349	100.0	68.3	30.7	.6	.4
Vagrancy	2,441	2,047	347	24	23	100.0	83.9	14.2	1.0	.9
All other offenses (except traffic)	272,408	194,152	72,027	1,655	4,573	100.0	71.3	26.4	.6	1.7
Suspicion	2,557	2,136	395	17	9	100.0	83.5	15.4	.7	.4
Curfew and loitering law violations	77,071	55,493	19,711	766	1,101	100.0	72.0	25.6	1.0	1.4
Runaways	134,806	112,393	19,191	1,279	1,943	100.0	83.4	14.2	.9	1.4

Source: *Crime in the United States*, 183.

Table 3.5
Lifetime Prevalence (by Percent) of Use of Sixteen Types of Drugs by Subgroups, Class of 1985

	Marijuana	Inhalants	Amyl/Butyl Nitrites	Hallucinogens	LSD	PCP	Cocaine	Heroin	Other Opiates	Stimulants (Adjusted)	Sedatives	Barbiturates	Methaqualone	Tranquilizers	Alcohol
All Seniors	54.2	15.4	7.9	10.3	7.5	4.9	17.3	1.2	10.2	26.2	11.8	9.2	6.7	11.9	92.2
Sex:															
Male	56.6	18.5	11.1	12.4	9.4	6.6	19.7	1.4	11.3	24.6	12.3	9.9	7.1	11.7	92.6
Female	51.5	12.4	4.9	8.0	5.6	3.1	14.8	0.8	9.1	27.6	11.0	8.3	6.0	11.7	91.9
College Plans:															
None or under 4 yrs	59.1	16.5	9.2	12.5	9.7	6.8	20.2	1.6	11.5	31.9	15.2	11.9	8.7	13.4	93.0
Complete 4 yrs	50.2	14.5	6.9	8.0	5.6	3.4	14.6	0.9	9.3	22.6	9.6	7.4	5.3	10.8	91.9
Region:															
Northeast	62.2	18.3	10.0	15.7	9.4	7.3	25.9	1.6	12.0	27.6	13.4	10.5	7.9	14.0	95.0
North Central	53.8	14.6	7.5	10.2	8.5	3.1	11.5	1.2	10.4	27.7	12.0	9.6	6.8	11.5	93.5
South	44.5	13.0	6.0	5.8	4.8	3.4	11.1	1.2	7.2	22.1	11.1	8.0	6.7	11.1	89.7
West	60.4	17.0	9.2	10.9	8.2	7.1	25.4	0.8	12.7	29.1	10.9	9.1	4.9	11.2	90.6
Population Density*															
Large SMSA*	59.2	14.9	8.8	13.9	8.1	6.2	24.1	1.4	9.8	25.8	12.3	9.8	7.0	11.9	93.5
Other SMSA*	54.6	15.6	8.7	9.6	8.0	4.3	16.2	1.2	11.0	26.2	12.0	8.9	7.2	11.7	91.4
Non-SMSA*	49.3	15.6	6.1	8.2	6.4	4.5	13.1	1.0	9.5	26.8	11.2	9.3	5.6	12.1	92.0

*Standard Metropolitan Statistical Area

Source: Johnston, O'Malley, and Bachman (1986): 32

As table 3.2 indicates, juveniles accounted for about 16 percent of the arrests for drug abuse violations in 1987 (down 33 percent from 1978), and they accounted for slightly more than one-fourth of the arrests for liquor law violations other than drunkenness in the same year (a decrease of 5 percent from 1978).

There has, of course, been a good deal written about the relationship between illegal drug use and crime. Similarly, there is considerable interest in the relationship between illegal drugs and gangs (we have more to say about this in chapter 13). Possession, sale, manufacture, and distribution of any of a number of illegal drugs are, in themselves, crimes. Purchase and consumption of some legal drugs, such as alcohol or tobacco, by juveniles are also illegal. Juveniles who violate statutes relating to these offenses may be labeled delinquent or status offenders. Equally important, however, are other illegal acts often engaged in by drug users in order to support their drug habits. Such offenses are thought to include theft, burglary, robbery, and prostitution, among others. It also is possible that use of certain drugs, such as cocaine and amphetamines, is related to the commission of violent crimes, though the exact nature of the relationship between drug abuse and crime is controversial. Some maintain that delinquents are more likely to use drugs than nondelinquents—that is, drug use follows rather than precedes delinquency, while others argue the opposite.[44]

Whatever the nature of the relationship between drug abuse and delinquency, the two are intimately intertwined for some delinquents, while for others drug abuse is not a factor. Why some youths become drug abusers while others in similar environments avoid such involvement is the subject of a great deal of research. The single most important determinant of drug abuse appears to be the interpersonal relationships in which the juvenile is involved, particularly interpersonal relationships with peers. Drug abuse is a social phenomenon that occurs in social networks accepting, tolerating, and/or encouraging such behavior. Though the available evidence suggests that peer influence is most important, there is also evidence to indicate that juveniles whose parents are involved in drug abuse are more likely to abuse drugs than juveniles whose parents are uninvolved. Further, behavior of parents and peers appears to be more important in drug abuse than the values and beliefs espoused.[45]

44. W. E. Thornton, L. Voight, and W. G. Doerner, *Delinquency and Justice,* 2d ed. (New York: Random House, 1987).

45. Schinke and Gilchrist, *Life Counseling Skills.*

There is no way of knowing how many juveniles suffering from school, parent, or peer-related depression and/or the general ambiguity surrounding adolescence turn to drugs as a means of escape, but the prevalence of teen suicide, combined with information obtained from self-reports of juveniles, indicate that the numbers are large. While juvenile involvement with drugs may have declined over the past decade, there is little doubt that such involvement remains a major problem.

Implications for Practitioners

Official profiles of juvenile offenders reflect only the characteristics of those who have been apprehended and officially processed. They tell little or nothing about the characteristics of all juveniles who actually commit delinquent acts. They may be useful in dealing with juveniles who have been officially processed, but are of less value in preventing and controlling delinquency outside the juvenile justice system.

Practitioners need to realize that it may not be the broken home itself that leads to delinquency, but the quality of life within the family in terms of consistency of discipline, level of tension, and ease of communication. Therefore, in some instances, it may be better to remove a child from an intact family that does not provide a suitable environment than to maintain the integrity of the family. In addition, it may not be necessary to automatically place juveniles from broken homes in institutions, foster homes, and so forth provided the quality of life within the broken home is acceptable.

Since education is an important determinant of occupational success in our society and since occupational success is an important determinant of life satisfaction, it is important that practitioners attempt to minimize the number of juveniles who are "pushed out" of the educational system. They should work for improvements in educational programs to minimize the number of juveniles who drop out. It may be that we are currently asking too much of educators when we require them to provide not only academic and vocational information, but also to promote psychological and social well-being, moral development, and a sense of direction for juveniles (formerly provided basically by the family). At the present time, if educators fail to provide for all these concerns, the juvenile often has nowhere else to turn except his or her peers, who may be experiencing similar problems. One result of this alienation from both the family and the educational system is the development of delinquent behavior patterns.

For too long we have concentrated our interest and research activities on the lower class and have generally ignored and denied the existence of middle-class delinquency. While we do not intend to minimize the importance of lower-class delinquency, it is time to realize that the problem may be similarly widespread in the middle class. We can no longer afford the luxury of viewing delinquency as only a problem of the lower social class neighborhoods in urban areas. Recent statistics indicate that the problem of delinquency is increasing at a more rapid rate in what were commonly considered to be "quiet middle-class suburban areas." Since motivations and types of offenses committed by middle-class delinquents may differ from those of their lower-class counterparts, new techniques and approaches for dealing with these problems may be required.

If practitioners develop more effective ways of promoting good relationships between juveniles and their families and making the importance of a relevant education clear to juveniles, concern with gang activities may be lessened. At the present time, however, understanding the importance of peer group pressure and the demands of the gang on the individual juvenile are extremely important in understanding drug abuse and related activities. If gangs could be used to promote legitimate rather than illegitimate concerns, one of the major sources of support for certain types of delinquent activities (for example, vandalism and drug abuse) could be weakened considerably. Reasonable alternatives to such current gang activities need to be developed and promoted.

Summary

None of the factors discussed in this chapter can be considered a direct cause of delinquency. It is important to remember that official statistics reflect only a small proportion of all delinquent activities. Profiles based on the characteristics discussed in this chapter are valuable to the extent that they alert us to a number of problem areas which may make it more or less easy for the juvenile to avoid delinquent behavior.

Attempts to improve the quality of family life and the relevancy of education and attempts to change discriminatory practices in terms of social class, race, and sex are needed badly. Improvements in these areas might go a long way toward reducing the frequency of certain types of delinquent activity.

Discussion Questions

1. What is the relationship between profiles of delinquents based on official statistics and the actual extent of delinquency?
2. Discuss the relationships among the family, the educational system, drugs, and gangs as they relate to delinquency.
3. Discuss some of the reasons for the overrepresentation of black juveniles in official delinquency statistics. What could be done to decrease the proportion of young blacks involved in delinquency?
4. How do area of the city, race, and social class combine to affect delinquency?

Selected Readings

Ageton, S. S. "The Dynamics of Female Delinquency, 1976–1980." *Criminology* 21, no. 4 (November 1983): 555–84.

Bookin, H., and R. Horowitz. "The End of the Youth Gang: Fad or Fact." *Criminology* 21, no. 4 (November 1983): 585–602.

Carpenter, C., B. Glassner, B. D. Johnson, and J. Loughlin. *Kids, Drugs, and Crime.* Lexington, Mass.: Lexington Books, 1988.

Fagan, J., E. Slaughter, and E. Hartstone. "Blind Justice: The Impact of Race on the Juvenile Justice Process." *Crime and Delinquency* 33, no. 2 (April 1987): 173–205.

Headley, B. D. "Black on Black Crime: The Myth and the Reality." *Crime and Social Justice* 20 (1984): 50–62.

Huizinga, D., and D. S. Elliot. "Juvenile Offenders: Prevalence, Offender Incidence, and Arrest Rates by Race." *Crime and Delinquency* 33 (1987): 206–23.

Johnson, R. E. "Family Structure and Delinquency: General Patterns and Gender Differences." *Criminology* 24 (1986): 64–80.

Krisberg, B., I. Swartz, G. Fishman, Z. Eisikovits, E. Guttman, and K. Joe. "The Incarceration of Minority Youth." *Crime and Delinquency* 33, no. 2 (April 1987): 173–205.

Lamb, J. H., and R. J. Sampson. "Unraveling Families and Delinquency: A Reanalysis of the Gluecks' Data." *Criminology* 26, no. 3 (August 1988): 355–80.

McGahey, R. M. "Economic Conditions, Neighborhood Organization, and Urban Crime." In *Communities and Crime,* ed. A. J. Reiss and M. Tonry. Chicago: University of Chicago Press, 1986.

Steinberg, L. "Latchkey Children and Susceptibility to Peer Pressure: An Ecological Analysis." *Developmental Psychology* 22 (1986): 439–443.

4 Theories of Causation

In this chapter, we will examine some of the so-called theories which have been developed in an attempt to explain juvenile delinquency (or adult criminality or some other form of deviance). While dozens of conceptual schemes have been proposed in attempts to specify the causes of delinquency, only a few of the more prominent attempts will be discussed here.

A theory may be defined as a set of deductively interrelated propositions, at least some of which are empirically testable, that describe and explain some phenomenon.[1] Although this definition may sound complex, it is really quite simple if we take it piece by piece. A proposition is simply a statement of a relationship between two or more variables. Propositions that are deductively interrelated are simply related in a logical manner so that some propositions can be derived (deduced) from others. For example:

Proposition #1—All delinquents are from broken homes.
Proposition #2—Harry is a delinquent.
Proposition #3—Harry is from a broken home.

In this case, Proposition #3 is derived from Propositions #1 and #2; that is, Proposition #3 is said to be explained by Propositions #1 and #2 and is logically correct. Our definition of a theory, however, requires that at least some of the propositions be empirically testable. To be acceptable, then, a theory must be both logically correct and accurately describe events in the real world. Suppose that Harry is not, in fact, from a broken home. Clearly our explanation of delinquency is erroneous and our theory must be revised or rejected. While conceptual schemes which do not meet our requirements for theory may be useful stepping stones in describing delinquency, only a logically correct and empirically accurate theory will

1. See George C. Homans, *The Nature of Social Science* (New York: Harcourt Brace Jovanovich, 1967); or F. S. C. Northrop, *The Logic of the Sciences and Humanities* (New York: World Publishing, 1966), especially chapter 4.

enable us to explain delinquency. As we discuss some of the so-called theories of delinquency in the following pages, you may find it useful to assess the extent to which they meet the requirements of our definition and the extent to which they are useful in helping us understand delinquency. We do not propose to discuss all attempts at explaining delinquency in the following sections. Our intent is simply to familiarize you with some such attempts and the strengths and weaknesses of these attempts. For those who desire greater details concerning selected theories, the Selected Readings list at the end of this chapter should prove useful.

Some Early Theories

Demonology

Early attempts to explain various forms of deviant behavior (crime, mental illness, and so forth) focused on demon or spirit possession. Individuals who violated societal norms were thought to be possessed by some evil spirit, which forced them to commit evil deeds through the exercise of mysterious supernatural power. Deviant behavior, then, was viewed not as a product of free will, but as determined by forces beyond the control of the individual (and thus the demonological theory of deviance is known as a "deterministic approach"). In order to cure or control deviant behavior, a variety of techniques were employed to drive the evil spirits from the mind and/or body of the deviant. One process that was employed was "trephining," which consisted of drilling holes in the skulls of deviants to allow the evil spirits to escape. Various rites of exorcism, including beating and burning, were practiced to make the body of the deviant such an uncomfortable place to reside that the evil spirit would leave, or to make the deviant confess his or her association with evil spirits. As might be expected, such tortures of the body often resulted in death or permanent disability to the individuals who were allegedly possessed. In addition, either confession or failure to confess could be taken as evidence of possession. Tortured sufficiently, many individuals confessed simply to prevent further torture. Those who persisted in claiming innocence were often thought to be so completely under the control of evil spirits that they could not tell the truth. Needless to say, the consequences for both categories of accused were frequently very unpleasant.

Some observers feel that belief in spirit possession as a cause of deviance is rare today. A recent study by Bourguignon, however, indicates that of 488 societies in the *Ethnographic Atlas,* 388 (or four-fifths of the sample) are characterized by belief in spirit/demon possession.[2] Further, our own analysis of newspaper articles over the past five years has turned up an average of an article per month dealing with attempts to exorcise evil spirits from children in the United States.

Perhaps demonology as a so-called explanation of deviance persists because, in some respects, attempts to deal with deviance thought to be caused by spirits are logical if the basic premise is accepted as true: that is, if one believes that spirit possession causes deviance, it makes sense to drive the spirits away if possible. While such an explanation of deviance seems simplistic to criminologists today, it cannot be scientifically disproved and it is still accepted as valid by a significant number of people in a substantial number of countries. However, because it is impossible to test scientifically the proposition that evil spirits which possess the mind and/or body cause delinquency, this attempt to explain delinquency is of little value from our theoretical perspective.

Classical Theory

In the last half of the eighteenth century, the classical school of criminology (often referred to as a "free-will" approach) emerged in Italy and England. This approach to explaining and controlling crime was based upon the belief that human beings exercise free will and that human behavior results from rationally calculating rewards and costs in terms of pleasure and pain. In other words, before an individual commits a specific act, he or she determines whether the consequences of the act will be pleasurable or painful. Presumably, acts that have painful consequences will be avoided. To control crime, then, society simply had to make the punishment for violators outweigh the benefits of their illegal actions. Thus, penalties became increasingly more severe as offenses became increasingly more serious. Under the classical theory, threat of punishment was considered to be a deterrent to criminals who rationally calculated the consequences of their illegal actions.

By 1765, Cesare Beccaria recognized that not all individuals were capable of rationally calculating rewards and costs and called for the exclusion of the insane and juveniles from punishment identical to that of sane adults. By definition, the insane were not capable of rational calculation and youth, up to a certain age at least, were thought to be less responsible than adults.

2. Erika Bourguignon, "Spirit Possession Belief and Social Structure," in *The Realm of the Extra-Human,* ed. A. Bharati (The Hague and Paris: Mouton, 1976), 19.

It is important to understand the classical approach, since its propositions (punishment deters crime, the punishment should fit the crime, and juveniles and the insane should be treated differently than sane adults) are basic to our current criminal and juvenile justice system. Unfortunately, the classical approach to controlling crime has never been very successful. While there seems to be some logic to the approach, the premise that the threat of punishment deters crime, at least as currently employed, is inaccurate. There are a variety of possible sources of error in this premise. First, it may be that man does not always rationally calculate rewards and costs. An individual committing what we commonly refer to as a "crime of passion" (as in the case of the murder of a spouse caught in an adulterous act) may not stop to think about the consequences. If this individual does not stop to make such calculations, then the threat of punishment (no matter how severe) will not affect that person's behavior. Second, an individual may calculate rewards and costs in a way that appears rational to him or her (but perhaps not to society) and may decide that certain illegal acts are worth whatever punishment he or she will receive if apprehended (as in the case of a starving person stealing food). Finally, the individual may rationally calculate rewards and costs, but have no fear of punishment because he or she feels the chances of apprehension are slight (as in the case of many juveniles involved with alcohol and minor vandalism). If the individual believes that he or she will not be apprehended for his or her illegal acts, the threat of punishment has little meaning. Additionally, the individual may believe that even if he or she is caught, punishment will not be administered (as in the case of many juveniles who are aware that most juvenile cases never go to court).

For whatever reasons, the classical approach to explaining and controlling crime has not proven successful. It would appear that whatever possibility of success this approach has rests with delivering punishment relatively immediately and with a great deal of certainty. Since our society largely continues to rely upon the classical approach and since neither immediacy of punishment nor certainty of apprehension exists, it is not surprising that we are unsuccessful in our attempts to control crime and delinquency.[3]

3. For further discussion of fear of punishment as a deterrent to crime, see Cesare Beccaria, *On Crimes and Punishments,* trans. Henry Paolucci (New York: Bobbs-Merrill Co., 1963); Gordon P. Waldo and Theodore G. Chiricos, "Perceived Penal Sanction and Self-Reported Criminality: A Neglected Approach to Deterrence Research," *Social Problems* 19 (Spring 1972): 522–40; or Hugo A. Bedau, "Death as Punishment," in his *The Death Penalty in America* (New York: Doubleday & Co., Inc., 1967), 214–31.

The Positive School

The positive school of criminology (also known as the Italian school) emerged in the second half of the nineteenth century. Cesare Lombroso is recognized as the founder of the positive school and also as the "father" of modern criminology. Lombroso, with other positivists such as Garofalo and Ferri, believed that criminals should be studied scientifically and emphasized determinism as opposed to free will (classical school) as the basis of criminal behavior. While a number of positivists believed that heredity is the determining factor in criminality, others believed the environment determined in large measure whether or not an individual became a criminal. The positivists emphasized the need for empirical research in criminology and some stressed the importance of environment as a causal factor in crime. While their methodology was unsophisticated by modern standards, their contributions to the development of modern criminology are undeniable. Lombroso may also be considered, earlier in his career at least, as one of the founders of the biological school of criminology.

The Biological School

The biological approach to delinquency was initially based on the assumption that delinquency (criminality) is inherited. Over the past century, the approach has tended to emphasize more the belief that heredity predisposes certain individuals toward delinquency rather than determines delinquency. This school has offered a number of different explanations of delinquency, ranging from glandular malfunctions to learning disabilities to racial heritage to nutrition. As we examine some of these explanations, keep in mind our definition of an acceptable theory.

Lombroso

Lombroso became known for the theory of the "born criminal." As a result of his research, he became convinced at one point in his career that criminals were *atavists,* or throwbacks to more primitive beings. According to Lombroso, these born criminals could be recognized by a series of external features, such as receding foreheads, enormous development of the jaw, and large or handle-shaped ears. These external traits were thought to be related to personality types characterized by laziness, moral insensitiveness, and absence of guilt feelings.[4] Individuals with a number of these criminal features or "anomalies" were thought to be incapable of resisting the impulse to commit crimes except under very favorable circumstances.

Later in his career, Lombroso modified his approach by recognizing the importance of social factors, but his emphasis on biological causes encouraged many other researchers to seek such causes. Lombroso remains important today largely because of his attempts to explain crime scientifically, rather than as a result of his particular theories.

Other Biological Theories

Following Lombroso, there were a number of attempts to find biological or genetic causes for crime and delinquency. Identical twin studies were conducted based on the belief that if genetics determine criminality, when one twin is criminal the other will also be. In general, these studies provide evidence that genetic structure is not the sole cause of crime, since none of them indicate that 100 percent of the twins studied were identical with respect to criminal behavior. Research on the relationship between genetics and crime in twins continues nonetheless.[5]

Dugdale made the Jukes family a famous test case in the late 1800s, when he demonstrated that over generations this family had been characterized by criminality. Dugdale felt that crime and heredity were related, but his own admission that over the years the family had established a reputation for deviant behavior points to the possibility that other factors (learning and labeling, for instance) might be of equal or greater importance in explaining his observations.[6]

Other researchers, including Ernst Kretschmer, William H. Sheldon, and Sheldon and Eleanor Glueck, turned to studies of the relationship between body type and delinquency/criminality.[7] Causes of

4. Sawyer F. Sylvester, Jr., *The Heritage of Modern Criminology* (Cambridge, Mass.: Schenkman Publishing Co., 1972), 67–78.

5. See, for example, O. D. Dalgard and E. Kringlen, "Criminal Behavior in Twins," in *Crime in Society,* ed. L. D. Savitz and N. Johnston (New York: John Wiley & Sons, Inc., 1978), 292–307.

6. R. L. Dugdale, *The Jukes: A Study in Crime, Pauperism, Disease and Heredity,* 4th ed. (New York: Putnam, 1888).

7. Ernst Kretschmer, *Physique and Character,* trans. W. Sprott (New York: Harcourt, Brace and World, 1925); William H. Sheldon, *Varieties of Delinquent Youth: An Introduction to Constitutional Psychiatry* (New York: Harper & Row, 1949); Sheldon and Eleanor Glueck, *Unraveling Juvenile Delinquency* (Cambridge, Mass.: Harvard University Press, 1950).

delinquency and body type were thought by Sheldon, for example, to be biologically determined and selective breeding was suggested as a solution to delinquency. The Gluecks continued the body type tradition of explaining delinquency, but have included in their analysis a variety of other factors as well. The basic conclusion of the Gluecks' work with respect to body type and crime is that a majority of delinquents are muscular as opposed to thin or obese. One possible explanation for this conclusion, which does not require any assumptions about biological determination, is that youth who are not particularly physically fit recognize this fact and therefore consciously tend to avoid at least those delinquent activities which might require strength and fitness. Additionally, measurements of body type are rather subjective and the data presented by the body typists does not account for different individuals with the same body type being delinquent on the one hand and nondelinquent on the other.

In the past several years emphasis in the biological school has shifted somewhat. Chromosome studies and studies examining the relationship between learning disabilities and chemical imbalances and delinquency have emerged. We have already discussed some of the literature on the relationship between learning disabilities and delinquency in chapter 2. Here, we will simply state that, as typically conceived, many learning disabilities are clearly psychosocial (as opposed to biological) in nature. Those which are organically based have not, at this point in time, been shown to be causally related to delinquency.

In the 1960s, a number of researchers explored the relationship between the presence of an extra Y chromosome in some males and subsequent criminal behavior.[8] Mednick et al. found that about 42 percent of the XYY cases identified in Denmark had criminal histories compared to only 9 percent of the XY population.[9] Research is still being conducted on the possible relationship between an extra Y chromosome and criminality, though little if any work has been done specifically on the relationship between delinquency and the extra Y chromosome. At present, it is safe to say that a direct relationship between chromosome structure and criminality has not been scientifically established and that many of the studies conducted to date are characterized by serious methodological problems.

8. See W. H. Price and P. B. Whatmore, "Behavior Disorders and Patterns of Crime Among XYY Males Identified at a Maximum Security Hospital," *British Medical Journal* (March 1967): 533–36.

9. S. Mednick and K. O. Christiansen, *Biosocial Bases of Criminal Behavior* (New York: Gardner, 1977).

C. R. Jeffery views behavior as the product of interaction between a physical environment and a physical organism and believes that contemporary criminology should represent a merger of biology, psychology, and sociology. The basis for Jeffery's argument is that most contemporary criminologists believe that criminal behavior is learned, but neglect the fact that learning involves physical (biochemical) changes in the brain. He contends that while criminality is not inherited, the biochemical preparedness for such behavior is present in the brain, and will, given a particular type of environment, produce criminal behavior.[10]

Ellis, after reviewing research bearing upon the relationship between genetics and criminality, concludes that "the evidence is extremely supportive of the proposition that human variation in tendencies to commit criminal behavior is significantly affected by some genetic factors."[11]

Others interested in crime and delinquency agree that these behaviors are likely to result from biochemical abnormalities or malfunctions. Walsh and Berlin, for example, indicate that they have linked the violent sexual behavior of some males with a chemical imbalance that can be controlled using the drug Depo-Provera to lower the sex drive in these males.[12] Lesch and Nyhan, some time ago, identified a syndrome, named after them, in which victims of the disease routinely kick, punch, and bite others. The disease was traced to an enzyme deficiency which was traced to a defective gene. Contemporary genetic engineering techniques have raised hopes that the victims of the Lesch-Nyhan Syndrome may soon be helped.[13]

Mednick et al. have recently studied EEG (electroencephalogram) records of juveniles and compared these with later delinquency. They conclude that slow Alpha frequencies reflected in EEGs predict delinquency (in this case theft) about as well as other variables which have

10. C. R. Jeffery, "Criminology as an Interdisciplinary Behavioral Science," *Criminology* 16, no. 2 (August 1978): 149–69.

11. Lee Ellis, "Genetics and Criminal Behavior: Evidence Through the End of the 1970s," *Criminology* 20, no. 1 (May 1982): 43–66.

12. Brent Staples, "Curbing Crime May Be a Matter of Biochemistry," *Chicago Sun-Times,* 18 December 1983, 19–20.

13. Ibid.

been used in studies of antisocial behavior. Hsu et al. (1985), however, found no relationship between brain abnormalities as measured by the EEG and delinquency.[14]

There are numerous other attempts to explain delinquency in terms of biology, genetics, and biochemistry. As early as 1939, Ernest Hooton wrote of the consequences of biological causes of crime for rehabilitation and control of offenders. According to Hooton, *if* criminality is inherited, the solutions to crime lie in isolation and/or sterilization of offenders to prevent them from remaining active in the genetic pool of a society. A third alternative, which Hooton opposed, is extermination, and a fourth is the practice of eugenics. At various times, European societies have isolated (Devil's Island, the Colonies), sterilized, and exterminated offenders. Experiments with eugenics have also been conducted on numerous occasions, but raise serious ethical and moral issues. The extent to which genetic engineering becomes acceptable as a means of dealing with a wide variety of social problems will likely determine its use in controlling criminality if genetic deficiencies or abnormalities are shown to be causes of crime and delinquency.[15]

Psychological Theories

Early varieties of psychological theories of delinquency and crime focused on lack of intelligence and/or personality disturbances as major causal factors. Several of the early pioneers in the psychological school were convinced that biological factors played a major role in determining intelligence, and they could therefore be considered proponents of both schools of thought. Goddard's studies of the Kallikak family and the intellectual abilities of reformatory inmates, for instance, led him to conclude that "feeblemindedness," which he believed to be inherited, was an important contributing factor in criminality. He suggested that "eliminating" a large proportion of mental defectives would reduce the number of criminals and other deviants in society.[16] Similarly, Charles

14. Sarnoff A. Mednick, Jan Volavka, William F. Gabrielli, Jr., and Turan M. Itil, "EEG as a Predictor of Antisocial Behavior," *Criminology* 19, no. 2 (August 1981): 219–29; and L. Hsu, K. Wisner, E. Richey, and C. Goldstein, "Is Juvenile Delinquency Related to an Abnormal EEG?" *Journal of American Academy of Child Psychiatry* 24 (1985): 310–15.

15. Ernest Hooton, *Crime and the Man* (Cambridge, Mass.: Harvard University Press, 1939).

16. Henry H. Goddard, *Feeblemindedness: Its Causes and Consequences* (New York: Macmillan Co., 1914).

Goring focused on defective intelligence and psychological characteristics as basic causes of crime in his attempt to refute Lombroso and the other positivists.[17] As we have indicated previously, research concerning the relationship between defective intelligence, IQ, or learning disabilities and delinquency continues.[18] Problems concerning the reliability and validity of IQ tests and other methodological shortcomings continue to plague such research and the psychological school as a whole has taken other directions.

Freud

Sigmund Freud, born in 1856, spent most of his life in Vienna, Austria. He is regarded as the founder of psychoanalysis, an approach to explaining behavior which relies heavily upon the techniques of introspection (looking inside one's self) and retrospection (reviewing past events). Freud's theories were introduced in the United States in the early 1900s. He divided personality into three separate components: the id, the ego, and the superego. The function of the id, according to Freud, is to provide for the discharge of energy which permits the individual to seek pleasure and reduce tension. The id is also said to be the seat of instincts in human beings and not thought to be governed by reason. The ego is said to be the part of the personality that controls and governs the id and the superego by making rational adjustments to real-life situations. For example, the ego might prevent the id from causing the individual to seek immediate gratification of his or her desires by deferring gratification to a later time. The development of the ego is said to be a product of interaction between the individual's personality and the environment, and is thought to be affected by heredity as well.[19] The superego is viewed as the moral branch of the personality and may be roughly equated with the concept of conscience. Both the ego and the superego are thought to develop out of the individual's interactions with his or her environment, while the id is said to be a product of evolution.

17. Charles Goring, *The English Convict* (London: H. M. Stationery Office, 1913).

18. See, for example, Robert A. Gordon, "Prevalence: The Rare Datum in Delinquency Measurement and Its Implications for the Theory of Delinquency," in *The Juvenile Justice System,* ed. Malcolm Klein (Beverly Hills, Calif.: Sage, 1976); or Travis Hirschi and Michael J. Hindelang, "Intelligence and Delinquency: A Revisionist Review," *American Sociological Review* 42 (1977): 571–87.

19. Calvin S. Hall, *A Primer of Freudian Psychology* (New York: World Publishing Co., 1954), 22–35.

In general, deviance is viewed as the product of an uncontrollable id, a faulty ego, an underdeveloped superego, or some combination of the three. Therefore, those who commit a criminal or delinquent act do so as the result of a personality disturbance. In order to correct or control this behavior, the causes of the personality disturbance are located primarily through introspection and retrospection, with a particular emphasis upon childhood experiences, and then eliminated through therapy.

Freud is one of the most important figures (if not *the* most important figure) in the history of psychology. There are, no doubt, many cases where psychoanalytic techniques prove effective in therapeutic treatment. As a system for explaining the causes of deviance, however, Freudian psychology has several shortcomings. First, the existence of the id, ego, and superego cannot be empirically demonstrated. Second, instincts, which Freud viewed as the driving forces in the id, are thought by many behavioral scientists to be extremely rare or nonexistent in humans.[20] Third, there seems to be faulty logic among practitioners using Freud's system. They accept the premise that those who commit deviant acts must be experiencing personality disturbances; that is, they employ circular reasoning rather than logical deduction. In response to the question, How do you know X has a disturbed personality? they often answer: Since he committed a deviant act, he must have been experiencing a personality disturbance. Such a response is more a statement of faith than a matter of fact. At present, it is safe to say that the psychoanalytic approach is of very little value in explaining crime and delinquency (or any other form of deviance, for that matter). Nonetheless, the Freudian approach remains popular in most of the Western world and Freud has had many disciples who have applied his techniques directly to delinquency.[21]

Among those emphasizing the psychoanalytic perspective was William Healy, who believed that the delinquent was a product of a personality disturbance resulting from unhealthy family relationships. He and his associate, Augusta Bronner, interviewed numerous juvenile offenders and came to the conclusion that 90 percent of them were emotionally disturbed.[22] Others, using a variety of personality inventories,

20. See Robert M. Goldenson, *The Encyclopedia of Human Behavior: Psychology, Psychiatry, and Mental Health,* vol. 1 (New York: Doubleday & Co., Inc., 1970), 620–22.

21. See, for example, August Aichorn, *Wayward Youth* (New York: The Viking Press, Inc., 1953); or Fritz Redl, *Children Who Hate* (New York: Free Press, 1951).

22. William Healy and Augusta Bronner, *New Light on Delinquency and Its Treatment* (New Haven: Yale University Press, 1936).

have concluded that such inventories do appear to discriminate between delinquents and nondelinquents, but the reasons for such discrimination are not at all clear-cut and neither are the numerous definitions of "abnormal" personality employed.[23]

One of the terms most commonly employed to describe certain types of criminals and delinquents is "psychopath." Typically, the term is used to describe aggressive criminals who act impulsively with no apparent reason. Sutherland and Cressey indicate that some fifty-five descriptive terms are consistently linked with the concept of psychopathy (sociopathy or antisocial personality).[24] While the concept is generally considered to be too vague and ambiguous to distinguish psychopaths from nonpsychopaths, at least one psychologist has attempted to operationalize the concept in more meaningful fashion. Gough has conceptualized psychopathy as the inability to take the role of the other (the inability to identify with others). The scales he has developed to measure role-taking ability generally result in lower scores for offenders than nonoffenders.[25] Whether or not such differences could have been detected before the offenders committed offenses is another matter.

Behaviorism and Learning Theory

In the later nineteenth century, a number of psychologists became increasingly concerned about weaknesses in the theory and techniques developed by Freud and his followers. They called for a change in focus from the internal workings of the mind to observable behavior. While the major work on the learning theory model as it relates to delinquency has been done by sociologists and will be discussed under that topic, the psychological underpinnings will be discussed here.

As we indicated above, behaviorists called for a change of techniques from the subjective, speculative approach based on introspection and retrospection to a more empirical, objective approach based on observing and measuring behavior. Perhaps the most important individual

23. See Michael Hakeem, "A Critique of the Psychiatric Approach to the Prevention of Juvenile Delinquency," *Social Problems* 5 (Winter 1957): 194–205; or Karl F. Schuessler and Donald R. Cressey, "Personality Characteristics of Criminals," *American Journal of Sociology* 55 (March 1950): 476–84.

24. Edwin H. Sutherland and Donald R. Cressey, *Criminology,* 10th ed. (New York: J. B. Lippincott Co., 1978).

25. Harrison G. Gough, "A Sociological Theory of Psychopathy," *American Journal of Sociology* 53 (March 1948): 359–66; or "Theory and Measurement of Socialization," *Journal of Consulting Psychology* 24 (1960): 23–30.

in the behaviorist tradition is B. F. Skinner, who directed his attention toward the relationship between a particular stimulus and a given response and to the learning processes involved in connecting the two.[26] Human social behavior, then, is viewed as a set of learned responses to specific stimuli. Criminal and delinquent behavior are viewed as varieties of human social behavior, learned in the same way as other social behaviors. Through the process of *conditioning* (rewarding for appropriate behavior and/or punishing for inappropriate behavior), any type of social behavior can be taught. Therefore, when an individual behaves in a delinquent manner (exhibits an inappropriate response in a given situation), his or her behavior can be modified using conditioning. To control and rehabilitate delinquents, then, the therapist employs behavior modification techniques to extinguish inappropriate behavior and/ or to replace it with appropriate behavior.

While behaviorists do not seek to explain the ultimate causes of social behavior except in the sense that they are learned, their approach holds considerably more promise for understanding and controlling delinquent behavior than the psychoanalytic approach. The behaviorist approach forces us to focus on the specific problem behavior and to recognize that it is learned, so it can—hypothetically at least—be unlearned. With this focus, we are dealing with observable behavior that can be measured, counted, and perhaps modified. Success in modifying behavior in the laboratory has been relatively consistent.[27] The extent to which this success can be transferred to the world outside the laboratory remains an empirical question. Think about the difficulties of transferring desirable behavior from the laboratory to the street in the following hypothetical case. Joe Foul Up, a juvenile, is repeatedly apprehended for fighting. Finally, he is turned over to a therapist who, over a period of several weeks, eliminates the undesirable behavior by punishing (with electric shock, for example) Joe when he begins to exhibit the undesirable behavior and by rewarding him when he exhibits appropriate alternative behavior. After therapy ends, Joe's behavior has been modified and he returns home to his old neighborhood and his old street gang. When Joe refuses to fight when the gang thinks it is appropriate they

26. B. F. Skinner, "What is Psychotic Behavior?" in Theodore Millon, *Theories of Psychopathology and Personality,* 2d ed. (Philadelphia: W. Saunders, 1973), 282–93.

27. For numerous examples, see L. Krasner and L. P. Ullman, *Research in Behavior Modification* (New York: Holt, Rinehart and Winston, Inc., 1965); or Garry Martin and Joseph Peas, *Behavior Modification: What It Is and How to Do It* (Englewood Cliffs, N.J.: Prentice-Hall, Inc., 1978).

punish him by calling him a coward and excluding him from gang activities. When he does fight, they reward him by treating him like a hero. What are the chances that the behavior modification that occurred in the laboratory will continue to exist?

We will have more to say about the learning theory or behaviorist approach in the following section on sociological theories.

Sociological Theories

There have been a number of different sociological theories of delinquency causation, some dealing with social class and/or family differences,[28] some with blocked educational and occupational goals,[29] some with neighborhood and peers,[30] and some with the effects of official labeling.[31] Most of these theories share the notion that delinquent behavior is the product of social interaction rather than the result of heredity or personality disturbance. For sociologists, delinquency must be understood in social context.

The Ecological Approach

The ecological approach to explaining crime and delinquency was developed in the 1930s and 1940s and is one of the oldest interest areas of American criminologists. The ecological approach focuses on the geographic distribution of delinquency. Clifford Shaw and Henry McKay, and later others, found that crime and delinquency rates were not distributed equally within cities. They mapped the areas marked by high crime and delinquency rates along with the socioeconomic problems of those areas.[32] Using Ernest Burgess's concentric zone theory of city

28. Albert K. Cohen, *Delinquent Boys: The Culture of the Gang* (New York: Free Press, 1955); Walter B. Miller, "Lower Class Culture as a Generating Milieu of Gang Delinquency," *Journal of Social Issues* 14, no. 3 (1958): 5–19; Richard A. Cloward and Lloyd E. Ohlin, *Delinquency and Opportunity: A Theory of Delinquent Gangs* (New York: Free Press, 1960); or Richard Quinney, *Criminology* (Boston: Little, Brown & Co., 1975).

29. Robert K. Merton, *Social Theory and Social Structure* (New York: Free Press, 1955), especially pp. 131–60.

30. Thrasher, *The Gang;* Cohen, *Delinquent Boys;* Miller, "Lower Class Culture"; and Clifford R. Shaw and Henry D. McKay, *Juvenile Delinquency and Urban Areas* (Chicago: University of Chicago Press, 1942).

31. Howard S. Becker, *The Outsiders* (New York: Free Press, 1963).

32. See note 30 above.

growth,[33] the ecological studies generally found that zones of transition between residential and industrial neighborhoods consistently had the highest rates of crime and delinquency. These zones are characterized by physical deterioration and are located adjacent to the business district of the central city. The neighborhoods in this zone are marked by deteriorating buildings, substandard housing with accompanying overcrowdedness, lack of sanitation, and generally poor health and safety features. In addition, the area is marked by a transient population, high unemployment rates, poverty, broken homes, and a high adult crime rate. In short, the area is characterized by a general lack of social stability and cohesion.

Judith Wilks best summarized the majority of ecological studies and their findings on the distribution of delinquency. Her findings were:

1. *Rates of delinquency and crime vary widely in different neighborhoods, within a city or town.*

2. *The highest crime and delinquency rates generally occur in the low-rent areas located near the center of the city and the rates decrease with increasing distance from the city center.*

3. *High delinquency rate areas tend to maintain their rates over time, although the population composition of the area may change radically within the same time period.*

4. *Areas which have high rates of truancy also have high rates of juvenile court cases and high rates of male delinquency, and usually have high rates of female delinquency.*

5. *The differences in area rates reflect differences in community background. High rate areas are characterized by such things as physical deterioration and declining population.*

6. *The delinquency rates for particular nationality and ethnic groups show the same general tendency as the entire population; namely to be high in the central area of the city and low as the groups move toward the outskirts of the city.*

7. *Delinquents living in areas of high delinquency rates are the most likely to become recidivists, and are likely to appear in court several times more often than those from areas with low delinquency rates.*

8. *In summary, delinquency and crime follow the pattern of social and physical structure of the city with concentration occurring in disorganized, deteriorated areas.*[34]

33. Ernest W. Burgess, "The Economic Factor in Juvenile Delinquency," *Journal of Criminal Law, Criminology, and Police Science* 43 (May–June 1952): 29–42.

34. Judith A. Wilks, "Ecological Correlates of Crime and Delinquency," in *Task Force Report: Crime and Its Impact—An Assessment,* President's Commission on Law Enforcement and the Administration of Justice (Washington, D.C.: U.S. Government Printing Office, 1967), A, 138–56.

According to Wilks, in order to predict delinquency using the ecological approach, it is necessary to be aware of the existing social structure, social processes, and the population composition as well as the area's position within the large urban societal complex, since these variables all affect the distribution of delinquency. In general, the ecological approach found that family and neighborhood stability were lacking and that the street environment was the prevailing determinant of behavior. If delinquent behavior is learned behavior, this learning would be maximized in environments such as those in transitional zones. In transitional zones, those agencies or institutions that traditionally produce stability, cohesion, and organization have often been replaced by the street environment of adult criminals and delinquent gangs.

The ecological approach to explaining delinquency has been challenged on the grounds that using only one variable to explain delinquency is not likely to lead to success. In Bernard Lander's study of Baltimore,[35] for example, he found anomie, or normlessness, to be a more appropriate explanation of delinquency rates than socioeconomic area. Nonetheless, follow-up studies by Shaw and McKay in other American cities (Boston, Philadelphia, Cleveland) support their contention that official delinquency rates decrease from the central city out to the suburbs.[36] Similarly, Lyerly and Skipper found that significantly less delinquent activity was reported by rural youths than by urban youths in their study of youths in detention.[37] Whatever the cause, the fact remains that high official delinquency rates are found in certain areas or types of areas where serious and repetitive misconduct is not only common, but appears to have become traditional and more or less acceptable.

Sutherland

Edwin Sutherland developed what is known as the "theory of differential association." Sutherland's approach combines some of the principles of behaviorism (or learning theory) with the notion that learning

---

35. Bernard Lander, "An Ecological Analysis of Baltimore," in *Sociology of Crime and Delinquency,* 2d ed., ed. Marvin E. Wolfgang et al. (New York: John Wiley & Sons, Inc., 1970), 247–65.

36. Clifford R. Shaw and Henry D. McKay, *Juvenile Delinquency and Urban Areas,* rev. ed. (Chicago: University of Chicago Press, 1969).

37. Robert R. Lyerly and James K. Skipper, Jr., "Differential Rates of Rural-Urban Delinquency," *Criminology* 19, no. 3 (November 1981): 385–99.

takes place in interaction within social groups. For Sutherland, the primary group (family or gang) is the focal point of learning social behavior, including deviant behavior. In this context, individuals learn how to define different situations as appropriate for law-abiding or law-violating behavior. Therefore, seeing an unattended newsstand might be defined as a situation appropriate to the theft of a newspaper by some passers-by, but not by others. The way that a given individual defines a particular situation depends upon that individual's prior life experiences. An individual who has a balance of definitions favorable to law-violating behavior in a given situation is likely to commit a law-violating act. The impact of learned definitions on the individual depends upon how early in life the definitions were learned (priority), how frequently the definitions are reinforced (frequency), the period of time over which such definitions are reinforced (duration), and the importance of the definition to the individual (intensity).[38]

Sutherland's approach has the advantage of discussing both "deviant" and "normal" social behavior as learned phenomena. The approach also indicates that the primary group is crucial in the learning process. In addition, Sutherland suggests some important variables to be considered in determining whether behavior will be criminal or noncriminal in given situations. Finally, Sutherland suggests that it is not differential association with criminal and noncriminal types that determines the individual's behavior, but differential association with, or exposure to, definitions favorable or unfavorable to law-violating behavior.

There are a number of criticisms of Sutherland's approach. It is clearly difficult to operationalize the terms "favorable to" and "unfavorable to." There are serious problems with trying to measure the variable "intensity." How many exposures to definitions favorable to law violation are required before definitions unfavorable to law violation are outweighed and the individual commits the illegal act? These and other weaknesses have been pointed out over the years by critics of differential association.[39] Nonetheless, there is a certain logic to Sutherland's approach. Some of the propositions are empirically testable, and the description of the learning process seems to be relatively accurate.

38. For a complete, detailed presentation of differential association, see Edwin H. Sutherland and Donald R. Cressey, *Criminology,* 9th ed. (New York: J. B. Lippincott Co., 1974), especially pp. 75–91.

39. For example, see James F. Short, Jr., "Differential Association and Delinquency," *Social Problems* 4 (January 1957): 233–39.

Sutherland has sensitized us to an approach to understanding crime/delinquency that may be built upon by future theorists and researchers.[40]

One attempt to improve upon Sutherland's theory has been made by Daniel Glaser. Glaser refers to his theory as the "theory of differential-anticipation" which, in his view, combines differential association and control theory and is compatible with biological and personality theories. "Differential-anticipation theory assumes that a person will try to commit a crime wherever and whenever the expectations of gratification from it—as a result of social bonds, differential learning, and perceptions of opportunity—exceed the unfavorable anticipations from these sources."[41] In short, expectations determine conduct and expectations are determined by social bonds, differential learning, and perceived opportunities. This theory is eclectic in the sense that it extends Sutherland while being compatible with most of the approaches we have discussed above and with labeling theory, to which we now turn our attention.

Labeling Theory

A number of social scientists have contributed to what might be called the "labeling school" of crime/delinquency causation. Howard S. Becker has discussed the process of labeling deviants as "outsiders."[42] Kai Erikson has pointed out the importance of what he calls the labeling "ceremony" for deviants.[43] These authors and others have shifted the focus of attention from the individual deviant (delinquent, criminal, mentally ill, and so forth) to the reaction of the audience observing and labeling the behavior as deviant. As we have indicated repeatedly, it is clear that many individuals commit deviant acts, but only some are dealt with officially. The time at which the act occurs, the place in which it

40. See, for instance, Robert L. Burgess and Ronald L. Akers, "A Differential Association-Reinforcement Theory of Criminal Behavior," *Social Problems* 14 (Fall 1968): 128–47; or Daniel Glaser, "Differential Association and Criminological Prediction," *Social Problems* 8 (Summer 1960): 6–14.

41. Daniel Glaser, *Crime in Our Changing Society* (New York: Holt, Rinehart and Winston, Inc., 1978), 126–27.

42. Howard S. Becker, *The Outsiders: Studies in the Sociology of Deviance* (New York: Free Press, 1963).

43. Kai Erikson, "Notes on the Sociology of Deviance," *Social Problems* 9 (1962): 301–14.

occurs, and the people who observe the act are all important in determining whether or not official action will be taken. Thus, the juvenile using heroin in the privacy of his gang's "hangout" in front of other gang members is not subject to official action. If, however, he used heroin in a public place in the presence of a police officer who was observing his behavior, official action would be most likely.

From the labeling theorist's point of view, then, society's reaction to deviant behavior is crucially important in understanding who becomes labeled deviant. Erikson discusses the ceremony that deviants typically go through once the decision to take official action has been made. First, the alleged deviant is apprehended (arrested or taken into custody). Second, the individual is confronted, generally at a trial or hearing. Third, the individual is judged (a verdict, disposition, or decision is rendered). Finally, he or she is placed (imprisoned, committed to an institution, or put back in society on probation).[44] The end result is that the individual is officially labeled deviant. One of the consequences of labeling in our society is that, once labeled, the individual may never be able to redeem himself or herself in the eyes of society. Therefore, John Q. Convict does not become John Q. Citizen upon release from prison. Instead, he becomes John Q. Ex-Convict. Having been labeled may make it extremely difficult for the "rehabilitated" deviant to find employment and establish successful family ties. The more difficult it becomes for the rehabilitated deviant to succeed in the larger society, the greater the chances that he or she will return to old associates and old ways. Of course, these are often the very associates and ways that led the individual to become officially labeled in the first place. Thus, the individual may be more or less forced to continue his or her career in deviance, partially as a result of the labeling itself.[45]

Research by Blankenship and Singh indicates that a juvenile's prior career of delinquent behavior (the extent to which he or she has been previously officially labeled) is indeed an important determinant of official action.[46] They, and Covington,[47] point out that labeling comes in different forms (legalistic versus peer group, for example) and has different consequences for different types of offenders (whites versus blacks, for instance).

44. Ibid.

45. Becker, *The Outsiders,* especially pp. 19–41.

46. Ralph L. Blankenship and B. Krishna Singh, "Differential Labeling of Juveniles: A Multivariate Analysis," *Criminology* 13, no. 4 (February 1976): 471–90.

47. Jeanette Covington, "Insulation from Labeling: Deviant Defenses in Treatment," *Criminology* 22, no. 4 (November 1984): 619–43.

If we could assume that society *never* makes a mistake in attaching the label "deviant" and that rehabilitation programs *never* succeed, we might regard the consequences of labeling as somewhat less alarming. As we have already seen in chapters 2 and 3, the assumption that society never makes a mistake is unwarranted. In chapters 11 and 12, we shall see that there is at least some hope that rehabilitation programs do succeed. If the end result of official labeling forces the labeled individual into a deviant career, then, in the case of juveniles at least, we are accomplishing exactly the opposite of what we intended when we created a separate juvenile justice system designed to protect, educate, and treat juveniles rather than to punish them. One of the consequences of negative societal reaction to the label of "delinquent" may be the changing of the delinquent's self-concept so the individual, like society, begins to think about himself or herself in negative terms. Possibilities for rehabilitation may be lessened as a result.

The labeling approach accurately describes how individuals become labeled, why some maintain deviant careers, and some of the possible consequences of labeling. It does not deal with the issue of why some individuals initially commit acts that lead them to be labeled. In addition, those who support the approach often lose sight of the fact that the individual is in some way responsible for the actions which are viewed as unacceptable: that is, social audiences do not appear to attach negative labels haphazardly. They are responding to some stimulus presented by the individual committing a crime for which he or she must accept some responsibility (unless we return to a completely deterministic concept of deviance).

Despite some weaknesses, the labeling approach contributes significantly to our understanding of deviance. Through this approach deviance is viewed as a product of social interaction, in which the actions of both the deviant and his or her audience must be considered. This view of deviance, and therefore delinquency, has a number of important implications for practitioners.

Conflict and Radical/Critical/Marxist Theories

Chambliss (1984) describes conflict theories of crime as focusing on whole political and economic systems and on class relations in those systems.[48] Conflict theorists argue that conflict is inherent in all societies,

48. W. J. Chambliss, *Criminal Law in Action,* 2d ed. (New York: John Wiley & Sons, Inc., 1984).

not just capitalist societies, and focus on conflict resulting from gender, race, ethnicity, power, and other relationships. Conflict results from competition for power among many groups. Those who are successful in this competition define criminality at any given time. Thus criminal behavior is not viewed as universal or inherent, but as situational and definitional. This view does not account for individual acts of criminality occurring outside the group context, but serves basically to alert us to the social factors which may be related to criminality.

The Marxist approach to criminology and delinquency finds the causes of these phenomena in the repression of the lower social classes by the "ruling class." In short, laws are passed and enforced by those who monopolize power against those who are powerless (the poor and minorities, for example). The causal roots of crime are assumed, by many proponents of this approach, to be inherent in the social structure of capitalistic societies. Crime control policies are developed and implemented by those who have power (own the means of production, have wealth, and so on), and these policies serve to criminalize those who threaten the status quo.[49] Labeling the discontented as criminals and delinquents allows the ruling class to call upon law enforcement officials to deal with such individuals without having to grant legitimacy to their discontent. While there are a number of variations on the theme as discussed here, these are the essential components of most radical or critical explanations of delinquency and crime.

Radical criminology became relatively popular in the United States in the 1960s and 1970s, but its popularity has declined over the past few years and some of its most important spokespersons have abandoned, in part at least, this approach as an explanation of crime and delinquency. Little empirical research has been done which supports the radical/critical approach. As we have indicated earlier, delinquency appears to be rather uniformly distributed across social classes, contrary to the teachings of the Marxist approach. In addition, as we have indicated earlier, this approach fails to recognize that the legal order serves the purpose of maintaining the system in all known types of societies, including those which claim to be Marxist/communist/socialist.[50] As

49. See, for example, *Whose Law What Order?*, ed. W. J. Chambliss and M. Mandoff (New York: John Wiley & Sons, Inc., 1976); Anthony Platt, *The Child Savers,* 2d ed. (Chicago: University of Chicago Press, 1977); Richard Quinney, *Critique of Legal Order: Crime Control in Capitalist Society* (Boston: Little, Brown & Co., 1974), or *Class, State, and Crime,* 2d ed., 1980; Austin Turk, *Criminality and Legal Order* (Chicago: Rand McNally & Co., 1969); P. Beirne and R. Quinney, *Marxism and the Law* (New York: John Wiley & Sons, Inc., 1982).

50. Steven M. Cox, "Review of *Critique of Legal Order,*" *Teaching Sociology* 3, no. 1 (October 1975): 98.

Klockars notes, "The leading figures of American Marxist criminology have not raised the details of Gulag or Cuban solutions to the problems of crime in America, nor have they seriously examined such solutions in states which legitimate them."[51] Finally, proponents of this approach have a difficult time dealing with the fact that crime and delinquency rates are as high or higher in some countries (Cuba and the USSR, for instance) which claim to be other than capitalistic as in the United States.

Control Theories

Control theories assume that all of us must be held in check or "controlled" if we are to resist the temptation to commit criminal or delinquent acts. The types of systems used to control or check delinquent behavior fall into two categories: personal (internal) and social (external). The containment theory of Walter Reckless, for instance, emphasizes the importance of both inner controls and external pressures on self-concept. A poor self-concept is thought to increase the chances that a youth will turn to delinquency; a positive self-concept is seen as insulating youth from delinquent activities.[52]

Hirschi's control theory places more emphasis on social factors (bonds and attachments) than on inner controls. For example, the term attachment is used to refer to the feelings one has toward other persons or groups. The stronger one's attachment to nondelinquent others, the less likely one is to engage in delinquency. The same type of argument is applied to commitment (profits associated with conformity versus losses associated with nonconformity), involvement (in conforming versus nonconforming activities), and beliefs (in the conventional value system versus some less conventional value system). Although these four components of control theory may vary independently, Hirschi believes that in general they vary together. Strong positive ties in each of these four areas minimizes the possibility of delinquency, while strong negative ties maximizes the likelihood of delinquency.[53]

While there is some empirical evidence to support portions of the control-theory approach, this approach leaves unanswered a number of

51. Carl B. Klockars, "The Contemporary Crises of Marxist Criminology," *Criminology* 16, no. 4 (February 1979): 477–515.

52. Walter C. Reckless, "A New Theory of Delinquency and Crime," *Federal Probation* 25 (1961): 42–46; or *The Crime Problem* (New York: Appleton-Century-Crofts, 1967).

53. Travis Hirschi, *Causes of Delinquency* (Berkeley, Calif.: University of California Press, 1969).

important questions. What is the exact nature of the relationship between self-concept and labeling? How is it that some youth who appear to be well insulated from negative attachments and bonds commit delinquent acts? Do such bonds and attachments themselves actually inhibit delinquent behavior, or are the bonds and attachments perceived by law enforcement and criminal justice personnel simply used to determine whether or not to take official action? Are there longitudinal data which support the approach?

Implications for Practitioners

The implications for practitioners of all the theoretical approaches discussed are numerous and important. Demonology as an explanation for delinquency is of little importance today. The classical approach to crime and delinquency remains important as the basis of our current juvenile and criminal justice systems, for much public opinion concerning control of delinquents, and because it has not and does not work very well in controlling deviant behavior. The notion that somehow more severe punishment will reduce or eliminate delinquency remains common among the public and, unfortunately, among many practitioners. As a result, the public clamors for more arrests, more prosecutions, more adjudications, and more severe punishment. Most practitioners are keenly aware that these increases are likely to have little or no positive effect on delinquents. They are also aware that with the limited resources available, certainty and immediacy of apprehension and punishment are not likely to be achieved. As a result, practitioners are once again caught in the middle, left to struggle within or attempt to change a system based on faulty or at least questionable grounds. Currently, the only effective deterrent to delinquency based upon the classical approach may be capital punishment, which would clearly deter the particular juvenile from further delinquency. Since there is little convincing evidence that capital punishment would deter other potential offenders and since we are concerned about rehabilitation of offenders, the classical approach (appealing though it might be in moments of anger) has little to offer in contemporary juvenile justice.

Biological theories of causation raise some important issues. While biological factors do not seem to be a direct cause of delinquency, practitioners should remain constantly alert to the possibility that biological malfunctions or abnormalities may be important in assessing juveniles' behavior. For example, a juvenile who has become increasingly more aggressive, more irrational, and/or less cooperative over time could conceivably be suffering from brain damage (tumor or lesion, for instance) which, in a sense, causes frequent fights with peers or parents. It is best, in cases where physical ailments might be related to delinquency problems, to provide for appropriate medical examinations to eliminate the possibility.

Recent evidence suggests that the amount of crime and delinquency among those characterized as mentally disordered is higher than in the population at large. Although such evidence is questionable as a result of the inability to operationally define and measure personality disturbances, the psychological approach remains important to practitioners in the delinquency field for a variety of reasons. There is, of course, always the possibility that some emotional or psychological problem might be causally related to delinquent behavior and, if suspected, this possibility should be fully explored. The psychological approach is also important because treatment in many institutions for delinquents is largely psychological—individual and/or group therapy or counseling. If we are correct in our assessment that the evidence does not overwhelmingly support the belief that psychological disturbances commonly cause delinquency, a large number of current treatment programs may be inappropriate. This may help explain our repeated failures in the area of rehabilitation. Finally, the psychological approach is important because it is employed by a large proportion of practitioners, with at least occasional success.

We believe that the implications of the sociological school and the psychological-learning school are crucial for practitioners (not surprising, since we are sociologists). First, there is a direct relationship between these theories, which view delinquency as learned social behavior resulting from social interaction, and the current juvenile justice system. If these theoretical approaches are correct, much of the juvenile justice system makes sense, but some of it does not. For example, if labeling is an important factor in delinquency, attempts to keep juvenile proceedings confidential would be beneficial. If delinquent behavior is learned from associations with adult offenders, it makes sense to separate the two groups. However, it does not make sense from this theoretical perspective to place delinquents in institutions with other delinquents, if we hope to eventually rehabilitate and release them. This may account for the failure of most institutions to cause a positive change among most delinquent inmates.

Second, the sociological approach in particular looks for causes of delinquency in the society as well as in the individual. It may be that the only way to significantly reduce delinquency rates is to change some societal policies, such as those leading to educational and racial discrimination and unemployment.

Finally, the sociological approach suggests methods of control and rehabilitation that do not require capital punishment, the practice of eugenics, or the complete restructuring of the juvenile's personality. This approach suggests that positive reinforcement, administered in the surroundings in which the juvenile lives and by those with whom the juvenile regularly interacts, may provide more positive results than many techniques currently employed. While the sociological approach is not a cure-all approach, it does provide a number of leads for future research and treatment that may prove beneficial, provided citizen and agency cooperation can be obtained.

Summary

We have provided a brief history of some of the attempts to explain delinquency. It should be clear at this point that, using our definition of theory, few, if any, of these attempts have resulted in explanations that are sound from a scientific point of view. Many have been more or less discarded over time, while others continue to provide leads that need to be pursued. Bridging the gap between theory and practice is crucial to the control of delinquency and to improvement of the juvenile justice system. The input of practitioners is extremely useful in testing our theoretical statements. The benefits to be reaped, if and when a sound theoretical base is established, are considerable. We can no longer afford to ignore the importance of theory, nor can we continue to rely upon "common sense" notions of causation, which are, as we have seen, very often inaccurate.

Discussion Questions

1. What is a scientific theory and why is the development of such theories crucial to the understanding and control of delinquency?
2. What are the strengths and weaknesses of our current juvenile justice system in terms of the learning theory and labeling theory approaches?

3. Discuss some of the reasons why the classical approach to the control of delinquency has been and continues to be ineffective. Why do you think the approach has remained popular in spite of its ineffectiveness?
4. What are the major strengths and weaknesses of the psychogenic approach to understanding and controlling delinquency?

Selected Readings

Cernkovich, Stephan A. "Evaluating Two Models of Delinquency Causation: Structural Theory and Control Theory." *Criminology* 16, no. 3 (November 1978): 335–52.

Hagan, J. *Crime, Criminal Behavior, and Its Control.* New York: McGraw-Hill, 1985.

Mannheim, Hermann. *Pioneers in Criminology.* Montclair, N.J.: Patterson Smith, 1966.

Monahan, John, and Henry J. Steadman. "Crime and Mental Disorder." *Research in Brief,* National Institute of Justice. Washington, D.C.: U.S. Government Printing Office, September 1984.

Nettler, Gwynn. *Explaining Crime.* 3d ed. New York: McGraw-Hill, 1984.

Quinney, Richard. *The Social Reality of Crime.* Boston: Little, Brown & Co., 1970.

Savitz, Leonard D., and Norman Johnston. *Contemporary Criminology.* New York: John Wiley & Sons, Inc., 1984.

Schur, Edwin M. *Labeling Deviant Behavior.* New York: Harper & Row, 1971.

Sheley, J. F. *Exploring Crime: Readings in Criminology and Criminal Justice.* Belmont, Calif.: Wadsworth, 1987.

Shoemaker, Donald J. *Theories of Delinquency: An Examination of Explanations of Delinquent Behavior.* New York: Oxford University Press, 1984.

Skinner, B. F. *Science and Human Behavior.* New York: Macmillan Co., 1953.

5 Purpose and Scope of Juvenile Court Acts

Every juvenile court act contains sections that discuss purpose and scope. The purpose statement of a juvenile court act spells out the intent or basic philosophy of the act. The scope of the act is indicated by sections dealing with definitions, age, jurisdiction, and waiver. In this chapter, we will focus on the Uniform Juvenile Court Act,[1] which was developed in an attempt to encourage uniformity of purpose, scope, and procedures in the juvenile justice system. For purposes of comparison, sections of various state juvenile codes will be presented and analyzed. Although the Uniform Juvenile Court Act has not been adopted in its entirety by any one state, recent revisions of some states' juvenile court acts are now in accord with the recommendations of the Uniform Juvenile Court Act.

Purpose

As indicated previously, the first juvenile court act in the United States was passed in Illinois in 1899. By 1945 all states had a juvenile court act within their statutory enactments or constitutions.[2] Juvenile court acts typically authorize the creation of a juvenile court with the legal power to hear designated kinds of cases, such as delinquency, neglect, abuse, dependency, and other special cases enumerated in the acts.

Typically, juvenile court acts establish both procedural and substantive law relative to youths within the court's jurisdiction. This law is to be administered in a general atmosphere of parental concern rather than with punitive overtones. As a result of reformers' interests in divorcing the juvenile court from the criminal court, a separate nomenclature has been developed, based upon the philosophy underlying juvenile courts as opposed to criminal courts.

1. National Conference of Commissioners on Uniform State Laws, *Uniform Juvenile Court Act* (August 1968). A copy of this act is included in appendix A.
2. Paul Tappan, *Juvenile Delinquency* (New York: McGraw-Hill, 1949), 172–73.

Table 5.1
Comparison of Adult Criminal Justice and Juvenile Justice Systems

Adult	Juvenile
Arrest	Taking into Custody
Preliminary Hearing	Preliminary Conference/ Detention Hearing (both optional)
Grand Jury/Information/ Indictment	Petition
Arraignment	--------
Criminal Trial	Adjudicatory Hearing
Sentencing Hearing	Dispositional Hearing
Sentence—Probation, Incarceration, etc.	Disposition—Probation, Incarceration, etc.
Appeal	Appeal

As table 5.1 indicates, we find "a petition alleging that the respondent may have committed a delinquent act," instead of "a complaint charging a defendant with a crime." We find "adjudicatory" and "dispositional" hearings, instead of a "criminal trial" and "sentencing hearing." The entire proceeding is initiated by a "petition" in the "interests of" the juvenile rather than by a "complaint against" him. The juvenile, therefore, may not be "found guilty" in juvenile court, but may be "adjudicated delinquent." Juvenile court acts are predicated on the basic assumption that all agencies involved in the juvenile justice system act in the best interests of the juvenile. There are, however, differences of opinion concerning how to best ensure the interests of the juvenile. In August 1968, in the hope of bringing some uniformity to legal definitions of delinquency and delinquency proceedings, the National Conference of Commissioners on Uniform State Laws drafted and recommended for enactment in all the states, a Uniform Juvenile Court Act. This act was approved by the American Bar Association at its annual meeting during the same year.

In essence, section 1 of the Uniform Juvenile Court Act reaffirms the basic philosophy of all juvenile court acts by specifically stating that the major purpose of the act is "to provide for the care, protection, and wholesome moral, mental, and physical development of children coming within its provisions."[3] The basic philosophy was first stated in the Cook

3. *Uniform Juvenile Court Act*, sec. 1. See appendix A.

County Juvenile Court Act of 1899 and has been stated in each state's juvenile court act adopted or revised since 1899. This philosophy has been controversial because of the questionable ability of the juvenile justice system to provide the specified benefits to juveniles. Considerable documentation exists on the deficiencies of the state's ability to provide for the welfare of juveniles. A week seldom passes where a column in a newspaper or an article in a journal or magazine does not relate an instance of neglect by the state in its parental role.[4] Although the philosophy of providing "care, guidance, and protection" is well entrenched in the juvenile justice system, it would appear that a reevaluation of the state's effectiveness in adhering to that philosophy is in order.

Other basic themes expressed in the Uniform Act include protecting juveniles who commit delinquent acts from the taint of criminality and punishment and substituting treatment, training, and rehabilitation; keeping the juvenile within the family whenever possible and separating the juvenile from his or her parents only when necessary for his or her welfare or in the interest of public safety; and providing a simple judicial procedure to execute and enforce the act, yet, one which assures a fair hearing with constitutional and other legal rights recognized and enforced. We will now discuss each of these philosophical themes. In "Implications for Practitioners," we will focus our attention on the ability of states to meet the goals expressed.[5]

Protecting the Juvenile from Stigmatization

For a long time, some states allowed a wide variety of activities to be labeled delinquent. However, a majority of states have revised their juvenile codes and changed their legal definitions of acts considered delinquent. At issue is the difference between unthinking, mischievous misbehavior of a nonserious nature and vicious, intentional conduct that endangers life and property. It is difficult to ascertain exactly when mischievous behavior ends and vicious conduct begins. As a result, we frequently encounter cases where the hard-core delinquent has benefited from the treatment/rehabilitation philosophy of the juvenile court to the point where any concept of justice or accountability has been eliminated.

4. For further readings see Patrick T. Murphy, *Our Kindly Parent. . . . The State* (New York: The Viking Press, Inc., 1974); and Howard James, *Children in Trouble: A National Scandal* (New York: Pocket Books, 1971).

5. We are using the term "state" here to mean that government agency with appropriate jurisdiction. Most often this is the county or municipality in juvenile cases.

Similarly, we sometimes note that mischievous youth are treated as hard-core delinquents. Clearly, the concepts of rehabilitation and treatment can be helpful to both the mischievous offender and the hard-core delinquent. For the mischievous offender, a variety of rehabilitative/treatment programs have been developed as alternatives to the punishment concept and are more or less effective in community-based agencies. For the hard-core offender, rehabilitative/treatment programs have been typically located in institutions housing more serious offenders. However, we sometimes find the mischievous offender labeled delinquent in an institution for delinquents, while his or her peers who are more serious offenders remain at large in community-based programs that were never intended to deal with hard-core cases. In short, some juveniles have learned how to "play the game" and are able to shift all responsibility for their actions to others or to society and therefore escape accountability under the rehabilitative/treatment philosophy. Others, less skilled at "playing the game," are unable to escape more serious consequences for acts that may be trivial in nature. The dilemma facing reformers of the juvenile court revolves around the obvious—avoid labeling juveniles who don't deserve the label "delinquent" and at the same time prevent the juvenile court from becoming so informal that those who are a threat to the community remain at large.

Maintaining the Family Unit

The concept that a child should remain in the family unit whenever possible is another basic element of the Uniform Juvenile Court Act. Without question the child and family should not be separated unless there is a serious threat to the welfare of the child or society. However, once there is an established necessity for removing the child, the juvenile court has the power to move swifty in that direction. Determining exactly when it is necessary to remove the youth is not, of course, an easy task. Careful investigation of the total family environment and its effect on the juvenile is typically required in cases of suspected abuse, neglect, and delinquency. Removal may be permanent or it may include an option to return the child if circumstances improve. Careful consideration is focused on the family's attitudes toward the child and the past record of relationships among other family members.

While most of us would agree that it is generally desirable to maintain the family unit, there are certainly circumstances when removal is in the best interests of both the juvenile and society. The welfare of the child is clearly jeopardized by keeping him or her in a family where gross neglect, abuse, or acts of criminality occur. The emphasis placed upon maintaining the integrity of the family unit seems at times to be taken so seriously by juvenile court judges that they maintain family ties even when removal is clearly the better alternative.

Preserving Constitutional Rights in Juvenile Court Proceedings

The Uniform Juvenile Court Act provides judicial procedures so all parties are assured fairness and recognition of legal rights. The early philosophy of informal hearings void of legal procedures has a limited place in the modern juvenile justice system. For example, if the issue is delinquency and the act for which the child has been accused is theft, then the procedural rules of evidence should support the allegation and the result would be an adjudication of delinquency. If the evidence does not support the allegation, no adjudication of delinquency should occur. In an informal hearing where there is an absence of established guilt and where an adjudication of delinquency is based upon the attitude of the child, the types of peers with whom that child associates, or his or her family's condition, the rights of the juvenile and perhaps other parties have been violated. The philosophy of a fair hearing, where constitutional rights are recognized and enforced and where a high standard of proof to establish delinquency is strictly enforced, has been generally established in juvenile court acts since 1967. Informality is generally accepted in post-adjudicatory hearings on disposition of the juvenile and is often permitted in pre-hearing stages. The adjudicatory hearing for delinquency must, however, be based on establishing "beyond a reasonable doubt" that the allegations are supported by the allowable evidence.

The general purpose of juvenile court acts, then, is to ensure the welfare of juveniles while protecting their constitutional rights in such a way that removal from the family unit is accomplished only for a reasonable cause and in the best interests of the juvenile and society.

Scope

In addition to the basic themes previously discussed, all juvenile court acts define the ages and subject matter within the scope of the court.

Age

Section 2 of the Uniform Juvenile Court Act defines a "child" as a person who is under the age of eighteen years; or under the age of twenty-one years, but who committed an act of delinquency before reaching the age of eighteen years; or under twenty-one years who committed an act of delinquency after becoming eighteen years and is transferred to the juvenile court by another court having jurisdiction over him or her.[6]

As stated in chapter 2, both upper and lower age limits vary among the states. The Uniform Juvenile Court Act establishes the age of eighteen as the legal age where actions of an illegal nature will be considered criminal and the wrongdoer will be considered accountable and responsible as an adult. Prior to the eighteenth birthday, illegal activities will be considered acts of delinquency with the wrongdoer processed by the juvenile court in a way that removes the taint of criminality and punishment and substitutes treatment, training, and rehabilitation in its place. The Uniform Juvenile Court Act allows two exceptions regarding the legal jurisdictional age of eighteen. Section 2(1, iii) states that a person under twenty-one, who commits an act of delinquency after becoming eighteen, can be transferred to the juvenile court by another court having jurisdiction and therefore would be accorded all of the protection and procedural guidelines of the juvenile court. Section 34 allows for a transfer to other courts of a child under eighteen, if serious acts of delinquency are alleged and the child was sixteen or older at the time of the alleged conduct.[7] There are stringent guidelines to follow before a waiver to adult court jurisdiction may be permitted. Waivers of juvenile jurisdiction will be discussed later in this chapter.

In establishing the age of eighteen as the legal breakpoint between childhood and adulthood, the Uniform Juvenile Court Act is consistent with a majority of state juvenile court acts, as the following table indicates.

Delinquent Acts

The Uniform Juvenile Court Act clearly limits the definition of delinquency by stating in essence that a delinquent act is an act designated

6. *Uniform Juvenile Court Act,* sec. 2. See appendix A.

7. *Uniform Juvenile Court Act,* sec. 34. See appendix A. These provisions, of course, are in keeping with the notions of "age of responsibility" discussed in chapter 1.

Table 5.2
Age at Which Criminal Courts Gain Jurisdiction of Young Offenders Ranges from 16 to 19*

Age of offender when under criminal court jurisdiction

16	17	18			19
Connecticut	Georgia	Alabama	Kansas	Ohio	Wyoming
New York	Illinois	Alaska	Kentucky	Oklahoma	
North Carolina	Louisiana	Arizona	Maine	Oregon	
	Massachusetts	Arkansas	Maryland	Pennsylvania	
	Missouri	California	Michigan	Rhode Island	
	South Carolina	Colorado	Minnesota	South Dakota	
	Texas	Delaware	Mississippi	Tennessee	
		District of	Montana	Utah	
		Columbia	Nebraska	Vermont	
		Florida	Nevada	Virginia	
		Hawaii	New Hampshire	Washington	
		Idaho	New Jersey	West Virginia	
		Indiana	New Mexico	Wisconsin	
		Iowa	North Dakota	Federal districts	

*Source: Linda A. Szymanski, "Upper age of juvenile court jurisdiction statutes analysis," National Center for Juvenile Justice, March 1987.

as a crime by local ordinance, state law, or federal law. Excluded from acts constituting delinquency are vague activities, such as incorrigibility, ungovernability, habitually disobedient, and other status offenses, which are legal offenses only applicable to children and not to adults. At the time the Uniform Juvenile Court Act was drafted in 1968, many states legally defined delinquency as encompassing a broad spectrum of behavior. The proposal by the drafters of the Uniform Juvenile Court Act excluded the broader definition of activities labeled as delinquent and focused only on violations of laws that are applicable to both adults and minors. This narrow interpretation was consistent with the legalistic trend occurring in the latter 1960s. By narrowing the legal definition of delinquency, the Uniform Juvenile Court Act did not ignore other types of activities that fall within the court's jurisdiction, but placed these activities outside the realm of delinquent acts. A minor who is "beyond the control of his parents," "habitually truant from school," or "habitually disobedient, uncontrolled, wayward, incorrigible, indecent, or deports himself or herself as to injure or endanger the morals or health of themself or others" was until recently included in the legal definition of delinquency in some states.[8] A major difficulty with including these vague activities within the delinquent behavior category concerns the issue of who defines what is incorrigible, indecent, or habitual misconduct and the nature of the standard used to determine this behavior. In most of the states using the broad definition of delinquency, there are no standardized definitions for "habitual," "wayward," "incorrigible," and so on.

It is interesting to note that prior to the development of the Uniform Juvenile Court Act in 1968, several states had already started restricting the definition of delinquency to include only those activities that would be punishable as crimes if committed by adults. For example, in New York under the pre-1962 Children's Court Act, the term "juvenile delinquency" included ungovernability and incorrigibility. However, in 1962, the Joint Legislative Committee on Court Reorganization, which drafted the Family Court Act,[9] developed the concept of a "person in need of supervision" to cover noncriminal status offenses and the term "juvenile delinquent" was narrowed to include only persons over seven and less than sixteen years who commit any act that, if committed by

8. *Indiana Code Annotated*, sec. 31–6–4–1, 1987; *South Carolina Code Annotated*, sec. 20–7–390, 20–7–400 (A) (1), 1976; *West Virginia Code Annotated*, sec. 49–1–4, 1986.

9. *New York Session Laws*, vol. 2, 3428, 3434 (McKinney 1962).

an adult, would constitute a crime.[10] With a more specific definition of delinquency, it was inevitable that due process procedures, rules of evidence, and constitutional rights would emerge as important issues in Supreme Court decisions involving the rights of juveniles in delinquency proceedings. As the states moved toward a more specific definition of delinquency, additional appellate decisions were rendered regarding "due process and fair treatment." The effect of this narrow interpretation of delinquency has been the advent of an adjudicatory process that is more formalized and that ensures and protects the juvenile's procedural and constitutional rights. This trend is clearly consistent with the spirit behind the creation of the Uniform Juvenile Court Act.

Section 2(3) of the Uniform Juvenile Court Act indicates that an adjudicated delinquent is in need of "treatment or rehabilitation." The development of narrower definitions of delinquency and more formalized "due process models" is not intended to cause the juvenile court to abandon rehabilitation and treatment. This philosophy was stated as early as 1909, when it was pointed out that "the goal of the juvenile court is not so much to crush but to develop, not to make the juvenile a criminal but a worthy citizen."[11] This initial concept of rehabilitation and treatment has been affirmed in many decisions and is briefly summarized by the Supreme Court case, in re *Gault*, where the Court reaffirms the original juvenile court philosophy that "the child is to be 'treated' and 'rehabilitated' and the procedures, from apprehension through institutionalization, are to be 'clinical' rather than 'punitive.' "[12] It is important to remember that although it operates under the "treatment and rehabilitation" concept, the juvenile court is also charged with protecting the community against unlawful and violent conduct. To fulfill this obligation the court may resort to incarceration or imprisonment. This clash between the rehabilitative ideal and the clear, present necessity to protect the community in certain situations has been described as the "schizophrenic nature of the Juvenile Court process."[13] It is clear that

10. Ibid., sec. 712(a).

11. *Consolidated Laws of New York Annotated,* bk. 29A, art. 7 (McKinney 1975), p. 543.

12. Frederic L. Faust and Paul J. Brantingham, "The Era of the 'Socialized Juvenile Court'—1899 to 1967," in *Juvenile Justice Philosophy,* ed. Frederic L. Faust and Paul J. Brantingham (St. Paul, Minn.: West Publishing Company, 1974), 369–70.

13. See *Consolidated Laws of New York Annotated,* bk. 29A, art. 7 (McKinney 1975), p. 547.

a majority of the states have moved toward a narrower definition of delinquency.[14] Inherent in this trend is the recent movement toward formalizing the legal procedures and processes accorded the accused delinquent. The importance of this trend is twofold. First, legal definitions of delinquency have become more standardized and by law require a violation or attempted violation of the criminal code. Second, the process of proving the allegation of delinquency may include only the same types of evidentiary materials that would be admitted if the same charges were leveled against an adult. This is a considerable change from past practices in many juvenile courts where much of the evidentiary material that was introduced to prove an act of delinquency was basically irrelevant material concerning the juvenile's family, peers, school behavior, and other information about his or her environment. The establishment of reasonable proof that the juvenile did violate the law was lost in the process. The case was often weighed and decided on factors other than establishing, beyond reasonable doubt, that the juvenile committed the act for which he or she had been accused. The juvenile court is a court of law. The juvenile adjudicatory process and the juvenile court must be totally dedicated to work within a legal framework that is conducive to reaching the truth and serving the ends of justice. To do otherwise would result in what is best described in an often-quoted passage of the Kent decision, where the Supreme Court stated:

> *There is evidence . . . that the child receives the worse of both worlds; that he gets neither the protections accorded to adults nor the solicitious care and regenerative treatment postulated for children.*[15]

Without a doubt, there is a place in the juvenile justice system for consideration of the adjudicated delinquent's family and his or her environment. However, such consideration should be given only after an adjudication of delinquency rather than being used as the basis for adjudication. For instance, suppose as an adult you have been accused of "breaking and entering" and throughout the pre-trial process and during the course of the trial almost all of the evidence and information introduced centers around your family, your associations, your attitude, and your overall environment. Furthermore, only a minimum amount of court time and effort is devoted toward establishing beyond a doubt that you

14. John L. Hutzler and Ellen Nimick, *Juvenile Court Jurisdiction Over Childrens' Conduct: 1982 Comparative Analysis of Juvenile and Family Codes and National Standards* (Pittsburg: National Center for Juvenile Justice, 1982).

15. Justice Fortas in *Kent* v. *United States*, 383 US 541, 546. See appendix C.

did in fact violate the law by breaking and entering and even then most of this evidence is hearsay, not subjected to cross-examination, and based on belief rather than proof. Yet, you are convicted. Such cases were fairly common in the juvenile justice system until the *Gault* decision in 1967. The focus on due process to protect the accused juvenile's constitutional rights is as important as determining whether the act was committed by the accused. The legal issue of delinquency must be determined not on the basis of a social investigation describing the minor's environment, but on the basis of whether the evidence supports or denies the allegation of delinquent acts.

Unruly Children (minors, juveniles, children, persons in need of or requiring supervision or intervention)

Section 2(4) of the Uniform Juvenile Court Act defines an unruly child as a child who

(i) *while subject to compulsory school attendance is habitually and without justification truant from school;*

(ii) *is habitually disobedient of the reasonable and lawful commands of his parent, guardian, or other custodian and is ungovernable; or*

(iii) *has committed an offense applicable only to a child; and*

(iv) *in any of the foregoing is in need of treatment or rehabilitation.*[16]

At one time, a majority of states included these activities in the category of delinquent behavior that often resulted in the official label of "delinquent" and led to the possibility of being incarcerated in a juvenile correctional institution for treatment and rehabilitation. The Uniform Juvenile Court Act recognizes that such activities may require the aid and services provided by the juvenile court but also recognizes that these minors should not be included in the category "delinquent." According to section 32 of the Uniform Juvenile Court Act, the unruly child cannot be placed in a correctional institution unless the court finds after a further hearing that the child is not amenable to treatment or rehabilitation under a previous noncorrectional disposition.[17] The "unruly child" is generally categorized by activities that are noncriminal or minor violations of law. Types of offenses, such as curfew violations or running away from home, are referred to as "status offenses" or acts that are offenses only because of the age of the offender. If the same act were committed

16. *Uniform Juvenile Court Act*, sec. 2(4). See appendix A.
17. *Uniform Juvenile Court Act*, sec. 32. See appendix A.

by an adult, it would not be a violation of law. A substantial number of states have separated the types of activities described as "unruly" by the Uniform Juvenile Court Act from delinquency and have placed them in the nondelinquent categories of "in need of supervision."[18] The labels of these categories differ and include titles such as, PINS (persons in need of supervision), JINS (juveniles in need of supervision), CHINS (children in need of supervision), and MRAI (minors requiring authoritative intervention).[19]

Regardless of the title, the importance of the development of this category lies in separating the delinquent from the nonserious violator and in realizing that the behavioral activities included in the categories "unruly child" or "child in need of assistance" are often symptomatic of problems in the juvenile's home life and environment and may not indicate criminal tendencies. The "unruly child" category allows the juvenile court to be involved with the minor who needs supervision and allows the court flexibility and options short of the label "delinquent." There is a potential problem to consider regarding the "unruly child" category. Some juvenile courts use this category as a means of plea bargaining. In doing this, they fail to pursue serious cases of misconduct as delinquency and then use the "unruly child" category as a form of plea bargaining when the prosecution has a weak case. The labels "unruly child" or "in need of supervision" tend to become terms of disrepute and often have a stigmatizing effect on the juvenile similar to the label "delinquent." As a result, one of the major benefits of the distinction is lost. been lost.

To further distinguish the differences between the delinquent and the "unruly child," most states have developed different procedural requirements. These requirements allow the civil standard of "preponderance of evidence" in the adjudicatory hearing for the latter, where the bulk of the evidence, but not necessarily all of it, must support the charges. They also provide for different dispositional options and for different upper ages for the category of "unruly" or "in need of supervision."

In distinguishing between juveniles whose misconduct is criminal and those whose misconduct is not, it is assumed that the "unruly child's"

18. Hutzler and Nimick, *Juvenile Court Jurisdiction over Children's Conduct,* 1–6. See also *District of Columbia Code,* sec. 16–2301(8), 1981; and *New York Family Court Act,* sec. 712(a) (McKinney 1983).

19. CHINS—*Wyoming Statutes Annotated,* sec. 14–6–201(a) (iv), 1981; JINS—*New Jersey Statutes Annotated,* sec. 2A: 4–45, 1981; MRAI—*Illinois Revised Statutes,* ch. 37, art. 3, sec. 803–3, 1988; PINS—*Consolidated Laws of New York Annotated,* bk. 29A, art. 7, sec. 712(b), 1983.

behavior may be of a pre-delinquent nature and that early, remedial treatment might prevent the incipient delinquency. However, it is becoming increasingly clear that the "unruly child" may have more intense emotional and behavioral problems than some delinquents who commit a single criminal act or a series of minor criminal acts.

The "unruly" or "in need of supervision" categories are generally written without specificity since it is difficult to define and describe all of the noncriminal (delinquent) conduct that could ultimately fall within these categories. The term "habitually" is frequently used to distinguish between isolated incidents and a recurring pattern of incorrigibility, ungovernability, or disobedience. The flagrant, repetitive nature of these behaviors often serves as the basis for filing a petition.

It was noted earlier that in some instances the behavior engaged in by the juvenile and alleged in a petition (often filed by the parents) may actually reflect "neglect" rather than an "unruly child." A lack of parental supervision, whether due to unwillingness or inability of the parents, may have created a situation within the family that resulted in the juvenile's behavior. This behavior, although alleged to be "unruly" in the petition, may have been precipitated by a family crisis resulting in the minor rebelling against the family.

Deprived, Neglected, or Dependent Children

In section 2(5) of the Uniform Juvenile Court Act a "deprived" child is defined as a child under the age of eighteen who

> (i) is without proper parental care or control, subsistence, education as required by law, or other care or control necessary for his physical, mental, or emotional health, or morals, and the deprivation is not due primarily to the lack of financial means of his parents, guardian, or other custodian;
> (ii) has been placed for care or adoption in violation of law; [or]
> (iii) has been abandoned by his parents, guardian, or other custodian; [or]
> [(iv) is without a parent, guardian, or legal custodian.][20]

A number of jurisdictions use a single classification to describe a child who is without a parent or who has been abandoned, abused, or is without adequate parental care or supervision. Such a child is variously referred to as a "dependent child,"[21] a "deprived child,"[22] or a "neglected child."[23]

20. *Uniform Juvenile Court Act*, sec. 2(5). See appendix A.
21. *Alabama Code*, sec. 12–15–1(10), 1985.
22. *Georgia Code Annotated*, sec. 15–11–2(8), 1985.
23. *District of Columbia Code*, sec. 16–2301(9), 1981.

Some states separate deprived children into several categories with specific labels. For example, in Illinois the category "neglected minor" includes

> any minor under 18 years of age who is neglected as to proper or necessary support, education as required by law, or as to medical or other remedial care recognized under state law or other care necessary for his/her well-being, including food, clothing, and shelter, or who is abandoned by his/her parents, guardian, or custodian.[24]

Within the section of the Illinois code dealing with neglected minors is a special section on abused minors, including

> any minor under 18 years of age whose parent or immediate family member, custodian, or any person living in the same family or household, or a paramour of the minor's parent: (1) inflicts, causes to be inflicted, or allows to be inflicted physical injury which causes death, disfigurement, impairment of physical or emotional health, or loss or impairment of any bodily function; or (2) creates a substantial risk of physical injury; or (3) commits or allows to be committed any sex offense; or (4) commits or allows to be committed acts of torture; or (5) inflicts excessive corporal punishment; or (6) whose environment is injurious to his or her welfare.[25]

In addition, Illinois has a separate category for the "dependent minor" who is under eighteen and

> (1) is without a parent, guardian or legal custodian; or
> (2) is without proper care because of the physical or mental disability of his or her parent, guardian or custodian; or
> (3) is without proper medical or remedial care or other care necessary for his or her well-being through no fault, neglect or lack of concern by his or her parents, guardian or custodian; or
> (4) who has a parent, guardian or legal custodian who with good cause, wishes to be relieved of all residual parental rights and responsibilities, guardianship or custody, and who desires the appointment of a guardian of the person with power to consent to the adoption of the 'minor.'[26]

Even though the Uniform Juvenile Court Act specifically disallows "a lack of financial means" as a basis for alleging that a minor is a "deprived child," some states, under circumstances where the deprivation is so extreme that it seriously endangers the well-being of the child, provide for handling these cases under the "neglected child" portion of the juvenile court act. Deprivation may be considered "gross neglect," if the

24. *Illinois Revised Statutes*, ch. 37, art. 2, sec. 802–3(1), 1988.
25. Ibid., sec. 802–2.
26. Ibid., sec. 802–4.

amount of parental income is sufficient, but the income is misappropriated and jeopardizes the well-being of the children within the family. Appropriate juvenile court remedies are generally available for this type of deprivation.

According to Sanford Fox, "where a statutory distinction is made between a neglected child and one who is dependent, the difference generally is a matter of the presence of some parental fault in the former case and its absence in the latter."[27] The Illinois distinction between the neglected child and dependent child clearly illustrates the difference between the "parental fault concept" for the "neglected" child and the "no fault concept" for the "dependent" child. Regardless of the statutory definitions of "deprived," "neglected," "abused," or "dependent child," it is quite clear that the situations described in these statutes exist basically through no fault of the child. The trend of legislation may follow the Uniform Juvenile Court Act's combining of dependency and neglect under the label of "deprived child." Iowa, for example, combined dependency and neglect into the category of "child in need of assistance."[28]

Jurisdiction

The jurisdiction of a court concerns persons, behavior, and relationships over which the court may exercise authority. The word jurisdiction also may be used to describe geographical areas or to describe the process through which the juvenile court acquires authority to make orders concerning particular individuals.[29] As Thomas Johnson points out, the question of jurisdiction is of basic importance to the juvenile court judge; without jurisdiction over the subject matter and the subject, that judge's court has no power to act. The term jurisdiction means, "the legal power, right, or authority to hear and determine a cause or causes."[30] Jurisdiction is created and defined in juvenile court acts.

There is a distinction between the juvenile court's inherent jurisdictional powers and its discretion to exercise jurisdiction over a case. For example, the statutory law creating the juvenile court in a state may give that court exclusive jurisdiction in any proceeding involving cases

27. Sanford J. Fox, *Juvenile Courts in a Nutshell* (St. Paul, Minn.: West Publishing Company, 1971), 58.

28. *Iowa Revised Statutes,* ch. 232, sec. 232.2,(13)9(14), 1975.

29. Fox, *Juvenile Courts in a Nutshell,* 13.

30. Thomas A. Johnson, *Introduction to the Juvenile Justice System* (St. Paul, Minn.: West Publishing Company, 1975), 20.

of delinquency, unruly children, dependency, or neglect, provided the respondent is within the age range and geographical area specified by the court. However, unless a petition is duly filed and the respondent receives a copy or summary of the petition as well as adequate notification of when and where the allegations against him or her will be presented and heard, the court has not exercised proper jurisdiction over the case.

In some states the juvenile court act has been repealed and a broader family court act has been created allowing for broader jurisdictional powers over virtually all problems directly involving families.[31] Adoptions, divorces, proceedings concerning mentally retarded or mentally ill children, custody and support of children, paternity suits, and certain criminal offenses committed by one family member against another are all within the jurisdiction of some family court acts.

Age is obviously an important factor in determining jurisdiction in all states. As previously stated, age limits for delinquency vary among the states for both the upper and lower limits. Eight states (Colorado, Kansas, Minnesota, Mississippi, Pennsylvania, South Dakota, Texas, and Vermont) have statutes establishing a lower age limit of ten years of age, while in Wisconsin the lower age limit is twelve. The majority of juvenile court acts are silent on the lower age limits; however, in some states the common-law age of seven has been established by statute as the lower age limit for delinquency. This is the case in New York and Massachusetts, where the jurisdictional age for delinquency begins at seven. In thirty-nine states the minimum age for delinquency is not specified.[32] In these states, it might be technically possible that a child could be adjudicated delinquent from birth. Such adjudication is unlikely if the juvenile court requires a reasonable degree of capacity, such as the ability to understand the act and to know or appreciate its consequences.

The "unruly child" or "child in need of supervision" has been generally subjected to the same upper age limit for jurisdictional purposes as the delinquent. Since common law does not deal directly with this category, the common-law age of seven has not been traditionally recognized as the minimum age for the "unruly child."

Determining the upper or lower age limits in delinquency raises difficult questions about the factor of responsibility and accountability in law. For example, a child of six, who is fully aware of the wrongfulness

31. For example, see *Consolidated Laws of New York Annotated,* bk. 29A (McKinney 1975).

32. U.S. Department of Justice, *Sourcebook of Criminal Justice Statistics 1987* (U.S. Government Printing Office: Washington, D.C., 1988): 94–95.

of a criminal act and its consequences and still commits the act, will be immune from prosecution if the jurisdictional age of seven is part of the state's juvenile court act. Another child, who is less mature at seven years, may commit the same act while unaware of its consequences and may have to face juvenile court.

States differ about whether a juvenile who commits a delinquent act while within the age jurisdiction of the juvenile court, but who is not apprehended until he or she has passed the maximum age of jurisdiction, can be handled as a juvenile. Some states have determined through court decisions or previous statutory enactments that it is the age at the time of the offense that determines jurisdiction and not the age at the time of apprehension. The Uniform Juvenile Court Act in section 2(1, iii) allows a person under twenty-one who commits an act of delinquency before reaching the age of eighteen to be considered a "child" and within the juvenile court's jurisdiction for delinquency proceedings.[33]

States differentiate between the upper ages for delinquency and other categories, they believe that a minor may still need the care and protection of the family even though he or she is beyond the age for an adjudication of delinquency. Similarly, the "deprived," "neglected," or "dependent child" is generally not subject to a lower age limit, since a younger child may have a greater need for the protection of the juvenile court than an older counterpart. Currently some states have set one age for all categories included in the juvenile court act, while others have different ages for each category. For example, California has established the upper jurisdictional age of eighteen for activities that could result in wardship. Illinois continues to follow different ages for delinquency up to the seventeenth birthday and for "minor requiring authoritative intervention," "dependency," "abused," and "neglect" up to the eighteenth birthday.[34] The Uniform Juvenile Court Act recommends in section 2 the establishment of an upper age of eighteen for all categories.[35]

Concurrent or Exclusive Jurisdiction

The issue of concurrent or exclusive jurisdiction of the juvenile court is generally determined by the legislature and specifically stated in the

33. *Uniform Juvenile Court Act,* sec. 2(1, iii). See appendix A.

34. *Welfare and Institutions Code Annotated, California,* Pocket Supplement, sec. 600, 601.1, and 602, 1985; and *Illinois Revised Statutes,* ch. 37, art. 2, sec. 802–3, 802–4, 803–3, and 805–3, 1988.

35. *Uniform Juvenile Court Act,* sec. 2. See appendix A.

juvenile court act. The Uniform Juvenile Court Act in section 3 provides the juvenile court with exclusive jurisdiction of certain proceedings listed in that section.[36] In effect, exclusive jurisdiction means that the juvenile court will be the only tribunal legally empowered to proceed and that all other courts are deprived of jurisdiction. In some juvenile court acts, concurrent jurisdiction may be present when certain specified situations exist. For example, certain criminal acts may be concurrently under the jurisdiction of the juvenile court and the criminal court. The court that acts first may exercise jurisdiction over a case, not because the court has exclusive jurisdiction but simply because it exercises its jurisdiction before the other court acts. In some states, juvenile court acts may allow exclusive jurisdiction over adults who play a role in encouraging a minor to violate a law. In other states, this jurisdiction may be concurrent with the criminal court. In still other states, the juvenile court may have no jurisdiction over such adults; so exclusive jurisdiction rests with the criminal courts. In order to determine if the juvenile court has exclusive or concurrent jurisdiction over the subject matter and the subject, it is necessary to refer to the juvenile court act of the state in question.

In section 4 of the Uniform Juvenile Court Act, provision is made for the juvenile court to have concurrent jurisdiction with another court where the proceedings are to treat or commit a mentally retarded or mentally ill child.[37]

Waiver

As previously stated, statutory provisions in juvenile court acts have given juvenile courts original and exclusive jurisdiction over certain cases if the subject is within the defined jurisdiction. However, in a majority of juvenile court acts, there are provisions for the waiver of the juvenile court's jurisdiction over certain offenses committed by minors of certain ages. The waiver should not be confused with concurrent jurisdiction where two courts have simultaneous jurisdiction over the subject matter and the subject. Waiver, in this case, refers to the process by which a juvenile over whom the juvenile court has original jurisdiction is transferred to adult criminal court. Most authorities agree that the waiver represents a critical stage of the juvenile justice process.[38] At this point,

36. Ibid., sec. 3.

37. Ibid., sec. 4.

38. Mortimer J. Stamm, "Transfer of Jurisdiction in Juvenile Court," *Kentucky Law Journal* 62 (1973):142–43.

the juvenile may lose the *parens patriae* protection of the juvenile court, including its emphasis on treatment and rehabilitation as opposed to punishment. Once transferred (waived) to the criminal justice system, the juvenile is subjected to contact with adult offenders, may obtain a criminal record, and finds himself or herself in a generally vulnerable position.[39] In some states an automatic waiver of the exclusive jurisdiction of the juvenile court occurs when specific offenses are allegedly committed by a juvenile. For example, in Illinois,

> *any minor alleged to have committed a traffic, boating or fish and game violation or an offense punishable by fine only, may be prosecuted therefore and if found guilty punished under any statute or ordinance relating thereto, without reference to the procedures set out in the Juvenile Court Act of this state.*[40]

Among jurisdictions which permit waivers, the provisions setting forth the circumstances under which such waivers may be granted are quite varied. Most jurisdictions require that the child be over a certain age and that he/she be charged with a particularly serious offense before jurisdiction may be waived.[41] In Indiana, if a juvenile over the age of ten commits the crime of murder, or if a juvenile is over sixteen and violates any traffic laws or ordinances of that state, he or she is not within the statutory definition of "delinquent child."[42]

For the most part, automatic waivers are restricted to the more serious offenses and to lesser offenses, such as traffic violations. Even in the most serious offenses, an automatic waiver may occur only if the youth involved is over a certain age. For example, in Indiana, the youth must be over the age of ten before a waiver is possible for murder. However, in Florida, there is no minimum age if the alleged offense is punishable by death or a life sentence.[43] In Illinois, the definition of delinquent minor does not apply to any youth who at the time of the offense was at

39. *A Comparative Analysis of Juvenile Codes,* Community Research Forum, University of Illinois, Grant No. 78–JS–AX–0046, U.S. Department of Justice, July 1980, p. 9.

40. *Illinois Revised Statutes,* ch. 37, art. 5, sec. 805–4, 1988.

41. *Colorado Revised Statutes Annotated,* sec. 19–1–104(4) (a), 1986, indicate the child must be fourteen or older and charged with a felony. *Louisiana Revised Statutes Annotated,* sec. 13:157–1(A), 1985, indicate the child must be fifteen or older, and the court must find probable cause to believe the child committed armed robbery, aggravated burglary, or aggravated kidnapping.

42. *Indiana Statutes Annotated,* ch. 5.

43. *A Comparative Analysis of Juvenile Codes,* 10.

least fifteen years old and who is charged with murder, aggravated criminal sexual assault, or armed robbery committed with a firearm.[44]

According to Davis, only three states (Arkansas, Nebraska, and New York) do not provide for a waiver. A clear majority allow waivers for youth over a specified age.[45] In Illinois, a waiver may occur if the minor is thirteen or older and the alleged act constitutes a crime under the laws of the state.[46] Other states authorize waivers similarly (see table 5.3), if the jurisdictional age is established and met and the specific offense is within the statutory allowance for such a waiver. Legislative trends are toward automatic waiver for serious offenses and more frequent use of the waiver proceeding to justify criminal prosecution of "juvenile criminals."

Another type of waiver is the "discretionary waiver." A number of states permit waiver of jurisdiction over children above a certain age without regard to the nature of the offense involved. In California, the juvenile court maintains exclusive jurisdiction in all cases where the minor is under eighteen and has been charged with committing a public offense or crime unless the juvenile court finds that the minor is not a fit and proper subject to be dealt with under the juvenile court act. In such cases, the juvenile court judge may order criminal proceeding to be instituted against the minor.[47]

Discretionary determination of waivers is generally left to juvenile court judges to decide after a petition for a waiver has been filed and a hearing has been conducted on the advisability of granting the waiver. In general, the criteria used by juvenile courts to determine the granting or denial of waivers of juveniles to criminal courts are rather vague and, for the most part, quite subjective. As previously stated, in California, "if the minor is not a fit and proper subject to be dealt with under the Juvenile Court," an order instituting criminal proceedings may be rendered by the juvenile court.[48] With respect to waivers, in the case of *Kent* v. *U.S.* (1966), the Supreme Court ruled that in order to protect the constitutional rights of the juvenile, the juvenile is entitled to

1. *a full hearing on the issue of transfer,*
2. *the assistance of legal counsel at the hearing,*

44. *Illinois Revised Statutes,* ch. 37, art. 2, sec. 702–7(6a), 1988.

45. Samuel M. Davis, *Rights of Juveniles* (New York: Clark: Boardman, 1988), sec. 4–1.

46. *Illinois Revised Statutes,* ch. 37, art. 5, sec. 805–4, 1988.

47. *Welfare and Institutions Code Annotated, California,* Pocket Supplement, ch. 2, art. 5, sec. 603 and 606 (Deering 1984).

48. Ibid., ch. 2, art. 5, sec. 606, 8.

Table 5.3
48 States, the District of Columbia, and the Federal Government have judicial waiver provisions

Youngest age at which juvenile may be transferred to criminal court by judicial waiver

No specific age	10 years	12	13	14	15	16
Alaska	Vermont	Montana	Georgia	Alabama	District of Columbia	California
Arizona			Illinois	Colorado	Louisiana	Hawaii
Arkansas			Mississippi	Connecticut	Michigan	Kansas
Delaware				Idaho	New Mexico	Nevada
Florida				Iowa	Ohio	Rhode Island
Indiana				Massachusetts	Oregon	Washington
Kentucky				Minnesota	Texas	Wisconsin
Maine				Missouri	Virginia	
Maryland				North Carolina		
New Hampshire				North Dakota		
New Jersey				Pennsylvania		
Oklahoma				South Carolina		
South Dakota				Tennessee		
West Virginia				Utah		
Wyoming						
Federal districts						

Note: Many judicial waiver statutes also specify offenses that are waivable. This chart lists the states by the youngest age for which judicial waiver may be sought without regard to offense.

Source: Linda A. Szymanski, "Waiver/transfer/certification of juveniles to criminal court. Age restrictions. Crime restrictions." National Center for Juvenile Justice, February 1987.

3. *full access to the social records, used to determine whether such transfer should be made,*

4. *statement of the reasons why the juvenile judge decided to waive the juvenile to (adult) criminal court.*[49]

Although the *Kent* decision applied only to the District of Columbia, most states that allow waivers have incorporated the waiver procedures of *Kent* into their juvenile court acts. A clear majority of states statutorily guarantee a waiver hearing.

Some states have attempted to establish at least some criteria that would aid the juvenile court judge in making a determination on a motion to waive the juvenile court's jurisdiction. For example, in Illinois, the court must consider the following:

1. *whether there is sufficient evidence upon which a grand jury may be expected to return an indictment;*
2. *whether there is evidence that the alleged offense was committed in an aggressive and premeditated manner;*
3. *the age of the minor;*
4. *the previous history of the minor;*
5. *whether there are facilities particularly available to the Juvenile Court for the treatment and rehabilitation of the minor;*
6. *whether the best interest of the minor and the security of the public may require that the minor continue in custody or under supervision for a period extending beyond his minority.*[50]

The juvenile court judge, as well as the prosecuting officials, must weigh the consequences of a waiver for the future of the juvenile. The question, concerning a waiver of a juvenile to the adult criminal court for prosecution of offenses that might result in a felony record, is extremely important due to the lasting effects that a felony record might have. To justify a waiver for criminal prosecution, the juvenile court must agree to accept the more punitive, retributive, and punishment-oriented approach of the adult court. In such cases, not only must the juvenile court judge act "in the best interest of the minor," but also in the best interest of the community by protecting the community against further unlawful and perhaps violent conduct by the juvenile offender. Juvenile court judges, realizing the full effect of a felony record (in terms of future employment, for example), generally permit a waiver for criminal prosecution only when the offense is so serious that relegating the offense to the realm of delinquency would be unconscionable and would result in

49. *Kent v. United States,* 383 U.S. 541, 1966. See appendix C.
50. *Illinois Revised Statutes,* ch. 37, art. 5, sec. 805–4, 1988.

a mockery of justice and when the offense is not an isolated act but a series of acts showing a trend toward becoming more serious.

After dealing with scope and purpose, most juvenile court acts go on to describe in detail the procedures to be employed by various components of the juvenile justice system in handling the juvenile. After a brief look at the implications of the scope, purpose, and philosophy of juvenile court acts for practitioners, we will discuss these procedural requirements.

Implications for Practitioners

A thorough understanding of both the purpose and scope of juvenile court acts is crucial for practitioners at all levels of the juvenile justice system. Without this understanding, the intent of the juvenile court acts cannot be carried out.

The primary purpose of juvenile court acts is to insure the welfare of the juvenile within a legal framework while maintaining the family unit and protecting the public. Most of us would agree that this is an admirable goal. At the same time, however, we should be aware of the inherent difficulties of achieving this goal. Consider, for example, the police officer who has apprehended a particular juvenile a number of times for increasingly serious offenses. Repeated attempts at enlisting the aid of the youth's family in correcting the undesirable behavior have failed. If the officer decides that protection of the public is now of primary importance, the officer may feel compelled to arrest the juvenile, even though this action may result in the juvenile being sent to a detention facility. As a result, the family unit is broken up and the welfare of the juvenile has been, to some extent, sacrificed by placing him or her in detention.

Also consider the dilemma of the juvenile court judge who must make the final decision concerning what is in the best interests of both the juvenile and the public. If he or she adheres to the philosophy of the juvenile court, the judge may be tempted to leave the juvenile with his or her family, even though the public may suffer. In addition, the judge and prosecutor are faced with the difficult task of making distinctions between "unruly" and "delinquent" juveniles. These distinctions are crucial, since different types of treatment, correctional, and rehabilitation programs are available, depending upon the label attached.

A thorough understanding of the scope of juvenile court acts is equally important. The police officer on the street must be aware of both the age limits and the different categories into which juveniles are separated, if the requirements of the juvenile court act are to be met. Prosecutors and judges must be certain that jurisdictional requirements have been met and must understand the consequences of requesting or granting waivers. In short, the purposes of juvenile court acts cannot be achieved without thorough knowledge of the subjects and behaviors dealt with in the scope of such acts. Table 5.4 provides a summary of selected characteristics of juvenile codes in the United States.

Summary

The purposes of juvenile court acts are, in general, to create courts with the authority to hear designated kinds of cases, to discuss the procedural rules to be used in such cases, and to provide for the best interests of juveniles while at the same time protecting the interests of the family and society. Unfortunately, it is not always possible to achieve all of these purposes in any one case. For example, it might be in the best interests of society to send a particular juvenile to a correctional facility, but this action is not likely to be in the best interests of the juvenile.

Sections in juvenile court acts dealing with "scope" generally include information on age requirements, geographical requirements, types of behaviors covered by the act, and waivers.

There is a general trend in the United States toward conforming to the standards of the Uniform Juvenile Court Act. The Uniform Juvenile Court Act requires legal accountability, narrows the definition of delinquency (excludes status offenses), and attempts to insure the best interests of juveniles while maintaining the family unit and protecting the public.

In 1967, the President's Commission on Law Enforcement and Administration of Justice recommended that serious thought be given to completely eliminating from juvenile court jurisdiction youth who commit noncriminal acts or "status offenses." Consistent with this recommendation, two national commissions (the American Bar Association Standards Project in 1977 and the Twentieth Century Task Force on

Table 5.4
Selected Characteristics of State Juvenile Legal Codes by Type of Code and State, as of September 1988

	Alabama	Alaska	Arizona	Arkansas	California	Colorado	Connecticut	Delaware	Florida	Georgia	Hawaii	Idaho	Illinois	Indiana	Iowa	Kansas	Kentucky	Louisiana	Maine	Maryland	Massachusetts	Michigan	Minnesota	Mississippi	Missouri
Minimum jurisdictional age																									
6 years		✓				✓										✓					✓		✓	✓	
7 years			✓		✓		✓															✓			✓
10 years																									
12 years																									
Either common law presumption of 7 or not specified	✓			✓				✓	✓	✓	✓	✓	✓	✓	✓		✓	✓	✓	✓					
Maximum jurisdictional age																									
Up to 16 years	✓									✓			✓					✓			✓	✓			✓
Up to 17 years		✓	✓	✓	✓		✓	✓	✓		✓	✓		✓	✓	✓	✓		✓	✓			✓	✓	
Up to 18 years					(c)																				
Up to 19 years																									
Duration of jurisdiction																									
Up to 18 years															✓										
Up to 19 years		✓	✓		✓	✓	✓	✓			✓	✓		✓			✓	✓	✓	✓	✓		✓		
Up to 20 years									✓															✓	
Up to 21 years	✓																					✓			✓
Waiver to adult court	✓		✓			✓	✓	✓	✓	✓	✓	✓	✓		✓	✓	✓					✓			
Minimum age required																									
16 years																									
15 years				(g)									(h)												
14 years			✓		✓	✓	✓					✓				✓					✓		✓		✓
13 years										(m)			✓							(d)				✓	

106

10 years

10 to 14 years for limited offenses

No minimum age

No waiver or reverse waiver

Other restrictions

Hearing requested

Investigation only

Not clear

Probable cause finding is required

Status offenses

States specifically providing for truancy as a status offense

States specifically providing for running away as a status offense

Pre-adjudication and adjudication process

Initial appearance for detained juveniles

Detention hearing

Bail available at detention hearing

Secure or non-secure custody determined by order of court

Pretrial detention

Allows preventive detention

To protect juveniles

To protect others

Protect others property

No specific reasons for detention

Conditions of release from detention

Right to bail

As a matter of right:

In all cases

In felony cases

At discretion of court

Bail prohibited

No mention

Table 5.4 (continued)

	Montana	Nebraska	Nevada	New Hampshire	New Jersey	New Mexico	New York	North Carolina	North Dakota	Ohio	Oklahoma	Oregon	Pennsylvania	Rhode Island	South Carolina	South Dakota	Tennessee	Texas	Utah	Vermont	Virginia	Washington	West Virginia	Wisconsin	Wyoming
Minimum jurisdictional age																									
6 years								✓																	
7 years							✓																		
10 years		✓											✓					✓		✓					
12 years																									
Either common law presumption of 7 or not specified	✓		✓	✓	✓	✓			✓	✓	✓	✓		✓	✓	✓	✓		✓		✓	✓	✓	✓	✓
Maximum jurisdictional age																									
Up to 16 years							✓	✓			✓ (a)							✓							
Up to 17 years		✓	✓	✓	✓	✓			✓	✓		✓	✓	✓	✓	✓	✓		✓		✓	✓	✓	✓	✓
Up to 18 years	✓										✓ (b)									✓					
Up to 19 years																									
Duration of jurisdiction																									
Up to 18 years							✓	✓																	
Up to 19 years		✓		✓	✓	✓																			
Up to 20 years	✓		✓						✓								✓	✓		✓					
Up to 21 years										✓	✓	✓	✓	✓	✓	✓			✓		✓	✓	✓	✓	✓
Waiver to adult court																									
Minimum age required																									
16 years					✓	✓ (i)		✓ (j)	✓ (j)			✓ (e)	✓	✓	✓ (k)	✓ (f)	✓	✓	✓			✓	✓	✓	✓
15 years			✓																		✓				
14 years																			✓						
13 years																✓ (l)	✓ (l)								

108

10 years
10 to 14 years for limited offenses
No minimum age
No waiver or reverse waiver
Other restrictions
Hearing requested
Investigation only
Not clear
Probable cause finding is required
Status offenses
States specifically providing for truancy as a status offense
States specifically providing for running away as a status offense
Pre-adjudication and adjudication process
Initial appearance for detained juveniles
Detention hearing
Bail available at detention hearing
Secure or non-secure custody determined by order of court
Pretrial detention
Allows preventive detention
To protect juveniles
To protect others
Protect others property
No specific reasons for detention
Conditions of release from detention
Right to bail
As a matter of right:
In all cases
In felony cases
At discretion of court
Bail prohibited
No mention

Table 5.4 (continued)

	Alabama	Alaska	Arizona	Arkansas	California	Colorado	Connecticut	Delaware	Florida	Georgia	Hawaii	Idaho	Illinois	Indiana	Iowa	Kansas	Kentucky	Louisiana	Maine	Maryland	Massachusetts	Michigan	Minnesota	Mississippi	Missouri
Non-bail conditions																									
Requires promise to bring juvenile before the court	✓	✓		✓	✓	✓		✓		✓	✓			✓				✓	✓	✓	✓		✓		✓
No mention of conditions			✓	✓	✓		✓		✓			✓			✓	✓					✓	✓	✓	✓	
Intake official may impose conditions		✓				✓													✓						✓
Other conditions may be imposed by court																									✓
Plea bargaining																									
No provision	✓	✓	✓	✓	✓	(s)	✓	✓		✓	✓	✓	✓	✓	✓	✓		✓		✓	✓	✓	✓	✓	✓
No plea required		✓	✓		✓	✓	✓		✓	✓	✓	✓	✓	✓	✓	✓		✓	✓		✓	✓	✓	✓	
Informal adjustment	✓	✓							✓							✓			✓				✓		
Jury trial																									
Defendant enjoys right if demanded (at adjudicatory hearing)	✓	✓	✓						✓	✓	✓	✓		✓	✓	✓		✓	✓	✓		✓		✓	
Defendant denied right					✓	✓	✓		✓																
No mention		✓	✓	(t)		✓																			✓
By court order																									
Rules of evidence																			✓	✓	✓		✓		
Burden of proof																									
Delinquency proceeding, burden on prosecution																				✓	✓				
No mention	✓	✓	✓	✓	✓	✓	✓	✓	✓	✓	✓	✓	✓	✓	✓	✓	✓	✓	✓			✓	✓	✓	✓

110

Standard of proof
Delinquency proceeding, beyond a reasonable doubt ✓ ✓ ✓ ✓ ✓ ✓ ✓ ✓ ✓ ✓ ✓ ✓ ✓ ✓ ✓ ✓ ✓ ✓
Preponderance of the evidence
No mention ✓ ✓ ✓ ✓ ✓ ✓ ✓ ✓ ✓ ✓ ✓ ✓ ✓ ✓ ✓ ✓
Admissibility
Evidence must be competent, relevant, and material ✓ ✓ ✓ ✓ ✓ ✓ ✓ ✓ ✓ ✓ ✓ ✓
In accord with civil cases
No mention ✓ ✓ ✓ ✓ ✓ ✓ ✓ ✓ ✓ ✓ ✓ ✓ ✓ ✓ ✓

Table 5.4 (continued)

	Montana	Nebraska	Nevada	New Hampshire	New Jersey	New Mexico	New York	North Carolina	North Dakota	Ohio	Oklahoma	Oregon	Pennsylvania	Rhode Island	South Carolina	South Dakota	Tennessee	Texas	Utah	Vermont	Virginia	Washington	West Virginia	Wisconsin	Wyoming
Non-bail conditions																									
Requires promise to bring juvenile before the court	√		√		√	√		√	√	√			√	√	√	√	√	√	√						√
No mention of conditions						√				√		√								√					
Intake official may impose conditions		√		√	√	√	√	√			√							√			√	√			
Other conditions may be imposed by court	√					√																			
Plea bargaining																									
No provision	√					√																			
No plea required		√	√		√			√	√	√		√	√	√	√	√	√	√	√	√	√	√	√		
Informal adjustment		√					√		√	√			√			√	√	√				√	√	√	
Jury trial																									
Defendant enjoys right if demanded (at adjudicatory hearing)	√	√	√	√	√			√	√	√	√	√	√		√			√	√	√	√	√		√	√
Defendant denied right							√									√									
No mention																									
By court order														(n)											
Rules of evidence																									
Burden of proof																									
Delinquency proceeding, burden on prosecution	√	√	√	√	√	√	√	√	√	√	√	√	√	√	√	√	√	√	√	√	√	√	√	√	√
No mention																									
Standard of proof																									
Delinquency proceeding, beyond a reasonable doubt	√	√	√	√		√		√	√	√		√	√	√	√	√	√	√	√	√	√	√	√	√	√

Preponderance of the evidence

No mention

Admissibility

Evidence must be competent, relevant, and material

In accord with civil cases

No mention

Note: These data were gathered through a cooperative effort of the Rose Institute of State and Local Government and the American Legislative Exchange Council. These agencies conducted extensive research into the juvenile codes for each State and surveyed district attorneys in each State. Only juvenile codes were included; court rules, attorney general opinions, and executive orders were excluded.

a. Males.

b. Females.

c. Up to 25 years.

d. Minimum age requirement varies with the seriousness of offense.

e. See ORS 419.533.

f. Child requests.

g. Prosecutor has authority to charge 15 to 18 year olds directly to adult court, plus 14 year olds who commit first and second degree murder or rape.

h. Murder, rape, robbery.

i. Murder.

j. Transfer to adult court may only occur for felonies. Transfer is mandatory for a capital felony (first degree murder).

k. Two prior adjudications for assault-type crimes.

l. Murder and rape.

m. Capital crimes.

n. Murder.

o. Required.

p. See ORS 419.533(l)(c) and (d).

q. Truancy and running away, although not specifically designated status offenses, are specifically listed as grounds under which the juvenile court can acquire jurisdiction. See MCL 712.2(a) and (a)4.

r. AS 47.10.141 addresses "runaways" and does not categorize the conduct as a status offense. Runaways are considered children in need of aid in Alaska.

s. A plea is required in a plea bargain and is governed by Rule 3 of the Colorado Rules of Juvenile Procedure.

t. See case law.

u. Juvenile trials are conducted without a jury.

Source: *Sourcebook of Criminal Justice Statistics 1987*, U.S. Department of Justice, Bureau of Justice Statistics (Washington, D.C.: U.S. Government Printing Office, 1988).

113

Sentencing Policy Toward Youthful Offenders, 1978) proposed the elimination of juvenile court jurisdiction over status offenders and a number of states have followed this recommendation in part at least.[51]

Discussion Questions

1. In addition to protecting the community from youthful offenders, what are the three major purposes or goals of juvenile court acts?
2. How and why did the Uniform Juvenile Court Act (see appendix A) come into existence? Has this act had much impact on the various state juvenile court acts? Give some examples to support your answer.
3. What are some of the considerations of jurisdiction that fall within the scope of juvenile court acts? Why are these considerations important?
4. Suppose a juvenile, age fifteen, is taken before juvenile court in the county in which he resides for allegedly repeatedly refusing to obey his parents' orders to be home before ten o'clock at night. Would such behavior fall within the scope of most juvenile court acts? Would the youth be dealt with as a delinquent under Uniform Juvenile Court Act recommendations? If not, why?

Selected Readings

Bishop, Donna M. "Legal and Extralegal Barriers to Delinquency." *Criminology* 22, no. 3 (August 1984): 403–19.

Guggenheim, Martin. "A Call to Abolish the Juvenile Justice System." *Children's Rights Report II*. New York: American Civil Liberties Union Foundation, June 1978.

Marshall, C. E., I. K. Marshall, and C. W. Thomas, "The Implementation of Formal Procedures in Juvenile Court Processing of Status Offenders." *Journal of Criminal Justice* 11, no. 3 (1983): 195–211.

Rubin, H. T. "Retain the Juvenile Court? Legislative Developments, Reform Directions, and the Call for Abolition." *Crime and Delinquency* 25 (July 1979): 281–98.

Teitelbaum, Lee E., and Aidan R. Gough. *Beyond Control: Status Offenders in the Juvenile Court.* Cambridge, Mass.: Ballinger, 1977.

51. C. E. Marshall, I. H. Marshall, and C. W. Thomas, "The Implementation of Formal Procedures in Juvenile Court Processing of Status Offenders," *Journal of Criminal Justice* 11 (1983): 195–96.

U.S. Department of Justice, Bureau of Justice Statistics. *Report to the Nation on Crime and Justice: The Data.* Washington, D.C.: U.S. Government Printing Office, May 1988.

U.S. Department of Justice, Office of Juvenile Justice and Delinquency Prevention. *Justice for Juveniles.* Washington, D.C.: U.S. Government Printing Office, 1986.

U.S. News and World Report, "Our Neglected Kids." 9 September 1982, 54–58.

Woodward, James G. "Making Criminals of Habitual Truants: Is It Cruel and Unusual?" *Illinois Bar Association Journal* (August 1983): 768–71.

6 Juvenile Justice Procedures

Juvenile court acts not only discuss the purposes and scope of the juvenile justice system, but also discuss the procedure the juvenile courts are to follow. Proceedings concerning juveniles officially begin with the filing of a petition alleging that a juvenile is delinquent, dependent, neglected, abused, or in need of supervision or intervention. Juvenile court acts clearly indicate those persons who are eligible to file a petition. For example, in Illinois,

> any adult person (over the age of 21), agency or association by its representative may file a petition, or the court on its own motion may direct the filing through the State's Attorney of a petition in respect to a minor under the Act.[1]

While it is true that a petition may be filed by any eligible person by going directly to the prosecutor (state's attorney, district attorney), a large proportion of petitions are filed following police action or by social service agencies dealing with minors. In order to understand the step-by-step procedures involved in processing juveniles, we will discuss the typical sequence of events occurring after the police take a juvenile into custody. We will rely heavily upon the procedures given in the Uniform Juvenile Court Act and the Illinois Juvenile Court Act, which closely resemble similar acts in many states. While a general discussion of juvenile justice procedures will be given, some states differ with respect to specific requirements. You should consult the juvenile court act or code relevant to your state for exact procedural requirements.

Regardless of the particular jurisdiction, juveniles in the United States have, since 1967, been guaranteed a number of basic rights. Thus, a juvenile who is alleged to be delinquent has at least the following rights:

> 1. the right to notice of the charges and time to prepare for the case;
> 2. the right to counsel;
> 3. the right to confrontation and cross-examination of witness; and
> 4. the right to remain silent in court.[2]

1. *Illinois Revised Statutes,* ch. 37. art. 2, sec. 802–13, 1988.
2. In re *Gault,* 387 U.S. 1, 49–50, 87S. Ct. 1428, 1455 (1967). See appendix B.

As a direct result of the *Gault* decision, the constitutional guarantees of the Fifth and Sixth Amendments are applicable to states through the Fourteenth Amendment and apply not only to delinquency matters but have been extended to some cases involving the need for supervision or intervention. The question remaining after the *Gault* decision concerned the extent to which its mandate logically extended to other stages of the juvenile justice process, particularly the police investigatory process. *Gault* has been extended to police interrogation of juveniles and lineups and has been interpreted to require the application of the Fourth Amendment and the exclusionary rule to the juvenile justice process. The most difficult issue has revolved around the juvenile's competency to waive his/her rights under *Miranda*. Generally, the courts have relied upon a "totality of circumstances" approach in determining the validity of the waiver. Circumstances considered include the age and educational level of the juvenile, his/her ability to understand the nature of the charges, and the methods used in and length of the interrogation.[3]

The Uniform Juvenile Court Act provides that all parties to juvenile court proceedings are entitled to representation by counsel.[4] In neglect and abuse cases, legal counsel for the juvenile is the state's attorney, who represents the state which has a duty to protect the child. In addition, the court may also appoint a *guardian ad litem* for a juvenile, if the juvenile has no parent or guardian appearing on his or her behalf or if the parents' or guardian's interests conflict with the juvenile's.

The protection afforded by the Fourth Amendment against illegal search and seizure extends to juveniles. All courts that have specifically considered the issue of the applicability of the Fourth Amendment to the juvenile justice process have found it applicable, or more correctly, none have found it inapplicable.[5] The Uniform Juvenile Court Act states that evidence seized illegally will not be admitted over objection. Similarly, a valid confession made by a juvenile out of court is, in the words of the Uniform Act, "insufficient to support an adjudication of delinquency unless it is corroborated in whole or in part by other evidence."[6] This extends some protection to juveniles not normally accorded to adults. In addition, the Uniform Juvenile Court Act recommends that a party

3. Davis, *Rights of Juveniles,* 3–52.

4. National Conference of Commissioners on Uniform States Laws, *Uniform Juvenile Court Act,* sec. 26 (August 1968). See appendix A.

5. Davis, *Rights of Juveniles,* 3–16.

6. *Uniform Juvenile Court Act,* sec. 27(b).

be entitled to introduce evidence and otherwise be heard in his or her own behalf and to cross-examine adverse witnesses.[7] Furthermore, a juvenile accused of a delinquent act need not be a witness against or otherwise incriminate himself or herself. A majority of juvenile court acts do not spell out a detailed code of evidence. However, most do specify whether the rules permit only competent, material, and relevant evidence and whether the rules of evidence that apply in criminal or civil cases are applicable in juvenile cases. A number of states provide that the rules of evidence applicable in criminal cases apply in delinquency proceedings, and the rules of evidence applicable in civil cases apply in other proceedings (i.e., neglect, dependency, and in need of supervision cases).[8]

The Children's Bureau of the Department of Health and Human Services has recommended that, unless the child is advised by counsel, the statements of a child made while in the custody of the police or probation officers, including statements made during a preliminary inquiry, predisposition study, or consent decree, not be used against the child prior to the determination of the petition's allegations in delinquency, in need of supervision/intervention cases, or in a criminal proceeding prior to conviction.[9]

It should be noted that some rights guaranteed adults are not guaranteed juveniles in most jurisdictions. As a result of the *McKeiver* decision,[10] juveniles are not generally guaranteed the right to a trial by jury or a public trial. The Supreme Court, in deciding *McKeiver,* indicated that a jury was not necessary for fact-finding purposes and left the issue of trial by jury up to the individual states. While the majority of jurisdictions provide for hearings without juries, some provide for jury trials by statute or judicial decision.[11] In addition, the *McKeiver* decision leaves open the question of whether juvenile court proceedings are necessarily

7. Ibid., sec. 27(a).

8. See, for example, *California Welfare and Institutions Code,* sec. 701, (Supp. 1984); *Illinois Revised Statutes,* ch. 37, sec. 802–18, 1988; *Iowa Code Annotated,* sec. 232.47(5), 232.96(3), Supp. 1985; *Florida Statutes Annotated,* sec. 39.09(1) (b), Supp. 1979.

9. Children's Bureau, Department of Health, Education, and Welfare, *Legislative Guide for Drafting Family and Juvenile Court Acts,* pub. no. 472–1969, sec. 26.

10. *McKeiver* v. *Pennsylvania,* 403 U.S. 528 (1971).

11. See, for example, *Colorado Revised Statutes Annotated,* sec. 19–1–106(4), 1986; *Montana Code Annotated,* sec. 41–5–521(1), 1987; *Wisconsin Statutes Annotated,* sec. 48.31(2), 1987.

adversary in nature, and left upon the states the burden of establishing that a separate justice system for juveniles represents a useful alternative to criminal processing. While proceedings may not be adversary when the issue before the court is neglect or dependency, there is a clear-cut trend toward treating all juvenile court procedures, resulting in adjudication of delinquency or deprivation of liberty, as adversarial.

The issue of bail for juveniles is also controversial at present. Some jurisdictions permit bail, whereas others do not on the grounds that the juvenile has not been charged with a crime and is, therefore, not entitled to bail. Because of special release provisions for juveniles (to the custody of parents or guardians), bail has not been a question of paramount concern in terms of litigation. A number of states forbid the use of bail with respect to juveniles, [12] several states authorize release on bail at the discretion of a judge, [13] and some states allow the same right to bail enjoyed by adults. [14]

Finally, most jurisdictions require that official records kept on juveniles be maintained in separate and confidential files. These may be opened only by court order or upon application of the juvenile for a law enforcement position.

Taking into Custody

The Uniform Juvenile Court Act states:

A child may be taken into custody pursuant to an order of the court under that Act, or pursuant to the laws of arrest; or, by a law enforcement officer if there are reasonable grounds to believe that the child is suffering from illness or injury or is in immediate danger from his surroundings and that his removal is necessary; or, by a law enforcement officer if there are reasonable grounds to believe that the child has run away from his parents or guardian. [15]

In general, any juvenile can be taken into custody without a warrant, if the law enforcement officer reasonably believes the juvenile to be delinquent, dependent, or neglected as defined within that state's juvenile court

12. *Hawaii Revised Statutes,* sec. 571–32(h), 1985; *Oregon Revised Statutes,* sec. 419.583, 1979; *Connecticut General Statutes Annotated,* sec. 466–133, 1986.

13. *Minnesota Statutes Annotated,* sec. 260.171(1), 1984; *Nebraska Revised Statutes,* sec. 43–253, 1985; *Tennessee Code Annotated,* sec. 37–1–117(e), 1984.

14. *Colorado Revised Statutes Annotated,* sec. 19–2–103(7), 1986; *Georgia Code Annotated,* sec. 15–11–19(d), 1986; *Oklahoma Statutes Annotated,* tit. 10, sec. 1112(c), 1987.

15. *Uniform Juvenile Court Act,* sec. 13.

act. However, some states have recognized that removing a juvenile from home before there has been any trial is a power to be used on a limited basis. For truancy, disobedience, and even neglect, the legal process should begin with a summons unless there is "imminent danger" involved and unless waiting for the court's permission would result in unnecessary and dangerous delay. In Illinois, a law enforcement officer may, without a warrant, take into temporary custody a minor whom the officer, with reasonable cause, believes to be a delinquent, minor requiring authoritative intervention, dependent, abused, or neglected child as defined within that state's juvenile court act.[16] In addition, the officer may take into custody any juvenile who has been adjudged a ward of the court and has escaped from any commitment ordered by the court. The officer may also take into custody any juvenile who is found in any street or public place suffering from any sickness or injury requiring care, medical treatment, or hospitalization.[17] The taking into temporary custody in Illinois and under the Uniform Juvenile Court Act does not constitute an official arrest.[18] Although statutes in various states provide that taking into custody is not deemed an arrest, this is somewhat a legal fiction since the juvenile is often held in involuntary custody. In light of recent court decisions, when delinquency is the alleged reason for custody, the law enforcement officers must adhere to appropriate constitutional guidelines. For categories other than delinquency, the *parens patriae* concern for protecting juveniles from dangerous surroundings will probably suffice constitutionally as reasonable grounds for taking minors into custody, when it is not abused by law enforcement officers.

While in custody, the juvenile has rights similar to those of an adult with respect to interrogation. Should the police desire to question the juvenile concerning a delinquent act, the juvenile should be given the Miranda warning and, many authorities agree, should be clearly told that a decision to remain silent will not be taken as an indication of guilt. Many police administrators, prosecutors, and juvenile court judges feel that it is best not to question the juvenile unless his or her parents or counselor are present. In Colorado, for example, "no statement or admission of a child made as a result of interrogation by law enforcement officials . . . shall be admissible . . . unless a parent, guardian, or custodian was present . . . and the child was advised of his right to remain

16. *Illinois Revised Statutes,* ch. 37, art. 2, sec. 802–5, 1988.
17. Ibid.
18. Ibid., and *Uniform Juvenile Court Act,* sec. 13(b).

silent."[19] Any confession obtained without these safeguards might be considered invalid on grounds that the juvenile did not understand his or her rights or was frightened.

Many juvenile court acts dictate that the police make an "immediate" and "reasonable" attempt to notify the juvenile's parents or guardian of his or her custody. The maximum length of time considered to be immediate is usually established by statute. The definition of reasonable usually includes attempts to phone and/or visit the residence of the juvenile's parents, place of employment, and any other known "haunts."

The Detention Hearing

If the juvenile is not released to his or her parents soon after being taken into custody, most states require that a detention hearing be held within a specified time period. Sufficient notification must, of course, be given to all parties concerned before the proceeding. Section 17 of the Uniform Juvenile Court Act indicates that, if a juvenile is brought before the court or delivered to a detention or shelter care facility, the intake or other authorized officer of the court will immediately make an investigation and release the juvenile unless it appears that further detention or shelter care is warranted or required.[20] If the juvenile is not released within seventy-two hours after being placed in detention, an informal detention hearing shall be held to determine whether further detention is warranted or required. Reasonable notice of the hearing must be given to the juvenile and to the parents or guardians. In addition, notification of the right to counsel and of the juvenile's right to remain silent regarding any allegations of delinquency or unruly conduct must also be given by the court to the respondents. States vary about the criteria used to determine the need for further detention, but they usually center around the need to insure the protection of society and the juvenile. For example, in Illinois, after a minor has been delivered to the place designated by the court,

> the in-take personnel shall immediately investigate the circumstances of the minor and the facts surrounding his being taken into custody. The minor shall be immediately released to the custody of his parents unless the in-take officer

19. *Colorado Revised Statutes Annotated*, sec. 19–2–102(3) (c) (I), 1986.
20. *Uniform Juvenile Court Act*, sec. 17(a).

finds that further detention is a matter of immediate and urgent necessity for the protection of the minor, or of the person or property of another or that he is likely to flee the jurisdiction of the court.[21]

Detention can be authorized by the in-take officer (generally a designated juvenile police officer or the juvenile probation officer) for up to thirty-six hours, at which time the minor is either released to his or her parents or brought before the court for a detention hearing. Failure to file a petition or to bring the juvenile before the court within thirty-six hours will result in a release from detention.[22] In Illinois, the detention hearing focuses first on whether there is probable cause to believe that the minor is within the category of delinquency, in need of supervision, neglected, or dependent. The court then decides, using the same criteria as the in-take officer, whether further detention is a matter of immediate and urgent necessity.[23]

Substantial numbers of juvenile cases are "unofficially adjusted" by law enforcement personnel at the initial encounter as well as at the station house. Among those juveniles who are turned over to the court's in-take personnel, a substantial number are disposed of at the in-take stage and at the detention hearings. In many instances the in-take personnel, the minor and his or her family, and the injured party are able to informally adjust the differences or problems that caused the minor to be taken into custody. Only the most serious cases of delinquency, "unruly" behavior, abuse, or neglect result in processing through the entire juvenile justice system. Currently, there are legal questions about unofficial dispositions for delinquents at the in-take stage and the assumption of guilt leading to some prescribed treatment program. While most practitioners make it clear that participation in informal dispositions is voluntary and that following advice or referrals is not mandatory, there may still be some official pressure perceived by the juvenile or the juvenile's parents that violates the presumption of innocence.

Detention/Shelter Care

Under the Uniform Juvenile Court Act,

a child taken into custody shall not be detained or placed in shelter care prior to the hearing on the petition unless such detention is required to protect the

---

21. *Illinois Revised Statutes*, ch. 37, sec. 805–7, 1988; *New York Family Court Act*, sec. 305.2 (McKinney Supp. 1988); and *Wisconsin Statutes Annotated*, sec. 48–19(2), 1987.

22. *Illinois Revised Statutes*, sec. 805–9, 1988.

23. Ibid., sec. 805–10, 1988.

person or property of others or of the child or because the child may abscond (flee) or be removed from the jurisdiction of the court or because he has no parent or guardian who is able to provide supervision and to return him to the court when required or an order for detention or shelter care has been made by the court pursuant to this Act.[24]

Absence of any of these conditions must result in the child's release to his or her parents or guardian with their promise to bring the child before the court as requested.[25] Failure to bring the child before the court will result in the issuance of a warrant directing that the child be taken into custody and brought before the court.[26]

The Uniform Juvenile Court Act is rather unique and adamant in its policy that the "person taking a child into custody, with all reasonable speed and without first taking the child elsewhere, shall release the child to his parents or guardian . . . unless detention or shelter care is warranted or required. . . ."[27] This section of the Uniform Juvenile Court Act is designed to reduce the number of children in detention by specifying criteria that would "require and warrant" further detention.

If reasonable cause for detention cannot be established, the juvenile should be released to his or her parents. In practice, and according to most juvenile court acts, the juvenile is taken to a police or juvenile facility at which time the parents are contacted. However, the Uniform Juvenile Court Act implies that the juvenile should be taken immediately to his or her parents unless detention appears to be warranted. This policy spares the juvenile from the experience of being held in the most depressing and intimidating of all custodial facilities, the jail or police lockup.

In Illinois, if the juvenile is not released to his or her parents, the juvenile must be taken without unnecessary delay to the court or to a place designated by the court to receive juveniles.[28] A juvenile under sixteen cannot legally be confined in a jail or place ordinarily used for the confinement of adults.[29] The Uniform Juvenile Court Act does allow detention in a local jail if, and only if, a detention home or center for delinquent children is unavailable.[30] If confined in a jail, detention must

24. *Uniform Juvenile Court Act,* sec. 14.
25. Ibid., sec. 15(1).
26. Ibid., sec. 15(b).
27. Ibid., sec. 15(a, 1).
28. *Illinois Revised Statutes,* ch. 37, art. 5, sec. 805–7, 1988.
29. Ibid., sec. 801–3(10).
30. *Uniform Juvenile Court Act,* sec. 16(a, 4).

be in a room separate and removed from those for adults. This required separation from confined adults is commonly found in statutes and extends to cell, room, or yard.

In all categories other than delinquency, the child is normally taken to a designated shelter care facility, which according to the Uniform Juvenile Court Act means a "physically unrestricted facility."[31] The procedures for contacting the parents and the criteria that are used to maintain custody in such a facility are the same as for the delinquent child. Shelter care facilities are generally licensed by the state and designated by the juvenile court to receive children who do not require the physically restrictive surroundings of a jail or juvenile detention center.

Maximum time limits for detention are set forth in the various juvenile court acts, so a juvenile will not be detained for lengthy periods without a review by the courts.

Once the juvenile has been taken into custody and either released to his or her parents or, with just cause, placed in a detention facility, an officer of the court may attempt to settle the case without a court hearing by arranging for a preliminary conference.

The Preliminary Conference

The Uniform Juvenile Court Act includes a provision that allows a probation officer or other officer designated by the court to hold a preliminary conference in order to give counsel or advice with a view toward an informal adjustment without filing a petition.[32] This preliminary conference is in order only if the admitted facts bring the case within the jurisdiction of the court and if such an informal adjustment, without an adjudication, is in the best interests of the public and the child. This conference is to be held only with the consent of the juvenile's parents or guardian. However, such a conference is not obligatory.[33] A similar provision is found in the Illinois Juvenile Court Act. It states that "the court may authorize the probation officer to confer in a preliminary conference with any person seeking to file a petition . . . concerning the advisability of filing the petition, with a view to adjusting suitable cases without the filing of a petition."[34] If agreement between the parties can

31. Ibid., sec. 2(6).
32. Ibid., sec. 10.
33. Ibid., sec. 10(a).
34. *Illinois Revised Statutes,* ch. 37, art. 5, sec. 805–12, 1988.

be reached at the preliminary conference, no further official action may be necessary. If judicial action seems necessary, then the probation officer may recommend the filing of a petition. However, should the injured party demand that a petition be filed, that demand must be satisfied. Although the preliminary conference or informal adjustment may be of value in eliminating cases that could be settled better outside of juvenile court, it has been subject to criticism as a method of engaging in legal coercion without trial.[35] Generally, information or evidence presented at the preliminary conference is not admissible at any later stage in the juvenile court proceedings.

The Petition

As indicated earlier, juvenile court proceedings begin with the filing of a petition naming the juvenile in question and alleging that this juvenile is delinquent, dependent, abused, neglected, or a minor in need of supervision. A copy of a typical petition is found in figure 6.1. Although states vary about who is eligible to file a petition, similarities do exist concerning the content of petitions and the initiation of follow-through activities as a result of the petition. In some states, a preliminary inquiry may be conducted by juvenile court personnel to determine whether the best interests of the child or the public will require a petition to be filed. In other states, this inquiry is accomplished after the petition has been filed and may result in the petition being dismissed by the court if the alleged facts are not supported. Regardless of whether the inquiry is conducted before or after the filing of a petition, a stipulation that is commonly found is one in which a court authorizes a person to endorse the petition as being in the best interest of the public and the child. The Uniform Juvenile Court Act specifies that "a petition may be made by any person who has knowledge of the facts alleged or is informed and believes that they are true."[36] The act also states that "the petition shall not be filed unless the court or designated person has determined and endorsed upon the petition that the filing is in the best interest of the child and the public."[37] It should be noted that the signing of a petition and the authority to file the petition may be separate and distinct acts.

35. Paul Tappan, *Juvenile Delinquency* (New York: McGraw-Hill, 1949), 310–11.
36. *Uniform Juvenile Court Act,* sec. 20.
37. Ibid., sec. 19.

FRANK THORNBER CO., CHICAGO J.1

STATE OF ILLINOIS

IN THE CIRCUIT COURT OF THE _____ JUDICIAL CIRCUIT

_____ COUNTY, JUVENILE DIVISION

In the interest of

No.

a minor

PETITION FOR ADJUDICATION OF WARDSHIP

I, _____, on oath state* on information and belief:
   (name of petitioner)

1. _____ is a _____ minor born on _____, 19____
                              (male) (female)

who resides or may be found in this county at _____
                                              (address)   (city)

2. The names and residence addresses of the minor's parents, legal guardian, custodian, and nearest known relative are:

	Name	Residence Address	City and State
Father			
Mother			
Legal guardian			
Custodian			
Nearest known relative			

The minor and the persons named in this paragraph are designated respondents.

3. The minor is delinquent, otherwise in need of supervision, neglected or dependent by reason of the following facts:

4. The minor _____ detained in custody.
             (is) (is not)

5. A detention hearing _____, 19____
                       (was held) (has been set for)

6. It is in the best interests of the minor and the public that the minor be adjudged a ward of the court.

I ask that the minor be adjudged a ward of the court and for other relief under the Juvenile Court Act.

_____
                      Petitioner

Signed and sworn to before me

_____, 19____

_____ Notary public

Name _____

Attorney for _____

Address _____

City _____

Telephone _____

* If any facts are not known, so state in the appropriate spaces.

Figure 6.1

This has led to some confusion. Some states require designated court personnel to sign the petition in order to establish some sufficiency of the allegations at the outset.

The contents of the petition are governed by statutory requirements in each juvenile court act. The petition may be filed on "information and belief" rather than on verified facts necessary for an adjudicatory hearing. The petition is generally prefaced with the words "in the interests of. . . ." The petition continues by giving the name and age of the child and frequently the names and addresses of the parents. It also indicates if the child is in detention. Also included in the petition is the statement of facts that bring the child within the jurisdiction of the juvenile court. This particular requirement has been a troublesome area since questions are often raised about whether sufficient facts have been stated and about the specificity of the charges. According to the Uniform Juvenile Court Act, the petition must also contain allegations that relate to the child's need of treatment or rehabilitation, if delinquency or unruly conduct is alleged.[38] States may require various kinds of information in the petition. The Illinois petition (fig. 6.1) is typical of the majority of petitions.

Once the petition has been filled out, it is filed with the prosecutor who then decides whether or not to prosecute. If the prosecutor decides to go ahead with the case, proper notice must be given to all concerned parties.

Notification

After a petition has been filed, the court will issue a summons to all concerned adult parties informing them of the time, date, and place of the adjudicatory hearing and of the right of all parties to counsel. In addition, many states direct a separate summons to the child who is above a certain age and is within a designated category such as "delinquent" or "unruly child." A copy of the petition will accompany the summons, unless the summons is served "by publication" (that is, printed in a newspaper of reasonable circulation). States vary about the length of time required between the serving of the summons and the actual proceedings. However, in accordance with the *Gault* decision,[39] a reasonable amount of time should be allowed in order to provide the parties with

38. Ibid., sec. 21(1).
39. In re *Gault,* 387 U.S. 1, 49–50, 87 S. Ct. 1428, 1455, (1967).

sufficient time to prepare. Unnecessary and long delays should be avoided particularly in those cases where a child is held in detention or shelter care. For example, Illinois allows at least three days before appearance when the summons is personally served to the parties, five days if notification is by certified mail, and ten days if notification is by publication. If it becomes necessary to change dates, notice of the new dates must be given, by certified mail or other reasonable means, to each respondent served with a summons.[40] The Illinois law and Uniform Juvenile Court Act provisions on service of summons are similar. The Uniform Juvenile Court Act allows at least twenty-four hours before the hearing when the summons is personally served, and five days if certified mail or publication is used.[41]

Service of the summons may be made by any person authorized by the court, usually a county sheriff, coroner, or juvenile probation officer. If the information received by the court indicates that the juvenile needs to be placed in detention or shelter care, the court may endorse upon the summons an order that the child should be taken into immediate custody and taken to the place of detention or shelter care designated by the court.

Following the filing of the petition and proper notification, the adjudicatory hearing is held. In delinquency cases, this is the juvenile court's equivalent of an adult criminal trial.

The Adjudicatory Hearing

The adjudicatory hearing is a fact-finding hearing to determine whether the allegations in the petition are valid. Although the Supreme Court has extended the legalistic principle of due process to the juvenile justice system, not all rights accorded under the Constitution and its Amendments have been incorporated into the juvenile system. For example, in 1971 the Supreme Court held that juveniles had no constitutional right to a jury trial since the "juvenile proceeding had not yet been held to be a 'criminal prosecution' within the meaning and reach of the Sixth Amendment. . . ."[42] The Court reiterated that the due process standard of "fundamental fairness" should be applied to juvenile

40. *Illinois Revised Statutes,* ch. 37, art. 5, sec. 805–15(5) and 805–16, 1988.
41. *Uniform Juvenile Court Act,* sec. 23 (a, b).
42. *McKeiver* v. *Pennsylvania,* 403 U.S. 528 (1971).

court proceedings. However, the Court further stated that it was unwilling to "remake the juvenile proceeding into a full adversary process."[43] As previously indicated, some states currently allow trial by juries. However, most cases are tried by a juvenile judge. The Uniform Juvenile Court Act recommends that hearings shall be conducted by the court without a jury.[44] The Supreme Court was clear in its holding that when the state undertakes to prove a child delinquent for committing a criminal act, it must do so "beyond a reasonable doubt."[45] The Uniform Juvenile Court Act not only advocates this standard of proof for the delinquency issue, but also extends this standard to the "unruly" category.[46] Some states have adopted this recommended standard.[47] The standard applicable to such categories as deprived, neglected, or dependent is usually the civil standard of "preponderance of evidence" or "clear and convincing evidence." For example, the Uniform Juvenile Court Act requires "beyond a reasonable doubt" to determine delinquency but allows the civil standard of "clear and convincing evidence" to determine if the adjudicated delinquent is in need of treatment or rehabilitation.[48] Generally, of course, it is more difficult to establish guilt beyond a reasonable doubt (no reasonable doubt in the mind of the judge) than it is to determine guilt based on a preponderance of evidence, that is, even though there may be some doubt remaining as to guilt.

The adjudicatory hearing is generally closed to the public. If the juvenile court judge agrees, certain persons, agencies, or associations who have a direct interest in the case may be admitted. Although the Sixth Amendment declares that "in all criminal prosecutions, the accused shall enjoy the right to a speedy and public trial," juvenile court acts prohibit these public hearings on the grounds that opening such hearings would be detrimental to the child. Although the application of the "public trial" concept of the Sixth Amendment has not been adopted by juvenile court acts, other due process provisions of the Amendment have been incorporated into juvenile court acts as a result of the *Gault* decision. The

43. Ibid.

44. *Uniform Juvenile Court Act*, sec. 24(a).

45. In re *Winship*, 397 U.S. 358, 90 S. Ct. 1068 (1970). See appendix D.

46. *Uniform Juvenile Court Act*, sec. 29(b).

47. *Georgia Code Annotated*, sec. 15–11–33(c), 1982; *New York Family Court Act*, sec. 342.2 (2), 744(b) (McKinney 1985); and *Texas Family Code Annotated*, sec. 54.03(f), 1986.

48. *Uniform Juvenile Court Act*, sec. 29(c).

Uniform Juvenile Court Act states that the general public shall be excluded except parties, counsel, witnesses, and other persons requested by a party and approved by the court as having an interest in the case or in the work of the court.[49] Those persons having an interest in the work of the court include members of the bar and press who may be admitted on the condition that they will refrain from divulging any information that could identify the child or family involved. The due process concept of "speedy trial" contained in the Sixth Amendment has been incorporated into juvenile court acts. Specific time frames are contained in most acts designating the length of time between custody, detention, adjudicatory, and disposition hearings. Requests for delays are entertained by the juvenile court whenever reasonable and justifiable motions are submitted. Unfortunately, it is common in some jurisdictions for the juvenile court judge to ignore the time limits established by the statute so a "speedy trial" may not result. Some judges have ignored the statutory requirement of an adjudicatory hearing within thirty days of the time the petition is filed (without detention) even when there is no motion for a continuance by defense counsel. In cases such as these, the juvenile might not be brought before the court for an adjudicatory hearing for as long as six months, a clear violation of the statutory requirement. It is possible, of course, for defense counsel to move for dismissal or to appeal, but very seldom are such actions taken. When motions to dismiss based upon procedural irregularities are made, they are almost routinely overruled. Once again, the gap between theory and practice comes to light.

According to section 29 of the Uniform Juvenile Court Act, after hearing the evidence on the petition the court shall make and file its findings about whether the child is deprived, delinquent, or unruly as alleged in the petition. If the evidence does not support the allegation, the petition shall be dismissed and the child discharged. If the court finds that the allegation is supported by evidence using the appropriate standard of proof for that hearing, the court may proceed immediately or hold an additional hearing to hear evidence and decide whether the child is in need of treatment or rehabilitation. In the absence of evidence to the contrary, the finding of delinquency where felonious acts were committed is sufficient to sustain a finding that the child is in need of treatment or rehabilitation. However, even though the court may find that the child is within the alleged criteria of the petition, the court may not

49. Ibid., sec. 24(d).

find that the child is in need of treatment or rehabilitation. The court may then dismiss the proceeding and discharge the child from any detention or other restrictions.[50]

It should also be noted that juvenile court judges in many states may decide prior to, or in the early stages of, the adjudicatory hearing to "continue the case under supervision." This usually means that the judge postpones adjudication and specifies a time period during which the judge (through court officers) will observe the juvenile. If the juvenile has no further difficulties during the specified time period, the petition will be dismissed. If the juvenile does get into trouble again, the judge will proceed with the original adjudicatory hearing. An example of an order for "continuance under supervision" is shown in figure 6.2.

Continuance under supervision may benefit the juvenile by allowing him or her to escape adjudication as delinquent. It is generally used by juvenile court judges for precisely this purpose. However, if the juvenile did not commit the alleged delinquent act, he or she may be unjustly subjected to court surveillance. If the juvenile's parents or counselor object to the procedure and request the judge to proceed with the adjudicatory hearing, the judge must, in most jurisdictions, comply with their wishes.

In the adjudicatory hearing, the Uniform Juvenile Court Act as well as the juvenile court acts of many states separates the issues of establishing whether the child is within the defined category and whether the state should exercise wardship or further custody. The determination of further custody or wardship is usually made on the basis of what type of treatment or rehabilitation the court feels is necessary.

The term "ward of the court" means simply that the court as an agency of the state has found it necessary to exercise its role of *in loco parentis*. The decisions that are normally made by the parents are now made by a representative of the court, usually the juvenile probation officer in consultation with the juvenile court judge. As indicated in the Uniform Juvenile Court Act, the determination for continued custody for treatment or rehabilitation purposes may be made as part of the adjudicatory hearing or in a separate hearing. The court in determining wardship will receive both oral and written evidence and will use this evidence to the extent of its probative value even though such evidence may not have been admissible in the adjudicatory hearing. The standard

50. Ibid., sec. 29(a and b).

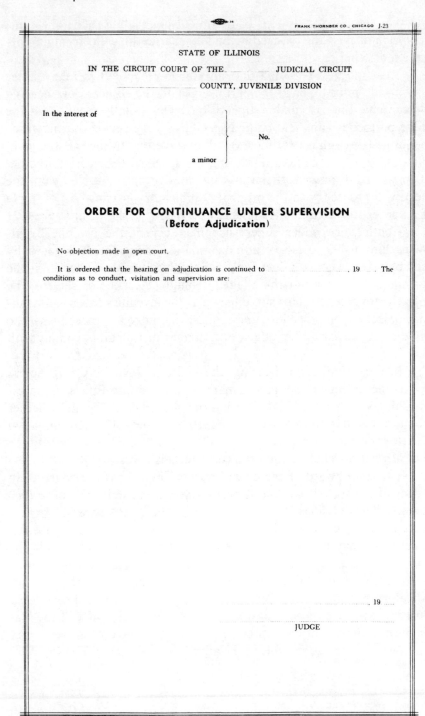

FRANK THORNBER CO., CHICAGO J-23

STATE OF ILLINOIS

IN THE CIRCUIT COURT OF THE_____ JUDICIAL CIRCUIT

_____ COUNTY, JUVENILE DIVISION

In the interest of

                                        } No.

              a minor }

ORDER FOR CONTINUANCE UNDER SUPERVISION
(Before Adjudication)

No objection made in open court.

It is ordered that the hearing on adjudication is continued to _____, 19____ The conditions as to conduct, visitation and supervision are:

_____, 19____

_____
JUDGE

Figure 6.2

of clear and convincing evidence is recommended by the Uniform Juvenile Court Act in determining wardship.[51] The Uniform Juvenile Court Act also permits a continuance of hearings for a reasonable period in order to receive reports and other evidence bearing on the disposition or the need of treatment or rehabilitation. The child may be continued in detention or released from detention and placed under the supervision of the court during the period of continuance. Priority in wardship or dispositional hearings shall always be given to those children who are in detention or have been removed from their homes pending a final dispositional order.[52]

According to Sanford Fox, in order to avoid giving a child a record, it has become a common practice for juvenile courts to place a child under probation supervision without reaching any formal finding.[53] This practice may be engaged in without filing any formal petition. Placing children under probation supervision should not be confused with continuances granted by the court in order to complete investigations for wardship or disposition proceedings. "Unofficial probation or supervision" has been subject to much criticism as the result of disregarding due process requirements.

The Social Background Investigation

After a determination in the adjudicatory hearing that the allegations in the petition have been established and that wardship is necessary, a dispositional hearing is set to determine final disposition of the case. There are differences among the states about whether the dispositional hearing must be separated from the adjudicatory hearing.[54] In some states the two hearings are separate since different procedures and rights are involved. For example, in an Illinois adjudicatory hearing on delinquency the standard of proof and the rules of evidence in the nature

---

51. Ibid., sec. 29(c and d).

52. Ibid., sec. 29(e).

53. Sanford J. Fox, *Juvenile Courts in a Nutshell* (St. Paul, Minn.: West Publishing Company, 1971), 192.

54. *Georgia Code Annotated*, sec. 15–11–33(b, c), 1985; *New York Family Court Act*, sec. 350.1, 746 (McKinney 1983); *California Welfare and Institutional Code*, sec. 701, 702, 1985.

of criminal proceedings are applicable; however, the civil rules of evidence and standard of proof are applicable to adjudicatory hearings on neglect, dependent, abuse, minor requiring authoritative intervention (in need of supervision) cases.[55] Yet, in the Illinois dispositional hearing for all categories, all evidence helpful in determining the disposition, including oral and written reports, may be admitted and relied upon to the extent of its probative value, even though it may not be competent for the purposes of the adjudicatory hearing.[56] Similar wording and evidentiary concepts are contained in the Uniform Juvenile Court Act's reference to determination of whether the adjudicated child requires treatment and rehabilitation and to the dispositional stage of the case.[57]

Between the adjudicatory hearing and the dispositional hearing, the court's staff (usually probation officers) is engaged in obtaining information useful in aiding the court to determine final disposition of a case. This information is obtained through social background investigations and is premised on the belief that individualized justice is a major function of the juvenile court. Social background investigations typically include information about the child, the child's parents, school, work, and general peer relations as well as other environmental factors. This information is gathered through interviews with relevant persons in the community and is compiled in report form to aid the judge in making a dispositional decision. The probative value of some information collected is questionable and is certainly challengable in the dispositional hearing. Some juvenile judges delegate the court's staff to make recommendations and to justify the elimination of some options or alternatives from consideration. Unfortunately, social investigations have been used by some courts prior to the adjudicatory hearing and have resulted in an adjudication of delinquency without proving that the accused juvenile did commit the acts of delinquency alleged in the petition. As a result of the *Kent* decision, counsel for the juvenile has been extended the right to review the contents of staff social investigations used in waiver hearings, since there is no irrefutable presumption of accuracy attached to staff reports.[58] This principle has been extended by most juvenile court acts to legal counsel representing the child in dispositional hearings.

55. *Illinois Revised Statutes,* ch. 37, art. 2, sec. 802–18, 1988.
56. Ibid., sec. 802–22.
57. *Uniform Juvenile Court Act,* sec. 29(d).
58. *Kent* v. *U.S.,* 383 U.S. 541. See appendix C.

The Dispositional Hearing

The dispositional alternatives available to the juvenile court judge are clearly stated in each state's juvenile court act. The state may differ in the dispositional alternatives available to juveniles in the separate categories. An option available for the deprived child may not be available for the delinquent child. According to section 30 of the Uniform Juvenile Court Act, the "deprived child" may remain with his or her parents, subject to conditions imposed by the court including supervision by the court. Also according to section 30 of the Uniform Juvenile Court Act, the "deprived child" may be temporarily transferred legally to any of the following:

(i) *any individual . . . found by the court to be qualified to receive and care for the child;*

(ii) *an agency or other private organization licensed or otherwise authorized by the law to receive and provide care for the child; or*

(iii) *the Child Welfare Department of the [county] [state] [or other public agency authorized by law to receive and provide care for the child];*

(iv) *an individual in another state with or without supervision. . . .*[59]

For the delinquent child, the Uniform Juvenile Court Act states that the court may make any disposition best suited to the juvenile's treatment, rehabilitation, and welfare including

(1) *any order authorized by section 30 for the disposition of a "deprived child";*

(2) *. . . probation under the supervision of the probation officer . . . under conditions and limitations the court prescribes;*

(3) *placing the child in an institution, camp, or other facility for delinquent children operated under the direction of the court [or other local public authority]; or*

(4) *committing the child to [designate the state department to which commitments of delinquent children are made or, if there is no department, the appropriate state institution for delinquent children].*[60]

The "unruly child" may be disposed of by the court in any authorized disposition allowable for the delinquent except commitment to the state correctional agency. However, if the "unruly child" is found not amenable to treatment under the disposition, the court, after another hearing, may make any disposition otherwise authorized for the delinquent.[61]

---

59. *Uniform Juvenile Court Act,* sec. 30.

60. Ibid., sec. 31.

61. Ibid., sec. 32.

A general trend occurring in juvenile court acts is to refrain from committing all categories, other than delinquents, to juvenile correctional institutions unless the "unruly" or "in need of supervision" child warrants such action after other alternatives have failed. Most juvenile court acts also provide for transferring a juvenile demonstrating mental retardation or mental illness to the appropriate authority within the state. A similar section is included in the Uniform Juvenile Court Act.[62] With the advent of a multiplicity of community treatment programs and child guidance centers, many of the current dispositions contain conditions for attendance at these centers. Dispositions of probation or suspended sentence often require compulsory attendance at a community-based treatment or rehabilitation program. Violation of these conditions may result in revocation of probation or a suspended sentence. This is accomplished through a revocation hearing. Most states now specify the maximum amount of time for confinement of a juvenile. Extensions of the original disposition generally require another hearing with all rights accorded in the original dispositional hearing. The court may, under some circumstances, terminate its dispositional order prior to the expiration date if it appears that the purpose of the order has been accomplished. Juvenile court acts generally terminate all orders affecting the juvenile upon reaching the age of majority in that state. This termination results in discharging the juvenile from further obligation or control. If the disposition is probation, both the conditions of probation and its duration are spelled out by the court. For copies of various dispositional orders which may be entered by the court see figures 6.3, 6.4, and 6.5.

Appeals

As Sanford Fox indicates, appeals from juvenile courts have been rare due to the absence of formality in the system until recently.[63] While a few states do not allow appeals of juvenile court decisions, most allow appeals on behalf of any aggrieved party. The Uniform Juvenile Court Act provides for such appeals.[64] A number of courts have held that, although there is no constitutional right to appeal from juvenile court orders, all statutory appeals procedures must be applied fairly to all persons to avoid denial of equal protection to a particular class of persons.[65]

62. Ibid., sec. 35.
63. Sanford J. Fox, *Juvenile Courts in a Nutshell* (St. Paul, Minn.: West Publishing Company, 1971), 244.
64. *Uniform Juvenile Court Act,* sec. 59(a and b).
65. Davis, *Rights of Juveniles,* sec. 6.10.

FRANK THORNBER CO., CHICAGO   J.25

STATE OF ILLINOIS

IN THE CIRCUIT COURT OF THE _____ JUDICIAL CIRCUIT

_____ COUNTY, JUVENILE DIVISION

In the interest of

No.

a minor

DISPOSITIONAL ORDER
(Probation)

The court considered the evidence and finds: it has jurisdiction of the subject matter and the parties; the minor has been adjudged a delinquent, that all statutory prerequisites have been complied with.

It is ordered.

1. Probation is granted to the minor, _____ , until _____ , 19 __ subject to the terms and conditions:

2. The minor is released to the custody of _____ , and shall not
(parent)   (guardian)   (legal custodian)
depart from his custody except upon written authorization of the probation officer or order of court.

_____ , 19 _____

_____
JUDGE

Figure 6.3

FRANK THORNBER CO., CHICAGO

STATE OF ILLINOIS

IN THE CIRCUIT COURT OF THE .... JUDICIAL CIRCUIT

.... COUNTY, JUVENILE DIVISION

In the interest of

}

No.

a minor

DISPOSITIONAL ORDER
(Commitment)

The court considered the evidence and finds: it has jurisdiction of the subject matter and the parties; the minor has been adjudged a delinquent; all statutory prerequisites have been complied with; placement under Section 5-7 of the Juvenile Court Act will not serve the best interest of the minor and the public; the parent, guardian, or legal custodian is unfit, unable, or unwilling to care for, protect, train or discipline the minor.

It is ordered:

1. The minor, ... , is committed to the Department of Corrections;

2. The Director, Juvenile Division, Department of Corrections, is appointed legal custodian of the minor;

3. The minor is placed under the guardianship of .... ;

4. The .... of this county convey the minor forthwith to the appropriate re-
   (appropriate officers)
   ception depot or other place designated by the Department of Corrections;

5. The clerk of the court deliver a certified copy of this order to the officer.

...., 19.......

JUDGE

I certify that the above is a copy of an order entered in this case on ...., 19 ......

...., 19........

Clerk of Court
[Seal of Court]

Figure 6.4

FRANK THORNBER CO., CHICAGO J-26

STATE OF ILLINOIS

IN THE CIRCUIT COURT OF THE................................JUDICIAL CIRCUIT

................................COUNTY, JUVENILE DIVISION

In the interest of

}

No.

a minor

DISPOSITIONAL ORDER
(Placement)

The court considered the evidence and finds: it has jurisdiction of the subject matter and the parties; the minor has been adjudged a delinquent, all statutory prerequisites have been complied with; the parent, guardian, or legal custodian is unfit, unable for some reason other than financial circumstances alone to care for, protect, train or discipline the minor, or is unwilling to do so, it is in the best interest of the minor to take him from such custody.

It is ordered:

1. The minor, ..., is:

   [ ] placed in the custody of ...., a suitable relative or other person,

   [ ] placed under the guardianship of ...., a probation officer,

   [ ] committed to ...., an agency for care or placement,

   [ ] committed to ...., a licensed training or industrial school,

   [ ] placed in the custody and guardianship of ...., Guardianship Administrator, Department of Children and Family Services, or his successor in office,

   [ ] placed ....

2. The clerk of the court deliver a certified copy of this order to the custodian or guardian as proof of his authority. No other process is necessary as authority for the keeping of the minor

3. This custody shall continue until the minor reaches age 21 unless otherwise ordered by the court.

4. The custodian .... authorized to consent to any required major medical and
   (is)   (is not)
   dental treatment recommended by a licensed physician.

....

I certify that the above is a copy of an order entered in this case on ...., 19......

........................, 19......

....
Clerk of Court
[Seal of Court]

Figure 6.5

Implications for Practitioners

It is essential for practitioners at all levels of the juvenile justice system to be completely familiar with appropriate procedures for dealing with juveniles. It is also important for practitioners to be aware of the rules governing other members of the juvenile justice system. This awareness helps to insure that the interests of juveniles will be protected within the guidelines established by society. It should not be too much to ask practitioners to be familiar with the juvenile court act that applies to them. Yet we have repeatedly seen practitioners from the level of the juvenile officer to the level of the juvenile court judge who are either ignorant of the procedural requirements for juveniles or who choose to ignore them. The consequences of such actions on behalf of juvenile justice personnel for juveniles, other practitioners in the system, and the public can be disastrous. Juveniles' rights may be violated, other practitioners may be put in a position where they cannot take appropriate action, and society may not be protected as a result of ignorance of proper procedure.

For example, a police officer may take a juvenile into custody for a serious delinquent act (robbery, for instance). The officer may, upon interrogation, obtain a confession from the juvenile. It may be impossible for the prosecutor to prosecute, if the police officer has failed to warn the juvenile of his or her rights according to *Miranda,* or if a reasonable attempt to contact the youth's parents was not made, or if the youth was frightened into confessing when his or her parents or legal representative were not present, or if the evidence in the case was obtained illegally. Of course, there will be no adjudication by the judge and rehabilitation/ corrections personnel will have no chance to rehabilitate, correct, or protect through detention. In the long run, then, neither the best interests of society nor those of the juvenile will be served.

Summary

Every state has a juvenile court act spelling out appropriate procedures for dealing with juveniles from the initial apprehension through final disposition. In looking at several juvenile court acts, we have seen that there are many uniformities in these acts as well as many points of disagreement. It is crucial, therefore, for all juvenile justice practitioners to become familiar with the juvenile court act under which they operate, so the best interests of juveniles, other practitioners, and society may be served to the maximum extent possible.

Discussion Questions

1. What are the constitutional rights guaranteed to adults in our society, which are not guaranteed juveniles in juvenile court proceedings? What is the rationale for depriving juveniles of these rights?
2. Discuss the benefits of the current trend toward a more legalistic stance in juvenile court proceedings for juveniles. Are there any disadvantages for juveniles in this trend? If so, what are they?
3. What are the strengths and weaknesses of informal adjustments, unofficial probation, and continuance under supervision?
4. Assume a fifteen-year-old male has been caught shoplifting a small transistor radio at a local discount store. The security guard at the store calls the police. The police officer arriving on the scene has settled similar disputes between this particular juvenile and the management of the chain store on several previous occasions. In addition, the police officer knows that, besides shoplifting frequently, the juvenile frequently runs away from home and is gone for days at a time. The security guard and store manager are determined to prosecute the juvenile. Based on the juvenile court act in your particular state, answer the following questions:
   a. What steps *must* the police officer take after he or she has taken the juvenile into custody?
   b. What steps *may* the probation officer take in an attempt to settle the dispute?
   c. If further custody is a consideration, what steps must be taken in order to continue such custody?
   d. Assuming a petition has been filed, what are the juvenile court's obligations with respect to all parties to the proceedings?
   e. What are the two major findings to be determined at the adjudicatory hearing? What degree of proof is required? What are the juvenile's rights during the hearing?
   f. At the dispositional hearing, what alternatives are available to the juvenile court judge and what information does the judge have at hand to help to arrive at the proper disposition?

Selected Readings

Binder, A. "The Juvenile Court, the U.S. Constitution, and Where the Twain Meet." *Journal of Criminal Justice* 10 (1984).

Davis, Samuel M. *Rights of Juveniles: The Juvenile Justice System.* New York: Clark Boardman Co., 1974 with 1988 supplement.

Gardner, Martin R. "Punishment and Juvenile Justice: A Conceptual Framework for Assessing Constitutional Rights of Youthful Offenders." *Vandervilt Law Review* 35 (1982).

Grisso, Thomas. *Juveniles' Waiver of Rights: Legal and Psychological Competence.* New York: Plenum Press, 1981.

McNally, R. B. "Juvenile Court: An Endangered Species." *Federal Probation* 47, no. 1 (1983): 32–37.

National Center for Juvenile Justice. *Juvenile Court Jurisdiction Over Childrens' Conduct: 1982 Comparative Analysis of Juvenile and Family Codes and National Standards.* Pittsburgh: National Center for Juvenile Justice, 1982.

National Juvenile Justice Assessment Center Report. "Jurisdiction and the Elusive Status Offender: A Comparison in Delinquent Behavior and Status Offenses." Washington, D.C.: U.S. Government Printing Office, 1980.

Robin, Gerald D. "Juvenile Interrogation and Confessions." *Journal of Police Science and Administration* 10, no. 2 (1982): 224–28.

7 Juveniles and the Police

The police are usually the first representatives of the juvenile justice system encountered by delinquents. The importance of the police in the juvenile justice system is considerable for this very reason. If the police decide not to take into custody or arrest a particular juvenile, none of the rest of the official legal machinery can go into operation.[1] It is well established that the police exercise a considerable amount of "discretion" (individual judgment) in handling juveniles. While the exercise of discretion is a necessary and normal part of police work, the potential for abuse exists, since there is no way to routinely review this practice. As a result, officers are often inconsistent in the decision-making process.

There are a number of cues to which most police officers respond in making decisions about whether to take official action against a particular juvenile. These cues include the following:

1. the wishes of the complainant;
2. the nature of the violation;
3. the race, attitude, and sex of the offender;
4. knowledge about prior police contacts with the juvenile in question;
5. the perceived ability and willingness of the juvenile's parents to cooperate in solving the problem;
6. the setting or location (private or public) in which the encounter occurs.[2]

---

1. Edwin H. Sutherland and Donald R. Cressey, *Criminology,* 9th ed. (New York: J. B. Lippincott Co., 1974), 374–75. Also see Joseph Goldstein, "Police Discretion Not to Invoke the Criminal Process: Low-Visibility Decisions in the Administration of Justice," *Yale Law Journal* 69 (March 1960): 543–88.

2. For further discussion of these variables, see Carl Wertham and Irving Piliavin, "Gang Members and the Police," in *The Police: Six Sociological Essays,* ed. David J. Bordua (New York: John Wiley & Sons, Inc., 1967), 56–98; Donald Black and Albert J. Reiss, Jr., "Police Control of Juveniles," *American Sociological Review* 35, no. 1 (February 1970): 67; and Irving Piliavin and Scott Briar, "Police Encounters with Juveniles," *American Journal of Sociology* 70 (September 1964): 206–14.

Figure 7.1 Police officer visiting elementary school (Photo courtesy of Macomb Police Department, Macomb, Illinois)

In general, the wishes of the complainant and the nature of the offense weigh heavily upon police officers' decisions. If the offense is serious (robbery and burglary, for example), the officer is generally expected by his or her department and by the public to arrest and, under most circumstances, the officer does so. There is some evidence, however, that the police may not arrest, even for serious offenses, if the complainant does not wish to pursue the matter.[3] If the offense is minor and the complainant does not desire to pursue the matter, the police will often handle the case unofficially. Again, in the case of a minor offense, the police will often intervene on behalf of the juvenile to persuade the complainant not to take official action. It should be noted, however, that in most jurisdictions the police cannot prevent a complainant from filing a petition if he or she insists.

3. See Kenneth Culp Davis, *Police Discretion* (St. Paul, Minn.: West Publishing Company, 1975), 3–7.

In general, juveniles who show "proper" respect for the police, have few if any known prior police contacts, and are perceived as having cooperative parents are more likely to be dealt with unofficially than those who show little respect, have a long history of encounters with the police, and are perceived as having uncooperative parents.[4] Most authorities agree that those juveniles who are most likely to have a "police record of arrest are those who conform to police preconceptions about delinquent types, who are perceived as a threat to others, and who are most visible to the police."[5] Morash indicates she found a "convincing demonstration of regular tendencies of the police to investigate and arrest males who have delinquent peers regardless of these youths' involvement in delinquency."[6] Moyer, while indicating that sex and race are not critical factors in the police decision-making process with respect to adults, indicates that the nature of the offense and demeanor of the offender when confronting the police are important in determining the type of action taken by the police.[7] Biases on behalf of the police may lead to more informal adjustments for certain types of juveniles (white, middle-class, polite) than for others (black, lower-class, rude). This is largely a matter of speculation, since no records of such dispositions are routinely kept. It is clear, however, that based upon their perceptions of a number of cues, police officers make decisions as to whether official action is in order or whether a particular juvenile can be dealt with "unofficially."

Unofficial Procedures

As Irving Piliavin and Scott Briar point out, police officers who encounter juveniles involved in delinquent activities have a number of alternatives available for handling such juveniles (see fig. 7.2).[8] Basically, the police officer may simply release the juvenile in question, or release the juvenile and submit a "juvenile card" briefly describing the

4. Donald J. Black and Albert J. Reiss, "Police Control of Juveniles," *American Sociological Review* 35 (February, 1970): 63–77.

5. Merry Morash, "Establishment of a Juvenile Police Record: The Influence of Individual and Peer Group Characteristics," *Criminology* 22, no. 1 (February 1984): 97–111.

6. Ibid., 110.

7. Imogene Moyer, "Demeanor, Sex, and Race in Police Processing," *Journal of Criminal Justice* 9, no. 3 (1981): 235.

8. Piliavin and Briar, "Police Encounters with Juveniles," 207–8.

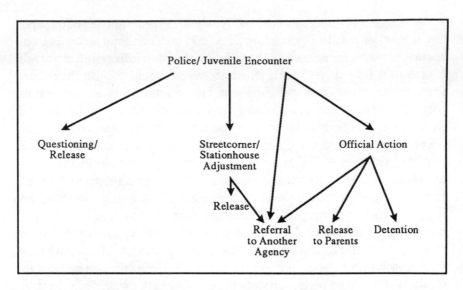

Figure 7.2   Police alternatives in handling juveniles

encounter, or reprimand the juvenile and release him or her, or the officer may take the juvenile into custody in order to file a petition in juvenile court. Only the last alternative involves official action. Each of the other three alternatives may occur either on the street or in a police facility. These informal adjustments are commonly referred to as "streetcorner" or "stationhouse" adjustments. A typical streetcorner adjustment might occur when the police have been notified by a homeowner that a group of juveniles have congregated on his property and have refused to leave when asked to do so. Since the offense is not serious and since the home-owner is likely to be satisfied once the juveniles have left, the officer may simply tell the juveniles to leave and not return. If, for some reason, the police officer is not satisfied that the orders to move on and not return will be obeyed, the officer may take the juveniles to the police station and request that the juveniles' parents meet with him or her there. If an agreement can be reached among the juveniles and their parents that the event leading to the complaint will not recur, the officer may release the juveniles in what is commonly referred to as a stationhouse adjust-ment. In either case, there is no official action taken and no official record of the encounter is kept. (While information cards kept on juveniles do not constitute official records, they are sometimes used by juvenile offi-cers to determine the number of prior contacts between a particular ju-venile and the police and therefore, may be used to determine whether official action will be taken.)

Informal adjustments such as these usually cause little controversy as long as all parties (complainant, police, parents, and juveniles) are reasonably satisfied. Some police officers, however, carry informal adjustments a step further and require repair of damages, monetary restitution, and visits to the police station, for example, as a condition of not taking official action. Although police officers often see solutions of this type as being better for the juvenile than official processing, some serious objections have been raised by parents, the courts, and sometimes the juveniles involved. Suppose a juvenile was allegedly involved in vandalism in which the juvenile spray-painted some derogatory comments on the front of a school building. Also suppose that, as a condition of not taking official action, a police officer instructs the youth to spend every night after school cleaning the paint off the school building with paint remover and brushes that are provided at the expense of the juvenile or his or her parents. Finally, suppose the juvenile persists in maintaining his or her innocence. The implications of this type of "treatment without trial" should be relatively clear. First, it has not been demonstrated that the juvenile did commit the delinquent act in question; that is, the juvenile has not been adjudicated delinquent in a court of law. Second, since it has not been demonstrated that he or she committed the vandalism, there is no legal basis for punishment. Third, even if the juvenile did in fact commit the offense, the police have no legal authority to impose punishment on alleged offenders. In a case of this type (which is not atypical), the juvenile may be upset at being punished for an act that he or she did not commit, the parents may be upset because their child did not receive a fair trial, and the juvenile court judge may be upset because the functions of the court have been usurped (taken over) by the police.

While many police officers who employ informal adjustments realize that they are acting illegally from a strict legal standpoint, an attempt to justify the use of informal adjustments is made on the basis that the treatment or punishment the juvenile entered into is voluntary. These officers reason that since the treatment or punishment is not mandatory and is in the juvenile's best interests, there does not need to be prior adjudication of delinquency. Many of these officers fail to recognize that the extent to which their "suggested" treatment or punishment programs are voluntary is highly questionable. The threat of taking official action, if unofficial suggestions are not acceptable to juveniles, largely removes any element of voluntarism.

In spite of the difficulties just mentioned, estimates are that as many as 85 percent of all police-juvenile contacts are resolved informally.[9] Police officers, who use informal dispositions, often see such dispositions as more desirable than official processing which is certain to leave the youth with a juvenile record and may lead to detention for some period of time. Most police officers agree that neither juvenile records nor attempts to rehabilitate juveniles who are detained are beneficial to juveniles. Thus, when police officers act informally, they often sincerely believe they are doing so in the best interests of the juveniles involved. This may be the case if we assume that all the juveniles apprehended did commit a delinquent act and if we assume that treatment and rehabilitation are of little or no value. However, if we recognize that sometimes the police do make mistakes, that some juveniles do need treatment of some type, that the police have no mandate to impose punishment or treatment, and that the juvenile court judge often has no way of knowing how many times a particular juvenile has been dealt with informally, the problems inherent in informal adjustments become very apparent.

Official Procedures

The official procedures to be followed when processing juveniles are clearly spelled out in juvenile court acts. These procedures have been outlined in chapter 6, but a number of additional observations should be made with respect to the role of the police in this processing.

It is important to note that police procedures for juvenile offenders differ in most jurisdictions from adult procedures. As a rule, these procedures are tailored specifically toward implementing the juvenile court philosophy of treatment, protection, and rehabilitation rather than punishment. As a result, in order to carry out proper procedures, specialized training is necessary. It has been our observation that many officers in most jurisdictions believe that being assigned as a juvenile officer is not particularly desirable. We have heard juvenile officers referred to as "kiddie cops" and seen distinctions made between "real" police officers and "juvenile" officers. Juvenile work, in many jurisdictions, is seen by male police officers and administrators as one of the few aspects of police work in which females can function successfully. These traditional police

9. Black and Reiss, "Police Control of Juveniles," 134.

attitudes have hampered the development of a professional corps of juvenile officers and have led many juvenile officers to see their role in an unfavorable light. We would like to point out that being a good juvenile police officer requires more skill than being a good patrol officer. In addition to learning the basics of policing, the juvenile officer needs to learn a great deal about the special requirements of juvenile law, about the nature of adolescence, about the nature of parent-child relationships, and about the social service agencies, public and private, to which juveniles may be referred for assistance. These skills are not easy to acquire, and those who have mastered them should take pride in their accomplishments. In addition, police organizations should reward those who possess and actively employ these skills in terms of both salary and promotion.

While the development of effective juvenile officers and juvenile bureaus is highly desirable, most initial contacts between juveniles and the police involve patrol officers. It would appear logical to provide at least minimal training in the area of juvenile law for all patrol personnel in order to safeguard the rights of juveniles and to ensure proper legal processing by the police. It does little good (either for the juvenile or for the prosecutor's case) to have a competent juvenile officer if the initial encounter between the juvenile and the police has been mishandled.

Police officers who are involved in the official processing of juveniles need to be aware that all of the guarantees in terms of self-incrimination and searches and seizures characteristic of adult proceedings also hold for juveniles. In addition, juveniles are, in most jurisdictions, extended even further protection by law. Thus the police are required to notify the juvenile's parents about their child's whereabouts and are required to release the juvenile to his or her parents unless good cause exists for detention. Detention in a lock-up routinely used for adult offenders is often illegal and the police must, in these cases, make special arrangements to transport and detain juveniles should further detention be necessary. Similarly, police records concerning juveniles must, in most jurisdictions, be kept separate from adult records and are more or less confidential (see chapter six). While fingerprints and photographs of juvenile offenders may be taken, there are often restrictions placed upon their use; that is, they may not be transmitted to other law enforcement agencies without a court order in many jurisdictions. Recent court decisions indicate that a juvenile charged with a delinquent act has a right to counsel prior to placement in a police line-up. There is some indication that a juvenile's waiver of his or her right to remain silent during interrogation is of questionable value.[10] As a result, many police departments delay interrogation until either a parent and/or an attorney is present. In many jurisdictions, police officers who have been designated juvenile officers have the task of ensuring that juveniles are properly handled. These juvenile officers are, presumably, specially trained in juvenile law and procedures.

Training and Competence of Juvenile Officers

For roughly the last seventy-five years, there have been repeated calls for professionalization of the police through increased education and training. The number of two- and four-year college programs in criminal justice and law enforcement has increased dramatically during the last decade, as has the number of special institutes, seminars, and workshops dealing with special police problems. Since juvenile cases present special problems for the police, one might expect considerable emphasis on training for juvenile officers at such institutes. Indeed, the number of police officers qualified by training to serve in juvenile bureaus has increased dramatically in recent years, especially in large metropolitan departments. In these departments promotion within the juvenile bureau is possible and both male and female officers deal with juvenile offenders brought to their attention by the public or by patrol officers. The possibilities of promotion and recognition for a job well done provide incentive and rewards for those choosing to pursue a career in juvenile law enforcement. The presence of officers of both sexes facilitates discussion of all types of juvenile problems as well as the transportation and search of juvenile offenders; that is, when a female offender is to be transported, a female officer can accompany her. Most departments without female officers require two male officers to transport female offenders, thereby removing an additional officer from other duty.

The situation of juvenile officers in smaller cities has also improved in recent years. More jurisdictions require compliance with laws mandating special training for juvenile officers, although personnel shortages and reduced financial resources sometimes make both training and specific assignment to purely juvenile matters difficult. There are still many smaller police departments with no female officers, so male officers must

10. Davis, *Rights of Juveniles,* pp. 3.44.10–3.49.

Figure 7.3 Police conducting bicycle safety program for youth (Photo courtesy of Galesburg Police Department, Galesburg, Illinois)

deal with juveniles of both sexes. Some rural departments have no officers specifically trained to deal with juveniles and others, in order to conform to statutory requirements, simply select and designate an officer, often one who has no prior training in juvenile matters, as juvenile officer. Considering the fact that juvenile officers are frequently expected to speak to civic action groups about juvenile problems, run junior police programs, visit schools and preschools, and investigate cases of abused and missing children, this lack of training is a very serious matter.

Smaller police departments face serious difficulties in providing adequately trained officers for twenty-four-hour-a-day service. When these departments do train and appoint officers to handle juvenile offenders, they can seldom afford to relieve these officers of other duties. This, in effect, makes it impossible for the appointed officers to become specialized in juvenile matters. This also eliminates the possibility of developing a stable juvenile bureau and removes the possibility of advancing based upon demonstrated skills in dealing with juvenile offenders. One result of these difficulties is that officers have little incentive to volunteer for service in juvenile bureaus. Consequently, juvenile officers are frequently appointed on the basis of a perceived affinity for "getting along" with youth. Unfortunately, this affinity is not a substitute for proper training, although it may appear to be to the police administrators who regard handling juvenile offenses as something less than real police work. The end product is often the assignment of untrained personnel as juvenile officers, which increases the possibility of mishandling juvenile offenders and demeans the juvenile officer's role when mistakes inevitably occur. An affinity or desire for working with juveniles is an important quality in any juvenile officer. This desire must, however, be supplemented by proper training in order to insure the interests of both juveniles in trouble and society. Therefore, it is essential that smaller police departments train officers to handle juvenile cases as rapidly as possible. Sending patrol officers to seminars, institutes, and workshops that deal with proper juvenile procedures is not a waste of time even when these officers cannot expect to be permanently assigned exclusively to juvenile bureaus.

Police/School Consultant and Liaison Programs

Over the past four decades, police departments and schools have worked together to develop programs to help prevent delinquency and improve relationships between juveniles and the police. These programs involve more than simply providing security through police presence in the schools. Rather, the programs attempt to foster a more personal relationship between youth and the police by using police officers in counseling settings, by improving communications between the police and school officials, and by increasing student knowledge of the law and the consequences of violations. One early police/school liaison program was developed in Flint, Michigan, in 1958. A 1972 evaluation of this program concluded that the police officers assigned had difficulties in being both authority figures and counselor/confidants.[11] Similar programs in Tuscon, Arizona, Montgomery, Alabama, Woodburn, Oregon, and Tampa, Florida, to mention a few, have shown similar results. More recent programs have focused on the latter role for officers assigned, who act as additional resource persons in the school setting, and who generally

11. R. Mulder, and D. Williams, *Cops in the School: A Look at Police School Liaison Programs in the State of Michigan,* Report to the Michigan Office of Criminal Justice Programs, Grand Valley State Colleges, 1975.

have been evaluated positively by school officials, though not always by students. These programs have proliferated, based on these evaluations, and the belief that the closer the relationship between police and juveniles in nonthreatening situations (those other than investigatory or crime intervention) the better in terms of improving the image of the police and decreasing deliquency. A number of schools and police agencies throughout the country are now involved with such programs, and they appear to be having more positive than negative effects on officers, juveniles, and school authorities, particularly when the officers involved have received special training to prepare them for their assignments.[12]

Police and Juvenile Court

The police are the primary source of referral to juvenile court and juvenile court judges rely heavily upon the police for background information concerning juveniles who come before them. As Hasenfeld points out, "The more dependent the court is on the police and the fewer the mechanisms for buffering itself from them, the greater the likelihood that court personnel will attempt to incorporate and conform to the expectations of the police in their everyday decisions about juvenile offenders."[13] Since the police and the court may have very different goals with respect to juveniles (e.g., control versus treatment), this may not always be in the best interests of juveniles. On the one hand, the juvenile court may become overly concerned with control. On the other, "The policeman who feels the court is unfair to the police or too lenient with offenders may fail to report cases to the court, since, in his opinion, nothing will be gained by such official referral."[14] In such cases, the police may attempt to resolve the case at hand themselves, which, as we have pointed out earlier, may or may not be in the best interests of the youth involved. In short, whether or not a particular juvenile is referred to juvenile court depends in part upon the police officer's attitude toward the court.

12. P. F. LeBreck, "An Evaluation of the Police Consultant Program in High School District 214" (Unpublished M.A. thesis, Western Illinois University, 1986).

13. Y. Hasenfeld, "The Juvenile Court and Its Environment," in *Introduction to Juvenile Delinquency,* ed. Cromwell et al. (St. Paul, Minn.: West Publishing Company, 1978), 208.

14. R. M. Emerson, *Judging Delinquents: Context and Process in the Juvenile Court* (Chicago: Aldine, 1968), 86.

Implications for Practitioners

In order to implement proper juvenile procedures and benefit from theoretical notions concerning prevention, causes, and correction of delinquent behavior, the juvenile officer must first know proper procedures and understand theories of causation. Since both types of knowledge are specialized, it is imperative that juvenile officers receive special training in these areas. This specialized training is advantageous for the police department, the juvenile, the justice system, and the community. The police department benefits in terms of creating a more professional image and in terms of efficiency, since mistakes in processing should be reduced. The juvenile benefits in that trained personnel can better carry out the intent of juvenile court acts, which were developed to protect the best interests of the juvenile. The justice system benefits from the proper initial processing of juveniles who are to be processed further in that system (for example, prosecuted). Finally, the community benefits from decisions made by police officers who are properly trained. In return for these benefits, it is essential to reward juvenile officers who perform well through the use of increased pay and/or rank.

Summary

The majority of police-juvenile contacts result in unofficial dispositions in the form of streetcorner or stationhouse adustments. It is important that decisions concerning proper disposition of juvenile cases by police officers be based upon a thorough knowledge of procedural requirements and the problems of youth. When trained, competent officers make such decisions, the imposition of punishment by the officers handling cases unofficially is reduced and the rights of juveniles are better protected. In those cases that require official disposition, further processing is facilitated by proper initial processing. In order to insure that police officers handle juvenile cases properly, specialized training programs need to be developed and utilized and incentives for good performance by juvenile officers need to be provided.

Discussion Questions

1. List and discuss some of the cues frequently used by police officers in deciding whether to handle a case officially or unofficially. What are some of the dangers in relying upon these cues from the point of view of the juvenile offender?

2. Joe Foul Up, a thirteen-year-old white male, has just been apprehended by a police officer for stealing a bicycle. Joe admits taking the bicycle, but says he only intended to go for a "joy ride" and was going to return the bicycle later in the day. Joe has no prior police contacts that the officer is aware of. The bicycle has been missing for only an hour and is unharmed. The owner of the bicycle is undecided about whether or not to proceed officially. Discuss the various options available to the police officer in handling this case. What options do you consider to be most appropriate and why?

3. In your opinion, what are the qualifications of a good juvenile officer? How can we best insure that juvenile officers possess these desirable qualities?

4. Why do you think juvenile officers handle the majority of contacts with juveniles unofficially even when they could clearly proceed officially? What are some of the advantages and disadvantages to both juveniles and society of unofficial dispositions?

Selected Readings

Agnew, Robert. "Appearance and Delinquency." *Criminology* 22, no. 3 (August 1984): 421–40.

Black, Donald J., and Albert J. Reiss, Jr. "Police Control of Juveniles." *American Sociological Review* 35 (February 1970): 63–77.

Ferdinand, T. N., and E. G. Luchterhand. "Inner-City Youth, the Police, the Juvenile Court, and Justice." *Social Problems* 17 (Spring 1970): 510–26.

Gavin, T., and W. Jacobs, "Adolescent Suicide and the School Resource Officer." *Police Chief* 54, no. 4 (April 1987): 42–44.

Griffiths, Curt T. "Law Enforcement-Juvenile Court Relations: The Impact of Decision Making." *Criminal Justice Review* 6, no. 1 (Spring 1981): 6–13.

Lundman, Richard L., R. E Sykes, and John P. Clark. "Police Control of Juveniles: A Replication." *Journal of Research in Crime and Delinquency* 15 (1978): 74–91.

Piliavin, Irving, and Scott Briar. "Police Encounters with Juveniles." *American Journal of Sociology* 70 (September 1964): 206–14.

Willis, C. L., and R. H. Welles. "The Police and Child Abuse: An Analysis of Police Decisions to Report Illegal Behavior." *Criminology* 26, no. 4 (November 1986): 695–715.

8 Key Figures in Juvenile Court Proceedings

One of the alternatives available to the police in dealing with juvenile offenders involves taking official action that can result in further processing through the juvenile justice system. Once the decision to take official action has been made, juvenile court personnel become involved in the case. We are using the term "juvenile court personnel" in the broad sense to include the prosecutor, defense counsel, the judge, and the juvenile probation officer.

The Prosecutor

The final decision about whether a juvenile will be brought into juvenile court rests with the prosecutor. Regardless of the source of the referral (police officer, teacher, parent, and so forth), the prosecutor may decide not to take the case into court and, for all practical purposes, no further official action may be taken on the case in question. The prosecutor, then, exercises an enormous amount of discretion in the juvenile (and adult) justice system. While the police officer may "open the gate" to the juvenile justice system, the prosecutor may close that gate. The prosecutor may do this without accounting for his or her reasons to anyone else in the system (except, of course, to the voters who elect the prosecutor to office, which is often long after the case has been decided).

Clearly, there are some circumstances under which the prosecutor would be foolish to proceed with court action. For example, lack of evidence, lack of probable cause, or lack of due process may make it virtually impossible to prosecute a delinquency case successfully. There are, however, a number of somewhat less legitimate reasons for failure to prosecute. There have been instances where prosecutors have failed to take cases to court for political or personal reasons (as when the juvenile in question is the son or daughter of a powerful and influential citizen) or because the case load of the prosecutor includes an "important" or "serious" case in which successful prosecution will result in favorable publicity. As a result, the prosecutor may screen out or dismiss a number of "less serious" cases, such as burglary and assault.[1] In short, the prosecutor is the key figure in the justice system and is recognized as such by both defendants and defense counsel.[2]

The prosecutor's key role in the American juvenile justice system has emerged slowly over time. Initially, the prosecutor (state's attorney) was seen as both unnecessary and harmful in juvenile court proceedings which were supposedly nonadversary proceedings "on behalf of the juvenile."[3] The *Gault* decision, along with the decisions in *Kent* and *Winship,* brought about a number of changes in juvenile court proceedings. Among these changes was a growing recognition of the need for legally trained individuals to represent both the state and the juvenile (and, in some instances, the juvenile's parents) in all stages of juvenile justice proceedings. The need resulted from increased emphasis upon procedural requirements and the adversary nature of the proceedings.[4]

Today, the prosecutor is a key figure in juvenile justice because he or she determines whether or not a case will go to court, waiver decisions, the nature of the petition and, to a large extent, the disposition of the case after an adjudication of delinquent (the judge seldom imposes more severe punishment than that recommended by the prosecutor). In addition, we have noted an alarming tendency of prosecutors to impose unofficial probation on juveniles. The prosecutor indicates to a juvenile that he or she has a prosecutable case, but also indicates that prosecution will be withheld if the juvenile in question agrees to behave according to certain guidelines. These are often the same guidelines handed down by probation officers subsequent to an adjudication of delinquent. While the use of unofficial probation is clearly beneficial to the prosecutor since it eliminates the need to prepare a case for court and may be beneficial for the juvenile court by reducing the number of official cases, unofficial

1. For a comprehensive discussion of prosecutorial discretion see *The Invisible Justice System: Discretion and the Law,* ed. Burton Atkins and Mark Pogrebin (Cincinnati: Anderson, 1978), ch. III.

2. See Jonathan Caspar, *American Criminal Justice: The Defendant's Perspective* (Englewood Cliffs, N.J.: Prentice-Hall, Inc., 1972).

3. U.S. Department of Justice, Law Enforcement Assistance Administration, *Prosecution in the Juvenile Courts: Guidelines for the Future* (Washington, D.C.: U.S. Government Printing Office, December 1973), 9.

4. Ibid. 10–11.

probation has the same disadvantages for juveniles as informal adjustments by the police. In short, unofficial probation imposed by the prosecutor amounts to punishment without trial, and the voluntary nature of this probation is highly questionable.

In addition to enforcing the law and representing the state, the prosecutor has many of the following duties in juvenile justice proceedings:

—investigates possible violations of the law
—cooperates with the police, in-take officers, and probation officers regarding the facts alleged in the petition
—authorizes, reviews, and prepares petitions for the court
—plays a role in the initial detention or temporary placement process
—represents the state in all pre-trial motions, probable cause hearings, and consent decrees
—represents the state at transfer and waiver hearings
—may recommend physical or mental examinations
—seeks amendments or dismissals of filed petitions if appropriate
—represents the state at the adjudication of the case
—represents the state at the disposition of the case
—enters into plea-bargaining discussions with the defense attorney
—represents the state on appeal or in habeas corpus *proceedings*
—is involved in hearings dealing with violation of probation.[5]

An attorney for the state (prosecutor) should participate in every proceeding of every stage of every case subject to the jurisdiction of the family court in which the state has an interest.

Defense Counsel

The American Bar Association has described the responsibility of the legal profession to the juvenile court in Standard 2.3 of "Standards Relating to Counsel for Private Parties." The ABA states that legal representation should be provided in all proceedings arising from or related to a delinquency or in-need-of-supervision action—including mental competency, transfer, postdisposition, probation revocation and classification, institutional transfer, and disciplinary or other administrative proceedings related to the treatment process—that may substantially affect the juvenile's custody, status, or course of treatment.[6]

5. Larry J. Siegal and Joseph J. Senna, *Juvenile Justice: Theory, Practice, and Law,* 2d ed. (St. Paul, Minn.: West Publishing Company, 1981), 439–40.

6. American Bar Association, "Standards Relating to Counsel for Private Parties" (Cambridge, Mass.: Ballinger, 1977).

Juvenile court proceedings involving delinquency are adversary in nature, in spite of the intent of the early developers of juvenile court philosophy. It is for this reason that the role of defense counsel has become increasingly more important. Today in large cities, at least 80 percent of all juveniles named in delinquency petitions are represented by counsel. In many cases the juvenile's parents also have legal representation. In more rural areas, the figures are considerably less impressive, but even here the frequency of legal representation for juveniles appears to be increasing.[7] In some cases a *guardian ad litem* may be appointed by the court. The *guardian ad litem* is a person appointed by the court "to promote and protect the interests of a child involved in a judicial proceeding, and to assure representation of those interests in the courts and throughout the social services and ancillary service systems."[8] Generally the *guardian ad litem* is used in abuse, neglect, and dependency cases where the minor is in need of representation because of immaturity.

There are two major categories of defense counsel. Private defense counselors are sometimes retained or appointed to represent the interests of juveniles in court. Frequently, however, juveniles are represented by public defenders, who are paid by the county or state or both, to represent defendants who do not have the money to retain private counsel. For many young lawyers interested in criminal law, the position of public defender represents a stepping stone. In most non-metropolitan areas the public defender is paid a relatively low salary, but the position guarantees a minimal income, which can be supplemented by private practice. As a rule, case loads are heavy, investigative resources are limited, and many clients are, by their own admission, guilty (or delinquent).[9] The public defender, therefore, spends a great deal of time negotiating pleas and often very little time with clients. In fact, sometimes public defenders in juvenile court have indicated to the judge that they were ready to proceed and then asked someone in the courtroom which of the several juveniles present was their client. As a result, public defenders often enjoy a less than favorable image among their clients.[10]

Some public defenders seem to have little interest in using every possible strategy to defend their clients. On numerous occasions legal errors are made by prosecutors and juvenile court judges to which the

7. H. Ted Rubin, "The Juvenile Court's Search for Identity and Responsibility," *Crime and Delinquency* 23, no. 1 (January 1977): 1–13.

8. Howard Davidson, "The Guardian ad Litem: An Important Approach to the Protection of Children," *Children Today* 10, no. 23 (1981).

9. Caspar, *American Criminal Justice,* 54–65.

10. Ibid., ch. 4.

public defender raises no objection. In addition, appeals initiated by public defenders in delinquency cases are quite rare even when chances of successful appeal seem to be good. There are also public defenders who pursue their clients' interests with all possible vigor, but on the whole, it appears that juveniles who have private counsel often fare better in juvenile court than those who are represented by public defenders.[11]

Whether defense counsel is private or public, his or her duties remain essentially the same. These duties are to see that the client is properly represented at all stages of the system, that the client's rights are not violated, and that the client's case is presented in the most favorable light possible, regardless of the client's involvement in delinquent activity.[12] In order to accomplish these goals, the defense counsel is expected to battle, at least in theory, the prosecutor in adversary proceedings. Here again, the difference between theory and practice is considerable.

The Relationship between the Prosecutor and Defense Counsel—Adversary or Cooperative?

In theory, adversary proceedings result when the "champion" of the defendant (defense counsel) and the "champion" of the state (prosecutor) do "battle" in open court where the "truth" is determined and "justice" is the result. In practice the situation is quite often different due to considerations of time and money on behalf of both the state and the defendant.

The ideal of adversary proceedings is perhaps most closely realized when a well-known private defense attorney does battle with the prosecutor. Prominent defense attorneys often have extremely competent investigative staffs and considerable resources in terms of time and money to devote to a case. Thus, the balance of power between the state and the defendant may be almost even. This is generally not the case when defense counsel is a public defender who is often paid less than the prosecutor, often has less experience than the prosecutor, and generally has

11. For a discussion of the differences between private and public defense counsels at the adult level, see John E. Conklin, *Robbery and the Criminal Justice System* (Philadelphia: J. B. Lippincott Co., 1972).

12. See Charles P. Curtis, "The Ethics of Advocacy," *Stanford Law Review* 4 (December 1951): 3–23; or F. Lee Bailey, *The Defense Never Rests* (New York: Signet, 1971).

more limited access to an investigative staff than the prosecutor. For a variety of reasons then, both defense counsel and the prosecutor may find it easier to negotiate a particular case rather than to fight it out in court, since court cases are costly in terms of both time and money.

The vast majority of adult criminal cases in the United States are settled by plea bargaining. A substantial proportion of delinquency cases is disposed of in this way as well. In fact, it has been suggested that justice in the United States is not the result of the adversary system, but is the result of a cooperative network of routine interaction between defense counsel, the prosecutor, the defendant, and, in many instances, the judge.[13]

In plea bargaining, both prosecutor and defense counsel hope to gain through compromise. The prosecutor wants the defendant to plead guilty, if not to the original charges then to some less serious offense. Defense counsel seeks to get the best deal possible for his or her client, which may range from an outright dismissal to a plea of guilty to some less serious offense than the original charge. The nature of the compromise depends upon conditions such as the strength of the prosecutor's case and the seriousness of the offense. Most often, the two counselors arrive at what both consider a "just" compromise, which is then presented to the defendant to accept or reject. As a rule, the punishment to be recommended by the prosecutor is also negotiated. Thus, the nature of the charges, the plea, and the punishment are negotiated and agreed upon before the defendant actually enters the courtroom. The adversary system, in its ideal form at least, has been circumvented. Perhaps a hypothetical example will help to clarify the nature and consequences of plea bargaining.

Suppose our friend, Joe Foul Up, is once again in trouble. This time, Joe is seen breaking into a house. The break-in is reported to the police who apprehend Joe in the house with a watch and some expensive jewelry belonging to the homeowner. This time, the police decide to take official action. Since Joe is over thirteen and since the offense is fairly serious, the prosecutor threatens to prosecute Joe as an adult in adult court. She also indicates that she intends to seek a prison sentence for Joe. Joe's attorney, realizing that the prosecutor has a strong case, knows that he cannot get Joe's case dismissed. He argues with the prosecutor

---

13. See Abraham S. Blumberg, *Criminal Justice* (Chicago: Quadrangle, 1967); or David Sudnow, "Normal Crimes: Sociological Features of the Penal Code in a Public Defender Office," *Social Problems* 12 (Winter 1965): 255–76.

that this is Joe's first appearance before the juvenile court and he is, after all, a juvenile. After some discussion, the prosecutor agrees to prosecute Joe in juvenile court, provided the allegation of delinquency is not contested. Joe's attorney agrees, provided the prosecutor recommends only a short stay in a private detention facility in the community. Joe's attorney then presents the "deal" to Joe and perhaps to Joe's parents, indicating that it is the best he can do and recommending that Joe accept, since he could be found guilty and sentenced to prison if he is tried in adult court. Joe accepts and the bargain is concluded. The case has been settled in the attorney's offices. All that remains is to make it official during the formal court appearance. Most judges will concur with the negotiated plea.

The benefits of plea bargaining to the prosecutor, defense counsel, and the juvenile court are clear. The prosecutor is successful in prosecuting a case (she obtains an adjudication of delinquency), defense counsel has reduced the charges and penalty against his client, and all parties have saved time and money by not contesting the case in court. The juvenile may benefit as well, since he might have been convicted of burglary in adult court (if the judge had accepted the prosecutor's motion to change jurisdiction) and might have ended up in prison with a felony record. The dangers in plea bargaining, however, should not be overlooked. First, there is always the possibility that the motion to change jurisdiction might have been denied. Second, Joe might have been found not guilty even if he had been tried in adult court or might have been found not delinquent if his case had been heard in juvenile court. Third, since negotiations occur most often in secret, there is a danger that the constitutional rights of the defendant may not be stringently upheld. For example, Joe did not have the chance to confront and cross-examine his accusers. Finally, the juvenile court judge is little more than a figurehead, left only to sanction the bargain, in cases settled by plea bargaining. The juvenile court judge has the responsibility to see that the hearings are conducted in the best interests of both the juvenile and society and has the responsibility to ensure due process. Neither of these can be guaranteed in cases involving plea bargaining. A final concern in all plea bargaining processes, whether adult or juvenile, is the victim who seldom feels good about the bargain.

The Juvenile Court Judge

Theoretically, the juvenile court judge is the most powerful and central figure in the juvenile justice system, although he or she does not always exercise this power. The juvenile court judge decides whether a juvenile will be adjudicated delinquent, abused, in need of intervention, dependent, or neglected. Since there is no jury in most instances, the decision of the judge is final unless an appeal overturns the judge's decision. In addition, the judge makes the final determination about the disposition of the juvenile. Therefore, the juvenile court judge decides matters of law, matters of fact, and the immediate future of those who come before the bench.

> *Juvenile judges perform the following functions: they rule on pretrial motions involving such legal issues as arrest, search and seizure, interrogation, and lineup identification; they make decisions about the continued detention of children prior to hearings; they determine the minor's right to bail/bond; they make decisions about plea-bargaining agreements and the informal adjustment of juvenile cases; they handle bench hearings, rule on appropriateness of conduct, settle questions of evidence and procedure, and guide the questioning of witnesses; they assure the responsibility for holding dispositional hearings and deciding on the treatment accorded the minor; they handle waiver proceedings and appeals where allowed by statute.*[14]

While judges in many jurisdictions are assigned to juvenile court on a full-time basis, there are also many juvenile court judges who serve on a part-time basis. The latter are circuit judges who perform judicial functions in civil, criminal, probate, and other divisions of the court and are assigned occasionally to juvenile court. It is difficult for such judges to become specialists in juvenile court proceedings, though many perform well, and some are not as well-versed in juvenile law as they might be.

Juvenile court judges may be placed along a continuum ranging from those who see themselves largely as "parent-figures" to those who are mainly concerned about the juvenile court as a legal institution. The parent-figure judge is often genuinely concerned about the total well-being of juveniles who appear before the court. He or she is likely to overlook some of the formalities of due process in an attempt to serve as a parent figure who both supports and disciplines juveniles. This judge's primary concern is serving what he or she perceives as the best interests of the juveniles who appear in court, based on the assumption that they

14. Siegal and Senna, *Juvenile Justice,* 440.

must have problems even though they may not have committed the specific acts that led to the filing of a petition. Often these judges talk to the juveniles in an attempt to obtain expressions of remorse or regret. Once these expressions are given, the acts involved can often be "forgiven," and attention centers on how to best help the youth to avoid future trouble. If these expressions of remorse or regret are not given, the judge frequently resorts to a role as disciplinarian, sometimes overlooking the facts in the case.

There is a tendency among parent-figure judges to continue juvenile cases under supervision for various lengths of time. These judges apparently assume that a delinquency adjudication is less desirable than using the threat of adjudication in an attempt to induce acceptable behavior in juveniles. While a number of juvenile court acts provide for judicial continuance, this action can be carried to the extreme in situations where the case against the juvenile is weak and the continuance period long. These continuances amount to punishment without trial in much the same way as informal adjustments and unofficial probation.

At the other end of the continuum is the "law-giver" judge who is primarily concerned that all procedural requirements are fulfilled. This type of judge has less interest in the total personality of the juvenile than in the evidence of the case at hand. He or she dismisses cases that the prosecutor cannot prove beyond a reasonable doubt and does not feel that it is his or her duty to prescribe treatment for juveniles who have not committed the offense for which they have been accused. The dispositions of the law-giver judge are based upon statutory requirements more than upon the personal characteristics of the youth involved.

Most juvenile court judges fall somewhere between the two extremes, reflecting the lack of consensus about the proper role of the juvenile court discussed in chapter one. Most judges make a sincere effort to maximize legal safeguards for juveniles while attempting to act in the best interests of both the juveniles and society. They insure that legal counsel is available, they try to arrive at an objective decision during the adjudicatory hearing, and they try to ensure that the disposition of each case takes into account the needs of the juvenile involved.

In attempting to arrive at an acceptable disposition, the juvenile court judge frequently relies heavily upon the recommendations of the juvenile probation officer.

The Juvenile Probation Officer

Probation is a disposition by the juvenile court in which the minor is placed and maintained in the community under the supervision of a duly authorized officer of the court, the juvenile probation officer. It allows the minor to remain with the family or a foster family under conditions prescribed by the court to insure acceptable behavior in a community setting.

The juvenile probation officer is a key figure at all levels of the juvenile justice system. He or she may arrange a preliminary conference among interested parties, which may result in an out-of-court settlement between an alleged delinquent and the injured party. After an adjudicatory hearing, the juvenile probation officer is often charged with conducting a social background investigation. This investigation will be used to help the judge make a dispositional decision. Probation officers are also charged with supervising those juveniles who are placed on probation and released in the community, and they have the power to request a revocation of probation if the juvenile violates the conditions of probation.

While sparsely populated rural counties may employ only one juvenile probation officer, more populated areas frequently employ a chief probation officer, or director of court services, and one or more caseworker probation officers. (Some areas have no juvenile probation officers.) The duties of chief probation officers generally include assignment of cases and supervision of subordinates. They may or may not handle cases themselves, depending upon available staff. In addition, they normally serve as a liaison with judges and other department heads. The better the rapport they are able to establish with the juvenile court judge and the more effective they are in transmitting information to subordinates and the judge, the better the opportunity to serve the interests of juveniles and the community.

The role of juvenile probation officers is an ambiguous one. They are officers of the court who must act as authority figures and disciplinarians on occasion. On the other hand, they are charged with helping the juvenile in trouble by attempting to keep him or her out of court, by recommending the most beneficial disposition, and by being available to help probationers solve problems encountered during their probationary period. If they are to be effective in their role as helping professionals,

Figure 8.1 Juvenile probation officer during weekly visit with a probationer (Photo reprinted by permission)

they must encourage open interaction and trust among the juveniles they encounter. If they seem too authoritarian, they may receive little cooperation from juveniles. If they become too friendly, they may find it difficult to take disciplinary steps when necessary.

As a result of the ambiguous role requirements, several different types of juvenile probation officers exist. Some think of themselves largely as law enforcement officers whose basic function is to detect violations of probation. Others see themselves as juvenile advocates whose basic function is to insure that the rights of juveniles are not violated by the police or potential petitioners. Still others view themselves as basically social workers whose function is to facilitate treatment and rehabilitation. The most effective juvenile probation officers exercise all of these options at different times under differing circumstances. Perhaps the most difficult task for most juvenile probation officers is the supervision of probationers. Many have excessive caseloads and have little actual contact with their clients other than short weekly or monthly meetings. Obviously, not a great deal of counseling or supervision can occur under these circumstances. When field contacts are made with probationers, probation officers are often considerably concerned about further stigmatizing their clients. Parents who have problems with their children frequently try to use the juvenile probation officer's official position to frighten the youth into compliance with their demands. As a result of these difficulties, most juvenile probation officers in discussing probation conditions with their clients make it clear that they are available to discuss whatever problems probationers feel are significant. Some juvenile probation officers using this technique allow clients to choose the time and place for conferences in order to minimize stigmatization.

The functions of the juvenile probation officer are clearly important to an effective juvenile justice program. Unfortunately, some rural areas have no juvenile probation officer to insure that the purposes of the juvenile justice system will be achieved.

Training and Competence of Juvenile Court Personnel

If the goals of the juvenile justice system are to be achieved, the system needs to be staffed by well-trained, competent practitioners. Unfortunately, a number of circumstances have prevented us from achieving total success in this area.

Prosecutors and defense attorneys who handle juvenile court cases generally have little to gain by large investments of time and money. Few defense attorneys have gained national renown as the result of their efforts in juvenile court. Few prosecutors can count on being reelected on the basis of successfully prosecuting juveniles. In addition, in many locales the juvenile court has been regarded as something less than a "real court of law" where technical proficiency in law is necessary. Prosecutors often assign inexperienced assistants to handle juvenile cases and few defense attorneys specialize in the practice of juvenile law. As a result, many cases presented in juvenile court are poorly prepared by both sides. Some prosecutors are not thoroughly familiar with the juvenile code governing their jurisdiction. Similarly, defense attorneys will at times accept hearsay evidence, fail to present witnesses for the defense, and fail to object to procedural violations which might result in the dismissal of the petition concerning their client. In short, although the frequency of legal representation for both the state and defense has increased considerably in the last decade, the quality of such representation often leaves something to be desired. There are some attorneys who do take juvenile court proceedings seriously, but they appear to be in the minority.

A recent article in the *Chicago Tribune* notes that Illinois' juvenile court system "suffers from an overload of cases and an attitude among lawyers that it is the "lowest social order." The report was based on observations of 4,107 juvenile court cases of which 3,900 were continued. Although Illinois law requires that cases handled by the juvenile court be processed within 120 days, the average waiting time in Cook County (the site of the study) was 14.4 months, and some cases were pending for as long as 3 years. Karen Gora, a court watcher in the study, observed, "It's not just the case load either. A lot of people in those courts don't know the terms, didn't know the law—some didn't even seem to care. Let's face it, juvenile court is the lowest social order when you're a lawyer. The assistant state's attorneys were in the hall half the time on the phone calling for other jobs."[15]

Even more alarming is the lack of competence and training among juvenile court judges. Many judges handle juvenile cases as a part-time assignment. While many clearly have the best interest of juveniles at heart, far too many show the same unfamiliarity with juvenile codes that characterizes many attorneys. In fact, some appear to disregard juvenile codes altogether and rule their jurisdictions as dictators whose decisions on the bench are law. Since many attorneys practicing before these judges know little about juvenile law, many judicial decisions go unchallenged. Even when they are challenged by the defense counsel, some judges dismiss motions in clear violation of juvenile codes. For example, some judges allow (over objections by defense counsel) prosecution of juveniles whose adjudicatory hearings had been scheduled much earlier, even though the juvenile code clearly states that such hearings must be held within a specified period after the filing of the petition.

A particularly disturbing example of judicial lack of familiarity with juvenile law was the case in which a part-time juvenile court judge was convinced by a juvenile officer to send a fourteen-year-old truant (MINS) to the department of corrections. This clearly violates the juvenile code prohibiting status offenders from being transferred to that department. Outside intervention prevented this illegal act, which would otherwise have gone unchallenged until the department of corrections refused to accept the juvenile.

It should not be too much to ask that attorneys and judges practicing in juvenile court read and become familiar with applicable juvenile codes. If they do not, none of the constitutional guarantees or court

15. "Report Notes Flaws in Juvenile Court," *Chicago Tribune*, 4 April 1988.

decisions regarding due process in juvenile cases will have any impact. Treating juvenile court cases as if they did not involve the "real practice of law" has made practice before the juvenile court unattractive to many lawyers and judges and will continue to do so in the future. Fortunately, there is some evidence that a corps of well-informed, sincere lawyers and judges is beginning to emerge. In order to encourage the growth of such a corps, proper recognition and rewards must be forthcoming.

Training and competence of juvenile probation officers varies as much as that of other juvenile court personnel. Many jurisdictions require a bachelor's degree for employment in this position and a number of juvenile probation officers in metropolitan areas have master's degrees. However, many areas have no educational requirements for such employment and, as indicated earlier, some areas have no juvenile probation services.

In *Standards for the Administration of Juvenile Justice,* various sections address the issue of training for juvenile court personnel. For example, one recommendation (section 1.4220) states that

> *family court judges should be provided with preservice training on the law and procedures governing subject matter by the family (juvenile) court, the causes of delinquency and family conflict, a thorough understanding of agencies responsible for intake and protective services. In addition, inservice education programs should be provided to judges to assure they are aware of changes in law, policy, and programs.*[16]

Other recommendations (sections 1.423, 1.424, and 1.425) address similar issues of preservice and inservice training in juvenile matters with prosecutors, public defenders, and other court personnel and their staffs.

Implications for Practitioners

It is the responsibility of all juvenile court personnel (and of all citizens as well) to help insure that all practitioners in the juvenile justice system are competent. Attorneys who appear in juvenile court uninformed and/or unprepared should be removed from juvenile cases by the juvenile court judge. Juvenile court judges who act in a dictatorial manner without regard for legal requirements established in juvenile court acts should be challenged by both the prosecutor and defense

16. National Advisory Committee for Juvenile Justice and Delinquency Prevention, *Standards for the Administration of Juvenile Justice,* U.S. Justice Department (Washington, D.C.: U.S. Government Printing Office, 1980), 130.

counsel and, where necessary, removed from the juvenile court by appropriate legal action. All jurisdictions should have the services of a juvenile probation officer available. Where no juvenile probation officer is currently employed, juvenile court personnel should make this need public.

Understanding the philosophy of juvenile justice, the various theories of causation, and the practical consequences of alternative courses of action is a necessity for juvenile court personnel. Shared understanding and cooperation among the various components of the juvenile justice system should result in a more effective system for juveniles and society.

Summary

Key figures in juvenile court proceedings include attorneys for the state and for the defendant, the judge, and the probation officer. While the frequency of legal representation in juvenile court is increasing, the quality of this representation needs to be improved. The practice of juvenile law must be taken more seriously. Competent lawyers and judges need to be rewarded for their performances in juvenile court proceedings. Whenever possible, juvenile court judges should be assigned exclusively to juvenile court for whatever period of time. Judges who combine the best elements of the parent figure and law giver roles are a definite asset to the juvenile justice system. Probation officers are crucial if juvenile justice philosophy is to be implemented. Their services to the court and to juveniles with problems complement the roles of the other juvenile court personnel.

While the overall quality of juvenile court personnel is clearly improving, there is still considerable variance. Continued emphasis on training and competence at all levels is essential.

Discussion Questions

1. Discuss the roles of the prosecutor and defense counsel in juvenile court. Why is the presence of legal representatives for both sides crucial in contemporary juvenile court?
2. Why is the judge such a powerful figure in juvenile court? What are the advantages and disadvantages of the judge as law giver and parent figure?

3. In what sense is the role of juvenile probation officer ambiguous? What are the consequences of this ambiguity?

4. In general, what is the current level of training and competence among juvenile court personnel? What improvements can you suggest?

Selected Readings

Aday, D. P. "Court Structure, Defense Attorney Use, and Juvenile Court Decisions." *Sociological Quarterly* 27, no. 1 (1986): 107–19.

Clarke, S. H., and G. G. Koch. "Juvenile Court: Therapy or Crime Control and Do Lawyers Make a Difference?" *Law and Society Review* 14 (1980): 263–308.

Coxe, Spencer. "Lawyers in Juvenile Court." *Crime and Delinquency* 13, no. 4 (October 1967): 488–93.

Fox, Stanford. *Juvenile Courts in a Nutshell.* St. Paul, Minn.: West Publishing Company, 1984.

Frank, Jerome. "The Judging Process and the Judge's Personality." In *Before the Law: An Introduction to the Legal Process,* ed. Bonsignore, Katsh, d'Errico, Pipkin, and Arons, 70–77. Boston: Houghton Mifflin Company, 1974.

Mahoney, A. R. "Jury Trial for Juveniles: Right or Ritual?" *Justice Quarterly* 2 (December 1985): 553–65.

Rubin, H. Ted. "The Juvenile Courts' Search for Identity and Responsibility." *Crime and Delinquency* 23, no. 1 (January 1977): 1–13.

———. "The Emerging Prosecutor Dominance of the Juvenile Court Intake Process." *Crime and Delinquency* 6 (July 1980): 229–318.

Walter, James D., and Susan A. Ostrander. "An Observational Study of a Juvenile Court." *Juvenile and Family Court Journal* 33, no. 3 (August 1982): 53–69.

9 Prevention and Diversion Programs

Our society annually spends millions of dollars attempting to apprehend, prosecute, and correct/rehabilitate delinquents. While some of these attempts prove more or less successful with some delinquents, the results are not particularly impressive on the whole. It would seem logical, therefore, to explore the possibilities of concentrating our resources on programs that might provide better returns. Many authorities interested in delinquency have come to believe that most of our money is spent at the wrong end of the juvenile justice process. "Evils do not disappear because people disapprove of them, unless conditions at their root are changed."[1]

In most cases we wait until a juvenile comes into official contact with the system before an attempt is made to modify behavior which has, by the time contact becomes official, become more or less ingrained. The task of corrections personnel, or personnel in functionally related agencies, is to modify this behavior after the fact. It would seem more logical to attempt to prevent the juvenile from engaging in illegal behavior in the first place, or, as early as possible, try to divert juveniles who do encounter the justice system. For example, consider the difficulty of trying to rehabilitate a juvenile addicted to heroin. The juvenile has probably developed, by the time he is addicted, apprehended, and processed, problems in his family, problems in school, and delinquent habits oriented toward insuring his supply of heroin (for example, burglary, mugging, and pushing drugs). In order to rehabilitate the juvenile, all of these problems must be dealt with. If, however, we had effective programs to detect and help to resolve problems that are likely to lead to heroin use, the necessity for solving all of these complicated, related problems would be eliminated. Suppose, for example, we found the juvenile in question dissatisfied with traditional education, but interested

1. Edgar Z. Friedenberg, *Coming of Age in America* (New York: Random House, Inc., 1965).

in pursuing a specific vocation. Suppose we were to provide an alternative education that enabled the juvenile to pursue his chosen vocation and heightened his interest in success within the system. We might, then, prevent the juvenile from dropping out of school, joining a heroin-abusing gang, and developing the undesirable behavior patterns mentioned above.

Prevention

There are two major types of delinquency prevention programs. The first type of program is directed toward preventing delinquent acts before they occur either by alleviating social conditions related to delinquency or by identifying juveniles who appear to be "predelinquent." The second type of program attempts to prevent delinquents from repeating delinquent acts once they have committed such acts. Neither type of program is a cure-all and there are a number of difficulties in attempting to develop and operate such programs. Nonetheless, many authorities are beginning to believe that our resources might be more effectively employed in prevention rather than correction of delinquent behavior.

In 1967, the President's Commission on Law Enforcement and Administration of Justice recommended the establishment of alternatives to the juvenile justice system. According to the report, service agencies capable of dealing with certain categories of juveniles should have these juveniles diverted to them. The report further recommended:

1. *The formal sanctioning system and pronouncement of delinquency should be used only as a last resort.*
2. *Instead of the formal system, dispositional alternatives to adjudication must be developed for dealing with juveniles, including agencies to provide and coordinate services and procedures to achieve necessary control without unnecessary stigma. Alternatives already available, such as those related to court intake, should be more fully exploited.*
3. *The range of conduct for which court intervention is authorized should be narrowed, with greater emphasis upon consensual and informal means of meeting the problems of difficult children.*[2]

In 1973, the National Advisory Commission on Criminal Justice Standards and Goals stated that "the highest attention must be given to preventing juvenile delinquency, minimizing the involvement of young

2. The President's Commission on Law Enforcement and Administration of Justice, *Task Force Report: Juvenile Delinquency and Youth Crime* (Washington, D.C.: U.S. Government Printing Office, 1967), 19–35.

offenders in the juvenile and criminal justice system, and reintegrating them into the community."[3] The commission further recommended minimizing the involvement of the offender in the system. This does not mean that we should "coddle" offenders. It recognizes that the further the offender penetrates into the system, the more difficult it becomes to divert the youth from a criminal career. Minimizing a youth's involvement with the juvenile justice system does not mean abandoning the use of confinement for certain individuals. Until more effective means of treatment are found, chronic and dangerous delinquents should be incarcerated to protect society. However, the juvenile justice system must search for beneficial programs outside institutions for juveniles who do not need confinement. Donald Cressey and Robert McDermott[4] feel that these recommendations are highly critical. They also indicate that contact with the juvenile justice system is undesirable, and stress the need to develop alternative programs.

Both labeling and learning "theories" stress the desirability of prevention rather than correction. The basic premise of the labeling "theory" is that juveniles find it difficult to escape the stigmatization of delinquent. Once apprehended and labeled, the juvenile is often forced out of interaction patterns with nondelinquents and forced into association with labeled delinquents. From this perspective, the agencies of the juvenile justice system that are established to correct delinquent behavior often contribute to its occurrence even as they try to cope with it. Learning "theory" holds that individuals engage in delinquent behavior because they experience an overabundance of interactions, associations, and reinforcements with definitions favorable to delinquency. Therefore, if agencies cast potential or first-time delinquents into interaction with more experienced delinquents, the process of learning delinquent behavior is greatly enhanced.

Alternatively, concentration on the problems of youth that tend to lead to delinquent behavior may not only result in preventing some youth from committing progressively more serious offenses, but might also allow

3. National Advisory Commission on Criminal Justice Standards and Goals, *A National Strategy to Reduce Crime* (Washington, D.C.: National Criminal Justice Reference Service, Department of Justice, Law Enforcement Assistance Administration, 1973), 34–36.

4. Donald R. Cressey and Robert A. McDermott, "Diversion from the Juvenile Justice System," Department of Justice, Law Enforcement Assistance Administration, National Institute of Law Enforcement and Criminal Justice (Washington, D.C.: U.S. Government Printing Office, January 1974, stock no. 2700-00241).

the formal juvenile justice system (for example, courts, law enforcement, corrections) to concentrate efforts on the hard-core delinquent whose label and stigmatization have been earned.

Since delinquency is a complex problem, no singular program is likely to emerge that will be effective in preventing all types of delinquency; that is, delinquency prevention involves many variables and no one program is likely to be foolproof. Inherent in the multifaceted problem of delinquency prevention is the fact that a great deal of delinquency has its roots in the basic social conditions of our society. Increasing urbanization with accompanying problems of poverty, inferior education, poor housing, health and sanitary problems, and unemployment are but a few social conditions that seem to be related to delinquency. Therefore, we should focus our attention on these problems, if delinquency prevention is to have a chance of success. While a number of programs are important for the prevention of delinquency, we would be remiss if we focused only on programs directed specifically at preventing delinquency and ignored these underlying conditions. Large-scale social change, which is clearly an important preventive measure, enables more people to achieve culturally approved goals without having to resort to illegal means.

In June 1970, a group was invited by the Youth Development and Delinquency Prevention Administration of the Department of Health, Education, and Welfare to meet in Scituate, Massachusetts, to consider the problem of youth development and delinquency prevention. The document produced at that meeting stated:

> We believe that our social institutions [school, family, church, etc.] are programmed in such a way as to deny large numbers of young people socially acceptable, responsible, and personally gratifying roles. These institutions should seek ways of becoming more responsible to youth needs.[5]

The group further stated that any strategy for youth development and delinquency prevention should give priority to

> . . . programs which assist institutions to change in ways that provide young people with socially acceptable, responsible, personally gratifying roles and assist young people to assume such roles.[6]

5. Youth Development and Delinquency Prevention Administration, Department of Health, Education, and Welfare, *National Strategy for Youth Development and Delinquency Prevention*, memo. Washington, D.C., 1971.
6. Ibid.

It follows from this premise that the development of a viable strategy for the prevention and reduction of delinquency rests on the identification, assessment, and alteration of those features of institutional functioning that impede development of youth, particularly those youth whose social situation makes them most prone to the development of delinquent careers and to participation in collective forms of withdrawal and deviancy.[7] This approach does not deny the occurrence of individual deviance, but it does assert that in many cases the deviance is traceable to the damaging experiences encountered by youths through their institutional encounters.[8]

As Daniel Katkin and his associates pointed out some time ago,

> . . . it is social institutions in the broader community—families, churches, schools, social welfare agencies, etc.—which have the primary mandate to control and care for young people who commit delinquent acts. It is only when individuals or institutions in the community fail to divert (or decide not to divert) that the formal processes of the juvenile justice system are called into action.[9]

The responsibility for dealing with juveniles who have problems has been too frequently placed on the juvenile justice practitioner. The public has been more than willing to place the blame for failures in preventing delinquency on these practitioners and quick to criticize their efforts. These practitioners are often faced with the task of attempting to modify undesirable behavior that has become habitual and deep-rooted and which a variety of other agencies have failed to modify. In addition, the time period available for rehabilitation is usually short. There are a number of agencies in our society with which juveniles come into contact earlier, more consistently, and with less stigmatization than the juvenile justice system. Some of these agencies or institutions are functionally related to the juvenile justice system. The term "functionally related agencies" is used to describe those agencies having goals similar to those of the juvenile justice system—improving the quality of life for juveniles by preventing offensive behavior, providing opportunities for success, and correcting undesirable behavior.

7. Ibid.

8. Department of Health, Education, and Welfare, Social and Rehabilitation Service, "Delinquency Prevention through Youth Development," DHEW publication no. 72–26013, 1972.

9. Daniel Katkin, Drew Hyman, and John Kramer, *Juvenile Delinquency and the Juvenile Justice System* (North Scituate, Mass.: Duxbury Press, 1976), 404.

Diversion

One form of prevention is diversion. Diversion has carried many different, and sometimes conflicting, meanings. The term is often used to describe pre-juvenile justice activities as well as post-juvenile justice activities. Some diversion programs are designed to suspend or terminate juvenile justice processing of youth in favor of release or referral to alternate services. Likewise, some diversionary activities involve referrals to programs outside the justice system prior to the youth entering the system. The latter is often referred to as "pure diversion" and programs of this type are not as numerous as those in the former or "secondary diversion" category. Diversion is not without pitfalls. It sometimes permits intervention into juvenile's lives with little or no formal processes and inadequate safeguards of individual liberties.

Before discussing specific diversion programs, a major problem in coordinating such problems and the agencies sponsoring them should be pointed out. The problem is one of "territorial jealousy." Territorial jealousy refers to a belief commonly held by agency personnel who feel that attempts to coordinate efforts are actually attempts to invade the territory they have "staked out" for themselves. Agency staff members have a tendency to view themselves as experts in their particular field, to resent suggestions for change made by "outsiders," and to fear that they will be found to be lacking in competence. As a result, these staff members tend to keep agency operations secret and reject attempts by personnel from other agencies to provide services or to suggest improvements. Perhaps an example will help to clarify the concept of territorial jealousy. An attempt was made by youth services agency personnel to provide services to a school district with one of the highest dropout rates in the state. The services offered included educational and vocational counseling, alternative educational programs, and some immediate employment opportunities. When contacted by the director of the youth services agency, the principal of the local high school indicated that the school system "really had no dropout problem," that school counselors handled any existing problems, and that he would initiate contact when he needed help from a "social work agency."

As the example clearly indicates, the consequences of territorial jealousy can be extremely serious for both juveniles and the taxpayer. Duplication of services is a costly enterprise in a time of budgetary cutbacks and financial restraints; however, denial of available services to youth with problems can be disastrous. Lack of cooperation, under-standing, and confidence among agency personnel greatly hamper at-tempts to provide for the welfare of youth. Again Katkin and his associates were correct when they indicated that programs exist at city, county, regional, state, and federal levels; in public, voluntary, and pri-vate sectors; and in a variety of categorical program areas—education, child welfare, youth services, health, law enforcement, employment, cor-rections, probation, court, etc. The animosities and conflicts that have emerged from this fragmentation have contributed, it seems, to the sad state of affairs regarding the care and treatment of troubled youth and youth in trouble.[10]

Some Examples of Prevention and Diversion Programs

School Programs

In chapter 3, the importance of school personnel in shaping the behavior of youth was discussed. No other institution in our society, with the possible exception of the family, has as much opportunity to observe, mold, and modify youthful behavior. Early detection of problems fre-quently leads to their solution before they become serious. The impor-tance of education as a stepping stone to future opportunities for success cannot be stressed too much. The provision of meaningful educational opportunities for youth who have been labeled delinquent or in need of supervision is of great importance in attempts to reintegrate these youth into society.

While it was once possible for educators to skirt their responsibil-ities in dealing with "problem youth" by "pushing" them out of the ed-ucational system, recent court decisions indicate that all youth have the right to an education. Therefore, youth who have been found delinquent and status offenders can no longer legally be dismissed from school at the whim of a teacher or administrator. While the impact of these court decisions does not appear to have reached all school districts,[11] it is only a matter of time until it does. School counselors who formerly concerned themselves with academic and career counseling, advising, and sched-uling also face the reality of coping with behavioral and/or emotional

10. Ibid., p. 405.
11. "Children Out of School in America" (Cambridge, Mass.: Defense Fund of the Washington Research Project, 1974).

problems. Hopefully, teachers who formerly passed juveniles with such problems on to their colleagues by refusing to fail "problem youth" will begin to seek other, more desirable alternatives. The crucial role that educational personnel play in preventing and correcting delinquent behavior by providing personal counseling or appropriate referrals should be appreciated.

There are numerous school programs designed to prevent youth from engaging in delinquent activities or to divert them from such activities once they become involved. We have previously mentioned (chapter 7) the police officer school liaison programs which have come into existence in recent years. In Houston, a School Task Force Program has been developed to help reduce truancy. Assistant school principals were designated as liaison personnel to work with members of the police task force in attempting to encourage youth to remain in the school environment by improving communications between youth and all agencies working with juveniles. In addition, the program attempted to reduce the opportunity for adult offenders to prey on juveniles through the sale of narcotics, sexually explicit materials, and alcohol. Survey data from 1,000 teachers and school administrators indicated that they expressed favorable attitudes toward the program, though they were not totally convinced that truancy was reduced by the effort.[12]

Alternative education programs have also become more widespread. Such programs include enhanced skills training, community internship programs, and more general attempts to integrate the schools and the community in the interests of serving the needs of marginal students and those who do not anticipate attending college. Many such programs also allow for more student input into curricula than has been traditionally encouraged.[13] Improved school counseling services and programs designed to encourage student and parent participation in combating violence and vandalism in the schools are indicative of other attempts to expand and improve the role of school personnel in preventing delinquency and diverting delinquents from further inappropriate actions.

Another program presented in the schools by police officers is the DARE (Drug Abuse Resistance Education) program. Originally developed in California, the program has now spread to other states. The goal

12. J. Martin, A. Schulze, and M. Valdex, "Taking Aim at Truancy," *FBI Law Enforcement Bulletin* 57, no. 5 (May 1988): 8–12.

13. J. Hawkins and J. Weis, *The Social Development Model: An Integrated Approach to Delinquency Prevention* (Seattle: University of Washington Center for Law and Justice, 1980).

of the semester-long program aimed at fifth and sixth graders is to equip juveniles with the skills to resist peer pressure to use drugs. Trained police officers present the program as a part of the regular school curriculum in an attempt to provide accurate information about drugs and alcohol, teach students decision-making skills, help them resist peer pressure, and provide alternatives to drug abuse.

Children and Family Services

Another agency with goals similar to those of the juvenile justice system is the state agency concerned with providing children and family services. As a rule, these agencies provide, among other services, day-care programs, foster care programs, and advice to unwed mothers. In addition, they often investigate reported cases of child abuse. Children and family service agencies deal with all categories of juveniles covered by most juvenile court acts, provide individual and family counseling services, and are normally set up to refer suitable cases to appropriate private agencies. In addition, they can provide financial aid to youth and families in need.

Like most state agencies, children and family services are often caught up in political change. While many of these agencies require bachelor's or master's degrees for employment and emphasize the need for professionalism among staff members, skillful and competent administrative personnel are often replaced when the political party in power changes. As a result, the continuity of policies implemented by these agencies frequently leaves much to be desired. Nonetheless, agencies concerned with providing services to children and families often have considerable power and, when administered appropriately, can provide multiple services to youth in trouble.

Youth Service Bureaus

In 1967, the President's Commission on Law Enforcement and Administration of Justice recommended the establishment of Youth Service Bureaus. They were created to provide a viable alternative to official juvenile court proceedings at the local level. They accept referrals concerning youth in trouble from other agencies including schools, the police,

A true friend is somebody who
can make us do what we can.

RALPH WALDO EMERSON

PLEASE,
BE A FRIEND—
VOLUNTEER

(The youth of McDonough
County need you.)

McDonough County Youth Service Bureau
Masonic Temple Building — Second Floor
133 S. Randolph — Macomb
Call: 837-5402

Figure 9.1 Volunteer appeal from a youth service bureau (Photo reprinted by permission of Chris Schoeninger, McDonough County Youth Service Bureau, Macomb, Illinois)

and other community agencies. In addition, they generally serve walk-in clientele (self-referrals) and frequently offer aid to juveniles who have already been adjudicated delinquent.

As a rule, youth service bureaus provide individual, family, and group counseling, job referral, recreation programs, drug treatment, legal services, and referrals to other agencies. Many also see advocacy for juveniles as an important function;[14] that is, youth service bureaus may represent juveniles who are having problems with other agencies (schools, public aid, and juvenile probation departments, for example).

The advocacy role is extremely important for a variety of reasons. When the advocate presents the juvenile's case to personnel from other agencies, the juvenile can see firsthand that the advocate is concerned about him or her and willing to fight to protect the juvenile's rights. In many cases, this may be the first indication the juvenile has that everyone in "the system" is not against him or her. Second, the advocate who is serious about his or her job helps to keep personnel in his or her and in other agencies "on their toes" by continually challenging their perceptions of their obligations. Perhaps most importantly, the advocate can

14. Department of Health, Education, and Welfare, Youth Development and Delinquency Prevention Administration, "The Challenge of Youth Service Bureaus" (Washington, D.C.: U.S. Government Printing Office, 1973).

serve as an important agent for change by challenging traditional practices which have routinely denied juvenile rights as a way of emphasizing
bureaucratic authority. When challenged in this way, agency personnel
frequently respond by characterizing the juvenile and the advocate as
"troublemakers" and frequently attempt to create obstacles for both. If
the advocate is dedicated and capable, most of these obstacles can be
overcome. Successful advocacy programs upset the system and consequently advocates are frequently unpopular with agency personnel who
feel secure only when the status quo is maintained. It is unfortunate that
many of these agency personnel have input into funding decisions and
are often able to cut off funds for advocacy programs when they find the
programs personally irritating even though they may benefit juveniles.

An example of the problems encountered by advocates might prove
beneficial. There was a case in which a juvenile was suspended from high
school for one month for allegedly smoking a cigarette in the school
parking lot. An advocate attended school board hearings conducted three
days after the suspension concerning readmitting the student. The advocate presented evidence that the juvenile in question was not the guilty
party. Still the school board was unwilling to ask the school principal to
reinstate the youth. The advocate then suggested that she intended to
take the case to court, if necessary, in order to get the juvenile read-
mitted, since he was due to graduate at the end of the semester. At this
point, the school board asked the principal to reconsider. He did so re-
luctantly. Later, he indicated to the advocate that her services would no
longer be utilized by the high school. He also indicated to personnel from
other agencies that the advocate had overstepped her authority and was
more concerned about demonstrating her power to juveniles than with
helping the school system solve some of its problems.

Youth service bureaus are financed by county and local funds.
Community involvement, then, is necessary for financial assistance as
well as for the success of the program in terms of appropriate referrals.
Staff members frequently consist of both full-time, paid professionals
and part-time volunteers from the community. Ideally, these staff members attempt to organize and coordinate existing community services
while providing direct services to youth.

As a result of its unique position, the youth service bureau is frequently in conflict with those agencies it is attempting to coordinate. It
is difficult to advocate the rights of juveniles without alienating agencies
attempting to take action against these youth. For example, a public aid
office delayed action on applications for aid until the applications were

filled out virtually perfectly. This process would often take several days because many of the applicants were school dropouts who had difficulty reading and writing. Advocates from the local youth service bureau began to help applicants complete the required forms so immediate processing was possible. Personnel in the public aid office were angered, since their power over youthful clients (delays in processing) was considerably reduced.

Youth service bureaus have had to spend considerable energy and resources in attempting to establish themselves as legitimate and viable service organizations in their communities. Although their goals may agree with those of other community agencies, they are often viewed as being competitors. As a result, little coordination has been accomplished by youth service bureaus and many have been eliminated or incorporated into long-established traditional agencies. This trend has been further enhanced by a gradual but critical reexamination of overlapping and multiple local "diversionary programs," all relatively expensive to operate and all subject to criticism with respect to success.

A major criticism of youth service bureaus has come from those who feel they attach labels to youth without due process. There are also those who question the youth service bureaus' voluntary nature when they are recommended as the only alternative to formal legal processing. This, and the withdrawal of federal funding for these programs, has led to diminished numbers of youth service bureaus.

Federal Programs

The federal government has sponsored many programs which, although not specifically designed as delinquency prevention programs, did encourage youths to accept and attain lawful objectives through institutionalized means of education and employment. A review by Martin Haskell and Lewis Yablonsky of some of the varied federal programs provides some insight into the value of these programs in preventing delinquency and crime.[15] A few examples will illustrate the focal points of these programs and their attempt to improve the social ills that result in delinquency.

There have been a number of federally funded programs aimed at improving educational and occupational opportunities for disadvantaged youth. A secondary benefit of many of these programs was believed to

15. Martin Haskell and Lewis Yablonsky, *Juvenile Delinquency,* 4th ed. (New York: Harper and Row, 1988), 435–59.

be a decrease in the likelihood of delinquency among the youth involved. Project Head Start was designed to help culturally deprived children "catch up" or "keep pace" in their preschool years. Previously, many children from culturally and/or economically deprived parents lagged behind other children in verbal and reading skills. Starting far behind in these basic skills, many of these children never caught up and school too often became an experience characterized by failure and rejection. As a result many dropped out of school as soon as possible, often during their first or second year of high school. Of those who did drop out, many went on to become delinquent.

Along slightly different lines, a number of federal laws providing assistance to the hard-core unemployed were passed. For example, the Manpower Development and Training Act, the Vocational Education Act, the Economic Opportunity Act, the Rehabilitation Program for Selective Service Rejectees, and the President's Youth Opportunities Campaign had the major objective of aiding youths to find employment by helping them to become more readily employable. The basic assumption underlying these programs has been that employment is an important key to solving the problems of many youths.

The emphasis of the youth opportunity centers is to increase employability through counseling or to provide vocational and prevocational training and work-training programs. This program recognizes that if young people, handicapped by inadequate education and lack of occupational skills, are to become employable, they must somehow be provided with additional training. Hopefully, these young people will then be absorbed into the labor market once their performance capabilities are improved.

Similarly, the Job Corps program was directed toward youths between sixteen and twenty-one with the principal objective of providing training in basic skills and a constructive work experience.

All of these programs have been geared toward providing youths with employment opportunities which will hopefully lead them to a better life. The basic, underlying assumption seems to be that youths employed in jobs for which they are suited are less likely to engage in delinquent or criminal activity than youths who are not employed and have little hope of finding any worthwhile employment.

The role of the federal government in programs specifically designed to prevent delinquency has been somewhat limited as a result of the belief that the primary responsibility for these programs rests with

the states. Although there have been scattered efforts in the field of juvenile justice by the federal government (for example, the development
of the Children's Bureau in 1912 and the development of various federal
commissions and programs in 1948, 1950, and 1961), the most relevant
to prevention occurred in 1968 with the Juvenile Delinquency Prevention
and Control Act and in 1974 with the Juvenile Justice and Delinquency
Prevention Act. The Juvenile Delinquency Prevention and Control Act
permits allocation of federal funds to the states for delinquency prevention programs and the Juvenile Justice and Delinquency Prevention Act
attempts to create a coordinated national program to prevent and control
delinquency.[16] The Juvenile Justice and Deliquency Control Act also
called for an evaluation of all federally assisted delinquency programs,
for a centralized research effort on problems of juvenile delinquency, and
for training programs for persons who work with delinquents. This law
directs spending of funds on diverting juveniles from the juvenile justice
system through the use of community-based programs, such as group
homes, foster care, and homemaker services. In addition, community-
based programs and services that work with parents and other family
members to maintain and strengthen the family unit are recommended.

The Juvenile Justice Amendments of 1977 made it clear that, in
the opinion of Congress, the evolution of juvenile justice in the United
States had resulted in excessive and abusive use of incarceration under
the rubric of "in the best interests of the child" and that the prohibitions
of contact with adult offenders and incarceration of status offenders and
nonoffenders (e.g., dependent and neglected youth) were to be taken seriously.[17] By 1980, fifty states and territories had demonstrated at least
some compliance with deinstitutionalization of such offenders and victims.

A wide variety of community and state agencies have become involved in delinquency prevention. Most efforts have been independent
and uncoordinated. By the 1950s the delinquency prevention effort in
virtually every state and large city was like a jigsaw puzzle of services

16. Office of Juvenile Justice and Delinquency Prevention, Law Enforcement Assistance Administration, Department of Justice, "First Analysis and Evaluation: Federal
Juvenile Delinquency Programs" (Washington, D.C.: U.S. Government Printing Office,
1976).

17. Office of Juvenile Justice and Delinquency Prevention, Law Enforcement Assistance Administration, Department of Justice, *Juvenile Justice: Before and After the
Onset of Delinquency* (Washington, D.C.: U.S. Government Printing Office, 1980),
5–6.

operating independently. The agencies concerned with delinquency prevention included the schools, recreation departments, public housing authorities, public welfare departments, private social agencies, health departments, and medical facilities.[18]

According to Robert Trojanowicz, there are two types of delinquency prevention programs. Pure prevention, or primary prevention, attempts to inhibit delinquency before it takes place. Rehabilitative prevention, or secondary prevention, treats the youth once he or she has come in contact with the formal justice system.[19]

Other typologies have been used to characterize delinquency prevention programs. For example, Peter Lejins differentiates between punitive prevention, corrective prevention, and mechanical prevention.[20] Punitive prevention is the threat of punishment under the hypothesis that punishment will presumably prevent the act. Corrective prevention refers to the attempt to eliminate potential causes, factors, or motivations before the delinquent behavior occurs. Mechanical prevention emphasizes placing obstacles in the way of the potential delinquent making it difficult or impossible to commit an offense. Increased security measures and "hardware" at retail stores are mechanical efforts at prevention.

Clyde Sullivan and Carrie Bash use a type of classification which differentiates prevention programs by their service orientation. For example,

1. *Programs that have explicit primary functions and goals involving deliberate intervention in the lives of identified individuals for the purpose of preventing the occurrence of behavior that would label them as antisocial or delinquent by the laws and rules of general society.*

2. *Programs that have explicit primary goals of planned intervention and participation in the development, employment, and organization of interrelationships of various social institutions, groups, and agencies within the community with the intention of preventing formation of patterns of delinquent behavior in specific individuals or groups.*

3. *Programs that have explicit primary goals of deliberate participation in the special processes of reviewing laws, social policies, and public attitudes that have a specific and direct relevance to activities designed to prevent delinquency.*[21]

18. Robert C. Trojanowicz, *Juvenile Delinquency: Concepts and Control* (New York: Prentice-Hall, Inc., 1973), 187–88.

19. Ibid., 188–89.

20. Peter Lejins, "The Field of Prevention," in *Delinquency Prevention: Theory and Practice,* ed. William Amos and Charles Wellford (Englewood Cliffs, N.J.: Prentice-Hall, Inc., 1967), 3.

21. Clyde Sullivan and Carrie Bash, "Current Programs for Delinquency Prevention," in *Delinquency Prevention: Theory and Practice,* 61–62.

Figure 9.2 Class being conducted by police officers (Photo courtesy of Galesburg Police Department, Galesburg, Illinois)

Youth service bureaus frequently attempt to perform all three of these functions. As envisioned by the President's Crime Commission, the youth service bureau is a substitute agency that allows diversion from the juvenile justice system.[22] Most successful bureaus offer practical programs of assistance to young people, such as tutoring, medical treatment, legal aid, temporary housing, and recreation. Some use referrals to other agencies or purchase those services they cannot provide directly. The effective youth service bureau involves good programming plus operational knowledge by the staff about how to effectively use the resources of the community. Successful bureaus use their knowledge to work through the red tape normally found in governmental bureaucracies.

While it would be impossible to list and discuss all prevention programs, we would like to mention a few more. Recreational and activity programs conducted by local police, civic, and religious groups are often

22. President's Commission on Law Enforcement and Administration of Justice, *The Challenge of Crime in a Free Society* (Washington, D.C.: U.S. Government Printing Office, 1967), 7.

aimed at preventing delinquency. Recently, the idea of preventing delinquency, or further delinquency, by family counseling has begun to take hold. An example of diversion from juvenile court through family counseling is the Sacramento Diversion Project, which began in 1970. Using family counseling, a specially trained probation officer attempts to convey the idea that a juvenile's problem is the responsibility of the entire family. Counseling is provided as early as possible in an attempt to mobilize the family to deal with the problem and to divert the juvenile from the court. Initial results indicate that juveniles who are dealt with through family counseling are less likely to have petitions filed on them in juvenile court, less likely to repeat the offense, and less likely to spend time in detention than juveniles who do not receive family counseling. In addition, the program is less expensive than more traditional alternatives.[23]

Another example of an attempt to prevent juveniles with prior records from recidivating is Project Pride, developed for use in Denver, Colorado. Project Pride selects juvenile probationers who are repeat offenders with social adjustment problems and provides a year of intensive, individualized treatment for them. Services provided include alternative schooling, correction of learning disabilities, vocational training, job placement, counseling, recreation, etc.[24] While success rates reported by program staff are not spectacular, they are somewhat better than success rates for juvenile offenders receiving no treatment. What success the Project has enjoyed is attributed to good relationships with the juvenile court, good community relations, and the combination of treatment services offered.

In addition to the prevention programs already mentioned, there have been a number of attempts to "scare" juveniles away from delinquent behavior. The best known, though not the earliest, of these programs was publicized nationally through a television film call *Scared Straight*. The film recorded a confrontation between juveniles brought into, and inmates housed in, Rahway State Prison in New Jersey. Such confrontation was based on the theory that inmates could frighten juveniles to the extent that they would be deterred from committing further delinquent acts. *Scared Straight* reported that of the 8,000 juveniles

23. Department of Justice, National Institute of Law Enforcement and Criminal Justice, Law Enforcement Assistance Administration, *Juvenile Diversion through Family Counseling* (Washington, D.C., January 1976).

24. National Institute of Law Enforcement and Criminal Justice, Law Enforcement Assistance Administration, U.S. Department of Justice, *Project Pride* (Washington, D.C.: U.S. Government Printing Office, 1977).

participating in such sessions through 1978, 90 percent had not been in trouble with the law again. Nationwide attention was focused on attempts to frighten youth out of delinquency and such programs were viewed by some as a panacea for delinquency problems.[25] However, more objective evaluations of this and other such programs have yielded, at best, mixed results. It is certain that such programs are not a panacea for delinquency, and some appear to increase rather than decrease the frequency of recidivism.[26]

Yet another attempt at preventing delinquency and diverting delinquent youth involves the use of community policing models oriented toward juveniles. These programs operate on the assumption that foot-patrol officers are more likely to favor problem-solving and peace-keeping roles with youth than their motorized counterparts. Officers who view their roles in these terms may be more likely to try to help youth before they get in trouble or to divert them away from the juvenile justice network.[27]

Other Programs

There are a host of other agencies providing services that complement those of the juvenile justice system. These include YMCAs and YWCAs, which often provide counseling and recreation programs. One alarming trend among these agencies is that membership fees have tended to eliminate the opportunity for some youth to use the services available. Some YMCA and YWCA programs seem to discourage rather than encourage the participation of youth who have little interaction with adults and have few resources.

In many areas, community mental health clinics provide services based on a sliding fee scale. Other agencies—such as Catholic Social Services, Vocational Rehabilitation Services, and the Boy and Girl Scouts of America—also use a sliding scale to determine fees for counseling, testing, and employment referrals. Still other agencies provide essentially the same services free of charge. These agencies typically include

25. James O. Finckenauer, *Scared Straight! and the Panacea Phenomenon* (Englewood Cliffs, N.J.: Prentice-Hall, Inc., 1982).

26. Richard J. Lundman, *Prevention and Control of Juvenile Delinquency* (New York: Oxford University Press, 1984), 136–52.

27. J. Belknap, M. Morash, and R. Trojanowicz, "Implementing of Community Policing Model for Work with Juveniles," *Criminal Justice and Behavior* 14, no. 2 (June 1987): 211–45.

community centers, Big Brother/Sister Volunteer Programs, alcohol and drug clinics, and hotline programs. In addition, many colleges and universities offer counseling services free of charge or based upon a sliding scale.

Straight, Inc., is a private chemical dependency program that originated in Florida in 1976. Today the program serves over eight hundred clients in seven cities. It is designed to deal with individuals ranging in age from early teens through early twenties by isolating such individuals from outside influences during initial treatment stages. Newcomers can receive no mail or phone calls initially, but the program soon moves to counseling sessions involving youth and their parents and assumes that chemical dependency is a family problem. Treatment usually takes about a year and costs more than $11,000. Program practices have been criticized as being authoritarian and selection procedures have been questioned as well. Straight, Inc., has made changes in these areas, but staff personnel indicate the program may be unsuitable for some youth.[28]

Some Criticisms

As we have indicated previously, delinquency prevention programs usually employ one of two strategies, either reform of society or individual treatment. Both strategies as generally employed have had difficulties. Programs oriented toward reforming society have been quite costly in terms of the results produced, depending on whether results are measured in terms of alleviating educational, occupational, or economic difficulties or in terms of reducing delinquency. Lack of coordination among various programs, inter-program jealousy, considerable duplication, and mismanagement have seriously hampered the effectiveness of these programs. As a result, much of the money intended for youth with problems ends up in staff salaries and many of the personnel hired to help supervise, train, and educate these youths are tied up dealing with administrative red tape. In addition, programs attempting to improve societal conditions may take a long time to show results. The extent to which any results can be attributed to a specific program is extremely difficult to measure. As a result, the public is frequently hesitant to finance prevention programs, since they have no immediately visible payoff.

28. Cliff Tarpy, "Straight: A Gloves-Off Treatment Program," *National Geographic* 175, no. 1 (January 1989): 48–51.

There are two basic types of prevention programs directed at providing individual treatment. The first deals with youth who have already
come into contact with the juvenile justice system and attempts to prevent further contact. There are inherent difficulties in attempting to
reform or rehabilitate youth after they have become delinquent. Many
of the basic assumptions about programs directed toward preventing
future delinquent acts by those already labeled "delinquent" are highly
questionable. For example, it is doubtful whether individual therapy will
be successful, if the juvenile's problems involve family, school, or peers.
Similarly, the belief that recreational or activity programs, in and of
themselves, are beneficial in reducing delinquency seems to be more a
matter of faith than fact at this time.

The second type of individual treatment program attempts to identify juveniles who are likely to become delinquent before a delinquent
act is committed. These programs may be called "early identification
programs" or "predelinquency detection programs." While these programs are clearly intended to "nip the problem in the bud," they may
be criticized for "creating" the very delinquency they propose to reduce;
that is, identifying a juvenile as predelinquent focuses attention on the
juvenile as a potential problem youth and, therefore, labels him or her
in much the same way official juvenile justice agencies label youth delinquent. In one sense, then, the juvenile is being treated (and sometimes
punished) for something which he or she has not yet done. Programs
directed toward pure prevention may, unintentionally, lead juveniles to
be labeled earlier by identifying them at an earlier stage.

Edwin M. Schur has encouraged the development of an approach
to delinquency prevention, which we believe (and have suggested at other
points in this book) has considerable merit. His approach is called "radical non-intervention."[29] According to Schur, "the primary target for delinquency policy should be neither the individual nor the local community
setting, but rather the delinquency-defining processes themselves."[30]
Rather than consistently increasing the number of behaviors society refuses to tolerate, policies should be developed that encourage society to
tolerate the "widest possible diversity of behaviors and attitudes." Much
of the behavior currently considered delinquent is characteristic of adolescence, nonpredatory in nature, and is offensive only because it is engaged in by juveniles. Since, in one sense, it is rules that produce

29. Edwin M. Schur, *Radical Non-Intervention: Rethinking the Delinquency Problem*
(Englewood Cliffs, N.J.: Prentice-Hall, Inc., 1973).
30. Ibid., 154.

deliquents, it may make more sense to change the rules (as we have done at the adult level in terms of alcohol consumption, abortion, and, in some states, homosexuality) than to attempt to change juveniles or the entire society overnight. One approach, then, would be to make fewer activities delinquent and to concentrate on enforcing rules for violations that may be harmful to the juvenile or society or both. In other cases, our best strategy may be to simply "leave kids alone wherever possible."[31]

Supporting Schur's contention is the fact that the Office of Juvenile Justice and Delinquency Prevention has found that a number of programs have no defensible basis whatever (e.g., those based on presumed personality differences or biological differences), others are poorly implemented (e.g., behavior modification programs in treatment settings without community follow-up), and still others of questionable merit are only based upon preliminary evidence (most predelinquency identification programs).[32]

Implications for Practitioners

All practitioners interested in the welfare of juveniles with problems should be familiar with the wide range of programs available in most communities. Teachers should not hesitate to consult youth service bureau staff members. In turn, youth service bureau staff members should not hesitate to contact appropriate personnel in other agencies. Practitioners within the juvenile justice system should both refer to and accept referrals from these agencies. It is important to remember that the goal of each of these agencies is the same—providing for the best interests of youth. Territorial jealousy must be eliminated and practitioners must learn to share their expertise with those outside their agency. It is not a sign of failure or weakness to recognize and admit that a particular problem could be dealt with more beneficially by personnel from an agency other than one's own. Concerned practitioners should provide direct services when it is possible and should not hesitate to make referrals when it is necessary or desirable.

Probably the best way to combat delinquency is to prevent it. There are at least three ways to accomplish some form of prevention. These

31. Ibid.

32. Office of Juvenile Justice and Delinquency Prevention, Law Enforcement Assistance Administration, U.S. Department of Justice, *Delinquency Prevention: Theories and Strategies* (Washington, D.C.: U.S. Government Printing Office, 1979).

include changing juvenile behavior, the rules governing that behavior, or societal conditions leading to that behavior. Practitioners may actively attempt changes in any of these three areas.

By establishing good working relationships with schools, families, and other juvenile justice practitioners, early detection of serious juvenile problems may be facilitated and proper referrals may be made. Clearly, if the old adage an "ounce of prevention is worth a pound of cure" is true, early detection and the support of the family as the primary institution influencing juvenile behavior are crucial to prevention programs. It is true that educational and vocational projects, community treatment programs, the use of volunteers and nonprofessionals, and youth service bureaus show signs of effectiveness. However, recreation, individual and group counseling, social casework, and the use of detached workers (gang workers) may be effective only under limited conditions. Improvement of societal conditions through judicious programs might increase the effectiveness of programs that handle juveniles who have failed to avoid delinquent activity.

At the same time, it seems that quite a few juvenile offenses are of a nonserious nature and that the statutes creating these offenses might be changed. The practitioner is in an excellent position to assess the necessity or desirability of many statutes and to move to change those that serve no useful purpose.

Practitioners are also in an excellent position to detect and report types of behavior which, in their experience, frequently lead to the commission of serious delinquent acts. Utilization of their experiences in combination with well-designed research projects will hopefully lead to modified, more satisfactory theories of causation. Finally, practitioners work on a day-to-day basis with juveniles who have already been labeled delinquent in an attempt to prevent further delinquency. Recognizing the variety of factors involved, the range of alternative programs available, and the strengths and weaknesses of prevention programs should lead to greater success in dealing with delinquent juveniles.

Summary

Preventing juvenile delinquency is more desirable than attempting to rehabilitate delinquents, both from an economic viewpoint and from the viewpoint of the juveniles involved and society. Successful prevention may depend upon societal changes, rule changes, and individual or group treatment. While a variety of more or less successful prevention programs exist, concentration on further research and improving theories of causation is crucial. Hopefully, commitment by government at all levels will facilitate effective prevention and lead to the abandonment of ineffective programs. Examination of some of the basic assumptions of current prevention programs is essential. Practitioners can provide valuable information that should benefit delinquency prevention programs.

There are a number of agencies operating programs that complement or supplement juvenile justice programs. Coordinating and organizing these programs to eliminate duplication and increase efficiency has proved difficult as the result of territorial jealousy. Nonetheless, the best way to insure the welfare of juveniles with problems is to share knowledge through interagency cooperation and referral, and budgetary restraints are currently dictating that this be accomplished.

Discussion Questions

1. What are the two major approaches to delinquency prevention? What are the strengths and weaknesses of each?
2. Discuss some contemporary attempts to prevent delinquency or divert delinquents, and tell why you feel they are effective or ineffective.
3. List some of the assumptions you feel are basic to delinquency prevention and diversion programs. To what extent do you feel each of these assumptions is justified?
4. Why is the public often unwilling to finance prevention programs and what are the consequences of this unwillingness?
5. What is territorial jealousy? Why does it occur and what are some of its consequences?
6. Discuss at least two agencies or programs with goals similar to those of the juvenile justice system. In your opinion, how successful are these agencies in achieving their goals?

Selected Readings

Binder, A., and G. Geis. "*Ad Populum* Argumentation in Criminology: Juvenile Diversion as Rhetoric." *Crime and Delinquency* 30, no. 2 (April 1984): 309–33.

Gold, Martin. "Scholastic Experience, Self-Esteem and Delinquent Behavior: A Theory for Alternative Schools." *Crime and Delinquency* 24 (July 1978): 290–308.

Howlett, Frederick W. "Is the YSB All It's Cracked Up to Be?" *Crime and Delinquency* 19, no. 4 (October 1973): 485–92.

Lab, S. P. *Crime Prevention: Approaches, Practices, and Evaluations.* Cincinnati, Ohio: Anderson Publishing Co., 1988.

Landau, Simha, and G. Nathan. "Selecting Delinquents for Cautioning." *British Journal of Criminology* 23 (1981): 128–89.

Law Enforcement Assistance Administration, U.S. Department of Justice. *Delinquency Prevention: Theories and Strategies.* Washington, D.C.: U.S. Government Printing Office, 1979.

Lemert, Edwin M. "Diversion in Juvenile Justice: What Has Been Wrought." *Journal of Research in Crime and Delinquency* (1981): 34–46.

Lundman, Richard J. *Prevention and Control of Juvenile Delinquency.* New York: Oxford University Press, 1984.

Polk, K. "Juvenile Diversion: A Look at the Record." *Crime and Delinquency* 30, no. 4 (October 1984): 684–59.

Schur, Edwin M. *Radical Non-Intervention: Rethinking the Delinquency Problem.* Englewood Cliffs, N.J.: Prentice-Hall, Inc., 1973.

Stumphauzer, J. S. *Helping Delinquents Change.* New York: Haworth Press, 1986.

Wright, W., and Michael C. Dixon. "Community Prevention and Treatment of Juvenile Delinquency." *Journal of Research in Crime and Delinquency* 14 (January 1977): 35–67.

10 Dispositional Alternatives

When attempts to divert youth from the juvenile justice network fail, an adjudicatory hearing is held to determine whether the youth should be dismissed or categorized as a delinquent, minor in need of supervision (or authoritative intervention), or an abused, neglected, or dependent child. At this time the judge must make a decision concerning appropriate disposition. The judge utilizes his/her own expertise and experience, the social background investigation report, and sometimes the probation officer's or caseworker's recommendation in arriving at a decision.

The alternatives available to the judge differ depending upon the category in which the youth has been placed, but in general they range from incarceration to foster-home placement to probation. In the Gault case, the Supreme Court specifically declined to comment on the applicability of due process requirements during the dispositional phase of juvenile court proceedings. Thus we must turn to state statutes and/or lower court decisions in analyzing this process. Keep in mind that the purpose of the dispositional hearing is to determine the best way to correct or treat the youth in question while protecting society. In order to accomplish these goals, the court must have available as much information as possible about the youth, his/her background (family, education, legal history), and available alternatives. Evidence pertaining to the welfare of the youth is generally admissible at this stage of the proceedings, and the youth should be represented by counsel.

While some nondelinquent youth, typically those found to be in need of supervision, may be confined temporarily in specifically designated facilities, the trend had been toward diverting them to other types of programs. In some cases the child is permitted to remain with the family under the supervision of the court; in others custody reverts to the state, with placement in a foster or adoptive home. The extent of state intervention has been a subject of considerable controversy, but when the welfare of the child is involved, termination of parental rights may be the only way to provide adequate protection.

Delinquent conduct always involves violation of law, unlike some of the other conduct dealt with by the juvenile court. There are numerous available dispositions for youth in this category, including probation under conditions prescribed by the court, placement in a restrictive/secure facility not operated by the department of corrections, or commitment to a public correctional facility. The latter disposition is generally used as a last resort, but may be necessary to protect society. In some cases restitution is used in addition to probation, or as a disposition in and of itself. In some cases weekend incarceration or community-based correctional programs are utilized. These programs allow the youth to remain in the community where he/she may attend school, work part-time, and participate in supervised activities. The effectiveness of such programs is an empirical question, and many are not adequately evaluated. In the following sections we will examine the various dispositions available for delinquents.

Probation

A juvenile on probation is released into the community with the understanding that his or her continued freedom depends upon good behavior and compliance with the conditions established by his or her probation officer and/or the judge. Probation, then, gives the juvenile a "second chance" to demonstrate that he or she can function in the community. A major finding of past presidential commissions has been that the earlier and deeper an offender goes into the juvenile justice system, the more difficult it is to get out successfully. Unnecessary commitments to correctional institutions often result in "criminalized" juveniles. The revolving door of delinquency and criminality is perpetuated as a result. The fact that there may be a short-term benefit from temporarily removing some juveniles from society should be tempered with the realization that, once released, some juveniles are more likely to jeopardize the community than if they had been processed under adequate probation services in the community where they must eventually prove themselves anyway. Since the goal of the juvenile court is therapeutic rather than punitive, probation is clearly in accord with the philosophy of the court. When circumstances warrant probation and when the juveniles for whom probation is a viable alternative are carefully selected, and when adequate supervision by probation officers is available, probation seems to have potential for success. Failure to take proper precautions in any of these areas, however, jeopardizes chances of success and adds to the criticism of probation as an alternative that "coddles delinquents."

Probation is clearly the most frequent disposition handed down by juvenile court judges. Despite pressures exerted by the mass media (in the form of coverage of some exceptionally disturbing offenses committed by probationers), juvenile court judges have generally adopted the philosophy that a youth will usually benefit more from remaining with his or her family or under the custody of other designated persons in the community than from incarceration.

In making a disposition, the juvenile court judge traditionally places heavy emphasis on the present offense, the wishes of the complainant, prior legal history, family background, personal history, peer associates, school record, and home and neighborhood. In addition, consideration is given to whether justice would be best served by granting probation or whether incarceration is necessary for the protection of the public. There are a multitude of other factors considered by judges, including the youth's attitude toward the offense and whether the youth participated in the offense in a principal or secondary capacity. The degree of aggravation and premeditation as well as mitigating circumstances are also considered.

Once probation has been decided upon, certain terms and conditions are imposed on the probationer. Within broad limits, these terms and conditions are left to the discretion of the judge and/or probation officer. The requirements that the probationer obey all laws of the land, avoid associating with criminals and other persons of ill repute, remain within jurisdiction, and report regularly to the probation officer are general terms and conditions usually imposed by statutory decree. Although the court has broad discretion in imposing other terms and conditions of probation, these terms and conditions must be reasonable and relevant to the offense for which probation is being granted. For example, a condition that a defendant cannot become pregnant while unmarried was not considered to be related to the robbery for which the female was adjudicated delinquent. The appellate court reasoned that a possible pregnancy had no reasonable relationship to future criminality.[1] An order of a juvenile court requiring regular attendance at Sunday school and

1. *People* v. *Dominquez*, 256 Cal. App. 2d 623 (1967).

church was held to be unconstitutional, as "no civil authority has the right to require anyone to accept or reject any religious belief or to contribute any support thereto."[2] However, conditions of probation that require a defendant to pay costs or make restitution are generally upheld, provided that the amounts ordered to be paid are not excessive in view of the financial condition of the defendant.[3] Any condition that cannot reasonably be fulfilled within the period fixed by the court is not likely to be upheld.

The importance of adhering to the terms and conditions of probation is stressed since violations constitute a basis for revocation of probation and the imposition or execution of the sentence which could have been given originally by the judge. There are generally three types of violations—technical, re-arrest for a new crime or act of delinquency, and absconding or fleeing jurisdiction. A technical violation is usually characterized by the probationer flagrantly ignoring the terms or conditions of probation, but not actually committing a new act of delinquency. For example, deliberately associating with delinquent peers might lead to revocation if such was prohibited as a condition of probation. Frequently, the technical violation is due to an excessive number of failures to meet with the probation officer. Technical violations are generally worked out between the probationer and probation officer and usually do not result in revocation action, unless the probationer develops a complete disregard for the terms or conditions of probation. A re-arrest or new custody action due to a new act of delinquency is obviously a serious breach of probation. The seriousness of the new act of delinquency is important in determining whether revocation proceedings will be initiated. Although absconding or fleeing the juvenile court's jurisdiction without approval of the court may be considered a technical violation, it is generally considered separately and may result in revocation action.

Release on probation is a conditional release; that is, the liberty of the probationer is not absolute but subject to the terms and conditions being met. Although the probation officer may seek a revocation of probation, the court will ultimately determine whether to revoke probation. When juveniles violate the conditions of supervised release and face revocation of probation, issues of due process with respect to right to counsel

---

2. *Jones* v. *Commonwealth,* 185 Va. 335, 38 S.E. 2d 444 (1946).

3. See G. Killinger, H. Kerper, and P. Cromwell, *Probation and Parole in the Criminal Justice System* (St. Paul, Minn.: West Publishing Company, 1976), especially pp. 69–93; or S. Davis, *Rights of Juveniles* (New York: Clark Boardman, 1988), 6.32–6.37.

and standard of proof arise. In *Morrissey* v. *Brewer*[4] the Supreme Court held that, although a parole revocation proceeding is not a part of the criminal prosecution, the potential loss of liberty involved is nevertheless significant enough to entitle the parolee to due process of law. First, the court held that the parolee is entitled to a preliminary hearing to determine if there is probable cause to believe that a violation of a condition has occurred. Second, an impartial examiner shall conduct the hearing. Finally, notice of the alleged violation, purpose of the hearing, disclosure of evidence to be used against the parolee, opportunity to present evidence on his or her own behalf, and limited right to cross examination are allowed under due process. Subsequently, in *Gagnon* v. *Scarpelli*[5] concerning the issue of probation revocation proceedings, the court held that a probationer was entitled to the same procedural safeguards announced in *Morrissey* v. *Brewer,* including requested counsel. Earlier, in *Mempa* v. *Rhay,*[6] the court had held that, where the petitioner had been placed on probation and his sentence deferred, he was entitled by due process of law to the right to counsel in a subsequent revocation proceeding, since the revocation proceeding was a continuation of the sentencing process and, therefore, the criminal prosecution itself. Most courts, in the absence of statute, have held that the probation violation need only be established by a preponderance of the evidence, even if the violation is itself an offense.

There are several dispositions available in revocation hearings. If the charges are vacated, the probationer may be restored to probation or the conditions may be altered, amended, or even remain the same. Finally, the revocation may be granted with a new disposition generally resulting in commitment to a juvenile correctional institution.

Although the length of probation varies among states, the maximum term of probation for the juvenile is usually not beyond the maximum jurisdiction of the juvenile court. Most terms of juvenile probation are between six months to one year with possible extensions in most states. Upon successful completion of the probation period or on the recommendation of the probation officer for early discharge, termination of probation releases the juvenile from the court's jurisdiction.

Although probation serves the purpose of keeping the juvenile in the community while rehabilitation attempts are being made, there are some potential dangers built into this disposition. Learning and labeling

4. *Morrissey* v. *Brewer,* 408 U.S. 471 (1972).
5. *Gagnon* v. *Scarpelli,* 411 U.S. 778 (1973).
6. *Mempa* v. *Rhay,* 389 U.S. 128 (1967).

"theories" indicate that proper supervision of probationers is essential if rehabilitation is to occur. Otherwise, the juvenile placed on probation may immediately return to the "old gang" or behavior patterns that initially led to that juvenile's adjudication as delinquent. Similarly, the juvenile placed on probation, while remaining with his or her family, may end up in the same negative circumstances that initially led to delinquent behavior, except that he or she has now been labeled and is more or less expected to misbehave. Problems in family, school, and peer relations may be exaggerated by the labeling process and the juvenile may find it difficult to meet the expectations established for him or her. In many cases, the only positive role model available is the probation officer, whose case load may preclude seeing the juvenile for more than a few minutes a week.

Juveniles placed on probation with families who are concerned and cooperative may, however, benefit far more from this disposition than from placement in a correctional facility. In an attempt to provide this solid family setting for juveniles whose own families are unconcerned, uncooperative, or the source of the delinquent activity in question, the juvenile court judge may place his or her client on probation in a foster home.

Foster Homes

When maintenance of the family unit is clearly not in the juvenile's best interests (or in the family's best interests, for that matter), the judge may place a juvenile on probation in a foster home. Ideally, foster homes are carefully selected through state and local inspection and are to provide a concerned, comfortable setting in which the delinquent's behavior may be modified. Foster parents provide the supervision and care that is often missing in the delinquent's own family, and provide a more constant source of supervision and support than the probation officer. As a result, the juvenile's routine contacts should provide a more positive environment for change than would be the case if the youth were free to associate with former delinquent companions or unconcerned or criminal parents. Likewise, foster homes are frequently used as viable alternatives for minors who have been abused, neglected, dependent or "in need of supervision." Since many of these youths are caught up in dangerous situations, it is often clearly in their best interests to be removed from their natural families.

The foster home clearly has a number of advantages for delinquent youth, provided the selection process for both foster parents and delinquents is adequate. Unfortunately, couples with low incomes frequently apply for foster parent status in the belief that the money paid by the state or county for housing the delinquent will supplement their income. If this added income is the basic interest of potential foster parents, limited guidance and assistance for foster children can be expected. In addition, many of these couples soon find that the money paid per foster child is barely adequate to feed and clothe the youth and therefore does nothing to supplement their income. Thus careful selection of foster parents is imperative.

No matter how careful the juvenile court judge is in selecting delinquent youth for foster home placement, some placements are likely to involve youth who commit further delinquent acts. Raising any adolescent presents problems, and caring for a delinquent youth frequently adds to these problems. As a result, the number of couples willing to provide foster care for delinquent youth is generally small. Foster families must be carefully screened through on-site visitations and interviews and have those physical and emotional attributes which will be supportive for any youth placed with them. Assuming responsibility for a delinquent youth placed in one's home requires a great deal of commitment and many juveniles who might benefit from this type of setting cannot be placed due to the lack of available families. Alternatives available to the judge in such cases include probation in a less desirable setting or incarceration in a juvenile correction facility.

Juvenile Corrections

Throughout this book, it has been indicated that juveniles should be diverted from the juvenile justice system when the offense involved is not serious and when viable alternatives are available. Status offenders, neglected, and dependent youth clearly should not be incarcerated. There may, of course, be times when the only option available to the court is to provide temporary placement in shelter care facilities, foster homes, or group homes when conditions preclude a return to the family. In cases where the juvenile in question may present a danger to himself or herself or to others, or may flee, temporary placement may be necessary. Placement may also be necessary in cases where the juvenile's family is completely negligent or incapable of providing appropriate care and/or control. Temporary custody of dependent, neglected, and in-need-of-supervision juveniles, as well as nonserious delinquents, should be in an environment conducive to normal relations and contact with the community. Numerous private and public programs directed at such youth have emerged in the 1980s. These include chemical dependency programs and residential treatment centers, among others.

There are, however, juveniles whose actions cannot be tolerated by the community. Those who commit predatory offenses or whose illegal behavior becomes progressively more serious may need to be institutionalized for the good of society. For these youth, alternative options may have already been exhausted and the only remedy available to insure protection of society may be incarceration. As previously indicated, incarceration is a serious business with a number of negative consequences for both juveniles and society which must be considered prior to placement.

The Dilemmas of Juvenile Corrections

While incarcerating juveniles for the protection of society is clearly necessary in some cases, correctional institutions frequently serve as the gateway to careers of crime and delinquency. The myth that sending juveniles to correctional facilities will result in rehabilitation must be destroyed. As Larry Cole indicates,

> . . . institutions that imprison children in America are both the result and the cause of more complex and socially disastrous problems. At best they are warehousing children like tiny time bombs, whom they ship out from time to time to explode with unpredictable injuries.[7]

In 1974, Robert M. Martinson completed a comprehensive review of rehabilitation efforts and provided a critical summary of all studies published since 1945. He concluded that there was "pitifully little evidence existing that any prevailing mode of correctional treatment had an appreciable effect on recidivism."[8] In spite of the fact that most of the research on the effects of juvenile correctional facilities substantiates Cole's statement, we have developed and frequently implement what may be termed an "away syndrome." When confronted with a youth who has

7. Larry Cole, *Our Children's Keepers* (Greenwich, Conn.: Fawcett Publications, 1974), 11.

8. Robert M. Martinson, "What Works? Questions and Answers about Prison Reform," *Public Interest* 35 (1974): 22–54.

Figure 10.1 Institutions new and old

committed a delinquent act, we all too frequently ask "Where can we send him?" This "away syndrome" represents part of a more general approach to deviant behavior that has prevailed for many years in America. The "away syndrome" applies not only to juveniles, but also to the mentally ill, the retarded, the aged, and the adult criminal. This approach frequently discourages attempts to find alternatives to incarceration and is frequently accompanied by an "out-of-sight, out-of-mind" attitude. Our hope seems to be that if we simply send deviants far enough away so they become invisible, then they or their problems will disappear. However, walls do not successfully hide such problems nor will they simply go away. Not only do "graduates" from correctional institutions reappear, but their experiences while incarcerated often seem to solidify delinquent or criminal attitudes and behavior. According to recent national statistics, from 74 to 80 percent of all juvenile offenders commit more crimes after release from incarceration.[9]

There are a number of alternative forms of incarceration available. For juveniles whose period of incarceration is to be relatively brief, there are many public and private detention facilities available. Treatment programs and security measures vary widely among these institutions. Both need to be considered when deciding where to place a juvenile. Generally speaking, private detention facilities house fewer delinquents and are less oriented toward strict custody than facilities operated by the state department of corrections. Many of these private facilities provide treatment programs aimed at modifying undesirable behavior as quickly as possible in order to facilitate an early release and to minimize the effects of isolation. The cost of maintaining a delinquent in an institution of this type may be quite high and not every community has access to such facilities.

Public detention facilities frequently are located near larger urban centers and often house large numbers of delinquents in either a cottage or dormitory setting. As a rule, these institutions are used only when all other alternatives have been exhausted. As a result, most of the more serious delinquents are sent to these facilities. It would certainly seem that concern with custody frequently outweighs concern with rehabilitation.

As the discussion of learning and labeling theories indicates, current correctional environments are not the best places to mold juvenile delinquents into useful, law-abiding citizens. As a rule, sending a delinquent to a correctional facility to learn responsible, law-abiding behavior is like sending a person to the desert to learn how to swim. If our specific intent is to demand revenge of youthful offenders through physical and emotional punishment and isolation, current correctional facilities will suffice. If we would rather have those incarcerated return to society "rehabilitated," a number of changes must be made.

First, we must be aware of the negative effects resulting from isolating juveniles from the larger society, especially for long periods of time. This isolation, while clearly necessary in certain cases, makes reintegration into society difficult. The transition from a controlled correctional environment to the relative freedom of society is not easy to make for those who have been labeled "delinquent."

9. Data supplied by American Correctional Association in 1983.

Second, it is essential to be aware of the continual, intense pressure to conform to institutional standards, which characterizes life in most correctional facilities. Although some juvenile institutions provide environments conducive to treatment and rehabilitation, many are warehouses concerned only with custody, control, and order maintenance. Correctional personnel frequently deceive the public, both intentionally and unintentionally, about what takes place in their institutions by providing tours that emphasize orderliness, cleanliness, and treatment orientation. Too often citizens fail to see or consider the harsh discipline, solitary confinement, and dehumanizing aspects of many correctional facilities. It has been recommended that concerned citizens, prosecutors, public defenders, and juvenile court judges spend a few days in such institutions to see if the state is really acting in the "best interests of the juvenile."

Third, the effects of peer group pressure in juvenile correctional facilities must be considered. There is little doubt that behavior modification will occur, but it will not necessarily result in the creation of a law-abiding citizen. The learning "theory" discussed earlier implies that the learning of delinquent behavior may be enhanced if the frequency of contact with those holding favorable attitudes toward law violation is increased. Juvenile correctional facilities are typically characterized by the existence of a delinquent subculture, which enhances the opportunity for dominance of the strong over the weak and gives impetus to the exploitation of the unsophisticated by the more knowledgeable. Into this quagmire we sometimes thrust nonserious delinquents who become involved in forced homosexual activities, who learn to settle disputes with physical violence or weapons, who learn the meaning of shakedowns and "the hole," and who discover how to "score" for narcotics and other contraband. Juvenile institutions have long been cited in cases of brutal beatings and other inhumane practices between residents (inmates) and between staff and residents.[10] We are then surprised when juveniles leave these institutions with more problems than they had prior to incarceration.

It is clearly counterproductive to send juveniles to educational or vocational training six to eight hours a day only to return them to a cottage or dormitory where "anything goes" except escape. Juveniles who

10. See Edward Walin, *Children Without Justice—A Report by the National Council of Jewish Women* (New York: National Council of Jewish Women, 1975), 43–55; Kenneth Wooden, *Weeping in the Playtime of Others* (New York: McGraw Hill, 1976); Kim Oates, *Child Abuse: A Community Concern* (New York: Brunner/Mazel: 1982); or George R. Parulski, Jr., "To the Point of Abuse," *Police Product News* (April 1983), 40.

are physically assaulted or "gang raped" in their cottage at night are seldom concerned about success in the classroom the next day. Howard Polsky indicated that the delinquent subculture existing in juvenile correctional facilities is based upon toughness and the ability to manipulate others. The status of the juvenile within the walls of the institution is largely determined by his or her position within this delinquent subculture.[11] This powerful reference group offsets the efforts of correctional staff members to effect positive attitudinal and/or behavioral change. As Dorwin Cartwright points out, "if the behavior of an individual is an intrinsic part of groups to which he belongs, attempts to change the behavior must be directed at the groups."[12] Since the behavior demanded within the delinquent subculture is frequently contrary to behavior acceptable to the larger society, techniques must be found for minimizing the negative impact of that subculture.

A fourth problem frequently encountered in juvenile correctional facilities is the assignment to cottages and/or existing programs based on vacancies rather than on the benefit to the juvenile. Juveniles who need remedial education may end up in vocational training. Any benefits to be derived from treatment programs are therefore minimized.

A fifth problem involves the mutual suspicion and distrust between staff members who see themselves as either rehabilitators or as custodians. Rehabilitators often believe that custodians have little interest and expertise in treatment, while custodians often believe that rehabilitators are "too liberal" and fail to appreciate the responsibilities of custody. The debate between these factions frequently makes it difficult to establish a cooperative treatment program. In addition, juveniles frequently use one staff group against the other. For example, they may tell the social worker that they have been unable to benefit from treatment efforts because the guards harass them physically and psychologically, keeping them constantly upset. This kind of report often contributes to the feud between guards and caseworkers who occasionally become so concerned with staff differences that the youth are left to do largely as they please.

Finally, the development of good working relationships between correctional staff and incarcerated juveniles is quite difficult. The delinquent subculture, the age difference, and the relative power positions of the two groups work against developing good rapport in most institutions. Frankly, there is often little contact between treatment personnel

11. Howard W. Polsky, *Cottage Six* (New York: Sage, 1962).
12. Dorwin Cartwright, "Achieving Change in People: Some Applications of Group Dynamics Theory," *Human Relations* 4 (1951): 381–92.

and their clients. It is very difficult for the caseworker, who sees his or her clients thirty minutes a week, to significantly influence juveniles, who spend the remainder of the week in the company of custodial staff and their delinquent peers. Since the custodial staff enforces institutional rules, there is a built-in mistrust between the staff members and their charges. Nonetheless, guards deal with the day-to-day problems of incarcerated youth most frequently, even though they are generally not regarded by caseworkers as particularly competent.

Under these circumstances, it is not difficult to see why rehabilitative efforts often end in failure.

Finding solutions to these problems is imperative if we are to improve the chances of rehabilitating youth who must be incarcerated.

Some Possible Solutions

Nearly all juvenile institutions utilize some form of treatment program for the youth in custody—counseling on an individual or group basis, vocational and educational training, various types of therapy, recreational programs, and religious counseling. In addition, most institutions provide medical and dental programs of some kind, as well as occasional legal service programs. Generally, the larger the institution, the greater the number of programs and services offered. The purpose of these various programs is to rehabilitate the youths within the institutions—to turn them into well-adjusted individuals and send them back into the community to be productive citizens. Despite generally good intentions, however, the goal of rehabilitation has rarely been attained.[13]

Solving the problems created by the effects of isolation on incarcerated juveniles is a difficult task. First, we need to be certain that all available alternatives to incarceration have been explored. We must remember that virtually all juveniles placed in institutions will eventually be released into society. If those juveniles are to be released with positive attitudes toward reintegration, we must orient institutional treatment programs toward that goal. This can be accomplished through educational and vocational programs brought into the institution from the outside and through "work or educational release" programs for appropriate juveniles. In addition, attempts to facilitate reintegration through the use of halfway houses or pre-release guidance centers seem to be somewhat successful.

13. Siegal and Senna, *Juvenile Justice,* 495–97.

Unfortunately, in many instances correctional staff members begin to see isolation as an end in itself. As a result, attempts at treatment are often oriented toward helping the juvenile adapt to institutional life rather than preparing the juvenile for reintegration. Ignoring life on "the outside" and failing to deal with problems that will be confronted upon release simply add to the problem. Provision of relevant educational and vocational programs, employment opportunities upon release, and programs provided by interested civic groups should take precedence over concentrating on strict schedules, mass movements, and punishment. The "out-of-sight, out-of-mind" attitude should be eliminated through the use of programs designed to increase community contact as soon as possible. This is not meant to belittle the importance of institutional educational, vocational, and recreational programs for the juvenile delinquent. However, they will fail unless they are supported by an intensive, continual orientation to success outside the walls of the institution. This will require both correctional personnel and concerned citizens to pull their heads "out of the sand" in a cooperative effort to serve the best interests of both incarcerated juveniles and society.

Changes are needed in rehabilitation and treatment programs within the walls of the institution as well. Some programs are based upon faulty assumptions. Others fail to consider the problems arising from the transition between the institution and the community upon release. Some examples should help to illustrate the advantages and disadvantages of different types of treatment programs.

Many institutions rely upon individual counseling or psychotherapy as treatment modalities. Treatment of this type is normally quite costly and contact with the therapist is generally quite limited. In addition, treatment programs of this type rest on two highly questionable assumptions: that the delinquents involved suffer from emotional or psychological distress and that psychotherapy is an effective means of relieving such distress. Most delinquents do not seem to suffer from such distress. Whether or not those who do are suffering from some underlying emotional difficulty or from the trauma of being apprehended, prosecuted, adjudicated, disposed of, and placed in an institution is not clear. Finally, whether psychotherapeutic techniques are effective in relieving emotional or psychological problems when they do exist is a matter of considerable disagreement.

Another type of program, which has become popular recently, is behavior modification. In programs of this type, the delinquent is rewarded for appropriate behavior and punished for inappropriate behavior. Rewards may be given by the staff, by peers, or by both. Perhaps rewards given by both show the best results. Research on behavior modification programs has shown encouraging results. It is reasonable to assume that most delinquent behavior can be modified under strictly controlled conditions. While it is possible to control many conditions within the walls of the institution, such controls cannot be applied to the same degree following release. In addition, as indicated earlier, behavior that is punished within the institution may be rewarded on the outside and vice versa. Again, transition from the institutional setting to the community is crucial. There are also ethical issues to consider in terms of granting institutional staff the power to modify behavior while still protecting the rights of the juveniles.

Other treatment techniques frequently employed in juvenile detention facilities center on change within the group. These include the use of reality therapy, group counseling sessions, psychodrama or role-playing sessions, and self-government programs. All of these techniques are aimed at getting the juveniles to talk through their problems, to take the role of other people in order to better understand why others react as they do, and to assume part of the responsibility for solving their own problems. All of these seem to be important, since lack of communication, lack of understanding other people's views, and failure to assume responsibility for their own actions characterize many delinquents. Continuing access to behavior modification programs after release could provide valuable help during and after the period of reintegration.

Assuming that we have worthwhile rehabilitation programs in juvenile institutions, serious attempts should be made to match juveniles with appropriate programs and to stop convenience assignments such as those based upon program vacancies and ease of transfer. A number of researchers have devised systems to classify offenders into "treatment-relevant types." A comparison of these differing typological approaches is presented in a National Institute of Mental Health publication.[14] Among the systems considered in this report is a method proposed by Herbert Quay, whose research in this area underlies the approach taken at the Kennedy Youth Center.[15] Youthful offenders are assigned scores

14. Department of Health, Education, and Welfare, Public Health Service, "Typological Approaches and Delinquency Control" (Washington, D.C.: U.S. Government Printing Office, 1967).

15. Kennedy Youth Center, Morgantown, West Virginia, is a federal center for youthful violators of federal laws. A complete description of the treatment strategies employed at the Center is contained in Herbert Quay, "Differential Treatment: A Way to Begin," U.S. Bureau of Prisons, Department of Justice (Washington, D.C.: U.S. Government Printing Office, 1970).

obtained from information based on the youth's present behavior, self-evaluation, and past history. The scores allow placement in any of four behavioral categories. Assignment of the youthful offender to a specific cottage is based on these behavioral categories. Each behavioral category and resultant cottage assignment is associated with a specific type of treatment and training program. The basic assumption at the Kennedy Youth Center is that different behavioral types require different types of treatment. Treatment programs vary according to the juvenile's behavioral characteristics, maturity level, and psychological orientation. Whereas one behavioral type may benefit from behavior modification based on immediate reinforcement (positive-negative), another behavioral type may benefit more through increasing levels of awareness and understanding. The immediate reinforcement conditioning approach has been utilized through token economy systems in many juvenile institutions where appropriate behavior is rewarded. Conversely, inappropriate behavior will result in a loss of privileges or points toward a specific goal. Although it may be risky to assume that there are clearly delineated behavioral categories with accompanying treatment for each category, at least some systematic effort is being made at the Kennedy Youth Center to work with the youths in their custody.

Since the peer group plays such an important role in correctional facilities, some way must be found to use its influence in a positive manner. Many institutions have adopted a "positive peer culture" orientation in which peers are encouraged to reward one another for appropriate behavior and to help one another eliminate inappropriate behavior. While correctional staffs frequently feel that these programs are highly successful, in many cases juveniles simply learn to play the game; that is, they make appropriate responses when being observed by staff members, but revert to undesirable behavior patterns upon their return to the dorm or cottage. This frequently happens because correctional personnel get taken in by their own institutional "babble." They sometimes begin to believe that the peer culture they see is positive when it is actually largely negative. One way to avert this problem is to view rehabilitation as more than an "eight-to-five" job. Unfortunately, the problems that confront incarcerated juveniles do not always arise at convenient times for staff members. Assistance in solving these problems should be available when it is needed.

Another beneficial step taken in some institutions has been to move away from the dormitory or large cottage concept to rooms occupied by two or three juveniles. These juveniles are carefully screened for the particular group in which they are included in terms of seriousness of offense, type of offense, past history of offenses, and so forth. This move holds some promise of success, since "rule by the toughest" may be averted for most inmates. In this way less serious offenders, such as auto thieves or burglars, run less risk of being "contaminated" by their more dangerous peers, those who commit offenses involving homicide, battery, or armed robbery, for example.

Finally, relationships between therapeutic and custodial staff members and between all staff members and inmates need to be improved. The solution is obvious. All staff members in juvenile correctional facilities should be employed on the basis of their sincere concern with preparing inmates for their eventual release and reintegration into society. Distinctions between custodial and treatment staffs should be eliminated, rehabilitation should be the goal of every staff member, and every staff member should be concerned about custody when necessary. Training and educational opportunities should be available to help staff members keep up with new techniques and research.

Providing correctional personnel of this type will not guarantee better relationships with all inmates, but should improve the quality of most relationships considerably. While initial costs of employment may be somewhat higher, the overall costs will not exceed those now incurred by taxpayers who often pay to have the same juvenile "rehabilitated" time and time again.

Implications for Practitioners

Juvenile court judges and probation officers should be aware of the possible negative consequences of the disposition most frequently used, probation. Without adequate supervision, delinquents on probation may find themselves in the same circumstances that initially led them to commit a delinquent act. They also have the additional problem of having been officially labeled. Adequate supervision and support of these juveniles by probation officers is often crucial to successful rehabilitation. Heavy case loads and unavailability in time of need hamper many probation officers and, as a result, a great deal of criticism has been aimed at probation as a viable dispositional alternative.

Support and supervision provided by carefully selected foster parents and community-based programs increase the chances of successful rehabilitation for delinquent youth and lighten the load on the juvenile probation officer. Routine inspections of foster homes and discussions of the quality of care provided among foster parents, foster children, and juvenile justice practitioners should maximize the benefits of this disposition.

Those practitioners who make decisions concerning the incarceration of juveniles (generally the juvenile probation officer, prosecutor, and juvenile court judge) have a tremendous responsibility. Recognizing that the consequences of incarceration are often highly negative, they should, and typically do, exhaust all possible alternatives before deciding to send juveniles to correctional facilities. These practitioners, however, cannot overlook their responsibility to society. Those juveniles whose behavior is actually dangerous to society must be isolated until some changes in that behavior occur.

Practitioners within the walls of juvenile correctional facilities should all have the same goal; the preparation of the juvenile for return to society. Background differences among staff members should not serve as the basis for petty squabbles, which are harmful to all concerned. Instead, such differences should provide new and different perspectives to achieve the goal of helping youth.

Correctional officials (and society as well) need to consider rehabilitation as more than an eight-hour-a-day job. It does little good to provide eight hours of treatment and then allow sixteen hours of opportunity for relapse. The control and influence of the delinquent subculture must be minimized. Within the walls of the institution, correctional staff must have the opportunity to change the attitudes and behaviors characteristic of that subculture.

All juvenile justice practitioners are crucial in helping to make the transition from correctional facility to society as easy as possible. If correctional practitioners strive for this goal, they deserve the support of other practitioners in the justice system and in functionally related agencies, as well as of concerned citizens.

Summary

Careful consideration should be given to available alternatives to incarceration of juveniles. Probation, whether within the juvenile's own family or in a foster home, has the advantage of maintaining ties between the juvenile and the community. Proper supervision and careful selection procedures to determine how a youth can benefit from probation are essential. When incarceration is necessary to protect society, programs directed toward the eventual return of the juvenile to society should be stressed.

Changes are required in society's belief that juveniles who are "out of sight" will automatically remain "out of mind." These youth will be returning to society and efforts should be made to insure that time spent in isolation produces beneficial, not negative, results.

Random assignment of juveniles to correctional treatment programs and the negative effects of the delinquent subculture which develops in most institutions seriously hamper rehabilitation efforts.

Discussion Questions

1. Discuss the negative consequences of placing juveniles in correctional facilities. In your opinion, what circumstances would warrant this placement? Why?
2. What are the major advantages and disadvantages of probation as a disposition? How are these advantages and disadvantages modified by foster home placement?
3. Why has so much criticism been aimed at probation as a dispositional alternative?
4. If you were superintendent of a juvenile correctional facility, what steps would you take to insure that juveniles will be better prepared for their return to society than they now are? Why would you take these steps?

Selected Readings

Abadinsky, Howard. *Probation and Parole: Theory and Practice*. 2d. ed. Englewood Cliffs, N.J.: Prentice-Hall, Inc., 1987.

Bureau of Justice Statistics. "Recidivism of Young Parolees." Washington, D.C.: U.S. Government Printing Office, May 1987.

Greenwood, P. W., and F. E. Zimring. *One More Change: The Pursuit of Promising Intervention Strategies for Chronic Juvenile Offenders*. Santa Monica, Calif.: Rand Corporation, 1985.

Krisberg B., I. Swartz, P. Litsky, and J. Austin. "The Watershed of Juvenile Justice Reform." *Crime and Delinquency* 32 (1986): 5–38.

Lab, S. P., and J. T. Whitehead. "An Analysis of Juvenile Correction Treatment." *Crime and Delinquency* 34 (1988): 60–83.

Reichel, P. L. "Getting to Know You: Decision-Making in an Institution for Juveniles." *Justice and Family Court Journal* (1985): 5–15.

Schneider, A. L. "Deinstitutionalization of Status Offenders: The Impact of Recidivism and Secure Confinement." *Criminal Justice Abstracts* (1984): 410–32.

11 Violence By and Against Youth

Over the past decade, violent crimes committed by juveniles and violence committed against juveniles have received a great deal of attention, much of which has focused on juvenile gangs and the crimes of violence they perpetrate. (We will have more to say on this subject in the next chapter.) As a result of this emphasis on juvenile violence, a number of states now have laws making it easier to try violent juveniles in adult courts, and making it possible to prescribe more severe penalties for such youth. In addition, numerous programs to assist abused youth have been initiated at the federal, state, and local levels, existing programs have been strengthened and expanded, and missing and abused children have received national media attention.

To what extent are the concerns outlined above based in fact? Should Americans be afraid of their children? Do adult Americans routinely commit violent acts against their children? Is there a relationship between being a victim of violence and committing violent acts? What, if anything, can be done to effectively reduce violence by and against youth? In the following sections, we will examine these and other questions concerning the involvement of youth in violent activities.

Violent Youth

"Kids in Crime: They Are Becoming More Violent" reads a newspaper headline.[1] This belief is widespread and is fostered in part by just such headlines, by television specials on youthful violence, by comments on behalf of political officials promising a "get tough" approach to young offenders, and by citizen action groups concerned about juvenile violence. Many of these articles and comments are allegedly based upon

1. N. Guarise, "Kids in Crime: They Are Becoming More Violent," *Peoria Journal Star,* 31 March 1985: 12.

analysis of official statistics, which, as we have pointed out elsewhere, can be highly misleading or misinterpreted when it comes to assessing juvenile delinquency. The use of such statistics may exaggerate the serious crime threat posed by juveniles since there is evidence that many nonserious juvenile offenses are simply overlooked and that juveniles are more likely than adults to be arrested for marginally criminal activity.[2]

If we consider violent juvenile offenders to be those who commit (and, in terms of official statistics, are arrested for) criminal homicide, rape, robbery, or aggravated assault/battery,[3] what has been the trend in recent years? Reviewing data collected using the National Crime Survey (NCS) for the years 1973 through 1977, Snyder and Hutzler conclude that "both the number and rate of personal victimizations committed by juveniles decreased while victimization by adults increased. In addition, there was no change in the seriousness of crime committed during the five year period. Personal victimizations committed by juveniles were less serious, in terms of weapon use, rate of injury, and financial loss than similar crimes committed by adults. The findings of NCS show that juvenile involvement in personal victimizations is substantial, however, they do not support the common belief regarding the increasing volume and seriousness of juvenile crime."[4]

Data from the Uniform Crime Reports (UCR) for the years from 1970 through 1981 indicate that although violent juvenile offense arrests increased during that period of time, adult rates increased more rapidly.[5] UCR data for the period from 1974 through 1983 indicate a 28 percent decrease in the number of youth arrested for Index offenses and a 15 percent decrease in the number arrested for violent crimes during that ten-year period. Comparable figures for adults (over age eighteen) increased 31 percent and 12 percent respectively. Not a single type of violent crime showed an increase in the under-eighteen group for the ten-year period in question, while all violent crimes except murder/nonnegligent manslaughter increased among the over-eighteen group.[6] In

2. P. Greenwood, J. Petersilia, and F. Zimring, *Age, Crime, and Sanctions: The Transition from Juvenile to Adult Court* (Santa Monica, Calif.: The Rand Corporation, 1980).

3. H. S. Synder and J. L. Hutzler, *The Serious Juvenile Offender: The Scope of the Problem and the Response of Juvenile Courts* (Pittsburgh: National Center for Juvenile Justice, 1981), 3.

4. Ibid., 4.

5. U.S. Department of Justice, Federal Bureau of Investigation, *Crime in the United States: 1982* (Washington, D.C.: U.S. Government Printing Office, 1983).

6. *Crime in the United States: 1983,* U.S. Department of Justice, Federal Bureau of Investigation (Washington, D.C.: U.S. Government Printing Office, 1984): 185.

1987, according to the UCR, youth under eighteen accounted for about 15 percent of violent crime, a 1.2 percent decrease from 1986.[7] It is possible, of course, that official statistics do not reflect the reality of violent juvenile crime, but to the extent that they do, they do not indicate increases in either the volume or seriousness of juvenile offenses over the past fifteen years.

Public Reaction

Nonetheless, the public perception that there has been a dramatic and disproportionate increase in violent and serious crime by juveniles during the 1980s has resulted in considerable pressure on legislators to pass new, more stringent laws relating to the prosecution and incarceration of violent juvenile offenders. The Juvenile Court Act in Illinois was amended to remove juveniles charged with criminal homicide, rape, and armed robbery from the jurisdiction of the juvenile court if they are over fifteen years of age at the time they commit the offense.[8] New York law excludes all offenders over the age of sixteen from Family Court jurisdiction. Delaware excludes all murder from juvenile court jurisdiction. Other states have followed or are following suit for these and other violent offenses. Further, in 1989 the United States Supreme Court agreed to arguments concerning the constitutionality of capital punishment for sixteen-and-seventeen-year-old youth, indicating the extent of concern surrounding violent youth. While there is little doubt that some violent juveniles must be dealt with harshly and incarcerated for the protection of society, we need to recognize that processing juveniles as adults clearly violates the philosophy of the juvenile court network by labeling these youth as criminals at an early age, and by placing them in incarceration with automatic transfer to adult facilities at the age of majority. Are there viable alternatives to giving up on youth so early in life?

Alternatives to Incarceration for Violent Juveniles

In his study of juvenile homicide, Sorrells found that a disproportionate number of juveniles who commit this offense come from communities with a high incidence of poverty and infant mortality. He also

7. *Crime in the United States: 1987,* U.S. Department of Justice, Federal Bureau of Investigation (Washington, D.C.: U.S. Government Printing Office, 1988): 172, 174.
8. *Illinois Revised Statutes,* ch. 37, 702–7(6)(a), 1984.

notes that such offenders are products of "violent, chaotic families."[9] He concludes that youth who kill are likely to fall into one of three categories:

1) *youngsters who lack the capacity to identify with other human beings;*
2) *prepsychotic juveniles who kill as an expression of intense emotional conflicts, and who are also high suicide risks, or;*
3) *neurotically fearful youngsters who kill in overreacting to a genuinely threatening situation.*[10]

Sorrells suggests as alternatives to simple incarceration the identification of high risk communities and the pooling of agency resources to combat specific problems characterizing each community, screening violent juveniles for emotional problems, treatment programs focusing on resolving such emotional problems, and removal of children from violent, chaotic families where possible.[11]

Other studies provide general support for Sorrells' findings and recommendations. One study of recidivism among juvenile offenders, for example, found that 100 percent of those recidivists had arrest records prior to the arrest upon which the recidivism was based, 88 percent had unstable home lives, 86 percent were unemployed, and over 90 percent had school problems.[12] Another study indicates that if early intervention is not effective, somewhere between two-thirds and three-fourths of violent juvenile offenders on probation will recidivate, committing essentially the same type of offense, within a few months.[13] Taylor concludes that it may be necessary to deal with juveniles who engage in progressively more serious assaultive behavior by commitment to a detention facility for a three- to six-month period (thus preventing recidivism in the community during this very high risk period) during which time the juvenile's behavior is "stabilized and brought under control."[14]

9. James Sorrells, Jr., "What Can Be Done About Juvenile Homicide?" *Crime and Delinquency* (April 1980): 152.

10. Ibid.

11. Ibid.

12. Richard M. Ariessohn, "Recidivism Revisited," *The Juvenile Family Court Journal* (November 1981): 65.

13. See, for example, W. Buikhuisen and R. W. Jongman, "A Legislative Classification of Juvenile Delinquents," *British Journal of Criminology* 10 (April 1970): 109–23; or Richard Areissohn and Gordon Gonion, "Reducing the Juvenile Detention Rate," *Juvenile Justice* (May 1973): 31.

14. Leah S. Taylor, "The Serious Juvenile Offender: Identification and Suggested Treatment Responses," *The Juvenile and Family Court Journal* (May 1980): 29.

The current dilemma surrounding violent juvenile offenders is indicated by the following quote. "We have clearly passed the time when juveniles who commit serious crimes could automatically count on being processed through juvenile court. That is not a happy circumstance to contemplate, and it automatically validates human failure somewhere down the line. But treating vicious juvenile criminals as criminals first and kids secondarily is a public policy which makes sober common sense."[15]

Recognizing the truth of this sentiment, the Office of Juvenile Justice and Delinquency Prevention recently sponsored a two-year program to identify, select, prosecute, and enhance treatment for serious, habitual juvenile offenders. Analysis showed that such programs result in more frequent findings of guilt and more correctional commitments; and that linking such efforts with special correctional treatment programs for youth is highly problematic due to the necessity of subcontractual relationships between prosecutors and service providers, and the unavailability of special correctional programs to meet the diverse needs of serious habitual offenders.[16]

Unfortunately, getting to and treating potentially violent juveniles is not an easy task. Most authorities agree that one of the major causes of violence among juveniles is being reared in a violent family, and most also agree that child abuse by parents and stepparents and other forms of domestic violence are at near epidemic proportions in the United States. The privacy of the home and the fear of retaliation and/or exposure make identifying and helping such youth extremely difficult. And, quite frankly, many juvenile court judges who hear cases of suspected child abuse are hesitant to break up the family by removing the child to other circumstances, a trait not difficult to understand in light of the emphasis of most juvenile court acts on preserving the integrity of the family. It may be, however, that preserving the family also preserves child abuse and perpetuates violence on the part of the abused children as they grow into adulthood.

15. *Lincoln Journal,* Lincoln, Nebraska, 7 December 1979.
16. National Institute of Justice, "Targeting Serious Juvenile Offenders for Prosecution Can Make a Difference," *NIJ Reports* (Washington, D.C.: U.S. Government Printing Office, Sept.–Oct. 1988): 9–12.

Violence Against Youth

Over the past three decades studies of the family have touched upon an aspect of the family which was rarely discussed before—domestic violence. The family, which had traditionally been viewed as an institution characterized by love, compassion, tenderness, and concern, proved to be an institution in which members are at considerable risk due to increasingly reported episodes of physical abuse and violence among members. Although the privacy of the home and family has made research on this topic difficult, there is now little doubt that the seeds of violence are frequently sown in this setting. Leaping divorce rates, increasing numbers of stepparents, increasing numbers of children reported as abused, the development of coalitions against domestic violence, and changes in state statutes dealing with domestic violence all indicate that family life is often problematic and sometimes violent.

Domestic violence takes many forms including spouse abuse, sibling abuse, parent abuse, and child abuse. Violent acts vary from hitting/battering (excluding any reasonable discipline of a minor child by a parent or guardian) to sexual abuse and exploitation. On the basis of a nationwide sample, Straus and associates estimate that during the year 1975, about 1.7 million children, out of a total of 46 million from ages three to seventeen who were living with both parents, were bitten, kicked, punched or beaten; or threatened with a gun or knife; or actually had a gun or knife used on them. The same survey reported that 6,000 parents out of every 100,000—husbands or wives or both—used serious types of violence against one another during a one-year time period. The authors conclude that when there is fighting between the parents, there is a greater likelihood that there will be fighting among children and aggression by children against parents.[17] The American Humane Association estimates that in 1985 almost two million children were abused and/or neglected. Between 1980 and 1985, homicide was the leading cause of injury-related death among children under one year of age.[18]

While the focus of attention has been on child and wife abuse, there is considerable evidence that abuse of husbands and grandparents occurs on a fairly frequent basis as well.[19] These same studies show that domestic violence is not limited by social class, race, religion, or education.

17. Murray A. Straus, Richard J. Gelles, and Susanne K. Steinmetz, *Behind Closed Doors: Violence in the American Family* (Garden City, N.Y.: Anchor Press, 1980).

18. Tim Friend, "Homicide Is Leading Baby Killer," *USA Today,* 1 March 1989, p. 52.

19. Jerry P. Flanzer, ed., *The Many Faces of Family Violence* (Springfield, Ill: Charles Thomas, 1982); Straus et al., *Behind Closed Doors.*

Violence is a learned behavior and those who behave violently toward their own family members as well as toward others are likely to have observed violent behavior in their own homes as children or to have been victims of domestic violence.[20] Estimates are that at least one in four persons who grew up in violent households uses some physical force against his or her spouse in any one year.[21] There is increasing evidence that domestic violence involving children is also far more common than we once thought.[22] Estimates are that at least one million children are physically abused annually and in 1978 some 5,000 children died as a direct result of child abuse.[23] Estimates as to the number of abused children in the United States range from 60,000 to 6.5 million.[24] Authorities estimate that seven children die each day from physical abuse and another twelve suffer some form of brain damage.[25] More children under five years of age die from mistreatment by parents than from tuberculosis, whooping cough, polio, measles, diabetes, rheumatic fever, and appendicitis combined.[26] Physical abuse is the most common cause of the death of a child in the United States today.[27] The vast majority of all such abuse occurs in the home and is committed by parents who were themselves victims of, or witnesses to, domestic violence. In short, domestic violence promotes domestic (and other forms of) violence.

Consider the following facts:

1) *a 31 percent increase in substantiated child abuse reports between 1981 and 1982 in Oregon, followed by an 8 percent increase between 1982 and 1983;*
2) *in Wisconsin a 41 percent increase in the number of children referred for protective services between 1983 and 1984;*
3) *a 76 percent increase between 1982 and 1983 in the number of suspected abuse and neglect reports filed in Vermont;*
4) *a 15 percent increase in the number of substantiated child abuse cases between 1982 and 1983 in Maine.*[28]

20. U.S. Commission on Civil Rights, *Under the Rule of Thumb: Battered Women and the Administration of Justice* (Washington, D.C.: U.S. Government Printing Office, 1982).

21. Ibid.

22. George R. Parulski, "To the Point of Abuse," *Police* 7 (1983): 40–43.

23. Shirley O'Brian, *Child Abuse: A Crying Shame* (Utah: Brigham Young University Press, 1980).

24. Charles Zastrow, *Introduction to Social Welfare Institutions, Social Problems, Services, and Current Issues* (Homewood, Ill.: Dorsey Press, 1982).

25. O'Brian, *Child Abuse.*

26. Zastrow, *Introduction to Social Welfare Institutions.*

27. O'Brian, *Child Abuse.*

28. Joe Muldoon, "A Time of Crisis in Child Abuse Community Intervention and Prevention," *Community Intervention* (Spring 1985): 1.

According to statistics from the National Center on Child Abuse and Neglect, only about 8,000 reports of child abuse were received nationally in 1967 and 1968, while some 700,000 such reports were received in 1978.[29] These statistics probably do not reflect an enormous increase in actual incidents of child abuse, but some authorities have estimated that as many as ten abuse cases occur for every one that is reported, and the dramatic increase in statistics most likely reflects increased awareness and willingness on behalf of the public to report child abuse.

In terms of sexual abuse alone, estimates are that between 100,000 and 500,000 children will be victimized this year (though relatively few of these cases will be reported), that 19 percent of all American women and 9 percent of all American men were sexually victimized as children, that 2 to 5 million American women have had incestuous relationships, and that over three-quarters of all these victims are abused by parents, family, or close friends, most of whom were abused as children themselves.[30]

There is little doubt, then, that violence committed against youth is causally related to violence committed by the victims at some later point in time. What, if anything, can be or is being done to break this cycle?

Programs Aimed at Altering the Potential for Abuse and Violence

In addition to the types of programs suggested by Sorrells and others outlined above, there have been numerous other attempts to develop ways of intervening early and effectively in domestic violence and child abuse in an attempt to save lives, prevent injuries, and break the intergenerational cycle of violence. Efforts to educate physicians and teachers as to the signs of child abuse and to promote laws which require these individuals to report suspected child abuse to the authorities exist in many, if not most, states. Parents Anonymous (PA) groups which provide a forum in which abusive parents can discuss their problems with others who share similar problems have been formed in many communities.

29. Ibid.
30. "A Hidden Epidemic," *Newsweek* (14 May 1984), pp. 30–36.

These groups claim high success rates, but it should be kept in mind that the statistics upon which these claims are based were collected by or for the agency sponsoring the program.[31]

In an attempt to prevent the sexual abuse of children and to rehabilitate offenders, two counties in Kansas have developed diversion programs for parents committing incest who meet certain stringent admission criteria (must not have used force in the abuse, must admit to the abuse, must have no prior felony convictions, must agree to pay all program costs, etc.). Although these two programs are too new to evaluate meaningfully, they may hold some promise out to those few offenders who meet the established criteria for entry into the programs.[32]

There have also been efforts to provide counseling and educational services to victims of child abuse, but as is the case with many if not most programs dealing with this sensitive subject, evaluation has been largely clinical as opposed to scientific. Still, even if each program helps only one child, many would consider it a success. As indicated previously, early and effective intervention is very difficult as the result of the fact that many parents, children, and helping professionals continue to view the sanctity of the family as extremely important.

Victims of Child Abuse in the Justice System

It would be inappropriate to conclude our discussion of violence against youth without mentioning the difficulties involved in dealing with them as victims. Effective advocacy for such youth is imperative for a variety of reasons. First, they are often ashamed, unable, or afraid to tell anyone about their plight. In many cases, even though they are being regularly and severely abused, children will not tell others because of the fear (sometimes instilled by the abuser) that their parents will be taken away from them if they do seek help. For many young children, this prospect is more frightening than their fear of continued abuse. Second, in many cases that do reach the courts, youth are unable to testify effectively due to fear and/or an inability to express themselves adequately (although some strides have been made with respect to the latter in recent years, particularly with respect to sexual abuse). Third, even when youth

31. "Program Aims to Alter the Potential for Abuse." *Community Intervention* (Spring 1985): 6.

32. Marvin R. Janssen, "Incest: Exploitative Child Abuse," *Police Chief* (February 1984): 46–47.

are able to adequately express themselves, perhaps as a result of the hesitancy to break up the family discussed earlier, judges may not remove them from the home. We are aware of cases where the evidence of abuse was overwhelming, based upon the testimony of teachers, caseworkers, and physicians, in which judges have returned the child to the home in which he or she was being abused. In several such cases, the abuse continued, and in at least one the child involved was killed by the abusing parents following the judge's decision not to remove him from the home. To avoid such occurrences, it is crucial that the rights of child abuse victims be insured by making certain that they have proper representation and counseling and that their testimony is taken seriously. If some American parents are bent on destroying their own children, it is imperative that the state exercise the right of *parens patriae* to protect such children. Last but not least, the state should proceed as rigorously as possible in the prosecution of abusers, if only to prevent them from abusing their own spouses and children again.

Implications for Practitioners

Practitioners need to be aware that, although a substantial proportion of violent crime is committed by juveniles, there is no current epidemic of violent juvenile offenses and no evidence that juveniles are becoming more violent. For those juveniles who do commit violent offenses, incarceration or effective intervention very early in the offense career appear to be the best means of protecting society. Evidence indicates that unless one of these two alternatives is employed, recidivism is very likely. Careful screening of juveniles to insure that only those who actually commit violent acts are processed according to laws intended to deal with such offenders is imperative in terms of costs to both the youth involved and society.

With respect to violence committed against youth, practitioners must be aware that the incidence of such violence is great even by the most conservative estimates. All suspected cases should be treated as extremely serious and given immediate attention in order to protect the life of the youth involved, in order to prevent the youth from learning violent behavior which he or she is likely to duplicate later in life, and in order to attempt to seek treatment or prosecution of the offender. Practitioners should also keep in mind that although family integrity is important, maintaining such integrity in cases of domestic violence or child abuse may be less important than saving life and limb. Most states now have legislation in place which enables the state to protect children from abuse, but many practitioners remain hesitant to take official action which would break up the family. One need only read any newspaper with a large circulation to note the sometimes deadly consequences of failure to remove abused children from the home of the abuser. Practitioners sometimes rationalize their failure to remove abused children from the homes in which they are abused by pointing to the uncertainty of appropriate foster home or shelter care placement. While it is true that such placement is sometimes problematic, leaving a child who has been or is being physically or sexually abused in the home of the abuser is unconscionable.

Summary

Violence by and against youth has received considerable attention over the past decade or so. Stories appearing in the mass media have led many to believe that violence committed by youth is epidemic, but official statistics and other sources of information indicate that violent acts committed by youth have actually declined in recent years. There is little doubt that those youths who do commit violent offenses deserve our immediate attention, since research indicates that they are likely to continue to commit such acts unless early, effective intervention occurs.

Violence committed against youth does in fact appear to be on the increase in the United States. Child abuse in its various forms is a relatively common occurrence, although only a small proportion of abuse cases are reported or discovered. Child abuse is particularly alarming because of the physical and psychological damage done to children, because most research indicates that parents who were abused as children often abuse their own children, and because, in spite of numerous programs designed to help prevent or halt child abuse, child abuse is by nature difficult to detect and control.

Discussion Questions

1. Is violence committed by youth on the increase in the United States? Support your answer. In your opinion, are adults in the United States afraid of youth? Why or why not?

2. Is probation likely to be effective in deterring violent youth from recidivating? Why or why not? Are there more effective programs for deterring violent youths?
3. It is often said that child abuse is intergenerational. Explain why this is the case.
4. Why is child abuse so difficult to deal with? What, in your opinion, would be required for us to deal more effectively with such abuse?

Selected Readings

Giles-Sims, Jean. "A Longitudinal Study of Battered Children of Battered Wives." *Family Relations* 34 (1985): 205–10.

Groth, A. N., R. E. Longo, and J. B. McFadin. "Undetected Recidivism among Rapists and Child Molesters." *Crime and Delinquency* (July 1982): 450–58.

McDermott, M. J., and Michael J. Hindelang. *Analysis of National Crime Victimization Survey Data to Study Serious Delinquent Behavior, Monograph One: Juvenile Criminal Behavior in the United States: Its Trends and Patterns.* U.S. Department of Justice, National Institute for Juvenile Justice and Delinquency Prevention. Washington, D.C.: U.S. Government Printing Office, 1981.

Oates, Kim. *Child Abuse: A Community Concern.* New York: Bruner/Mazel, 1982.

Osbun, Lee A., and Peter A. Rode. "Prosecuting Juveniles as Adults: The Quest for 'Objective' Decisions." *Criminology* 22, no. 2 (May 1984): 187–202.

Parulski, George R., Jr. "To the Point of Abuse." *Police* 7 (1983): 40–43.

Petersilia, Joan, Susan Turner, James Kahan, and Joyce Peterson. *Granting Felons Probation: Public Risks and Alternatives.* Santa Monica, Calif.: The Rand Corporation, 1985.

Rockey, A. A. "Minor Violence: Major Dilemma." *Police Product News* (June 1986): 25–31.

Rosenbaum, J. L. "Social Control, Gender, and Delinquency: An Analysis of Drug, Property, and Violent Offenders." *Justice Quarterly* 4 (1987): 117–32.

Rudman, C., E. Harstone, J. Fagan, and M. Moore. "Violent Youth in Adult Court: Process and Punishment." *Crime and Delinquency* 32 (1986): 75–96.

12 Gangs

This chapter briefly examines the history of gangs in the United States and the nature and extent of their involvement in delinquent and criminal activities. We will explore the attraction of gangs to juveniles, and the unique problems that gangs present to law enforcement, court, and correctional officials, as well as some prevention strategies. At the outset, it should be noted that while we once could have referred to these gangs as "juvenile" gangs, such a distinction is no longer totally appropriate since many gangs now include older adults among their membership. The "turf" gangs of yesteryear have been replaced in many instances by sophisticated criminal organizations involved in drug trafficking, extortion, murder, and other illegal activities. These "street" gangs destroy entire neighborhoods, maiming and killing their residents. They destroy family life, render school and social programs ineffective, deface property, and terrify decent citizens. Last, but not least, they have grown into national organizations that support and encourage criminal activities not only in local neighborhoods, but across the country and internationally.

A Brief History of Gangs

As we have seen previously (chapter 3), gang activity is not a recent phenomenon. Thrasher's classic study of juvenile gangs was published in 1927 and included information based on over thirteen hundred gangs in the Chicago area, including fraternities, play groups, and street-corner gangs. His study was the first to emphasize the organized, purposeful behavior of youth gangs. He found that gangs emerged from the interstitial areas as a result of social and economic conditions, became integrated through conflict, gradually developed an espirit de corps or solidarity, and protected their territory against outsiders, much like today's gangs.[1]

1. Frederick Thrasher, *The Gang: A Study of 1313 Gangs in Chicago* (Chicago: University of Chicago Press, 1927).

Albert Cohen, Walter Miller, and others (see chapter 3) further developed theories of gang delinquency in the 1950s and 1960s. During this period, delinquency came to be regarded as a product of social forces rather than individual deviance. Gang members were viewed as basically normal youth who, under difficult circumstances, adopted a gang sub-culture to deal with their disadvantaged socioeconomic positions.[2] Gangs attracted a good deal of attention as a result of their apparent opposition to conventional norms and sometimes were romanticized, as in the popular *West Side Story.*

By the late 1960s and early 1970s, the United States was in a period of social upheaval marked by civil disturbances, racial protests, antiwar demonstrations, and student protests. Gangs were largely forgotten by the media and sociologists. Definitions of crime and delinquency came into question. Political liberals focused on abuse of power and crimes by the wealthy. Labeling theory came into vogue, postulating that members of the lower social class are more likely to be labeled deviant than those in the middle and upper classes as a result of the balance of power resting with the latter. Gangs were viewed as a response to injustice and oppression. Conservatives, however, viewed crime and delinquency as products of immorality, poor socialization, or lack of sufficient deterrence. Control theory was popular with this political faction because it postulated that delinquency was largely an individual matter, developing early in life, and occurring due to a lack of internal as well as external controls. Failure of institutions such as the family, police, and corrections became the focal point of those representing the conservative viewpoint, obviating the need to deal with the social structure and conditions that were the focus of the liberal camp. The latter group continued to view gang members as youth in need of help rather than punishment. While these groups argued over the source of responsibility for crime and delinquency in general, developments were occurring that would soon lead society to take another look at the gang phenomenon.

In the 1960s, a Chicago gang known as the Blackstone Rangers (later called the Black P Stone Nation, and currently known as El Rukn) emerged as a group characterized by a high degree of organization and considerable influence. The Blackstone Rangers sought and were granted federal funds as well as funds from private enterprises to support their activities. This funding gave the gang an appearance of political and

2. See Cohen and Miller, note 24, Chapter 3.

social respectability. Street gangs in America were becoming "politicized." As Miller stated, the notion of "transforming gangs by diverting their energies from traditional forms of gang activities—particularly illegal forms—and channelling them into 'constructive' activities is probably as old, in the United States, as gangs themselves. Thus, in the 1960s, when a series of social movements aimed at elevating the lot of the poor through ideologically oriented, citizen-executed political activism became widely current, it was perhaps inevitable that the idea be applied to gangs."[3] Jacobs offered three explanations as to why Chicago street gangs, as well as those in many other urban areas, became politicized in the 1960s:

1) *Street gangs adopted a radical ideology from the militant civil rights movement;*
2) *Street gangs became committed to social change for their community as a whole;*
3) *Street gangs became politically sophisticated, realizing that the political system could be used to further their own needs—money, power, and organized growth.*[4]

Jacobs maintains that the third explanation is applicable to the Blackstone Rangers and many other large gangs in metropolitan areas. The leadership learned how to use the system to provide capital for their illegal activities. Gangs showed increased sophistication in organizing their activities along the lines of organized crime. Individual felonies were replaced by major criminal activity involving drugs, weapons, extortion, prostitution, and gambling. Fist fights were replaced by violent acts involving the use of weapons.

In the 1980s, society became increasingly concerned with violence and prescriptions for crime control. Attention once again focused on crime and delinquency as resulting from failures of social institutions, inadequate deterrence, and insufficient incapacitation. Deterrence research became popular, focusing on police, probation, and corrections activities rather than on gang dynamics. Current emphasis is on preventing youth from joining gangs through community education and involvement, and bringing to a halt the violent activities of gangs through stricter laws, better prosecution, and more severe sanctions.

3. Walter Miller, "American Youth Gangs, Past and Present," in *Current Perspectives on Criminal Behavior,* ed. A. Blumberg (New York: Alfred A. Knopf, 1974), 210–37.
4. James Jacobs, *Stateville: The Penitentiary in Mass Society* (Chicago: University of Chicago Press, 1977), 145.

The Nature of Street Gangs

Generally speaking, street gangs may be identified by the following characteristics:

1) *they are organized groups with recognized leaders who command the less powerful*
2) *they are unified at peace and at war*
3) *they demonstrate unity in obvious, recognizable ways (i.e., wearing of colors, certain types of graffiti)*
4) *they claim a geographic area and economic and/or criminal enterprise (i.e., turf, drugs)*
5) *they engage in activities that are delinquent and/or criminal, or are somehow threatening to the larger society*[5]

Short and Strodtbeck have developed a somewhat similar set of criteria for gang members:

1) *recurrent congregation outside the home*
2) *self-defined inclusion/exclusion criteria*
3) *a territorial basis consisting of customary hanging and ranging areas, including self-defined use and occupancy rights*
4) *a versatile activity repertoire*
5) *organizational differentiation, e.g., by authority, roles, prestige, friendship, etc.*[6]

Delinquent and Criminal Gang Activities

Antisocial and criminal conduct by members of juvenile gangs is not a new phenomenon. Early immigrant groups arriving in this country frequently found themselves located in the worst slums of urban areas and gangs soon emerged. Among the earliest juvenile gangs were those of Irish background, followed later by Italian and Jewish gangs, and eventually gangs of virtually all ethnic and racial backgrounds. Typically, members of these gangs left gang activities behind as they grew older, married, found employment, and raised families. Some, however, gravitated to adult gangs and into organized criminal activities. The path from juvenile gang membership to adult crime seems to have broadened in recent years, so while it is true that some street gangs are still little

5. Illinois Department of Corrections Training Manual, *Gang Activity* (Springfield, IL: July 1985).

6. James Short, Jr., and Fred Strodbeck, *Group Process and Gang Delinquency* (Chicago: University of Chicago Press, 1965).

more than collections of neighborhood youth with penchants for macho posturing, many are emerging as drug-terrorism gangs that terrify residents of inner-city neighborhoods.

Street gangs violate civilized rules of behavior, engaging in murder, rape, robbery, intimidation, extortion, burglary, prostitution, drug trafficking, and, more recently, in a phenomenon known as "wilding," in which gang members attack individuals at random, committing any of the above mentioned offenses. In recent years the activities of gangs have become increasingly serious, more sophisticated, and more violent, and are more likely to involve the use of weapons. Gangs have become so problematic in California, for example, that the legislature there has recently passed a law making it a felony to belong to a gang known to engage in criminal activities. While the constitutionality of this law has yet to be established, its mere existence indicates how serious the gang problem is perceived to be. *Newsweek* magazine (1988) describes the drug gangs found in urban ghettos and barrios as consisting of young men "whose poverty and deprivation have immunized them to both hope and fear. The result is a casual acceptance of—and sometimes enthusiasm for—torture and murder, 'drive-by shootings' and public mayhem. 'If they don't kill you, they'll kill your mother.' The days when rival gangs fought each other over 'turf' and 'colors' are fading fast. Today, gang conflicts are more of the form of urban-guerilla warfare over drug trafficking. Gang turf is now drug sales territory. Informers, welchers, and competitors are ruthlessly punished or assassinated. Street warfare and the bloody rampage of gang violence is the norm in many inner cities."[7]

Gang members commit a disproportionate share of crime for their numbers. Statistical data indicate that although gang membership in a given jurisdiction may not be high, and gang members constitute a small percentage of all criminals, they typically commit more offenses than their nongang-member criminal counterparts. For example, a 1983 study in San Diego County, California, showed that although gang members accounted for only one tenth of one percent of the criminal population, they accounted for 15 percent of the homicides in the county.[8] In spite of law enforcement efforts, an estimated one out of every eight murders committed in Chicago is gang related, with the average age of victims

7. "The Drug Gangs," *Newsweek,* 28 March 1988, pp. 20–29.
8. Keith Burt, "Prosecution of Street Gangs," presentation at National College of District Attorneys (1987).

being eighteen.[9] In 1984, there were 97 gang-related homicides of young people between the ages of eleven and twenty in Chicago. There were 75 in 1983; 53 in 1982.[10]

Gang violence is increasing in intensity and spreading throughout the country. In large metropolitan areas such as Chicago, New York, Miami, and Los Angeles, gang-related homicides number in the hundreds annually. Many of these homicides result from gang wars and retaliations, and often the victims are innocent bystanders or those unable to defend themselves. The macho image of gang members confronting each other in open warfare is largely a creation of the media. More often, gang killings occur on the streets, in the dark, as a result of gang members in a speeding vehicle firing shots at their intended victim(s).

Major gangs have made narcotics trafficking an important source of income, and activities in this area have become even more lucrative with the advent of a street market for cocaine and crack. We might speculate that some of the increase in gang violence is a result of competition over turf ownership related to the sales of these products. Gangs involved in profit-oriented schemes frequently resort to violence to protect their illicit businesses. With this shift to more business-oriented activities, some gangs have gone underground in the sense that members no longer openly display colors or graffiti, sometimes leading to the mistaken assumption that gang activity in a particular area has ceased. On other occasions, even when officials know gangs are behind a good deal of the illegal activity occurring in their jurisdictions, for political reasons they deny the importance of gangs. Political officials, including some police chiefs, would prefer to not make themselves look bad by admitting that gang activity in their areas is uncontrollable.

An illustration of the emerging drug-gang problem can be seen in south-central Los Angeles where the Bloods and Crips reign. These gangs consist of confederations of neighborhood gangs, each with a relatively small number of members. The Bloods (whose color is red) and the Crips (whose color is blue) consist of "rollers" or "gang bangers" who are in their twenties and thirties, gang veterans who have made it big in the drug trade. These veterans supervise and control the activities of younger members who are involved in drug trafficking and operating and supplying crack houses, activities that bring in millions of dollars a week.

9. Richard M. Daley, Gang Prosecution Unit, Cook County State's Attorney's Office, Chicago (1985).

10. David Williams, "Gang Crime Outline," Division of Criminal Investigation, State of Illinois (1985).

Recently the drug trafficking of the Bloods and Crips has spread out of Los Angeles and into other cities, including Portland, Denver, Minneapolis, Des Moines, and even Anchorage. In response, the FBI and DEA (Drug Enforcement Administration) have initiated a joint project to deal with the expanding drug trafficking in twenty cities.[11] It also must be noted that gang-related activities have been increasingly common in smaller metropolitan areas (cities with populations of 100,000–250,000).[12]

Other examples of gang activities include the following:

1. Vandalism—graffiti, wanton destruction
2. Harassment and intimidation—to recruit members, to exact revenge on those who report their activities, etc.
3. Armed robbery and burglary—targets include the elderly and, more recently, suburban communities
4. Extortion of:
   a. Students in schools (protection money)
   b. Businesses—protection money to avoid burglaries, fires, vandalism, general destruction
   c. Narcotics dealers—protection money to operate in a specific geographic area and a percentage of the "take"
   d. Neighborhood residents—who pay for the ability to come and go without being harassed, and for the "privilege" of not having their property destroyed

Gang crime continues to grow in smaller suburban and even rural communities, which are frequently perceived as easy marks for theft, burglary, robbery, and shoplifting, among other crimes. In other cases, gangs migrate to these areas to avoid the intense competition of drug trafficking in the cities.

In many communities, gangs have been largely ignored. Part of the reason for the continued expansion of gang activities is the view that such activity is "not our problem." Since many street gangs are ethnically oriented, it is easy to perceive the problem as affecting only certain groups or neighborhoods. Since members are predominantly from the lower social class, gangs are perceived as problematic basically in lower-social-class areas. However, if gang activity is not dealt with quickly, the consequences soon spread to the larger community and the problem may become unmanageable.

11. *Crime Control Digest,* Washington News Service (Washington, D.C., 5 September 1988).
12. Ibid., 28 November 1988.

Gang Membership

Among the generally accepted reasons for gang development and membership are the following:

1. The gang provides peer support during the transition from adolescence to adulthood
2. The gang results from a lower-class cultural reaction to the values or goals of the dominant society
3. The gang provides the opportunity to attain goals adopted by the larger society, but through alternative (illicit) means
4. The gang provides self-esteem, economic opportunities, a sense of belonging, affection, etc., which are missing from the lives of many youth

Further, individual motivations for joining gangs have been categorized as follows:

1. Identity/recognition. Allows the member to achieve a status he/she believes is impossible outside the gang. Many are failures in legitimate endeavors such as academics, athletics, etc.
2. Protection/survival. Many feel it is impossible to survive living in a gang-dominated area without becoming a member.
3. Intimidation. Youth are told and shown (through beatings, etc.) by gang members that membership is essential.
4. Fellowship and brotherhood. The gang offers psychological support to its members and provides the companionship which may be lacking in the home environment. As Jacobs explains, "Time and again gang members explained that, whether on the street or in prison, the gang allows you to feel like a man; it is a family with which you can identify. Many times young members have soberly stated that the organization is something, the only thing, they would die for."[13]

Bloch and Neiderhoffer (1958) believed that gangs were cohesive and organized and therefore satisfied deep-seated needs of adolescents.[14] Whyte (1955) portrayed the gang as a "street-corner family."[15]

---

13. James Jacobs, *Stateville*, 150–53.

14. Herbert Bloch and Arthur Neiderhoffer, *The Gang: A Study in Adolescent Behavior* (New York: Philosophical Library, 1958).

15. William Whyte, *Street Corner Society* (Chicago: University of Chicago Press, 1943).

Due to gang secrecy and the code of silence, it is extremely difficult to determine the number of gangs in a given area. It appears there are nearly one thousand gangs in California, and the state experienced approximately the same number of gang-related homicides in 1980.[16] In Chicago, 110 identified gangs exist with an estimated membership of over ten thousand.[17]

Characteristics

Generally, gang membership can be divided into three categories: leaders, hard-core members, and marginal members. The leaders within gangs usually acquire their positions of power through one of two methods—either by being the "baddest/meanest" member, or by possessing charisma and leadership abilities. In addition, the leaders tend to be older members who have built up seniority. Hard-core members are those whose lives center around the totality of gang activity. They are generally the most violent, streetwise, and knowledgeable in legal matters.

Marginal members drift in and out of gang activity. They are attached to the gang but have not developed a real commitment to the gang life-style. They associate with gang members for status and recognition and tend to gravitate toward hard-core membership if no intervention from outside sources occurs.

Age

Gang members generally range from eight to fifty-five years of age. For many younger youth, gang members serve as role models whose behavior is to be emulated as soon as possible in order to become full-fledged "gang-bangers." Consequently, these children are often exploited by members of gangs, manipulated into commiting offenses such as theft and burglary in order to benefit the gang as part of their initiation or rite of passage. As gang crimes become more profitable, as in the case of drug franchises, the membership tends to be older. As members become older, they move away from street crime and move up in stature within

16. James Davis, *Street Gangs: Youth, Biker, and Prison Groups* (Dubuque, Iowa: Kendall-Hunt, 1982), 2.
17. David Williams. See note 10.

the gang hierarchy. The younger members maintain the turf-oriented activities and the adults move into more organized and sophisticated activities.

Gender

Street gangs are predominantly male. Although there are female gang members, most often their roles are peripheral, and this is not likely to change rapidly due to the chauvinistic nature of most gangs.

Monikers

Many gang members have monikers or nicknames that are different from their given names. Generally these monikers reflect physical or personality characteristics or connote something bold or daring. Often gang members do not know the true identities of other members, making detection and apprehension difficult for law enforcement officials.

Graffiti

Street-gang graffiti is unique in its significance and symbolism. Graffiti serves several functions: it is used to delineate gang turf as well as turf in dispute, it proclaims who the top-ranking gang members are, it issues challenges, and it proclaims the gang's philosophy. Some examples of gang graffiti and symbols are presented in figure 12.1.

Placing graffiti in the area of a rival gang is considered an insult and a challenge to the rival gang, which inevitably responds. The response may be anything from crossing out the rival graffiti to drive-by shootings or other forms of violence. The correct interpretation of graffiti by the police can offer valuable information as to gang activities.

Jargon

Gang members frequently use jargon to exchange information. In fact, understanding gang jargon may be critical to obtaining convictions for gang-related crimes. In 1986, Jeff Fort and several high-ranking members of the Chicago-based El Rukn were charged with plotting acts of terrorism in the United States for a sum of $2.5 million from Libya. The FBI recorded thirty-five hundred hours of telephone conversations, most of which were in code, in this case. A former high-ranking member of El Rukn, who turned prosecution witness, translated portions of the confusing conversations for jurors. Fort was convicted and sentenced to an extended prison term.

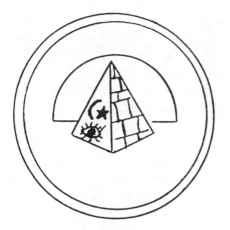

El Rukn

Conservative Vice Lord Nation

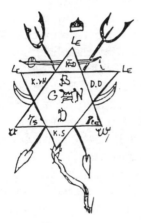

Disciples

Latin Kings

Simon City Royals

Figure 12.1 Gang Symbols/Graffiti

Response of Justice Network to Gangs

The problems presented by juvenile gangs are not easily addressed. In large part, the origins of these problems are inherent in the social and economic conditions of inner-city neighborhoods across the United States, and the issue is complicated by the continued existence of racial and ethnic discrimination in the educational and social arenas. These conditions are largely beyond the control of justice officials, whose efforts are greatly hampered as a result. Since we appear unwilling to confront the basic socioeconomic factors underlying gang involvement, our options are limited largely to responding to the actions of gang members after they have occurred. In general, the response in these terms has been to propose, and often pass, legislation creating more severe penalties for the offenses typically involved; specifically, drug-related and weapons-related offenses. Recognizing the fact that gangs are now more mobile and that splinter gangs exist in numerous communities, law enforcement officials have attempted to respond by establishing cooperative task forces of combined federal, state, and local authorities who share information and other resources in order to combat gang-related activities. At the federal level, President Bush has called for a war on drug trafficking and has appointed a "drug czar" to oversee efforts in this area. Prosecutors at the federal and state levels have become involved in extremely complex, expensive cases in order to incarcerate known gang leaders and to send a message to gangs that their behavior is not to be tolerated. Gang-crimes units and specialists have emerged in most large urban and some medium-sized city police departments. School liaison programs, previously discussed, have been implemented in the hope of reducing gang influence in the schools. Parent groups have mobilizied to combat the influence of gangs on children, and media attention has focused on the consequences of ignoring gang-related crimes. In short, there is now considerable effort directed toward controlling gang activities. Whether such effort is properly organized, coordinated, and directed, and whether the effort will have the desired consequences, remain empirical questions.

Implications for Practitioners

Practitioners are confronted by a multitude of problems relating to gangs. Preventing youth from becoming involved in gang activities, particularly in inner-city neighborhoods, is extremely difficult if not impossible. Youth who don't join gangs voluntarily risk their lives, as well as the lives of their family members. Thus early identification of new recruits and comprehensive knowledge concerning the membership and actions of existing gangs are essential. Information of this type is necessary if practitioners are to intervene early in the careers of young gang members. But often such intervention does not insure that gang influence will be reduced, since the youth in question is most likely to be returned to the neighborhood in which the gang operates. Incarceration of adult gang leaders may have some impact, but evidence indicates that these leaders often continue to control gang activities while they are in prison, and frequently control gangs within the prisons themselves.

Perhaps the best available strategy is to identify the signs of gang activities as early as possible and prosecute gang members to the full extent of the law in order to send gang leaders the message that their actions will not be tolerated by a given community. Such action by the justice network may convince gang leaders looking to expand their spheres of influence to move elsewhere. Where gangs are already clearly established, as in most metropolitan areas, a massive, coordinated effort, addressing socioeconomic conditions as well as criminal behavior, will be required if gang behavior is to be brought under some degree of control. Some such efforts are now being made and careful evaluation of their impact is crucial.

Summary

Gang activities have a long history in the United States, but attention has been redirected recently toward gangs as a result of their involvement with drug trafficking and gun-running, which are multi-million dollar enterprises. The complexion of gangs has changed somewhat over the years, and referring to gangs as "juvenile" gangs is not totally appropriate at this time due to the strong influence of adult gang leaders who supervise, organize, and control gang activities.

Juveniles continue to join gangs in order to attain status and prestige lacking in the domestic and educational arenas. They also continue to fight territorial wars, wear colors, extort protection money, and exclude from membership those from different racial/ethnic groups. They exist in all urban areas, in some cases have taken over prisons, and are spreading out to medium-sized and even smaller cities.

Gang involvement in violent activities, sometimes random, sometimes carefully planned, has received a good deal of attention from both media and justice officials. The latter are organizing to better combat gang activities, but their success has yet to be carefully evaluated. Similarly, "get-tough" legislation has been passed at all levels, but the impact of such legislative action remains in question.

Discussion Questions

1. Describe the conditions under which gang membership is most likely to be attractive to youth.
2. How are drug trafficking, gang membership, and violence interrelated?
3. What kinds of responses do we as a society need to make in order to help control gangs?
4. Why is the term "juvenile gangs" no longer totally appropriate?
5. Who are the leaders of street gangs, how do they recruit new members, and why is imprisonment ineffective in curbing their influence in many instances?

Selected Readings

Campbell, A. *The Girls in the Gang.* New York: Basil Blackwell, 1984.

Cornell, D. G., E. P. Benedek, and D. M. Benedek. "Juvenile Homicide: Prior Adjustment and a Proposed Typology." *American Journal of Orthopsychiatry* 57 (1987): 383–93.

Curry, G. D., and I. A. Spergel. "Gang Homicide, Delinquency, and Community." *Criminology* 26, no. 3 (August 1988): 381–405.

Fagan, J., E. Piper, and M. Moore. "Violent Delinquents and Urban Youth." *Criminology* 24, no. 3 (August 1986): 439–66.

Klein, M. W., M. A. Gordon, and C. L. Maxson. "The Import of Police Investigations of Police-Reported Rates of Gang and Nongang Homicides." *Criminology* 24, no. 3 (August 1986): 489–512.

Miller, W. B. *Violence by Youth Gangs and Youth Groups as a Crime Problem in Major American Cities.* Washington, D.C.: U.S. Government Printing Office, 1975.

Yablonsky, L. *The Violent Gang.* Baltimore: Penguin Books, 1970.

13 Summary and Conclusions

Throughout this book we have discussed in varying detail the philosophies of the juvenile justice system, the procedural requirements of that system, and some of the major problems with the system as it now operates. We have seen that the juvenile justice system is subject to numerous stresses and strains from within and without and that change, trial and error, and good intentions with sometimes less than desirable results characterize the system. We have arrived at a number of conclusions, some of which are supported by empirical evidence, others of which are more or less speculative based upon our observations and those of concerned practitioners and citizens.

The initial underlying assumption of the juvenile justice system is that juveniles with problems should be treated and/or educated rather than punished. Adult and juvenile justice systems in the United States were separated because of the belief that courts should act in the best interests of juveniles, and because of the belief that association with adult offenders would increase the possibility that juveniles would become involved in criminal careers. By developing a separate terminology and a separate, relatively confidential set of procedures for the juvenile justice system, early reformers hoped to minimize stigmatization of juvenile offenders. As concern for the rights of juveniles increased, two different approaches to dealing with juveniles emerged. The therapeutic or casework approach favored informal proceedings based upon concern for the juvenile's total personality. The legalistic approach favored seeking the best interests of juveniles, but only within a constitutional framework. The dilemma caused by differences between the two approaches continues to plague us today.

In many instances, we practice the opposite of what we preach. Some actions of practitioners deny the rights of juveniles ("informal adjustments," "unofficial probation," and some "continuances under supervision") and other actions lead to exactly those conditions we wish to prevent (incarceration of juveniles in detention facilities, for example).

We continue to label and stigmatize many juveniles for whom less stigmatizing alternatives should be found. Our inability to accurately determine the best type of treatment for juveniles with different types of problems has led some serious offenders to be released, therefore creating a risk to society, and others to be incarcerated who could benefit from less severe dispositions.

Some question whether the juvenile justice system can survive as a separate entity.

> *After half a century of conquest and occupation the juvenile court has in recent years entered a valley in which it has been caught in a withering cross-fire which may ultimately destroy it. From its left, the canons of the civil libertarians fired the first volleys in the form of Supreme Court decisions imposing due process requirements upon the juvenile court. From the right, the forces of law and order have moved, through legislation, to force fundamental changes in the purposes of the juvenile justice system and the substantive provisions of the juvenile law. The conflict between the principles of civil liberty and social control has long been a part of the criminal justice system. Now, apparently, it is being waged in the context of the juvenile justice system. . . . The juvenile justice system, if it survives at all, may soon become not a separate and philosophically different approach from the criminal justice system, but merely a separate criminal justice system for criminals under the age of eighteen.[1]*

This is in part due to the fear that serious delinquency is increasing at a rapid rate (belied by the facts) and, perhaps, in part due to the fact that some of the more widely accepted theories of delinquency causation and a great deal of practical experience suggest that much of what we now do to and/or for delinquents is the opposite of what needs to be done. In part, this is because there is still no accurate means of determining the actual extent and nature of delinquency, making treatment, prevention, and control difficult to achieve. This, coupled with the fact that the public apparently wants the system to both punish and rehabilitate offenders, ensures that many of the dilemmas currently confronting juvenile justice will continue to exist creating a variety of complications for those formulating juvenile law and implementing policy.[2] Thus, for example, there is currently an emphasis on a more adversarial model of juvenile justice typified by automatic waivers to adult court and the controversy surrounding capital punishment for older

1. John L. Hutzler, "Canon to the Left, Canon to the Right: Can the Juvenile Court Survive?" *Today's Delinquent* 1 (1982): 37–38.

2. Francis T. Cullen, Kathryn M. Golden, and John B. Cullen, "Is Child Saving Dead? Attitudes Toward Juvenile Rehabilitation in Illinois," *Journal of Criminal Justice* II, no. 1 (1983): 1–13.

juveniles. While this transition away from the *parens patriae* foundation of the juvenile justice network has been gradual, it has been clear-cut, enhanced by an atmosphere of public and political opinion focusing on a punitive approach to criminality and delinquency. Control, detention, and incarceration have become more popular due to an actual or perceived increase in the seriousness of juvenile offenses, and treatment/rehabilitation are currently perceived as being too lenient and, perhaps, unlikely to be successful in preventing recidivism. Whether or not these currently favored alternatives are in the best interest of the juveniles involved—or, for that matter, of the community—is an issue less frequently addressed, and a very complicated issue at that.

And so, in many ways, juvenile justice has come full cycle, for these are the very considerations which initially led to the development of a separate, unique juvenile justice network. Almost one hundred years later, we remain uncertain as to the best rehabilitation techniques, the value of probation, and the impact of incarceration in our attempts to protect youth and society simultaneously.

With respect to prevention, we still hang many of our hopes on both specific and general deterrence based upon increasingly severe punishments for increasingly severe offenses. The evidence with respect to the effects of such deterrence is mixed at best and the public is often unwilling to pay for programs with no directly measurable results.[3] In fact, some have suggested that both traditional prevention methods and attempts to frighten youth out of delinquency be abandoned.[4]

We have discussed juvenile justice as a system. By the term system we mean a group of agencies cooperatively involved in the pursuit of common goals. Juvenile justice philosophy provides for such a system, but in practice the police, courts, and corrections often act independently. There is often little communication of a positive nature among these agencies, and between these agencies and the functionally related agencies outside the official system. "Territorial jealousies" often impede efforts to work cooperatively in the best interests of juveniles. Practitioners working in the juvenile justice system are frequently still regarded as somehow less professional than their colleagues working with adult offenders. Uniformity of juvenile law has yet to be achieved. Many citizens still adopt an "out-of-sight, out-of-mind" attitude toward youth with problems, and both citizens and practitioners are often frustrated

3. H. Frances Pestello, "Deterrence: A Reconceptualization," *Crime and Delinquency* 30, no. 4 (October 1984): 593–609.

4. Lundman, *Prevention and Control of Juvenile Delinquency*, 221–35.

by our supposed failure to curb delinquency in spite of the millions of dollars invested in the enterprise. Unfortunately, the Juvenile Justice Act diverts most federal funding to objectives that have little to do with criminal aspects of delinquency and, since 1974, very little federal money has been directed toward controlling chronic, serious delinquents.[5]

Still, there are some rays of hope. First, it is apparent that serious delinquency (at least as reported) is in fact declining and that a very small number of youth account for a very large proportion of serious juvenile crime.[6] Our frustration here appears to be primarily a result of the fact that we cannot pinpoint exactly why this is the case. Second, status and other minor offenders are generally diverted from juvenile court in most states, thus freeing the courts to deal with more serious delinquents and perhaps leading to better treatment for those youth who are diverted. Third, public attention has been focused on youth who are victimized by adults and we have begun to realize the extent of such victimizations and to initiate programs to help youth avoid and/or deal with such incidents. As a corollary, some judges appear to be more willing than in the past to remove children from dangerous homes. Fourth, empirical research has shown that some treatment and prevention programs simply don't work, while others (such as community based programs which offer a wide range of services delivered rapidly) appear to have some promise. Fifth, although uniformity in juvenile law still eludes us, a recent twenty volume series on Juvenile Justice Standards is being used as a model by several states in establishing and revising laws and procedures in their juvenile justice systems.[7] Finally, practitioners working in juvenile justice appear to be taking more pride in their work as they create their own professional organizations, develop training programs, and exchange ideas.

We must not, however, rest on our laurels. There is room for a great deal of improvement in juvenile justice. To some extent, such improvement depends upon changes in societal conditions, such as poverty, unemployment, and discrimination. Changes in the family and in the educational network which improve our ability to meet the needs of youth

5. National Advisory Committee for Juvenile Justice and Delinquency Prevention, *Serious Juvenile Crime: A Redirected Federal Effort* (Washington, D.C.: U.S. Government Printing Office, 1984).

6. Ibid.

7. Joint Commission on Juvenile Justice Standards, Institute of Judicial Administration and the American Bar Association, *Juvenile Justice Standards,* 20 volumes (New York: Ballinger, 1980).

are also crucial. Changes in the rules which govern youth may be appropriate in some instances. Making better use of the information made available to us by researchers and practitioners is yet another way to improve the system. Last, taking a rational, calculated approach to delinquency will pay better dividends than adhering to policies developed and implemented as a result of fear and misunderstanding.

Selected Readings

Dwyer, D. C., and R. B. McNally. "Juvenile Justice: Reform, Retain, and Reaffirm." *Federal Probation Quarterly* (September 1987): 47–51.

Hellum, Frank. "Juvenile Justice: The Second Revolution." *Crime and Delinquency* (July 1979): 299–312.

National Council on Crime and Delinquency. "Special Issue: Rethinking Juvenile Justice." *Crime and Delinquency* 29, no. 3 (July 1983).

Roberts, A. R. *Juvenile Justice: Policies, Programs, and Services.* Chap. 13. Chicago: Dorsey Press, 1989.

Rubin, H. Ted. "Retain the Juvenile Court?" *Crime and Delinquency* (July 1979): 281–98.

Seib, Lawrence, and W. F. Schmoll. "Using Law-Related Education to Reduce Juvenile Delinquency." *Police Chief* LII, no. 1 (January 1985): 39–41.

A Uniform Juvenile Court Act

The Uniform Juvenile Court Act was drafted by the National Conference of Commissioners on Uniform State Laws and approved and recommended for enactment in all the states at its annual conference meeting in its seventy-seventh year, Philadelphia, Pennsylvania, July 22-August 1, 1968. Approved by the American Bar Association at its meeting at Philadelphia, Pennsylvania, August 7, 1968.

Section 1. *[Interpretation.]* This Act shall be construed to effectuate the following public purposes:

(1) to provide for the care, protection, and wholesome moral, mental, and physical development of children coming within its provisions;

(2) consistent with the protection of the public interest, to remove from children committing delinquent acts the taint of criminality and the consequences of criminal behavior and to substitute therefor a program of treatment, training, and rehabilitation;

(3) to achieve the foregoing purposes in a family environment whenever possible, separating the child from his parents only when necessary for his welfare or in the interest of public safety;

(4) to provide a simple judicial procedure through which this Act is executed and enforced and in which the parties are assured a fair hearing and their constitutional and other legal rights recognized and enforced; and

(5) to provide simple interstate procedures which permit resort to cooperative measures among the juvenile courts of the several states when required to effectuate the purposes of this Act.

Section 2. *[Definitions.]* As used in this Act:

(1) "child" means an individual who is:

(i) under the age of 18 years; or

(ii) under the age of 21 years who committed an act of delinquency before reaching the age of 18 years; [or]

[(iii) under 21 years of age who committed an act of delinquency after becoming 18 years of age and is transferred to the juvenile court by another court having jurisdiction over him;]

(2) "delinquent act" means an act designated a crime under the law, including local [ordinances] [or resolutions] of this state, or of another state, if the act occurred in that state, or under federal law, and the crime does not fall under paragraph (iii) of subsection (4) [and is not a juvenile traffic offense as defined in section 44] [and the crime is not a traffic offense as defined in Traffic Code of the State] other than [designate the more serious offenses which should be included in the jurisdiction of the juvenile court such as drunken driving, negligent homicide, etc.];

(3) "delinquent child" means a child who has committed a delinquent act and is in need of treatment or rehabilitation;

(4) "unruly child" means a child who:
    (i) while subject to compulsory school attendance is habitually and without justification truant from school;
    (ii) is habitually disobedient of the reasonable and lawful commands of his parent, guardian, or other custodian and is ungovernable; or
    (iii) has committed an offense applicable only to a child; and
    (iv) in any of the foregoing is in need of treatment or rehabilitation;

(5) "deprived child" means a child who:
    (i) is without proper parental care or control, subsistence, education as required by law, or other care or control necessary for his physical, mental, or emotional health, or morals, and the deprivation is not due primarily to the lack of financial means of his parents, guardian, or other custodian;
    (ii) has been placed for care or adoption in violation of law; [or]
    (iii) has been abandoned by his parents, guardian, or other custodian; [or]
    [(iv) is without a parent, guardian, or legal custodian;]

(6) "shelter care" means temporary care of a child in physically unrestricted facilities;

(7) "protective supervision" means supervision ordered by the court of children found to be deprived or unruly;

(8) "custodian" means a person, other than a parent or legal guardian, who stands in *loco parentis* to the child or a person to whom legal custody of the child has been given by order of a court;

(9) "juvenile court" means the [here designate] court of this state.

Section 3. *[Jurisdiction.]*

(a) The juvenile court has exclusive original jurisdiction of the following proceedings, which are governed by this Act:

    (1) proceedings in which a child is alleged to be delinquent, unruly, or deprived [or to have committed a juvenile traffic offense as defined in section 44;]

    (2) proceedings for the termination of parental rights except when a part of an adoption proceeding; and

    (3) proceedings arising under section 39 through 42.

(b) The juvenile court also has exclusive original jurisdiction of the following proceedings, which are governed by the laws relating thereto without regard to the other provisions of this Act:

    [(1) proceedings for the adoption of an individual of any age;]

    (2) proceedings to obtain judicial consent to the marriage, employment, or enlistment in the armed services of a child, if consent is required by law;

    (3) proceedings under the Interstate Compact of Juveniles; [and]

    (4) proceedings under the Interstate Compact on the Placement of Children; [and]

    [(5) proceedings to determine the custody or appoint a guardian of the person of a child.]

[**Section 4.** *[Concurrent Jurisdiction.]* The juvenile court has concurrent jurisdiction with [- - - - -] court of proceedings to treat or commit a mentally retarded or mentally ill child.]

Section 5. *[Probation Services.]*

[(a) [In [counties] of over - - - - - - - - - - - - - population] the [- - - - - - -] court may appoint one or more probation officers who shall serve [at the pleasure of the court] [and are subject to removal under the civil service laws governing the county]. They have the powers and duties stated in section 6. Their salaries shall be fixed by the court with the approval of the [governing board of the county]. If more than one probation officer is appointed, one may be designated by the court as the chief probation officer or director of court services, who shall be responsible for the administration of the probation services under the direction of the court.]

[(b) In all other cases the [Department of Corrections] [state [county] child welfare department] [or other appropriate state agency] shall provide suitable probation services to the juvenile court of each [county.] The cost thereof shall be paid out of the general revenue funds of the [state] [county]. The probation officer or other qualified person assigned to the court by the [Department of Corrections] [state [county] child welfare department] [or other appropriate state agency] has the powers and duties stated in section 6.]

Section 6. *[Powers and Duties of Probation Officers.]*

(a) For the purpose of carrying out the objectives and purposes of this Act and subject to the limitations of this Act or imposed by the Court, a probation officer shall:

(1) make investigations, reports, and recommendations to the juvenile court;

(2) receive and examine complaints and charges of delinquency, unruly conduct or deprivation of a child for the purpose of considering the commencement of proceedings under this Act;

(3) supervise and assist a child placed on probation or in his protective supervision or care by order of the court or other authority of law;

(4) make appropriate referrals to other private or public agencies of the community if their assistance appears to be needed or desirable;

(5) take into custody and detain a child who is under his supervision or care as a delinquent, unruly or deprived child if the probation officer has reasonable cause to believe that the child's health or safety is in imminent danger, or that he may abscond or be removed from the jurisdiction of the court, or when ordered by the court pur-

suant to this Act. Except as provided by this Act a probation officer does not have the powers of a law enforcement
officer. He may not conduct accusatory proceedings under
this Act against a child who is or may be under his care or
supervision; and

(6) perform all other functions designated by this Act or by
order of the court pursuant thereto.

(b) Any of the foregoing functions may be performed in another
state if authorized by the court of this state and permitted by the
laws of the other state.

[Section 7. *[Referees.]*

(a) The judge may appoint one or more persons to serve at the
pleasure of the judge as referees on a full or part-time basis. A
referee shall be a member of the bar [and shall qualify under the
civil service regulations of the County.] His compensation shall
be fixed by the judge [with the approval of the [governing board
of the County] and paid out of [- - - - - - - -]].

(b) The judge may direct that hearings in any case or class of cases
be conducted in the first instance by the referee in the manner
provided by this Act. Before commencing the hearing the
referee shall inform the parties who have appeared that they are
entitled to have the matter heard by the judge. If a party objects
the hearing shall be conducted by the judge.

(c) Upon the conclusion of a hearing before a referee he shall
transmit written findings and recommendations for disposition
to the judge. Prompt written notice and copies of the findings
and recommendations shall be given to the parties to the proceeding. The written notice also shall inform them of the right
to a rehearing before the judge.

(d) A rehearing may be ordered by the judge at any time and shall
be ordered if a party files a written request therefor within 3
days after receiving the notice required in subsection (c).

(e) Unless a rehearing is ordered the findings and recommendations
become the findings and order of the court when confirmed in
writing by the judge.]

Section 8. *[Commencement of Proceedings.]* A proceeding under
this Act may be commenced:

(1) by transfer of a case from another court as provided in
section 9;

[(2) as provided in section 44 in a proceeding charging the violation of a traffic offense;] or

(3) by the court accepting jurisdiction as provided in section 40 or accepting supervision of a child as provided in section 42; or

(4) in other cases by the filing of a petition as provided in this Act. The petition and all other documents in the proceeding shall be entitled "In the interest of - - - - - - - - -, a [child] [minor] under [18] [21] years of age."

Section 9. *[Transfer from Other Courts.]* If it appears to the court in a criminal proceeding that the defendant [is a child] [was under the age of 18 years at the time the offense charged was alleged to have been committed], the court shall forthwith transfer the case to the juvenile court together with a copy of the accusatory pleading and other papers, documents, and transcripts of testimony relating to the case. It shall order that the defendant be taken forthwith to the juvenile court or to a place of detention designated by the juvenile court, or release him to the custody of his parent, guardian, custodian, or other person legally responsible for him, to be brought before the juvenile court at a time designated by that court. The accusatory pleading may serve in lieu of a petition in the juvenile court unless that court directs the filing of a petition.

Section 10. *[Informal Adjustment.]*

(a) Before a petition is filed, the probation officer or other officer of the court designated by it, subject to its direction, may give counsel and advice to the parties with a view to an informal adjustment if it appears:

(1) the admitted facts bring the case within the jurisdiction of the court;

(2) counsel and advice without an adjudication would be in the best interest of the public and the child; and

(3) the child and his parents, guardian or other custodian consent thereto with knowledge that consent is not obligatory.

(b) The giving of counsel and advice cannot extend beyond 3 months from the day commenced unless extended by the court for an additional period not to exceed 3 months and does not authorize the detention of the child if not otherwise permitted by this Act.

(c) An incriminating statement made by a participant to the person
     giving counsel or advice and in the discussions or conferences
     incident thereto shall not be used against the declarant over
     objection in any hearing except in a hearing on disposition in a
     juvenile court proceeding or in a criminal proceeding against
     him after conviction for the purpose of a pre-sentence investiga-
     tion.

Section 11. *[Venue.]* A proceeding under this act may be commenced
in the [county] in which the child resides. If delinquent or unruly
conduct is alleged, the proceeding may be commenced in the
[county] in which the acts constituting the alleged delinquent or
unruly conduct occurred. If deprivation is alleged, the proceeding
may be brought in the [county] in which the child is present when it is
commenced.

Section 12. *[Transfer to Another Juvenile Court Within the State.]*
(a) If the child resides in a [county] of the state and the proceeding
     is commenced in a court of another [county], the court, on
     motion of a party or on its own motion made prior to final
     disposition, may transfer the proceeding to the county of the
     child's residence for further action. Like transfer may be made
     if the residence of the child changes pending the proceeding.
     The proceeding shall be transferred if the child has been
     adjudicated delinquent or unruly and other proceedings involv
     ing the child arc pending in the juvenile court of the [county] of
     his residence.
(b) Certified copies of all legal and social documents and records
     pertaining to the case on file with the clerk of the court shall
     accompany the transfer.

Section 13. *[Taking into Custody.]*
(a) A child may be taken into custody:
     (1) pursuant to an order of the court under this Act;
     (2) pursuant to the laws of arrest;
     (3) by a law enforcement officer [or duly authorized officer of
          the court] if there are reasonable grounds to believe that the
          child is suffering from illness or injury or is in immediate
          danger from his surroundings, and that his removal is
          necessary; or

(4) by a law enforcement officer [or duly authorized officer of the court] if there are reasonable grounds to believe that the child has run away from his parents, guardian, or other custodian.

(b) The taking of a child into custody is not an arrest, except for the purpose of determining its validity under the constitution of this State or of the United States.

Section 14. *[Detention of Child.]* A child taken into custody shall not be detained or placed in shelter care prior to the hearing on the petition unless his detention or care is required to protect the person or property of others or of the child because the child may abscond or be removed from the jurisdiction of the court or because he has no parent, guardian, or custodian or other person able to provide supervision and care for him and return him to the court when required, or an order for his detention or shelter care has been made by the court pursuant to this Act.

Section 15. *[Release or Delivery to Court.]*

(a) A person taking a child into custody, with all reasonable speed and without first taking the child elsewhere, shall:

(1) release the child to his parents, guardian, or other custodian upon their promise to bring the child before the court when requested by the court, unless his detention or shelter care is warranted or required under section 14; or

(2) bring the child before the court or deliver him to a detention or shelter care facility designated by the court or to a medical facility if the child is believed to suffer from a serious physical condition or illness which requires prompt treatment. He shall promptly give written notice thereof, together with a statement of the reason for taking the child into custody, to a parent, guardian, or other custodian and to the court. Any temporary detention or questioning of the child necessary to comply with this subsection shall conform to the procedures and conditions prescribed by this Act and rules of court.

(b) If a parent, guardian, or other custodian, when requested, fails to bring the child before the court as provided in subsection (a) the court may issue its warrant directing that the child be taken into custody and brought before the court.

Section 16. *[Place of Detention.]*
(a) A child alleged to be delinquent may be detained only in:
  (1) a licensed foster home or a home approved by the court;
  (2) a facility operated by a licensed child welfare agency;
  (3) a detention home or center for delinquent children which is under the direction or supervision of the court or other public authority or of a private agency approved by the court; or
  (4) any other suitable place or facility, designated or operated by the court. The child may be detained in a jail or other facility for the detention of adults only if the facility in paragraph (3) is not available, the detention is in a room separate and removed from those for adults, it appears to the satisfaction of the court that public safety and protection reasonably require detention, and it so orders.
(b) The official in charge of a jail or other facility for the detention of adult offenders or persons charged with crime shall inform the court immediately if a person who is or appears to be under the age of 18 years is received at the facility and shall bring him before the court upon request or deliver him to a detention or shelter care facility designated by the court.
(c) If a case is transferred to another court for criminal prosecution the child may be transferred to the appropriate officer or detention facility in accordance with the law governing the detention of persons charged with crime.
(d) A child alleged to be deprived or unruly may be detained or placed in shelter care only in the facilities stated in paragraphs (1), (2), and (4) of subsection (a) and shall not be detained in a jail or other facility intended or used for the detention of adults charged with criminal offenses or of children alleged to be delinquent.

Section 17. *[Release from Detention or Shelter Care—Hearing— Conditions of Release.]*
(a) If a child is brought before the court or delivered to a detention or shelter care facility designated by the court the intake or other authorized officer of the court shall immediately make an investigation and release the child unless it appears that his

detention or shelter care is warranted or required under section 14.

(b) If he is not so released, a petition under section 21 shall be promptly made and presented to the court.

An informal detention hearing shall be held promptly and not later than 72 hours after he is placed in detention to determine whether his detention or shelter care is required under section 14. Reasonable notice thereof, either oral or written, stating the time, place, and purpose of the detention hearing shall be given to the child and if they can be found, to his parents, guardian, or other custodian. Prior to the commencement of the hearing, the court shall inform the parties of their right to counsel and to appointed counsel if they are needy persons, and of the child's right to remain silent with respect to any allegations of delinquency or unruly conduct.

(c) If the child is not so released and a parent, guardian, or custodian has not been notified of the hearing, did not appear or waive appearance at the hearing, and files his affidavit showing these facts, the court shall rehear the matter without unnecessary delay and order his release unless it appears from the hearing that the child's detention or shelter care is required under section 14.

[**Section 18.** *[Subpoena.]* Upon application of a party the court or the clerk of the court shall issue, or the court on its own motion may issue, subpoenas requiring attendance and testimony of witnesses and production of papers at any hearing under this Act.]

Section 19. *[Petition—Preliminary Determination.]* A petition under this Act shall not be filed unless the [probation officer,] the court, or other person authorized by the court has determined and endorsed upon the petition that the filing of the petition is in the best interest of the public and the child.

Section 20. *[Petition—Who May Make.]* Subject to section 19 the petition may be made by any person, including a law enforcement officer, who has knowledge of the facts alleged or is informed and believes that they are true.

Section 21. *[Contents of Petition.]* The petition shall be verified and may be on information and belief. It shall set forth plainly:

    (1) the facts which bring the child within the jurisdiction of the court, with a statement that it is in the best interest of the child and the public that the proceeding be brought and, if delinquency or unruly conduct is alleged, that the child is in need of treatment or rehabilitation;

    (2) the name, age, and residence address, if any, of the child on whose behalf the petition is brought;

    (3) the names and residence addresses, if known to petitioner, of the parents, guardian, or custodian of the child and of the child's spouse, if any. If none of his parents, guardian, or custodian resides or can be found within the state, or if their respective places of residence address are unknown, the name of any known adult relative residing within the [county,] or, if there be none, the known adult relative residing nearest to the location of the court; and

    (4) if the child is in custody and, if so, the place of his detention and the time he was taken into custody.

Section 22. *[Summons.]*

(a) After the petition has been filed the court shall fix a time for hearing thereon, which, if the child is in detention, shall not be later than 10 days after the filing of the petition. The court shall direct the issuance of a summons to the parents, guardian, or other custodian, a guardian ad litem, and any other persons as appear to the court to be proper or necessary parties to the proceeding, requiring them to appear before the court at the time fixed to answer the allegations of the petition. The summons shall also be directed to the child if he is 14 or more years of age or is alleged to be a delinquent or unruly child. A copy of the petition shall accompany the summons unless the summons is served by publication in which case the published summons shall indicate the general nature of the allegations and where a copy of the petition can be obtained.

(b) The court may endorse upon the summons an order directing the parents, guardian or other custodian of the child to appear personally at the hearing and directing the person having the physical custody or control of the child to bring the child to the hearing.

(c) If it appears from affidavit filed or from sworn testimony before the court that the conduct, condition, or surroundings of the child are endangering his health or welfare or those of others, or that he may abscond or be removed from the jurisdiction of the court or will not be brought before the court, notwithstanding the service of the summons, the court may endorse upon the summons an order that a law enforcement officer shall serve the summons and take the child into immediate custody and bring him forthwith before the court.

(d) The summons shall state that a party is entitled to counsel in the proceedings and that the court will appoint counsel if the party is unable without undue financial hardship to employ counsel.

(e) A party, other than the child, may waive service of summons by written stipulation or by voluntary appearance at the hearing. If the child is present at the hearing, his counsel, with the consent of the parent, guardian or other custodian, or guardian ad litem, may waive service of summons in his behalf.

Section 23. *[Service of Summons.]*

(a) If a party to be served with a summons is within this State and can be found, the summons shall be served upon him personally at least 24 hours before the hearing. If he is within the State and cannot be found, but his address is known or can with reasonable deligence be ascertained, the summons may be served upon him by mailing a copy by registered or certified mail at least 5 days before the hearing. If he is without this State but he can be found or his address is known, or his whereabouts or address can with reasonable diligence be ascertained, service of the summons may be made either by delivering a copy to him personally or mailing a copy to him by registered or certified mail at least 5 days before the hearing.

(b) If after reasonable effort he cannot be found or his post office address ascertained, whether he is within or without this State, the court may order service of the summons upon him by publication in accordance with [Rule] [Section] - - - - - - - - [the general service by publication statutes]. The hearing shall not be earlier than 5 days after the date of the last publication.

(c) Service of the summons may be made by any suitable person under the direction of the court.

(d) The court may authorize the payment from [county funds] of the costs of service and of necessary travel expenses incurred by persons summoned or otherwise required to appear at the hearing.

Section 24. *[Conduct of Hearings.]*

(a) Hearings under this Act shall be conducted by the court without a jury, in an informal but orderly manner, and separate from other proceedings not included in section 3.

(b) The [prosecuting attorney] upon request of the court shall present the evidence in support of the petition and otherwise conduct the proceedings on behalf of the state.

(c) If requested by a party or ordered by the court the proceedings shall be recorded by stenographic notes or by electronic, mechanical, or other appropriate means. If not so recorded full minutes of the proceedings shall be kept by the court.

(d) Except in hearings to declare a person in contempt of court [and in hearings under section 44], the general public shall be excluded from hearings under this Act. Only the parties, their counsel, witnesses, and other persons accompanying a party for his assistance, and any other persons as the court finds have a proper interest in the proceeding or in the work of the court may be admitted by the court. The court may temporarily exclude the child from the hearing except while allegations of his delinquency or unruly conduct are being heard.

Section 25. *[Service by Publication—Interlocutory Order of Disposition.]*

(a) If service of summons upon a party is made by publication the court may conduct a provisional hearing upon the allegations of the petition and enter an interlocutory order of disposition if:

   (1) the petition alleges delinquency, unruly conduct, or deprivation of the child;

   (2) the summons served upon any party (i) states that prior to the final hearing on the petition designated in the summons a provisional hearing thereon will be held at a specified time and place, (ii) requires the party who is served other than by publication to appear and answer the allegations of the petition at the provisional hearing, (iii) states further that findings of fact and orders of disposition made pur-

suant to the provisional hearing will become final at the final hearing unless the party served by publication appears at the final hearing, and (iv) otherwise conforms to section 22; and

   (3) the child is personally before the court at the provisional hearing.

(b) All provisions of this Act applicable to a hearing on a petition, to orders of disposition, and to other proceedings dependent thereon shall apply under this section, but findings of fact and orders of disposition have only interlocutory effect pending the final hearing on the petition. The rights and duties of the party served by publication are not affected except as provided in subsection (c).

(c) If the party served by publication fails to appear at the final hearing on the petition the findings of fact and interlocutory orders made become final without further evidence and are governed by this Act as if made at the final hearing. If the party appears at the final hearing the findings and orders shall be vacated and disregarded and the hearing shall proceed upon the allegations of the petition without regard to this section.

Section 26. *[Right to Counsel.]*

(a) Except as otherwise provided under this Act a party is entitled to representation by legal counsel at all stages of any proceedings under this Act and if as a needy person he is unable to employ counsel, to have the court provide counsel for him. If a party appears without the counsel the court shall ascertain whether he knows of his right thereto and to be provided with counsel by the court if he is a needy person. The court may continue the proceeding to enable a party to obtain counsel and shall provide counsel for an unrepresented needy person upon his request. Counsel must be provided for a child not represented by his parent, guardian, or custodian. If the interests of 2 or more parties conflict, separate counsel shall be provided for each of them.

(b) A needy person is one who at the time of requesting counsel is unable without undue financial hardship to provide for full payment of legal counsel and all other necessary expenses for representation.

Section 27. *[Other Basic Rights.]*

(a) A party is entitled to the opportunity to introduce evidence and otherwise be heard in his own behalf and to cross-examine adverse witnesses.

(b) A child charged with a delinquent act need not be a witness against or otherwise incriminate himself. An extrajudicial statement, if obtained in the course of violation of this Act or which would be constitutionally inadmissible in a criminal proceeding, shall not be used against him. Evidence illegally seized or obtained shall not be received over objection to establish the allegations made against him. A confession validly made by the child out of court is insufficient to support an adjudication of delinquency unless it is corroborated in whole or in part by other evidence.

Section 28. *[Investigation and Report.]*

(a) If the allegations of a petition are admitted by a party or notice of a hearing under section 34 has been given the court, prior to the hearing on need for treatment or rehabilitation and disposition, may direct that a social study and report in writing to the court be made by the [probation officer] of the court, [Commissioner of the Court or other like officer] or other person designated by the court, concerning the child, his family, his environment, and other matters relevant to disposition of the case. If the allegations of the petition are not admitted and notice of a hearing under section 34 has not been given the court shall not direct the making of the study and report until after the court has heard the petition upon notice of hearing given pursuant to this Act and the court has found that the child committed a delinquent act or is an unruly or deprived child.

(b) During the pendency of any proceeding the court may order the child to be examined at a suitable place by a physician or psychologist and may also order medical or surgical treatment of a child who is suffering from a serious physical condition or illness which in the opinion of a [licensed physician] requires prompt treatment, even if the parent, guardian, or other custodian has not been given notice of a hearing, is not available, or without good cause informs the court of his refusal to consent to the treatment.

Section 29. *[Hearing—Findings—Dismissal.]*

(a) After hearing the evidence on the petition the court shall make and file its findings as to whether the child is a deprived child, or if the petition alleges that the child is delinquent or unruly, whether the acts ascribed to the child were committed by him. If the court finds that the child is not a deprived child or that the allegations of delinquency or unruly conduct have not been established it shall dismiss the petition and order the child discharged from any detention or other restriction theretofore ordered in the proceeding.

(b) If the court finds on proof beyond a reasonable doubt that the child committed the acts by reason of which he is alleged to be delinquent or unruly it shall proceed immediately or at a postponed hearing to hear evidence as to whether the child is in need of treatment or rehabilitation and to make and file its findings thereon. In the absence of evidence to the contrary evidence of the commission of acts which constitute a felony is sufficient to sustain a finding that the child is in need of treatment or rehabilitation. If the court finds that the child is not in need of treatment or rehabilitation it shall dismiss the proceeding and discharge the child from any detention or other restriction theretofore ordered.

(c) If the court finds from clear and convincing evidence that the child is deprived or that he is in need of treatment or rehabilitation as a delinquent or unruly child, the court shall proceed immediately or at a postponed hearing to make a proper disposition of the case.

(d) In hearings under subsections (b) and (c) all evidence helpful in determining the questions presented, including oral and written reports, may be received by the court and relied upon to the extent of its probative value even though not otherwise competent in the hearing on the petition. The parties or their counsel shall be afforded an opportunity to examine and controvert written reports so received and to cross-examine individuals making the reports. Sources of confidential information need not be disclosed.

(e) On its motion or that of a party the court may continue the hearings under this section for a reasonable period to receive reports and other evidence bearing on the disposition or the need for treatment or rehabilitation. In this event the court shall make an appropriate order for detention of the child or his release from detention subject to supervision of the court during the period of the continuance. In scheduling investigations and hearings the court shall give priority to proceedings in which a child is in detention or has otherwise been removed from his home before an order of disposition has been made.

Section 30. *[Disposition of Deprived Child.]*

(a) If the child is found to be a deprived child the court may make any of the following orders of disposition best suited to the protection and physical, mental, and moral welfare of the child:

   (1) permit the child to remain with his parents, guardian, or other custodian, subject to conditions and limitations as the court prescribes, including supervision as directed by the court for the protection of the child;

   (2) subject to conditions and limitations as the court prescribes transfer temporary legal custody to any of the following:

      (i) any individual who, after study by the probation officer or other person or agency designated by the court, is found by the court to be qualified to receive and care for the child;

      (ii) an agency or other private organization licensed or otherwise authorized by law to receive and provide care for the child; or

      (iii) the Child Welfare Department of the [county] [state,] [or other public agency authorized by law to receive and provide care for the child;]

      (iv) an individual in another state with or without supervision by an appropriate officer under section 40; or

   (3) without making any of the foregoing orders transfer custody of the child to the juvenile court of another state if authorized by and in accordance with section 39 if the child is or is about to become a resident of that state.

(b) Unless a child found to be deprived is found also to be delinquent he shall not be committed to or confined in an institution or other facility designed or operated for the benefit of delinquent children.

Section 31. *[Disposition of Delinquent Child.]* If the child is found to be a delinquent child the court may make any of the following orders of disposition best suited to his treatment, rehabilitation, and welfare:

(1) any order authorized by section 30 for the disposition of a deprived child;

(2) placing the child on probation under the supervision of the probation officer of the court or the court of another state as provided in section 41, or [the Child Welfare Department operating within the county,] under conditions and limitations the court prescribes;

(3) placing the child in an institution, camp, or other facility for delinquent children operated under the direction of the court [or other local public authority;] or

(4) committing the child to [designate the state department to which commitments of delinquent children are made or, if there is no department, the appropriate state institution for delinquent children].

Section 32. *[Disposition of Unruly Child.]* If the child is found to be unruly the court may make any disposition authorized for a delinquent child except commitment to [the state department or state institution to which commitment of delinquent children may be made]. [If after making the disposition the court finds upon a further hearing that the child is not amenable to treatment or rehabilitation under the disposition made it may make a disposition otherwise authorized by section 31.]

Section 33. *[Order of Adjudication—Non-Criminal.]*

(a) An order of disposition or other adjudication in a proceeding under this Act is not a conviction of crime and does not impose any civil disability ordinarily resulting from a conviction or operate to disqualify the child in any civil service application or appointment. A child shall not be committed or transferred to a penal institution or other facility used primarily for the execution of sentences of persons convicted of a crime.

(b) The disposition of a child and evidence adduced in a hearing in juvenile court may not be used against him in any proceeding in any court other than a juvenile court, whether before or after reaching majority, except in dispositional proceedings after conviction of a felony for the purposes of a pre-sentence investigation and report.

Section 34. *[Transfer to Other Courts.]*
(a) After a petition has been filed alleging delinquency based on conduct which is designated a crime or public offense under the laws, including local ordinances, [or resolutions] of this state, the court before hearing the petition on its merits may transfer the offense for prosecution to the appropriate court having jurisdiction of the offense if:
  (1) the child was 16 or more years of age at the time of the alleged conduct;
  (2) a hearing on whether the transfer should be made is held in conformity with sections 24, 26, and 27;
  (3) notice in writing of the time, place, and purpose of the hearing is given to the child and his parents, guardian, or other custodian at least 3 days before the hearing;
  (4) the court finds that there are reasonable grounds to believe that
      (i) the child committed the delinquent act alleged;
      (ii) the child is not amenable to treatment or rehabilitation as a juvenile through available facilities;
      (iii) the child is not committable to an institution for the mentally retarded or mentally ill; and
      (iv) the interests of the community require that the child be placed under legal restraint or discipline.
(b) The transfer terminates the jurisdiction of the juvenile court over the child with respect to the delinquent acts alleged in the petition.
(c) No child, either before or after reaching 18 years of age, shall be prosecuted for an offense previously committed unless the case has been transferred as provided in this section.
(d) Statements made by the child after being taken into custody and prior to the service of notice under subsection (a) or at the hearing under this section are not admissible against him over objection in the criminal proceedings following the transfer.
(e) If the case is not transferred the judge who conducted the hearing shall not over objection of an interested party preside at

the hearing on the petition. If the case is transferred to a court of which the judge who conducted the hearing is also a judge he likewise is disqualified from presiding in the prosecution.

Section 35. *[Disposition of Mentally Ill or Mentally Retarded Child.]*

(a) If, at a dispositional hearing of a child found to be a delinquent or unruly child or at a hearing to transfer a child to another court under section 34, the evidence indicates that the child may be suffering from mental retardation or mental illness the court before making a disposition shall commit the child for a period not exceeding 60 days to an appropriate institution, agency, or individual for study and report on the child's mental condition.

(b) If it appears from the study and report that the child is committable under the laws of this state as a mentally retarded or mentally ill child the court shall order the child detained and direct that within 10 days after the order is made the appropriate authority initiate proceedings for the child's commitment.

(c) If it does not so appear, or proceedings are not promptly initiated, or the child is found not to be committable, the court shall proceed to the disposition or transfer of the child as otherwise provided by this Act.

Section 36. *[Limitations of Time on Orders of Disposition.]*

(a) An order terminating parental rights is without limit as to duration.

(b) An order of disposition committing a delinquent or unruly child to the [State Department of Corrections or designated institution for delinquent children,] continues in force for 2 years or until the child is sooner discharged by the [department or institution to which the child was committed]. The court which made the order may extend its duration for an additional 2 years, subject to like discharge, if:

  (1) a hearing is held upon motion of the [department or institution to which the child was committed] prior to the expiration of the order;

  (2) reasonable notice of the hearing and an opportunity to be heard is given to the child and the parent, guardian, or other custodian; and

(3) the court finds that the extension is necessary for the treatment or rehabilitation of the child.

(c) Any other order of disposition continues in force for not more than 2 years. The court may sooner terminate its order or extend its duration for further periods. An order of extension may be made if:

    (1) a hearing is held prior to the expiration of the order upon motion of a party or on the court's own motion;

    (2) reasonable notice of the hearing and opportunity to be heard are given to the parties affected;

    (3) the court finds that the extension is necessary to accomplish the purposes of the order extended; and

    (4) the extension does not exceed 2 years from the expiration of prior order.

(d) Except as provided in subsection (b) the court may terminate an order of disposition or extension prior to its expiration, on or without an application of a party, if it appears to the court that the purposes of the order have been accomplished. If a party may be adversely affected by the order of termination the order may be made only after reasonable notice and opportunity to be heard have been given to him.

(e) Except as provided in subsection (a) when the child reaches 21 years of age all orders affecting him then in force terminate and he is discharged from further obligation or control.

Section 37. *[Modification or Vacation of Orders.]*

(a) An order of the court shall be set aside if (1) it appears that it was obtained by fraud or mistake sufficient therefor in a civil action, or (2) the court lacked jurisdiction over a necessary party or of the subject matter, or (3) newly discovered evidence so requires.

(b) Except an order committing a delinquent child to the [State Department of Corrections or an institution for delinquent children,] an order terminating parental rights, or an order of dismissal, an order of the court may also be changed, modified, or vacated on the ground that changed circumstances so require in the best interest of the child. An order granting probation to a child found to be delinquent or unruly may be revoked on the ground that the conditions of probation have not been observed.

(c) Any party to the proceeding, the probation officer or other person having supervision or legal custody of or an interest in the child may petition the court for the relief provided in this section. The petition shall set forth in concise language the grounds upon which the relief is requested.

(d) After the petition is filed the court shall fix a time for hearing and cause notice to be served (as a summons is served under section 23) on the parties to the proceeding or affected by the relief sought. After the hearing, which may be informal, the court shall deny or grant relief as the evidence warrants.

Section 38. *[Rights and Duties of Legal Custodian.]* A custodian to whom legal custody has been given by the court under this Act has the right to the physical custody of the child, the right to determine the nature of the care and treatment of the child, including ordinary medical care and the right and duty to provide for the care, protection, training, and education, and the physical, mental, and moral welfare of the child, subject to the conditions and limitations of the order and to the remaining rights and duties of the child's parents or guardian.

Section 39. *[Disposition of Non-Resident Child.]*

(a) If the court finds that a child who has been adjudged to have committed a delinquent act or to be unruly or deprived is or is about to become a resident of another state which has adopted the Uniform Juvenile Court Act, or a substantially similar Act which includes provisions corresponding to sections 39 and 40, the court may defer hearing on need for treatment or rehabilitation and disposition and request by any appropriate means the juvenile court of the [county] of the child's residence or prospective residence to accept jurisdiction of the child.

(b) If the child becomes a resident of another state while on probation or under protective supervision under order of a juvenile court of this State, the court may request the juvenile court of the [county] of the state in which the child has become a resident to accept jurisdiction of the child and to continue his probation or protective supervision.

(c) Upon receipt and filing of an acceptance the court of this State shall transfer custody of the child to the accepting court and cause him to be delivered to the person designated by that court

to receive his custody. It also shall provide that court with certified copies of the order adjudging the child to be a delinquent,
unruly, or deprived child, of the order of transfer, and if the
child is on probation or under protective supervision under
order of the court, of the order of disposition. It also shall provide that court with a statement of the facts found by the court
of this State and any recommendations and other information it
considers of assistance to the accepting court in making a
disposition of the case or in supervising the child on probation
or otherwise.

(d) Upon compliance with subsection (c) the jurisdiction of the
court of this State over the child is terminated.

Section 40. *[Disposition of Resident Child Received from Another
State.]*

(a) If a juvenile court of another state which has adopted the
Uniform Juvenile Court Act, or a substantially similar Act
which includes provisions corresponding to sections 39 and 40,
requests a juvenile court of this State to accept jurisdiction of a
child found by the requesting court to have committed a delinquent act or to be an unruly or deprived child, and the court of
this State finds, after investigation that the child is, or is about
to become, a resident of the [county] in which the court pre-
sides, it shall promptly and not later than 14 days after receiving
the request issue its acceptance in writing to the requesting court
and direct its probation officer or other person designated by it
to take physical custody of the child from the requesting court
and bring him before the court of this State or make other appropriate provisions for his appearance before the court.

(b) Upon the filing of certified copies of the orders of the
requesting court (1) determining that the child committed a
delinquent act or is an unruly or deprived child, and (2) committing the child to the jurisdiction of the juvenile court of this
State, the court of this State shall immediately fix a time for a
hearing on the need for treatment or rehabilitation and disposition of the child or on the continuance of any probation or protective supervision.

(c) The hearing and notice thereof and all subsequent proceedings
are governed by this Act. The court may make any order of
disposition permitted by the facts and this Act. The orders of

the requesting court are conclusive that the child committed the delinquent act or is an unruly or deprived child and of the facts found by the court in making the orders, subject only to section 37. If the requesting court has made an order placing the child on probation or under protective supervision, a like order shall be entered by the court of this State. The court may modify or vacate the order in accordance with section 37.

Section 41. *[Ordering Out-of-State Supervision.]*

(a) Subject to the provisions of this Act governing dispositions and to the extent that funds of the [county] are available the court may place a child in the custody of a suitable person in another state. On obtaining the written consent of a juvenile court of another state which has adopted the Uniform Juvenile Court Act or a substantially similar Act which includes provisions corresponding to sections 41 and 42 the court of this State may order that the child be placed under the supervision of a probation officer or other appropriate official designated by the accepting court. One certified copy of the order shall be sent to the accepting court and another filed with the clerk of the [Board of County Commissioners] of the [county] of the requesting court of this State.

(b) The reasonable cost of the supervision including the expenses of necessary travel shall be borne by the [county] of the requesting court of this State. Upon receiving a certified statement signed by the judge of the accepting court of the cost incurred by the supervision the court of this State shall certify if it so appears that the sum so stated was reasonably incurred and file it with [the appropriate officials] of the [county] [state] for payment. The [appropriate officials] shall thereupon issue a warrant for the sum stated payable to the [appropriate officials] of the [county] of the accepting court.

Section 42. *[Supervision Under Out-of-State Order.]*

(a) Upon receiving a request of a juvenile court of another state which has adopted the Uniform Juvenile Court Act, or a substantially similar act which includes provisions corresponding to sections 41 and 42 to provide supervision of a child under the jurisdiction of that court, a court of this State may issue its written acceptance to the requesting court and designate its probation or other appropriate officer who is to provide supervision, stating the probable cost per day therefor.

(b)   Upon the receipt and filing of a certified copy of the order of the requesting court placing the child under the supervision of the officer so designated the officer shall arrange for the reception of the child from the requesting court, provide supervision pursuant to the order and this Act, and report thereon from time to time together with any recommendations he may have to the requesting court.

(c)   The court in this state from time to time shall certify to the requesting court the cost of supervision that has been incurred and request payment therefor from the appropriate officials of the [county] of the requesting court to the appropriate officials of the [county] of the accepting court.

(d)   The court of this State at any time may terminate supervision by notifying the requesting court. In that case, or if the supervision is terminated by the requesting court, the probation officer supervising the child shall return the child to a representative of the requesting court authorized to receive him.

Section 43. *[Powers of Out-of-State Probation Officers.]* If a child has been placed on probation or protective supervision by a juvenile court of another state which has adopted the Uniform Juvenile Court Act or a substantially similar act which includes provisions corresponding to this section, and the child is in this State with or without the permission of that court, the probation officer of that court or other person designated by that court to supervise or take custody of the child has all the powers and privileges in this State with respect to the child as given by this Act to like officers or persons of this State including the right of visitation, counseling, control, and direction, taking into custody, and returning to that state.

[Section 44. *[Juvenile Traffic Offenses.]*

(a)   *Definition.* Except as provided in subsection (b), a juvenile traffic offense consists of a violation by a child of:

    (1)   a law or local ordinance [or resolution] governing the operation of a moving motor vehicle upon the streets or highways of this State, or the waterways within or adjoining this State; or

(2) any other motor vehicle traffic law or local ordinance [or resolution] of this State if the child is taken into custody and detained for the violation or is transferred to the juvenile court by the court hearing the charge.

(b) A juvenile traffic offense is not an act of delinquency unless the case is transferred to the delinquency calendar as provided in subsection (g).

(c) *Exceptions.* A juvenile traffic offense does not include a violation of: [Set forth the sections of state statutes violations of which are not to be included as traffic offenses, such as the so-called negligent homicide statute sometimes appearing in traffic codes, driving while intoxicated, driving without, or during suspension of, a driver's license, and the like].

(d) *Procedure.* The [summons] [notice to appear] [or other designation of a ticket] accusing a child of committing a juvenile traffic offense constitutes the commencement of the proceedings in the juvenile court of the [county] in which the alleged violation occurred and serves in place of a summons and petition under this Act. These cases shall be filed and heard separately from other proceedings of the court. If the child is taken into custody on the charge, sections 14 to 17 apply. If the child is, or after commencement of the proceedings becomes, a resident of another [county] of this State, section 12 applies.

(e) *Hearing.* The court shall fix a time for hearing and give reasonable notice thereof to the child, and if their address is known to the parents, guardian, or custodian. If the accusation made in the [summons] [notice to appear] [or other designation of a ticket] is denied an informal hearing shall be held at which the parties have the right to subpoena witnesses, present evidence, cross-examine witnesses, and appear by counsel. The hearing is open to the public.

(f) *Disposition.* If the court finds on the admission of the child or upon the evidence that he committed the offense charged it may make one or more of the following orders:

  (1) reprimand or counsel with the child and his parents;

  (2) [suspend] [recommend to the [appropriate official having the authority] that he suspend] the child's privilege to drive under stated conditions and limitations for a period not to exceed that authorized for a like suspension of an adult's license for a like offense;

    (3) require the child to attend a traffic school conducted by public authority for a reasonable period of time; or

    (4) order the child to remit to the general fund of the [state] [county] [city] [municipality] a sum not exceeding the lesser of $50 or the maximum applicable to an adult for a like offense.

(g) In lieu of the preceding orders, if the evidence indicates the advisability thereof, the court may transfer the case to the delinquency calendar of the court and direct the filing and service of a summons and petition in accordance with this Act. The judge so ordering is disqualified upon objection from acting further in the case prior to an adjudication that the child committed a delinquent act.]

[Section 45. *[Traffic Referee.]*

(a) The court may appoint one or more traffic referees who shall serve at the pleasure of the court. The referee's salary shall be fixed by the court [subject to the approval of the [Board of County Commissioners]].

(b) The court may direct that any case or class of cases arising under section 44 shall be heard in the first instance by a traffic referee who shall conduct the hearing in accordance with section 44. Upon the conclusion of the hearing the traffic referee shall transmit written findings of fact and recommendations for disposition to the judge with a copy thereof to the child and other parties to the proceedings.

(c) Within 3 days after receiving the copy the child may file a request for a rehearing before the judge of the court who shall thereupon rehear the case at a time fixed by him. Otherwise, the judge may confirm the findings and recommendations for disposition which then become the findings and order of disposition of the court.]

[Section 46. *[Juvenile Traffic Offenses—Suspension of Jurisdiction.]*

(a) The [Supreme] court, by order filed in the office of the [   ] of the [county,] may suspend the jurisdiction of the juvenile courts over juvenile traffic offenses or one or more classes effective and offenses committed thereafter shall be tried by the appropriate court in accordance with law without regard to this Act. The child shall not be detained or imprisoned in a jail or other facility for the detention of adults unless the facility conforms to subsection (a) of section 16.

(b) The [Supreme] court at any time may restore the jurisdiction of the juvenile courts over these offenses or any portion thereof by like filing of its order of restoration. Offenses committed thereafter are governed by this Act.]

Section 47. *[Termination of Parental Rights.]*

(a) The court by order may terminate the parental rights of a parent with respect to his child if:

    (1) the parent has abandoned the child;

    (2) the child is a deprived child and the court finds that the conditions and causes of the deprivation are likely to continue or will not be remedied and that by reason thereof the child is suffering or will probably suffer serious physical, mental, moral, or emotional harm; or

    (3) the written consent of the parent acknowledged before the court has been given.

(b) If the court does not make an order of termination of parental rights it may grant an order under section 30 if the court finds from clear and convincing evidence that the child is a deprived child.

Section 48. *[Proceeding for Termination of Parental Rights.]*

(a) The petition shall comply with section 21 and state clearly that an order for termination of parental rights is requested and that the effect thereof will be as stated in the first sentence of section 49.

(b) If the paternity of a child born out of wedlock has been established prior to the filing of the petition, the father shall be served with summons as provided by this Act. He has the right to be heard unless he has relinquished all parental rights with reference to the child. The putative father of the child whose paternity has not been established, upon proof of his paternity of the child, may appear in the proceedings and be heard. He is not entitled to notice of hearing on the petition unless he has custody of the child.

Section 49. *[Effect of Order Terminating Parental Rights.]* An order
terminating the parental rights of a parent terminates all his rights

and obligations with respect to the child and of the child to him arising from the parental relationship. The parent is not thereafter entitled to notice of proceedings for the adoption of the child by another nor has he any right to object to the adoption or otherwise participate in the proceedings.

Section 50. *[Commitment to Agency.]*

(a) If, upon entering an order terminating the parental rights of a parent, there is no parent having parental rights, the court shall commit the child to the custody of the [State County Child Welfare Department] or a licensed child-placing agency, willing to accept custody for the purpose of placing the child for adoption, or in the absence thereof in a foster home or take other suitable measures for the care and welfare of the child. The custodian has authority to consent to the adoption of the child, his marriage, his enlistment in the armed forces of the United States, and surgical and other medical treatment for the child.

(b) If the child is not adopted within 2 years after the date of the order and a general guardian of the child has not been appointed by the [- - - - - - - - -] court, the child shall be returned to the court for entry of further orders for the care, custody, and control of the child.

Section 51. *[Guardian ad litem.]* The court at any stage of a proceeding under this Act, on application of a party or on its own motion, shall appoint a guardian ad litem for a child who is a party to the proceeding if he has no parent, guardian, or custodian appearing on his behalf or their interests conflict with his or in any other case in which the interests of the child require a guardian. A party to the proceeding or his employee or representative shall not be appointed.

Section 52. *[Costs and Expenses for Care of Child.]*

(a) The following expenses shall be a charge upon the funds of the county upon certification thereof by the court:

    (1) the cost of medical and other examinations and treatment of a child ordered by the court;

    (2) the cost of care and support of a child committed by the court to the legal custody of a public agency other than an institution for delinquent children, or to a private agency or individual other than a parent;

(3) reasonable compensation for services and related expenses of counsel appointed by the court for a party;

(4) reasonable compensation for a guardian ad litem;

(5) the expense of service of summons, notices, subpoenas, travel expense of witnesses, transportation of the child, and other like expenses incurred in the proceedings under this Act.

(b) If, after due notice to the parents or other persons legally obligated to care for and support the child, and after affording them an opportunity to be heard, the court finds that they are financially able to pay all or part of the costs and expenses stated in paragraphs (1), (2), (3), and (4) of subsection (a), the court may order them to pay the same and prescribe the manner of payment. Unless otherwise ordered payment shall be made to the clerk of the juvenile court for remittance to the person to whom compensation is due, or if the costs and expenses have been paid by the [county] to the [appropriate officer] of the [county].

Section 53. *[Protective Order.]* On application of a party or on the court's own motion the court may make an order restraining or otherwise controlling the conduct of a person if:

(1) an order of disposition of a delinquent, unruly, or deprived child has been or is about to be made in a proceeding under this Act;

(2) the court finds that the conduct (1) is or may be detrimental or harmful to the child and (2) will tend to defeat the execution of the order of disposition; and

(3) due notice of the application or motion and the grounds therefor and an opportunity to be heard thereon have been given to the person against whom the order is directed.

Section 54. *[Inspection of Court Files and Records.]* [Except in cases arising under section 44] all files and records of the court in a proceeding under this Act are open to inspection only by:

(1) the judge, officers, and professional staff of the court;

(2) the parties to the proceeding and their counsel and representatives;

(3) a public or private agency or institution providing supervision or having custody of the child under order of the court;

(4) a court and its probation and other officials or professional staff and the attorney for the defendant for use in preparing a pre-sentence report in a criminal case in which the defendant is convicted and who prior thereto had been a party to the proceeding in juvenile court;

(5) with leave of court any other person or agency or institution having a legitimate interest in the proceeding or in the work of the court.

Section 55. *[Law Enforcement Records.]* Law enforcement records and files concerning a child shall be kept separate from the records and files of arrests of adults. Unless a charge of delinquency is transferred for criminal prosecution under section 34, the interest of national security requires, or the court otherwise orders in the interest of the child, the records and files shall not be open to public inspection or their contents disclosed to the public; but inspection of the records and files is permitted by:

(1) a juvenile court having the child before it in any proceeding;

(2) counsel for a party to the proceeding;

(3) the officers of public institutions or agencies to whom the child is committed;

(4) law enforcement officers of other jurisdictions when necessary for the discharge of their official duties; and

(5) a court in which he is convicted of a criminal offense for the purpose of a pre-sentence report or other dispositional proceeding, or by officials of penal institutions and other penal facilities to which he is committed, or by a [parole board] in considering his parole or discharge or in exercising supervision over him.

Section 56. *[Children's Fingerprints, Photographs.]*

(a) No child under 14 years of age shall be fingerprinted in the investigation of a crime except as provided in this section. Fingerprints of a child 14 or more years of age who is referred to the court may be taken and filed by law enforcement officers in investigating the commission of the following crimes: [specifically such crimes as murder, non-negligent manslaughter, forcible rape, robbery, aggravated assault, burglary, housebreaking, purse snatching, and automobile theft].

(b) Fingerprint files of children shall be kept separate from those of adults. Copies of fingerprints known to be those of a child shall be maintained on a local basis only and not sent to a central state or federal depository unless in the interest of national security.

(c) Fingerprint files of children may be inspected by law enforcement officers when necessary for the discharge of their official duties. Other inspections may be authorized by the court in individual cases upon a showing that it is necessary in the public interest.

(d) Fingerprints of a child shall be removed from the file and destroyed if:

    (1) a petition alleging delinquency is not filed, or the proceedings are dismissed after either a petition is filed or the case is transferred to the juvenile court as provided in section 9, or the child is adjudicated not to be a delinquent child; or

    (2) the child reaches 21 years of age and there is no record that he committed a criminal offense after reaching 16 years of age.

(e) If latent fingerprints are found during the investigation of an offense and a law enforcement officer has probable cause to believe that they are those of a particular child he may fingerprint the child regardless of age or offense for purposes of immediate comparison with the latent fingerprints. If the comparison is negative the fingerprint card and other copies of the fingerprints taken shall be immediately destroyed. If the comparison is positive and the child is referred to the court, the fingerprint card and other copies of the fingerprints taken shall be delivered to the court for disposition. If the child is not referred to the court, the fingerprints shall be immediately destroyed.

(f) Without the consent of the judge, a child shall not be photographed after he is taken into custody unless the case is transferred to another court for prosecution.

Section 57. *[Sealing of Records.]*

(a) On application of a person who has been adjudicated delinquent or unruly or on the court's own motion, and after a hearing, the court shall order the sealing of the files and records in the proceeding, including those specified in sections 55 and 56, if the court finds:

(1) 2 years have elapsed since the final discharge of the person;
(2) since the final discharge he has not been convicted of a felony, or of a misdemeanor involving moral turpitude, or adjudicated a delinquent or unruly child and no proceeding is pending seeking conviction or adjudication; and
(3) he has been rehabilitated.

(b) Reasonable notice of the hearing shall be given to:

(1) the [prosecuting attorney of the county];
(2) the authority granting the discharge if the final discharge was from an institution or from parole; and
(3) the law enforcement officers or department having custody of the files and records if the files and records specified in sections 55 and 56 are included in the application or motion.

(c) Upon the entry of the order the proceeding shall be treated as if it never occurred. All index references shall be deleted and the person, the court, and law enforcement officers and departments shall properly reply that no record exists with respect to the person upon inquiry in any matter. Copies of the order shall be sent to each agency or official therein named. Inspection of the sealed files and records thereafter may be permitted by an order of the court upon petition by the person who is the subject of the records and only by those persons named in the order.

[**Section 58.** *[Contempt Powers.]* The court may punish a person for contempt of court for disobeying an order of the court or for obstructing or interfering with the proceedings of the court or the enforcement of its orders subject to the laws relating to the procedures therefor and the limitations thereon.]

Section 59. *[Appeals.]*
(a) An aggrieved party, including the state or a subdivision of the state, may appeal from a final order, judgment, or decree of the juvenile court to the [Supreme Court] [court of general jurisdiction] by filing written notice of appeal within 30 days after entry of the order, judgment, or decree, or within any further time the [Supreme Court] [court of general jurisdiction] grants, after entry of the order, judgment, or decree. [The appeal shall be heard

by the [court of general jurisdiction] upon the files, records, and minutes or transcript of the evidence of the juvenile court, giving appreciable weight to the findings of the juvenile court.] The name of the child shall not appear on the record on appeal.

(b) The appeal does not stay the order, judgment, or decree appealed from, but the [Supreme Court] [court of general jurisdiction] may otherwise order on application and hearing consistent with this Act if suitable provision is made for the care and custody of the child. If the order, judgment or decree appealed from grants the custody of the child to, or withholds it from, one or more of the parties to the appeal it shall be heard at the earliest practicable time.

Section 60. *[Rules of Court.]* The [Supreme] Court of this State may adopt rules of procedure not in conflict with this Act governing proceedings under it.

Section 61. *[Uniformity of Interpretation.]* This Act shall be so interpreted and construed as to effectuate its general purpose to make uniform the law of those states which enact it.

Section 62. *[Short Title.]* This Act may be cited as the Uniform Juvenile Court Act.

Section 63. *[Repeal.]* The following Acts and parts of Acts are repealed:

(1)

(2)

(3)

Section 64. *[Time of Taking Effect.]* This Act shall take effect. . . .

B The Gault Decision

IN RE GAULT

Supreme Court of the United States, 1967.
387 U.S. 1, 87 S.Ct. 1428, 18 L.Ed.2d 527.

Mr. Justice Fortas delivered the opinion of the Court.

This is an appeal under 28 U.S.C. § 1257(2) from a judgment of the Supreme Court of Arizona affirming the dismissal of a petition for a writ of habeas corpus. 99 Ariz. 181, 407 P.2d 760 (1965). The petition sought the release of Gerald Francis Gault, appellants' 15-year-old son, who had been committed as a juvenile delinquent to the State Industrial School by the Juvenile Court of Gila County, Arizona. The Supreme Court of Arizona affirmed dismissal of the writ against various arguments which included an attack upon the constitutionality of the Arizona Juvenile Code because of its alleged denial of procedural due process rights to juveniles charged with being "delinquents." The court agreed that the constitutional guarantee of due process of law is applicable in such proceedings. It held that Arizona's Juvenile Code is to be read as "impliedly" implementing the "due process concept." It then proceeded to identify and describe "the particular elements which constitute due process in a juvenile hearing." It concluded that the proceedings ending in commitment of Gerald Gault did not offend those requirements. We do not agree, and we reverse. We begin with a statement of the facts.

I.

On Monday, June 8, 1964, at about 10 a. m., Gerald Francis Gault and a friend, Ronald Lewis, were taken into custody by the Sheriff of Gila County. Gerald was then still subject to a six months' probation order which had been entered on February 25, 1964, as a result of his having been in the company of another boy who had stolen a wallet from a lady's purse. The police action on June 8 was taken as the result of a verbal complaint by a neighbor of the boys, Mrs. Cook, about a telephone call made to her in which the caller or callers made lewd or indecent remarks. It will suffice for purposes of this opinion to say that the remarks or questions put to her were of the irritatingly offensive, adolescent, sex variety.

At the time Gerald was picked up, his mother and father were both at work. No notice that Gerald was being taken into custody was left at the home. No other steps were taken to advise them that their son had, in effect, been arrested. Gerald was taken to the Children's Detention Home. When his mother arrived home at about 6 o'clock, Gerald was not there. Gerald's older brother was sent to look for him at the trailer home of the Lewis family. He apparently learned then that Gerald was in custody. He so informed his mother. The two of them went to the Detention Home. The deputy probation officer, Flagg, who was also superintendent of the Detention Home, told Mrs. Gault "why Gerry was there" and said that a hearing would be held in Juvenile Court at 3 o'clock the following day, June 9.

Officer Flagg filed a petition with the court on the hearing day, June 9, 1964. It was not served on the Gaults. Indeed, none of them saw this petition until the habeas corpus hearing on August 17, 1964. The petition was entirely formal. It made no reference to any factual basis for the judicial action which it initiated. It recited only that "said minor is under the age of eighteen years, and is in need of the protection of this Honorable Court; [and that] said minor is a delinquent minor." It prayed for a hearing and an order regarding "the care and custody of said minor." Officer Flagg executed a formal affidavit in support of the petition.

On June 9, Gerald, his mother, his older brother, and Probation Officers Flagg and Henderson appeared before the Juvenile Judge in chambers. Gerald's father was not there. He was at work out of the city. Mrs. Cook, the complainant, was not there. No one was sworn at this hearing. No transcript or recording was made. No memorandum or record of the substance of the proceedings was prepared. Our information about the proceedings and the subsequent hearing on June 15, derives entirely from the testimony of the Juvenile Court Judge, Mr. and Mrs. Gault and Officer Flagg at the habeas corpus proceeding conducted two months later. From this, it appears that at the June 9 hearing Gerald was questioned by the judge about the telephone call. There was conflict as to what he said. His mother recalled that Gerald said he only dialed Mrs. Cook's number and handed the telephone to his friend, Ronald. Officer Flagg recalled that Gerald had admitted making the lewd remarks. Judge McGhee testified that Gerald "admitted making one of these [lewd] statements." At the conclusion of the hearing, the judge said he would "think about it." Gerald was taken back to the Detention Home. He was not sent to his own home with his parents. On June 11 or 12, after having been detained since June 8, Gerald was released and driven home. There is no explanation in the record as to why he was kept in the Detention Home or why he was released. At 5 p. m. on the day of Gerald's release, Mrs. Gault received a note signed by Officer Flagg. It was on plain paper, not letterhead. Its entire text was as follows:

> "Mrs. Gault:
>
> "Judge McGHEE has set Monday June 15, 1964 at 11:00 A.M. as the date and time for further Hearings on Gerald's delinquency
>
> "/s/ Flagg"

At the appointed time on Monday, June 15, Gerald, his father and mother, Ronald Lewis and his father, and Officers Flagg and Henderson were present before Judge McGhee. Witnesses at the habeas corpus proceeding differed in their recollections of Gerald's testimony at the June 15 hearing. Mr. and Mrs. Gault recalled that Gerald again testified that he had only dialed the number and that the other boy had made the remarks. Officer Flagg agreed that at this hearing Gerald did not admit making the lewd remarks. But Judge McGhee recalled that "there was some admission again of some of the lewd statements. He—he didn't admit any of the more serious lewd statements." Again, the complainant, Mrs. Cook, was not present. Mrs. Gault asked that Mrs. Cook be present "so she could see which boy that done the talking, the dirty talking over the phone." The Juvenile Judge said "she didn't have to be present at that hearing." The judge did not speak to Mrs. Cook or communicate with her at any time. Probation Officer Flagg had talked to her once—over the telephone on June 9.

At this June 15 hearing a "referral report" made by the probation officers was filed with the court, although not disclosed to Gerald or his parents. This listed the charge as "Lewd Phone Calls." At the conclusion of the hearing, the judge committed Gerald as a juvenile delinquent to the State Industrial School "for the period of his minority [that is, until 21], unless sooner discharged by due process of law." An order to that effect was entered. It recites that "after a full hearing and due deliberation the Court finds that said minor is a delinquent child, and that said minor is of the age of 15 years."

No appeal is permitted by Arizona law in juvenile cases. On August 3, 1964, a petition for a writ of habeas corpus was filed with the Supreme Court of Arizona and referred by it to the Superior Court for hearing.

At the habeas corpus hearing on August 17, Judge McGhee was vigorously cross-examined as to the basis for his actions. He testified that he had taken into account the fact that Gerald was on probation. He was asked "under what section of * * * the code you found the boy delinquent?"

His answer is set forth in the margin.[1] In substance, he concluded that Gerald came within ARS § 8—201, subsec. 6(a), which specifies that a "delinquent child" includes one "who has violated a law of the state or an ordinance or regulation of a political subdivision thereof." The law which Gerald was found to have violated is ARS § 13—377. This section of the Arizona Criminal Code provides that a person who "in the presence or hearing of any woman or child * * * uses vulgar, abusive or obscene language, is guilty of a misdemeanor * * *." The penalty specified in the Criminal Code, which would apply to an adult, is $5 to $50, or imprisonment for not more than two months. The judge also testified that he acted under ARS § 8—201, subsec. 6(d) which includes in the definition of a

---

1. "Q. All right. Now, Judge, would you tell me under what section of the law or tell me under what section of—of the code you found the boy delinquent?"

"A. Well, there is a—I think it amounts to disturbing the peace. I can't give you the section, but I can tell you the law, that when one person uses lewd language in the presence of another person, that it can amount to—and I consider that when a person makes it over the phone, that it is considered in the presence, I might be wrong, that is one section. The other section upon which I consider the boy delinquent is Section 8—201, Subsection (d), habitually involved in immoral matters."

"delinquent child" one who, as the judge phrased it, is "habitually involved in immoral matters."[2]

Asked about the basis for his conclusion that Gerald was "habitually involved in immoral matters," the judge testified, somewhat vaguely, that two years earlier, on June 2, 1962, a "referral" was made concerning Gerald, "where the boy had stolen a baseball glove from another boy and lied to the Police Department about it." The judge said there was "no hearing," and "no accusation" relating to this incident, "because of lack of material foundation." But it seems to have remained in his mind as a relevant factor. The judge also testified that Gerald had admitted making other nuisance phone calls in the past which, as the judge recalled the boy's testimony, were "silly calls, or funny calls, or something like that."

The Superior Court dismissed the writ, and appellants sought review in the Arizona Supreme Court. That court stated that it considered appellants' assignments of error as urging (1) that the Juvenile Code, ARS § 8—201 to § 8—239, is unconstitutional because it does not require that parents and children be apprised of the specific charges, does not require proper notice of a hearing, and does not provide for an appeal; and (2) that the proceedings and order relating to Gerald constituted a denial of due process of law because of the absence of adequate notice of the charge and the hearing; failure to notify appellants of certain constitutional rights including the rights to counsel and to confrontation, and the privilege against self-incrimination; the use of unsworn hearsay testimony; and the failure to make a record of the proceedings. Appellants further asserted that it was an error for the Juvenile Court to remove Gerald from the custody of his parents without a showing and finding of their unsuitability, and alleged a miscellany of other errors under state law.

2. ARS § 8—201, subsec. 6, the section of the Arizona Juvenile Code which defines a delinquent child, reads:

" 'Delinquent child' includes:

"(a) A child who has violated a law of the state or an ordinance or regulation of a political subdivision thereof.

"(b) A child who, by reason of being incorrigible, wayward or habitually disobedient, is uncontrolled by his parent, guardian or custodian.

"(c) A child who is habitually truant from school or home.

"(d) A child who habitually so deports himself as to injure or endanger the morals or health of himself or others."

The Supreme Court handed down an elaborate and wide-ranging opinion affirming dismissal of the writ and stating the court's conclusions as to the issues raised by appellants and other aspects of the juvenile process. In their jurisdictional statement and brief in this Court, appellants do not urge upon us all of the points passed upon by the Supreme Court of Arizona. They urge that we hold the Juvenile Code of Arizona invalid on its face or as applied in this case because, contrary to the Due Process Clause of the Fourteenth Amendment, the juvenile is taken from the custody of his parents and committed to a state institution pursuant to proceedings in which the Juvenile Court has virtually unlimited discretion, and in which the following basic rights are denied:

1. Notice of the charges;
2. Right to counsel;
3. Right to confrontation and cross-examination;
4. Privilege against self-incrimination;
5. Right to a transcript of the proceedings; and
6. Right to appellate review.

We shall not consider other issues which were passed upon by the Supreme Court of Arizona. We emphasize that we indicate no opinion as to whether the decision of that court with respect to such other issues does or does not conflict with requirements of the Federal Constitution.

II.

The Supreme Court of Arizona held that due process of law is requisite to the constitutional validity of proceedings in which a court reaches the conclusion that a juvenile has been at fault, has engaged in conduct prohibited by law, or has otherwise misbehaved with the consequence that he is committed to an institution in which his freedom is curtailed. This conclusion is in accord with the decisions of a number of courts under both federal and state constitutions.

This Court has not heretofore decided the precise question. In Kent v. United States, 383 U.S. 541, 86 S.Ct. 1045, 16 L.Ed.2d 84 (1966), we considered the requirements for a valid waiver of the "exclusive" jurisdiction of the Juvenile Court of the District of Columbia so that a juvenile could be tried in the adult criminal court of the

District. Although our decision turned upon the language of the statute, we emphasized the necessity that "the basic requirements of due process and fairness" be satisfied in such proceedings. Haley v. State of Ohio, 332 U.S. 596, 68 S.Ct. 302, 92 L.Ed. 224 (1948), involved the admissibility, in a state criminal court of general jurisdiction, of a confession by a 15-year-old boy. The Court held that the Fourteenth Amendment applied to prohibit the use of the coerced confession. Mr. Justice Douglas said, "Neither man nor child can be allowed to stand condemned by methods which flout constitutional requirements of due process of law." To the same effect is Gallegos v. State of Colorado, 370 U.S. 49, 82 S.Ct. 1209, 8 L.Ed.2d 325 (1962). Accordingly, while these cases relate only to restricted aspects of the subject, they unmistakably indicate that, whatever may be their precise impact, neither the Fourteenth Amendment nor the Bill of Rights is for adults alone.

We do not in this opinion consider the impact of these constitutional provisions upon the totality of the relationship of the juvenile and the state. We do not even consider the entire process relating to juvenile "delinquents." For example, we are not here concerned with the procedures or constitutional rights applicable to the pre-judicial stages of the juvenile process, nor do we direct our attention to the post-adjudicative or dispositional process. We consider only the problems presented to us by this case. These relate to the proceedings by which a determination is made as to whether a juvenile is a "delinquent" as a result of alleged misconduct on his part, with the consequence that he may be committed to a state institution. As to these proceedings, there appears to be little current dissent from the proposition that the Due Process Clause has a role to play. The problem is to ascertain the precise impact of the due process requirement upon such proceedings.

In view of this, it would be extraordinary if our Constitution did not require the procedural regularity and the exercise of care implied in the phrase "due process." Under our Constitution, the condition of being a boy does not justify a kangaroo court. The traditional ideas of Juvenile Court procedure, indeed, contemplated that time would be available and care would be used to establish precisely what the juvenile did and why he did it—was it a prank of adolescence or a brutal act threatening serious consequences to himself or society unless corrected? Under traditional notions, one would assume that in a case like that of Gerald Gault, where the juvenile appears to have a home, a working mother and father, and an older brother, the Juvenile Judge would have made a careful inquiry and judgment as to the possibility that the boy could be disciplined and dealt with at home, despite his previous transgressions.[3] Indeed, so far as appears in the record before us, except for some conversation with Gerald about his school work and his "wanting to go to * * * Grand Canyon with his father," the points to which the judge directed his attention were little different from those that would be involved in determining any charge of violation of a penal statute. The essential difference between Gerald's case and a normal criminal case is that safeguards available to adults were discarded in Gerald's case. The summary procedure as well as the long commitment was possible because Gerald was 15 years of age instead of over 18.

If Gerald had been over 18, he would not have been subject to Juvenile Court proceedings. For the particular offense immediately involved, the maximum punishment would have been a fine of $5 to $50, or imprisonment in jail for not more than two months. Instead, he was committed to custody for a maximum of six years. If he had been over 18 and had committed an offense to which such a sentence might apply, he would have been entitled to substantial rights under the Constitution of the United States as well as under Arizona's laws and constitution. The United States Constitution would guarantee him rights and protections with respect to arrest, search, and seizure, and pretrial interrogation. It would assure him of specific notice of the charges and adequate time to decide his course of action and to prepare his defense. He would be entitled to clear advice that he could be represented by counsel, and, at least if a felony were in-

3. The Juvenile Judge's testimony at the habeas corpus proceeding is devoid of any meaningful discussion of this. He appears to have centered his attention upon whether Gerald made the phone call and used lewd words. He was impressed by the fact that Gerald was on six months' probation because he was with another boy who allegedly stole a purse—a different sort of offense, sharing the feature that Gerald was "along." And he even referred to a report which he said was not investigated because "there was no accusation" "because of lack of material foundation." With respect to the possible duty of a trial court to explore alternatives to involuntary commitment in a civil proceeding, cf. Lake v. Cameron, 124 U.S. App.D.C. 264, 364 F.2d 657 (1966), which arose under statutes relating to treatment of the mentally ill.

volved, the State would be required to provide counsel if his parents were unable to afford it. If the court acted on the basis of his confession, careful procedures would be required to assure its voluntariness. If the case went to trial, confrontation and opportunity for cross-examination would be guaranteed. So wide a gulf between the State's treatment of the adult and of the child requires a bridge sturdier than mere verbiage, and reasons more persuasive than cliche can provide. As Wheeler and Cottrell have put it, "The rhetoric of the juvenile court movement has developed without any necessarily close correspondence to the realities of court and institutional routines."

In Kent v. United States, supra, we stated that the Juvenile Court Judge's exercise of the power of the state as *parens patriae* was not unlimited. We said that "the admonition to function in a 'parental' relationship is not an invitation to procedural arbitrariness." With respect to the waiver by the Juvenile Court to the adult court of jurisdiction over an offense committed by a youth, we said that "there is no place in our system of law for reaching a result of such tremendous consequences without ceremony—without hearing, without effective assistance of counsel, without a statement of reasons." We announced with respect to such waiver proceedings that while "We do not mean * * * to indicate that the hearing to be held must conform with all of the requirements of a criminal trial or even of the usual administrative hearing; but we do hold that the hearing must measure up to the essentials of due process and fair treatment." We reiterate this view, here in connection with a juvenile court adjudication of "delinquency," as a requirement which is part of the Due Process Clause of the Fourteenth Amendment of our Constitution.[4]

We now turn to the specific issues which are presented to us in the present case.

---

4. The Nat'l Crime Comm'n Report recommends that "Juvenile courts should make fullest feasible use of preliminary conferences to dispose of cases short of adjudication." Id., at 84. See also D.C.Crime Comm'n Report, pp. 662-665. Since this "consent decree" procedure would involve neither adjudication of delinquency nor institutionalization, nothing we say in this opinion should be construed as expressing any views with respect to such procedure. The problems of pre-adjudication treatment of juveniles, and of post-adjudication disposition, are unique to the juvenile process; hence what we hold in this opinion with regard to the procedural requirements at the adjudicatory stage has no necessary applicability to other steps of the juvenile process.

III. Notice of Charges

Appellants allege that the Arizona Juvenile Code is unconstitutional or alternatively that the proceedings before the Juvenile Court were constitutionally defective because of failure to provide adequate notice of the hearings. No notice was given to Gerald's parents when he was taken into custody on Monday, June 8. On that night, when Mrs. Gault went to the Detention Home, she was orally informed that there would be a hearing the next afternoon and was told the reason why Gerald was in custody. The only written notice Gerald's parents received at any time was a note on plain paper from Officer Flagg delivered on Thursday or Friday, June 11 or 12, to the effect that the judge had set Monday, June 15, "for further Hearings on Gerald's delinquency."

A "petition" was filed with the court on June 9 by Officer Flagg, reciting only that he was informed and believed that "said minor is a delinquent minor and that it is necessary that some order be made by the Honorable Court for said minor's welfare." The applicable Arizona statute provides for a petition to be filed in Juvenile Court, alleging in general terms that the child is "neglected, dependent or delinquent." The statute explicitly states that such a general allegation is sufficient, "without alleging the facts." There is no requirement that the petition be served and it was not served upon, given to, or shown to Gerald or his parents.

The Supreme Court of Arizona rejected appellants' claim that due process was denied because of inadequate notice. It stated that "Mrs. Gault knew the exact nature of the charge against Gerald from the day he was taken to the detention home." The court also pointed out that the Gaults appeared at the two hearings "without objection." The court held that because "the policy of the juvenile law is to hide youthful errors from the full gaze of the public and bury them in the graveyard of the forgotten past," advance notice of the specific charges or basis for taking the juvenile into custody and for the hearing is not necessary. It held that the appropriate rule is that "the infant and his parents or guardian will receive a petition only reciting a conclusion of delinquency. But no later than the initial hearing by the judge, they must be advised of the facts involved in the case. If the charges are denied, they must be given a reasonable period of time to prepare."

We cannot agree with the court's conclusion that adequate

notice was given in this case. Notice, to comply with due process requirements, must be given sufficiently in advance of scheduled court proceedings so that reasonable opportunity to prepare will be afforded, and it must "set forth the alleged misconduct with particularity." It is obvious, as we have discussed above, that no purpose of shielding the child from the public stigma of knowledge of his having been taken into custody and scheduled for hearing is served by the procedure approved by the court below. The "initial hearing" in the present case was a hearing on the merits. Notice at that time is not timely; and even if there were a conceivable purpose served by the deferral proposed by the court below, it would have to yield to the requirements that the child and his parents or guardian be notified, in writing, of the specific charge or factual allegations to be considered at the hearing, and that such written notice be given at the earliest practicable time, and in any event sufficiently in advance of the hearing to permit preparation. Due process of law requires notice of the sort we have described—that is, notice which would be deemed constitutionally adequate in a civil or criminal proceeding. It does not allow a hearing to be held in which a youth's freedom and his parents' right to his custody are at stake without giving them timely notice, in advance of the hearing, of the specific issues that they must meet. Nor, in the circumstances of this case, can it reasonably be said that the requirement of notice was waived.

IV. Right to Counsel

Appellants charge that the Juvenile Court proceedings were fatally defective because the court did not advise Gerald or his parents of their right to counsel, and proceeded with the hearing, the adjudication of delinquency and the order of commitment in the absence of counsel for the child and his parents or an express waiver of the right thereto. The Supreme Court of Arizona pointed out that "[t]here is disagreement [among the various jurisdictions] as to whether the court must advise the infant that he has a right to counsel." It noted its own decision in Arizona State Dept. of Public Welfare v. Barlow, 80 Ariz. 249, 296 P.2d 298 (1956), to the effect "that *the parents* of an infant in a juvenile proceeding cannot be denied representation by counsel of their choosing." (Emphasis added.) It referred to a provision of the Juvenile Code which it characterized as requiring "that the probation officer shall look

after the interests of neglected, delinquent and dependent children,''
including representing their interests in court. The court argued that
''The parent and the probation officer may be relied upon to protect
the infant's interests.'' Accordingly it rejected the proposition that
''due process requires that an infant have a right to counsel.'' It said
that juvenile courts have the discretion, but not the duty, to allow
such representation; it referred specifically to the situation in which
the Juvenile Court discerns conflict between the child and his parents
as an instance in which this discretion might be exercised. We do not
agree. Probation officers, in the Arizona scheme, are also arresting
officers. They initiate proceedings and file petitions which they
verify, as here, alleging the delinquency of the child; and they
testify, as here, against the child. And here the probation officer was
also superintendent of the Detention Home. The probation officer
cannot act as counsel for the child. His role in the adjudicatory hearing, by statute and in fact, is as arresting officer and witness against
the child. Nor can the judge represent the child. There is no material
difference in this respect between adult and juvenile proceedings of
the sort here involved. In adult proceedings, this contention has been
foreclosed by decisions of this Court. A proceeding where the issue is
whether the child will be found to be ''delinquent'' and subjected to
the loss of his liberty for years is comparable in seriousness to a
felony prosecution. The juvenile needs the assistance of counsel to
cope with problems of law, to make skilled inquiry into the facts, to
insist upon regularity of the proceedings, and to ascertain whether he
has a defense and to prepare and submit it. The child ''requires the
guiding hand of counsel at every step in the proceedings against
him.'' Just as in Kent v. United States, supra, 383 U.S., at 561-562,
86 S.Ct., at 1057-1058, we indicated our agreement with the United
States Court of Appeals for the District of Columbia Circuit that the
assistance of counsel is essential for purposes of waiver proceedings,
so we hold now that it is equally essential for the determination of
delinquency, carrying with it the awesome prospect of incarceration
in a state institution until the juvenile reaches the age of 21.[5]

During the last decade, court decisions, experts, and legislatures
have demonstrated increasing recognition of this view. In at least
one-third of the States, statutes now provide for the right of

5. This means that the commitment, in virtually all cases, is for a minimum of three
years since jurisdiction of juvenile courts is usually limited to age 18 and under.

representation by retained counsel in juvenile delinquency proceedings, notice of the right, or assignment of counsel, or a combination of these. In other States, court rules have similar provisions.

The President's Crime Commission has recently recommended that in order to assure "procedural justice for the child," it is necessary that "Counsel * * * be appointed as a matter of course wherever coercive action is a possibility, without requiring any affirmative choice by child or parent."[6] As stated by the authoritative "Standards for Juvenile and Family Courts," published by the Children's Bureau of the United States Department of Health, Education, and Welfare:

> *"As a component part of a fair hearing required by due process guaranteed under the 14th amendment, notice of the right to counsel should be required at all hearings and counsel provided upon request when the family is financially unable to employ counsel."* Standards, p. 57.

6. Nat'l Crime Comm'n Report, pp. 86-87. The Commission's statement of its position is very forceful:

"The Commission believes that no single action holds more potential for achieving procedural justice for the child in the juvenile court than provision of counsel. The presence of an independent legal representative of the child, or of his parent, is the keystone of the whole structure of guarantees that a minimum system of procedural justice requires. The rights to confront one's accusers, to cross-examine witnesses, to present evidence and testimony of one's own, to be unaffected by prejudicial and unreliable evidence, to participate meaningfully in the dispositional decision, to take an appeal have substantial meaning for the overwhelming majority of persons brought before the juvenile court only if they are provided with competent lawyers who can invoke those rights effectively. The most informal and well-intentioned of judicial proceedings are technical; few adults without legal training can influence or even understand them; certainly children cannot. Papers are drawn and charges expressed in legal language. Events follow one another in a manner that appears arbitrary and confusing to the uninitiated. Decisions, unexplained, appear too official to challenge. But with lawyers come records of proceedings; records make possible appeals which, even if they do not occur, impart by their possibility a healthy atmosphere of accountability.

"Fears have been expressed that lawyers would make juvenile court proceedings adversary. No doubt this is partly true, but it is partly desirable. Informality is often abused. The juvenile courts deal with cases in which facts are disputed and in which, therefore, rules of evidence, confrontation of witnesses, and other adversary procedures are called for. They deal with many cases involving conduct that can lead to

This statement was "reviewed" by the National Council of Juvenile Court Judges at its 1965 Convention and they "found no fault" with it. The New York Family Court Act contains the following statement:

> *"This act declares that minors have a right to the assistance of counsel of their own choosing or of law guardians in neglect proceedings under article three and in proceedings to determine juvenile delinquency and whether a person is in need of supervision under article seven. This declaration is based on a finding that counsel is often indispensable to a practical realization of due process of law and may be helpful in making reasoned determinations of fact and proper orders of disposition."*

The Act provides that "At the commencement of any hearing" under the delinquency article of the statute, the juvenile and his parent shall be advised of the juvenile's "right to be represented by counsel chosen by him or his parent * * * or by a law guardian

incarceration or close supervision for long periods, and therefore juveniles often need the same safeguards that are granted to adults. And in all cases children need advocates to speak for them and guard their interests, particularly when disposition decisions are made. It is the disposition stage at which the opportunity arises to offer individualized treatment plans and in which the danger inheres that the court's coercive power will be applied without adequate knowledge of the circumstances.

"Fears also have been expressed that the formality lawyers would bring into juvenile court would defeat the therapeutic aims of the court. But informality has no necessary connection with therapy; it is a device that has been used to approach therapy, and it is not the only possible device. It is quite possible that in many instances lawyers, for all their commitment to formality, could do more to further therapy for their clients than can the small, overworked social staffs of the courts.

* * *

"The Commission believes it is essential that counsel be appointed by the juvenile court for those who are unable to provide their own. Experience under the prevailing systems in which children are free to seek counsel of their choice reveals how empty of meaning the right is for those typically the subjects of juvenile court proceedings. Moreover, providing counsel only when the child is sophisticated enough to be aware of his need and to ask for one or when he fails to waive his announced right [is] not enough, as experience in numerous jurisdictions reveals.

"The Commission recommends:

"COUNSEL SHOULD BE APPOINTED AS A MATTER OF COURSE WHEREVER COERCIVE ACTION IS A POSSIBILITY, WITHOUT REQUIRING ANY AFFIRMATIVE CHOICE BY CHILD OR PARENT."

assigned by the court * * *.'' The California Act (1961) also requires appointment of counsel.

We conclude that the Due Process Clause of the Fourteenth Amendment requires that in respect of proceedings to determine delinquency which may result in commitment to an institution in which the juvenile's freedom is curtailed, the child and his parents must be notified of the child's right to be represented by counsel retained by them, or if they are unable to afford counsel, that counsel will be appointed to represent the child.

At the habeas corpus proceeding, Mrs. Gault testified that she knew that she could have appeared with counsel at the juvenile hearing. This knowledge is not a waiver of the right to counsel which she and her juvenile son had, as we have defined it. They had a right expressly to be advised that they might retain counsel and to be confronted with the need for specific consideration of whether they did or did not choose to waive the right. If they were unable to afford to employ counsel, they were entitled in view of the seriousness of the charge and the potential commitment, to appointed counsel, unless they chose waiver. Mrs. Gault's knowledge that she could employ counsel was not an "intentional relinquishment or abandonment" of a fully known right.[7]

V. Confrontation, Self-Incrimination, Cross-Examination

Appellants urge that the writ of habeas corpus should have been granted because of the denial of the rights of confrontation and cross-examination in the Juvenile Court hearings, and because the privilege against self-incrimination was not observed. The Juvenile Court Judge testified at the habeas corpus hearing that he had proceeded on the basis of Gerald's admissions at the two hearings. Appellants attack this on the ground that the admissions were obtained in disregard of the privilege against self-incrimination. If the confession is disregarded, appellants argue that the delinquency conclusion, since it was fundamentally based on a finding that Gerald had made lewd remarks during the phone call to Mrs. Cook, is fatally defective for failure to accord the rights of confrontation and cross-

---

7. Johnson v. Zerbst, 304 U.S. 458, 464, 58 S.Ct. 1019, 1023, 82 L.Ed. 1461 (1938); Carnley v. Cochran, 369 U.S. 506, 82 S. Ct. 884, 8 L.Ed.2d 70 (1962); United States ex rel. Brown v. Fay, 242 F. Supp. 273 (D.C.S.D.N.Y.1965).

examination which the Due Process Clause of the Fourteenth Amendment of the Federal Constitution guarantees in state proceedings generally.

Our first question, then, is whether Gerald's admission was improperly obtained and relied on as the basis of decision, in conflict with the Federal Constitution. For this purpose, it is necessary briefly to recall the relevant facts.

Mrs. Cook, the complainant, and the recipient of the alleged telephone call, was not called as a witness. Gerald's mother asked the Juvenile Court Judge why Mrs. Cook was not present and the judge replied that "she didn't have to be present." So far as appears, Mrs. Cook was spoken to only once, by Officer Flagg, and this was by telephone. The judge did not speak with her on any occasion. Gerald had been questioned by the probation officer after having been taken into custody. The exact circumstances of this questioning do not appear but any admissions Gerald may have made at this time do not appear in the record. Gerald was also questioned by the Juvenile Court Judge at each of the two hearings. The judge testified in the habeas corpus proceeding that Gerald admitted making "some of the lewd statements * * * [but not] any of the more serious lewd statements." There was conflict and uncertainty among the witnesses at the habeas corpus proceeding—the Juvenile Court Judge, Mr. and Mrs. Gault, and the probation officer—as to what Gerald did or did not admit.

We shall assume that Gerald made admissions of the sort described by the Juvenile Court Judge, as quoted above. Neither Gerald nor his parents were advised that he did not have to testify or make a statement, or that an incriminating statement might result in his commitment as a "delinquent."

The Arizona Supreme Court rejected appellants' contention that Gerald had a right to be advised that he need not incriminate himself. It said: "We think the necessary flexibility for individualized treatment will be enhanced by a rule which does not require the judge to advise the infant of a privilege against self-incrimination."

In reviewing this conclusion of Arizona's Supreme Court, we emphasize again that we are here concerned only with a proceeding to determine whether a minor is a "delinquent" and which may result in commitment to a state institution. Specifically, the question is whether, in such a proceeding, an admission by the juvenile may be used against him in the absence of clear and unequivocal evidence that the admission was made with knowledge that he was not obliged to speak and would not be penalized for remaining silent. In light of Miranda v. State of Arizona, 384 U.S. 436, 86 S.Ct. 1602, 16 L.Ed.2d 694 (1966), we must also consider whether, if the privilege against self-incrimination is available, it can effectively be waived unless counsel is present or the right to counsel has been waived.

It has long been recognized that the eliciting and use of confessions or admissions require careful scrutiny. Dean Wigmore states:

"The ground of distrust of confessions made in certain situations is, in a rough and indefinite way, judicial experience. There has been no careful collection of statistics of untrue confessions, nor has any great number of instances been even loosely reported * * * but enough have been verified to fortify the conclusion, based on ordinary observation of human conduct, that under certain stresses a person, especially one of defective mentality or peculiar temperament, may falsely acknowledge guilt. This possibility arises wherever the innocent person is placed in such a situation that the untrue acknowledgment of guilt is at the time the more promising of two alternatives between which he obliged to choose; that is, he chooses any risk that may be in falsely acknowledging guilt, in preference to some worse alternative associated with silence.

"The principle, then, upon which a confession may be excluded is that it is, under certain conditions, testimonially untrustworthy * * *. [T]he essential feature is that the principle of exclusion is a testimonial one, analogous to the other principles which exclude narrations as untrustworthy * * *."

This Court has emphasized that admissions and confessions of juveniles require special caution. In Haley v. State of Ohio, 332 U.S. 596, 68 S.Ct. 302, 92 L.Ed. 224, where this Court reversed the conviction of a 15-year-old boy for murder, Mr. Justice Douglas said:

"What transpired would make us pause for careful inquiry if a mature man were involved. And when, as here, a mere child—an easy victim of the law—is before us, special care in scrutinizing the record must be used. Age 15 is a tender and difficult age for a boy of any race. He cannot be judged by the more exacting standards of maturity. That which would leave a man cold and unimpressed can overawe and overwhelm a lad in his early teens. This is the period of great instability which the crisis of adolescence produces. A 15-year-old lad, questioned through the dead of night by relays of police, is a ready victim of the inquisition. Mature men possibly might stand the ordeal from midnight to 5 a.m. But we cannot believe that a lad of tender years is a match for the police in such a contest. He needs counsel and support if he is

not to become the victim first of fear, then of panic. He needs someone on whom to lean lest the overpowering presence of the law, as he knows it, crush him. No friend stood at the side of this 15-year-old boy as the police, working in relays, questioned him hour after hour, from midnight until dawn. No lawyer stood guard to make sure that the police went so far and no farther, to see to it that they stopped short of the point where he became the victim of coercion. No counsel or friend was called during the critical hours of questioning.''

In *Haley,* as we have discussed, the boy was convicted in an adult court, and not a juvenile court. In notable decisions, the New York Court of Appeals and the Supreme Court of New Jersey have recently considered decisions of Juvenile Courts in which boys have been adjudged "delinquent" on the basis of confessions obtained in circumstances comparable to those in *Haley.* In both instances, the State contended before its highest tribunal that constitutional requirements governing inculpatory statements applicable in adult courts do not apply to juvenile proceedings. In each case, the State's contention was rejected, and the juvenile court's determination of delinquency was set aside on the grounds of inadmissibility of the confession. In Matters of W. and S., 19 N.Y.2d 55, 277 N.Y.S.2d 675, 224 N.E.2d 102 (1966) (opinion by Keating, J.), and In Interests of Carlo and Stasilowicz, 48 N.J. 224, 225 A.2d 110 (1966) (opinion by Proctor, J.).

The privilege against self-incrimination is, of course, related to the question of the safeguards necessary to assure that admissions or confessions are reasonably trustworthy, that they are not the mere fruits of fear or coercion, but are reliable expressions of the truth. The roots of the privilege are, however, far deeper. They tap the basic stream of religious and political principle because the privilege reflects the limits of the individual's attornment to the state and—in a philosophical sense—insists upon the equality of the individual and the state. In other words, the privilege has a broader and deeper thrust than the rule which prevents the use of confessions which are the product of coercion because coercion is thought to carry with it the danger of unreliability. One of its purposes is to prevent the state, whether by force or by psychological domination, from overcoming the mind and will of the person under investigation and depriving him of the freedom to decide whether to assist the state in securing his conviction.

It would indeed be surprising if the privilege against self-incrimination were available to hardened criminals but not to children. The language of the Fifth Amendment, applicable to the States by operation of the Fourteenth Amendment, is unequivocal and without exception. And the scope of the privilege is comprehensive. As Mr. Justice White, concurring, stated in Murphy v. Waterfront Commission, 378 U.S. 52, 94, 84 S.Ct. 1594, 1611, 12 L.Ed.2d 678 (1964):

> *"The privilege can be claimed in* any proceeding, *be it criminal or civil, administrative or judicial, investigatory or adjudicatory.* * * * *it protects* any disclosures *which the witness may reasonably apprehend* could be used in a criminal prosecution or which could lead to other evidence that might be so used." *(Emphasis added.)*

With respect to juveniles, both common observation and expert opinion emphasize that the "distrust of confessions made in certain situations" to which Dean Wigmore referred in the passage quoted supra, at 1453, is imperative in the case of children from an early age through adolescence. In New York, for example, the recently enacted Family Court Act provides that the juvenile and his parents must be advised at the start of the hearing of his right to remain silent. The New York statute also provides that the police must attempt to communicate with the juvenile's parents before questioning him, and that absent "special circumstances" a confession may not be obtained from a child prior to notifying his parents or relatives and releasing the child either to them or to the Family Court. In In Matters of W. and S., referred to above, the New York Court of Appeals held that the privilege against self-incrimination applies in juvenile delinquency cases and requires the exclusion of involuntary confessions, and that People v. Lewis, 260 N.Y. 171, 183 N.E. 353, 86 A.L.R. 1001 (1932), holding the contrary, had been specifically overruled by statute.

The authoritative "Standards for Juvenile and Family Courts" concludes that, "Whether or not transfer to the criminal court is a possibility, certain procedures should always be followed. Before being interviewed [by the police], the child and his parents should be informed of his right to have legal counsel present and to refuse to answer questions or be fingerprinted if he should so decide."

Against the application to juveniles of the right to silence, it is argued that juvenile proceedings are "civil" and not "criminal," and therefore the privilege should not apply. It is true that the statement of the privilege in the Fifth Amendment, which is applicable to the States by reason of the Fourteenth Amendment, is that no person "shall be compelled in any *criminal case* to be a witness against himself." However, it is also clear that the availability of the privilege does not turn upon the type of proceeding in which its protection is invoked, but upon the nature of the statement or admission and the exposure which it invites. The privilege may, for example, be claimed in a civil or administrative proceeding, if the statement is or may be inculpatory.

It would be entirely unrealistic to carve out of the Fifth Amendment all statements by juveniles on the ground that these cannot lead to "criminal" involvement. In the first place, juvenile proceedings to determine "delinquency," which may lead to commitment to a state institution, must be regarded as "criminal" for purposes of the privilege against self-incrimination. To hold otherwise would be to disregard substance because of the feeble enticement of the "civil" label-of-convenience which has been attached to juvenile proceedings. Indeed, in over half of the States, there is not even assurance that the juvenile will be kept in separate institutions, apart from adult "criminals." In those States juveniles may be placed in or transferred to adult penal institutions after having been found "delinquent" by a juvenile court. For this purpose, at least, commitment is a deprivation of liberty. It is incarceration against one's will, whether it is called "criminal" or "civil." And our Constitution guarantees that no person shall be "compelled" to be a witness against himself when he is threatened with deprivation of his liberty—a command which this Court has broadly applied and generously implemented in accordance with the teaching of the history of the privilege and its great office in mankind's battle for freedom.

In addition, apart from the equivalence for this purpose of exposure to commitment as a juvenile delinquent and exposure to imprisonment as an adult offender, the fact of the matter is that there is little or no assurance in Arizona, as in most if not all of the States, that a juvenile apprehended and interrogated by the police or even by the Juvenile Court itself will remain outside of the reach of adult courts as a consequence of the offense for which he has been taken into custody. In Arizona, as in other States, provision is made for

Juvenile Courts to relinquish or waive jurisdiction to the ordinary criminal courts. In the present case, when Gerald Gault was interrogated concerning violation of a section of the Arizona Criminal Code, it could not be certain that the Juvenile Court Judge would decide to "suspend" criminal prosecution in court for adults by proceeding to an adjudication in Juvenile Court.

It is also urged, as the Supreme Court of Arizona here asserted, that the juvenile and presumably his parents should not be advised of the juvenile's right to silence because confession is good for the child as the commencement of the assumed therapy of the juvenile court process, and he should be encouraged to assume an attitude of trust and confidence toward the officials of the juvenile process. This proposition has been subjected to widespread challenge on the basis of current reappraisals of the rhetoric and realities of the handling of juvenile offenders.

In fact, evidence is accumulating that confessions by juveniles do not aid in "individualized treatment," as the court below put it, and that compelling the child to answer questions, without warning or advice as to his right to remain silent, does not serve this or any other good purpose. In light of the observations of Wheeler and Cottrell, and others, it seems probable that where children are induced to confess by "paternal" urgings on the part of officials and the confession is then followed by disciplinary action, the child's reaction is likely to be hostile and adverse—the child may well feel that he has been led or tricked into confession and that despite his confession, he is being punished.

Further, authoritative opinion has cast formidable doubt upon the reliability and trustworthiness of "confessions" by children. This Court's observations in Haley v. State of Ohio are set forth above. The recent decision of the New York Court of Appeals referred to above, In Matters of W. and S. deals with a dramatic and, it is to be hoped, extreme example. Two 12-year-old Negro boys were taken into custody for the brutal assault and rape of two aged domestics, one of whom died as the result of the attack. One of the boys was schizophrenic and had been locked in the security ward of a mental institution at the time of the attacks. By a process that may best be described as bizarre, his confession was obtained by the police. A psychiatrist testified that the boy would admit "whatever he thought was expected so that he could get out of the immediate situation." The other 12-year-old also "confessed." Both confessions were in specific detail, albeit they contained various inconsistencies. The Court of Appeals, in an opinion by Keating, J., concluded that the confessions were products of the will of the police instead of the boys. The confessions were therefore held involuntary and the order of the Appellate Division affirming the order of the Family Court adjudging the defendants to be juvenile delinquents was reversed.

A similar and equally instructive case has recently been decided by the Supreme Court of New Jersey. In Interests of Carlo and Stasilowicz, supra. The body of a 10-year-old girl was found. She had been strangled. Neighborhood boys who knew the girl were questioned. The two appellants, aged 13 and 15, confessed to the police, with vivid detail and some inconsistencies. At the Juvenile Court hearing, both denied any complicity in the killing. They testified that their confessions were the product of fear and fatigue due to extensive police grilling. The Juvenile Court Judge found that the confessions were voluntary and admissible. On appeal, in an extensive opinion by Proctor, J., the Supreme Court of New Jersey reversed. It rejected the State's argument that the constitutional safeguard of voluntariness governing the use of confessions does not apply in proceedings before the Juvenile Court. It pointed out that under New Jersey court rules, juveniles under the age of 16 accused of committing a homicide are tried in a proceeding which "has all of the appurtenances of a criminal trial," including participation by the county prosecutor, and requirements that the juvenile be provided with counsel, that a stenographic record be made, etc. It also pointed out that under New Jersey law, the confinement of the boys after reaching age 21 could be extended until they had served the maximum sentence which could have been imposed on an adult for such a homicide, here found to be second-degree murder carrying up to 30 years' imprisonment. The court concluded that the confessions were involuntary, stressing that the boys, contrary to statute, were placed in the police station and there interrogated; that the parents of both boys were not allowed to see them while they were being interrogated; that inconsistencies appeared among the various statements of the boys and with the objective evidence of the crime; and that there were protracted periods of questioning. The court noted the State's contention that both boys were advised of their constitutional rights before they made their statements, but it held that this should not be given "significant weight in our determination of voluntariness." Accordingly, the judgment of the Juvenile Court was reversed.

In a recent case before the Juvenile Court of the District of Columbia, Judge Ketcham rejected the proffer of evidence as to oral statements made at police headquarters by four juveniles who had been taken into custody for alleged involvement in an assault and attempted robbery. In the Matter of Four Youths, Nos. 28—776—J, 28—778—J, 28—783—J, 28—859—J, Juvenile Court of the District of Columbia, April 7, 1961. The court explicitly stated that it did not rest its decision on a showing that the statements were involuntary, but because they were untrustworthy. Judge Ketcham said:

"Simply stated, the Court's decision in this case rests upon the considered opinion—after nearly four busy years on the Juvenile Court bench during which the testimony of thousands of such juveniles has been heard—that the statements of adolescents under 18 years of age who are arrested and charged with violations of law are frequently untrustworthy and often distort the truth."

We conclude that the constitutional privilege against self-incrimination is applicable in the case of juveniles as it is with respect to adults. We appreciate that special problems may arise with respect to waiver of the privilege by or on behalf of children, and that there may well be some differences in technique—but not in principle—depending upon the age of the child and the presence and competence of parents. The participation of counsel will, of course, assist the police, Juvenile Courts and appellate tribunals in administering the privilege. If counsel was not present for some permissible reason when an admission was obtained, the greatest care must be taken to assure that the admission was voluntary, in the sense not only that it was not coerced or suggested, but also that it was not the product of ignorance of rights or of adolescent fantasy, fright or despair.

The "confession" of Gerald Gault was first obtained by Officer Flagg, out of the presence of Gerald's parents, without counsel and without advising him of his right to silence, as far as appears. The judgment of the Juvenile Court was stated by the judge to be based on Gerald's admissions in court. Neither "admission" was reduced to writing, and, to say the least, the process by which the "admissions" were obtained and received must be characterized as lacking the certainty and order which are required of proceedings of such formidable consequences. Apart from the "admission," there was nothing upon which a judgment or finding might be based. There was no sworn testimony. Mrs. Cook, the complainant, was not present. The Arizona Supreme Court held that "sworn testimony must be required of all witnesses including police officers, probation officers and others who are part of or officially related to the juvenile court structure." We hold that this is not enough. No reason is suggested or appears for a different rule in respect of sworn testimony in juvenile courts than in adult tribunals. Absent a valid confession adequate to support the determination of the Juvenile Court, confrontation and sworn testimony by witnesses available for cross-examination were essential for a finding of "delinquency" and an order committing Gerald to a state institution for a maximum of six years.

The recommendations in the Children's Bureau's "Standards for Juvenile and Family Courts" are in general accord with our conclusions. They state that testimony should be under oath and that only competent, material and relevant evidence under rules applicable to civil cases should be admitted in evidence. The New York Family Court Act contains a similar provision.

As we said in Kent v. United States, 383 U.S. 541, 554, 86 S.Ct. 1045, 1053, 16 L.Ed.2d 84 (1966), with respect to waiver proceedings, "there is no place in our system of law for reaching a result of such tremendous consequences without ceremony * * *." We now hold that, absent a valid confession, a determination of delinquency and an order of commitment to a state institution cannot be sustained in the absence of sworn testimony subjected to the opportunity for cross-examination in accordance with our law and constitutional requirements.

VI. Appellate Review and Transcript of Proceedings

Appellants urge that the Arizona statute is unconstitutional under the Due Process Clause because, as construed by its Supreme Court, "there is no right of appeal from a juvenile court order * * *." The court held that there is no right to a transcript because there is no right to appeal and because the proceedings are confidential and any record must be destroyed after a prescribed period of time. Whether a transcript or other recording is made, it held, is a matter for the discretion of the juvenile court.

This Court has not held that a State is required by the Federal Constitution "to provide appellate courts or a right to appellate review at all." In view of the fact that we must reverse the Supreme Court of Arizona's affirmance of the dismissal of the writ of habeas corpus for other reasons, we need not rule on this question in the present case or upon the failure to provide a transcript or recording of the hearings—or, indeed, the failure of the Juvenile Judge to state the grounds for his conclusion. Cf. Kent v. United States, supra, 383 U.S., at 561, 86 S.Ct., at 1057, where we said, in the context of a decision of the juvenile court waiving jurisdiction to the adult court, which by local law, was permissible: "* * * it is incumbent upon the Juvenile Court to accompany its waiver order with a statement of the reasons or considerations therefor." As the present case illustrates, the consequences of failure to provide an appeal, to record the proceedings, or to make findings or state the grounds for the juvenile court's conclusion may be to throw a burden upon the machinery for habeas corpus, to saddle the reviewing process with the burden of attempting to reconstruct a record, and to impose upon the Juvenile Judge the unseemly duty of testifying under cross-examination as to the events that transpired in the hearings before him.

For the reasons stated, the judgment of the Supreme Court of Arizona is reversed and the cause remanded for further proceedings not inconsistent with this opinion. It is so ordered.

Judgment reversed and cause remanded with directions.

Mr. Justice Black, concurring.

The juvenile court laws of Arizona and other States, as the Court points out, are the result of plans promoted by humane and forward-looking people to provide a system of courts, procedures, and sanctions deemed to be less harmful and more lenient to children than to adults. For this reason such state laws generally provide less formal and less public methods for the trial of children. In line with this policy, both courts and legislators have shrunk back from labeling these laws as "criminal" and have preferred to call them "civil." This, in part, was to prevent the full application to juvenile court cases of the Bill of Rights safeguards, including notice as provided in the Sixth Amendment, the right to counsel guaranteed by the Sixth, the right against self-incrimination guaranteed by the Fifth, and the right to confrontation guaranteed by the Sixth. The Court here holds, however, that these four Bill of Rights safeguards apply to protect a juvenile accused in a juvenile court on a charge under which he can be imprisoned for a term of years. This holding strikes a well-nigh fatal blow to much that is unique about the juvenile courts in the Nation. For this reason, there is much to be said for the position of my Brother Stewart that we should not pass on all these issues until they are more squarely presented. But since the majority of the Court chooses to decide all of these questions, I must either do the same or leave my views unexpressed on the important issues determined. In these circumstances, I feel impelled to express my views.

The juvenile court planners envisaged a system that would practically immunize juveniles from "punishment" for "crimes" in an effort to save them from youthful indiscretions and stigmas due to criminal charges or convictions. I agree with the Court, however, that this exalted ideal has failed of achievement since the beginning of the system. Indeed, the state laws from the first one on contained provisions, written in emphatic terms, for arresting and charging juveniles with violations of state criminal laws, as well as for taking juveniles by force of law away from their parents and turning them over to different individuals or groups or for confinement within some state school or institution for a number of years. The latter occurred in this case. Young Gault was arrested and detained on a charge of violating an Arizona penal law by using vile and offensive language to a lady on the telephone. If an adult, he could only have been fined or imprisoned for two months for his conduct. As a juvenile, however, he was put through a more or less secret, informal hearing by the court, after which he was ordered, or more realistically, "sentenced," to confinement in Arizona's Industrial School until he reaches 21 years of age. Thus, in a juvenile system designed to lighten or avoid punishment for criminality, he was ordered by the State to six years' confinement in what is in all but name a penitentiary or jail.

Where a person, infant or adult, can be seized by the State, charged, and convicted for violating a state criminal law, and then ordered by the State to be confined for six years, I think the Constitution requires that he be tried in accordance with the guarantees of all the provisions of the Bill of Rights made applicable to the States by the Fourteenth Amendment. Undoubtedly this would be true of an adult defendant, and it would be a plain denial of equal protection of the laws—an invidious discrimination—to hold that others subject to heavier punishments could, because they are children, be denied these same constitutional safeguards. I consequently agree with the Court that the Arizona law as applied here denied to the parents and their son the right of notice, right to counsel, right against self-incrimination, and right to confront the witnesses against young Gault. Appellants are entitled to these rights, not because "fairness, impartiality and orderliness—in short, the essentials of due process"—require them and not because they are "the procedural rules which have been fashioned from the generality of due process," but because they are specifically and unequivocally granted by provisions of the Fifth and Sixth Amendments which the Fourteenth Amendment makes applicable to the States.

A few words should be added because of the opinion of my Brother Harlan who rests his concurrence and dissent on the Due Process Clause alone. He reads that clause alone as allowing this Court "to determine what forms of procedural protection are necessary to guarantee the fundamental fairness of juvenile proceedings" "in a fashion consistent with the 'traditions and conscience of our people.'" Cf. Rochin v. People of California, 342 U.S. 165, 72 S.Ct. 205, 96 L.Ed. 183. He believes that the Due Process Clause gives this Court the power, upon weighing a "compelling public interest," to impose on the States only those specific constitutional rights which the Court deems "imperative" and "necessary" to comport with the Court's notions of "fundamental fairness."

I cannot subscribe to any such interpretation of the Due Process Clause. Nothing in its words or its history permits it, and "fair distillations of relevant judicial history" are no substitute for the words and history of the clause itself. The phrase "due process of law" has through the years evolved as the successor in purpose and meaning to the words "law of the land" in Magna Charta which more plainly intended to call for a trial according to the existing law of the land in effect at the time an alleged offense had been committed. That provision in Magna Charta was designed to prevent defendants from being tried according to criminal laws or proclamations specifically promulgated to fit particular cases or to attach new consequences to old conduct. Nothing done since Magna Charta can be pointed to as intimating that the Due Process Clause gives courts power to fashion laws in order to meet new conditions, to fit the "decencies" of changed conditions, or to keep their consciences from being shocked by legislation, state or federal.

And, of course, the existence of such awesome judicial power cannot be buttressed or created by relying on the word "procedural." Whether labeled as "procedural" or "substantive," the Bill of Rights safeguards, far from being mere "tools with which" other unspecified "rights could be fully vindicated," are the very vitals of a sound constitutional legal system designed to protect and safeguard the most cherished liberties of a free people. These safeguards were written into our Constitution not by judges but by Constitution makers. Freedom in this Nation will be far less secure the very moment that it is decided that judges can determine which of these safeguards "should" or "should not be imposed" according to their notions of what constitutional provisions are consistent with the "traditions and conscience of our people." Judges with such power, even though they profess to "proceed with restraint," will be above the Constitution, with power to write it, not merely to interpret it, which I believe to be the only power constitutionally committed to judges.

There is one ominous sentence, if not more, in my Brother Harlan's opinion which bodes ill, in my judgment, both for legislative programs and constitutional commands. Speaking of procedural safeguards in the Bill of Rights, he says:

> "These factors in combination suggest that legislatures may properly expect only a cautious deference for their procedural judgments, but that, conversely, courts must exercise their special responsibility for procedural guarantees with care to permit ample scope for achieving the purposes of legislative programs. * * * [T]he court should necessarily proceed with restraint."

It is to be noted here that this case concerns Bill of Rights Amendments; that the "procedure" power my Brother Harlan claims for the Court here relates solely to Bill of Rights safeguards; and that he is here claiming for the Court a supreme power to fashion new Bill of Rights safeguards according to the Court's notions of what fits tradition and conscience. I do not believe that the Constitution vests any such power in judges, either in the Due Process Clause or anywhere else. Consequently, I do not vote to invalidate this Arizona law on the ground that it is "unfair" but solely on the ground that it violates the Fifth and Sixth Amendments made obligatory on the States by the Fourteenth Amendment. Cf. Pointer v. State of Texas, 380 U.S. 400, 412, 85 S.Ct. 1065, 1072, 13 L.Ed.2d 923 (Goldberg, J., concurring). It is enough for me that the Arizona law as here applied collides head-on with the Fifth and Sixth Amendments in the four respects mentioned. The only relevance to me of the Due Process Clause is that it would, of course, violate due process or the "law of the land" to enforce a law that collides with the Bill of Rights.

Mr. Justice White, concurring.

I join the Court's opinion except for Part V. I also agree that the privilege against compelled self-incrimination applies at the adjudicatory stage of juvenile court proceedings. I do not, however, find an adequate basis in the record for determining whether that privilege was violated in this case. The Fifth Amendment protects a person from being "compelled" in any criminal proceeding to be a witness against himself. Compulsion is essential to a violation. It may be that when a judge, armed with the authority he has or which people think he has, asks questions of a party or a witness in an adjudicatory hearing, that person, especially if a minor, would feel compelled to answer, absent a warning to the contrary or similar information from some other source. The difficulty is that the record made at the habeas corpus hearing, which is the only information we have concerning the proceedings in the juvenile court, does not directly inform us whether Gerald Gault or his parents were told of Gerald's right to remain silent; nor does it reveal whether the parties were aware of the privilege from some other source, just as they were already aware that they had the right to have the help of counsel and to have witnesses on their behalf. The petition for habeas corpus did not raise the Fifth Amendment issue nor did any of the witnesses focus on it.

I have previously recorded my views with respect to what I have deemed unsound applications of the Fifth Amendment. See, for example, Miranda v. State of Arizona, 384 U.S. 436, 526, 86 S.Ct. 1602, 1654, 16 L.Ed.2d 694, and Malloy v. Hogan, 378 U.S. 1, 33, 84 S.Ct. 1489, 1506, 12 L.Ed.2d 653, dissenting opinions. These views, of course, have not prevailed. But I do hope that the Court will proceed with some care in extending the privilege, with all its vigor, to proceedings in juvenile court, particularly the nonadjudicatory stages of those proceedings.

In any event, I would not reach the Fifth Amendment issue here. I think the Court is clearly ill-advised to review this case on the basis of Miranda v. State of Arizona, since the adjudication of delinquency took place in 1964, long before the Miranda decision. See Johnson v. State of New Jersey, 384 U.S. 719, 86 S.Ct. 1772, 16 L.Ed.2d 882. Under these circumstances, this case is a poor vehicle for resolving a difficult problem. Moreover, no prejudice to appellants is at stake in this regard. The judgment below must be reversed on other grounds and in the event further proceedings are to be had, Gerald Gault will have counsel available to advise him.

For somewhat similar reasons, I would not reach the questions of confrontation and cross-examination which are also dealt with in Part V of the opinion.

Mr. Justice Harlan, concurring in part and dissenting in part.

Each of the 50 States has created a system of juvenile or family courts, in which distinctive rules are employed and special consequences imposed. The jurisdiction of these courts commonly extends both to cases which the States have withdrawn from the ordinary processes of criminal justice, and to cases which involve acts that, if performed by an adult, would not be penalized as criminal. Such courts are denominated civil, not criminal, and are characteristically said not to administer criminal penalties. One consequence of these systems, at least as Arizona construes its own, is that certain of the rights guaranteed to criminal defendants by the Constitution are withheld from juveniles. This case brings before this Court for the first time the question of what limitations the Constitution places upon the operation of such tribunals.[8] For reasons which follow, I have concluded that the Court has gone too far in some respects, and fallen short in others, in assessing the procedural requirements demanded by the Fourteenth Amendment.

I.

I must first acknowledge that I am unable to determine with any certainty by what standards the Court decides that Arizona's juvenile courts do not satisfy the obligations of due process. The Court's premise, itself the product of reasoning which is not described, is

---

8. Kent v. United States, 383 U.S. 541, 86 S.Ct. 1045, 16 L.Ed.2d 84, decided at the 1965 Term, did not purport to rest on constitutional grounds.

that the "constitutional and theoretical basis" of state systems of juvenile and family courts is "debatable"; it buttresses these doubts by marshaling a body of opinion which suggests that the accomplishments of these courts have often fallen short of expectations.[9] The Court does not indicate at what points or for what purposes such views, held either by it or by other observers, might be pertinent to the present issues. Its failure to provide any discernible standard for the measurement of due process in relation to juvenile proceedings unfortunately might be understood to mean that the Court is concerned principally with the wisdom of having such courts at all.

If this is the source of the Court's dissatisfaction, I cannot share it. I should have supposed that the constitutionality of juvenile courts was beyond proper question under the standards now employed to assess the substantive validity of state legislation under the Due Process Clause of the Fourteenth Amendment. It can scarcely be doubted that it is within the State's competence to adopt measures reasonably calculated to meet more effectively the persistent problems of juvenile delinquency; as the opinion for the Court makes abundantly plain, these are among the most vexing and ominous of the concerns which now face communities throughout the country.

The proper issue here is, however, not whether the State may constitutionally treat juvenile offenders through a system of specialized courts, but whether the proceedings in Arizona's juvenile courts include procedural guarantees which satisfy the requirements of the Fourteenth Amendment. Among the first premises of our constitutional system is the obligation to conduct any proceeding in which an individual may be deprived of liberty or property in a fashion consistent with the "traditions and conscience of our people." Snyder v. Commonwealth of Massachusetts, 291 U.S. 97, 105, 54 S.Ct. 330, 332, 78 L.Ed. 674. The importance of these procedural guarantees is doubly intensified here. First, many of the problems

---

9. It is appropriate to observe that, whatever the relevance the Court may suppose that this criticism has to present issues, many of the critics have asserted that the deficiencies of juvenile courts have stemmed chiefly from the inadequacy of the personnel and resources available to those courts. See, e.g., Paulsen, Kent v. United States: The Constitutional Context of Juvenile Cases, 1966 Sup.Ct.Rev. 167, 191-192; Handler, The Juvenile Court and the Adversary System: Problems of Function and Form, 1965 Wis.L.Rev. 7, 46.

with which Arizona is concerned are among those traditionally confined to the processes of criminal justice; their disposition necessarily affects in the most direct and substantial manner the liberty of individual citizens. Quite obviously, systems of specialized penal justice might permit erosion, or even evasion, of the limitations placed by the Constitution upon state criminal proceedings. Second, we must recognize that the character and consequences of many juvenile court proceedings have in fact closely resembled those of ordinary criminal trials. Nothing before us suggests that juvenile courts were intended as a device to escape constitutional constraints, but I entirely agree with the Court that we are nonetheless obliged to examine with circumspection the procedural guarantees the State has provided.

The central issue here, and the principal one upon which I am divided from the Court, is the method by which the procedural requirements of due process should be measured. It must at the outset be emphasized that the protections necessary here cannot be determined by resort to any classification of juvenile proceedings either as criminal or as civil, whether made by the State or by this Court. Both formulae are simply too imprecise to permit reasoned analysis of these difficult constitutional issues. The Court should instead measure the requirements of due process by reference both to the problems which confront the State and to the actual character of the procedural system which the State has created. The Court has for such purposes chiefly examined three connected sources: first, the "settled usages and modes of proceeding," Den ex dem. Murray v. Hoboken Land & Improvement Co., 18 How. 272, 277, 15 L.Ed. 372; second, the "fundamental principles of liberty and justice which lie at the base of all our civil and political institutions." Hebert v. State of Louisiana, 272 U.S. 312, 316, 47 S.Ct. 103, 104, 71 L.Ed. 270 and third, the character and requirements of the circumstances presented in each situation. FCC v. WJR, The Goodwill Station, 337 U.S. 265, 277, 69 S.Ct. 1097, 1104, 93 L.Ed. 1353; Yakus v. United States, 321 U.S. 414, 64 S.Ct. 660, 88 L.Ed. 834. See, further, my dissenting opinion in Poe v. Ullman, 367 U.S. 497, 522, 81 S.Ct. 1752, 1765, 6 L.Ed.2d 989, and compare my opinion concurring in the result in Pointer v. State of Texas, 380 U.S. 400, 408, 85 S.Ct. 1065, 1070. Each of these factors is relevant to the issues here, but it is the last which demands particular examination.

The Court has repeatedly emphasized that determination of the constitutionally required procedural safeguards in any situation requires recognition both of the "interests affected" and of the "circumstances involved." FCC v. WJR, The Goodwill Station, supra, 337 U.S. at 277, 69 S.Ct. at 1104. In particular, a "compelling public interest" must, under our cases, be taken fully into account in assessing the validity under the due process clauses of state or federal legislation and its application. See, e.g., Yakus v. United States, supra, 321 U.S. at 442, 64 S.Ct. at 675; Bowles v. Willingham, 321 U.S. 503, 520, 64 S.Ct. 641, 650, 88 L.Ed. 892; Miller v. Schoene, 276 U.S. 272, 279, 48 S.Ct. 246, 247, 72 L.Ed. 568. Such interests would never warrant arbitrariness or the diminution of any specifically assured constitutional right, Home Bldg. & Loan Assn. v. Blaisdell, 290 U.S. 398, 426, 54 S.Ct. 231, 235, 78 L.Ed. 413, but they are an essential element of the context through which the legislation and proceedings under it must be read and evaluated.

No more evidence of the importance of the public interests at stake here is required than that furnished by the opinion of the Court; it indicates that "some 601,000 children under 18, or 2% of all children between 10 and 17, came before juvenile courts" in 1965, and that "about one-fifth of all arrests for serious crimes" in 1965 were of juveniles. The Court adds that the rate of juvenile crime is steadily rising. All this, as the court suggests, indicates the importance of these due process issues, but it mirrors no less vividly that state authorities are confronted by formidable and immediate problems involving the most fundamental social values. The state legislatures have determined that the most hopeful solution for these problems is to be found in specialized courts, organized under their own rules and imposing distinctive consequences. The terms and limitations of these systems are not identical, nor are the procedural arrangements which they include, but the States are uniform in their insistence that the ordinary processes of criminal justice are inappropriate, and that relatively informal proceedings, dedicated to premises and purposes only imperfectly reflected in the criminal law, are instead necessary.

It is well settled that the Court must give the widest deference to legislative judgments that concern the character and urgency of the problems with which the State is confronted. Legislatures are, as this Court has often acknowledged, the "main guardian" of the public interest, and, within their constitutional competence, their understanding of that interest must be accepted as "well-nigh" conclusive.

Berman v. Parker, 348 U.S. 26, 32, 75 S.Ct. 98, 102, 99 L.Ed. 27. This principle does not, however, reach all the questions essential to the resolution of this case. The legislative judgments at issue here embrace assessments of the necessity and wisdom of procedural guarantees; these are questions which the Constitution has entrusted at least in part to courts, and upon which courts have been understood to possess particular competence. The fundamental issue here is, therefore, in what measure and fashion the Court must defer to legislative determinations which encompass constitutional issues of procedural protection.

It suffices for present purposes to summarize the factors which I believe to be pertinent. It must first be emphasized that the deference given to legislators upon substantive issues must realistically extend in part to ancillary procedural questions. Procedure at once reflects and creates substantive rights, and every effort of courts since the beginnings of the common law to separate the two has proved essentially futile. The distinction between them is particularly inadequate here, where the legislature's substantive preferences directly and unavoidably require judgments about procedural issues. The procedural framework is here a principal element of the substantive legislative system; meaningful deference to the latter must include a portion of deference to the former. The substantive-procedural dichotomy is, nonetheless, an indispensable tool of analysis, for it stems from fundamental limitations upon judicial authority under the Constitution. Its premise is ultimately that courts may not substitute for the judgments of legislators their own understanding of the public welfare, but must instead concern themselves with the validity under the Constitution of the methods which the legislature has selected. See, e.g., McLean v. State of Arkansas, 211 U.S. 539, 547, 29 S.Ct. 206, 208, 53 L.Ed. 315; Olsen v. State of Nebraska, 313 U.S. 236, 246-247, 61 S.Ct. 862, 865, 85 L.Ed. 1305. The Constitution has in this manner created for courts and legislators areas of primary responsibility which are essentially congruent to their areas of special competence. Courts are thus obliged both by constitutional command and by their distinctive functions to bear particular responsibility for the measurement of procedural due process. These factors in combination suggest that legislatures may properly expect only a cautious deference for their procedural judgments, but that, conversely, courts must exercise their special responsibility for procedural guarantees with care to permit ample scope for achieving the purposes of legislative programs. Plainly, courts can exercise such care only if they have in each case first studied thoroughly the objectives and implementation of the program at stake; if, upon completion of those studies, the effect of extensive procedural restrictions upon valid legislative purposes cannot be assessed with reasonable certainty, the court should necessarily proceed with restraint.

The foregoing considerations, which I believe to be fair distillations of relevant judicial history, suggest three criteria by which the procedural requirements of due process should be measured here: first, no more restrictions should be imposed than are imperative to assure the proceedings' fundamental fairness; second, the restrictions which are imposed should be those which preserve, so far as possible, the essential elements of the State's purpose; and finally, restrictions should be chosen which will later permit the orderly selection of any additional protections which may ultimately prove necessary. In this way, the Court may guarantee the fundamental fairness of the proceeding, and yet permit the State to continue development of an effective response to the problems of juvenile crime.

II.

Measured by these criteria, only three procedural requirements should, in my opinion, now be deemed required of state juvenile courts by the Due Process Clause of the Fourteenth Amendment: first, timely notice must be provided to parents and children of the nature and terms of any juvenile court proceeding in which a determination affecting their rights or interests may be made; second, unequivocal and timely notice must be given that counsel may appear in any such proceeding in behalf of the child and its parents, and that in cases in which the child may be confined in an institution, counsel may, in circumstances of indigency, be appointed for them; and third, the court must maintain a written record, or its equivalent, adequate to permit effective review on appeal or in collateral proceedings. These requirements would guarantee to juveniles the tools with which their rights could be fully vindicated, and yet permit the States to pursue without unnecessary hindrance the purposes which they believe imperative in this field. Further, their imposition now would later permit more intelligent assessment of the necessity under the Fourteenth Amendment of additional requirements, by creating suitable records from which the character and deficiencies of juvenile proceedings could be accurately judged. I turn to consider each of these three requirements.

The Court has consistently made plain that adequate and timely notice is the fulcrum of due process, whatever the purposes of the proceeding. See, e.g., Roller v. Holly, 176 U.S. 398, 409, 20 S.Ct. 410, 413, 44 L.Ed. 520; Coe v. Armour Fertilizer Works, 237 U.S. 413, 424, 35 S.Ct. 625, 628, 59 L.Ed. 1027. Notice is ordinarily the prerequisite to effective assertion of any constitutional or other rights; without it, vindication of those rights must be essentially fortuitous. So fundamental a protection can neither be spared here nor left to the "favor or grace" of state authorities. Central of Georgia Ry. v. Wright, 207 U.S. 127, 138, 28 S.Ct. 47, 51, 52 L.Ed. 134; Coe v. Armour Fertilizer Works, supra, 237 U.S. at 425, 35 S.Ct. at 628.

Provision of counsel and of a record, like adequate notice, would permit the juvenile to assert very much more effectively his rights and defenses, both in the juvenile proceedings and upon direct or collateral review. The Court has frequently emphasized their importance in proceedings in which an individual may be deprived of his liberty, see Gideon v. Wainwright, 372 U.S. 335, 83 S.Ct. 792, 9 L.Ed. 2d 799, and Griffin v. People of State of Illinois, 351 U.S. 12, 76 S.Ct. 585, 100 L.Ed. 891; this reasoning must include with special force those who are commonly inexperienced and immature. See Powell v. State of Alabama, 287 U.S. 45, 53 S.Ct. 55, 77 L.Ed. 158. The facts of this case illustrate poignantly the difficulties of review without either an adequate record or the participation of counsel in the proceeding's initial stages. At the same time, these requirements should not cause any substantial modification in the character of juvenile court proceedings: counsel, although now present in only a small percentage of juvenile cases, have apparently already appeared without incident in virtually all juvenile courts;[10] and the maintenance of a record should not appreciably alter the conduct of these proceedings.

The question remains whether certain additional requirements, among them the privilege against self-incrimination, confrontation, and cross-examination, must now, as the Court holds, also be im-

10. The statistical evidence here is incomplete, but see generally Skoler & Tenney, Attorney Representation in Juvenile Court, 4 J.Fam.Law 77. They indicate that some 91% of the juvenile court judges whom they polled favored representation by counsel in their courts. Id., at 88.

posed. I share in part the views expressed in my Brother White's concurring opinion, but believe that there are other, and more deep-seated, reasons to defer, at least for the present, the imposition of such requirements.

Initially, I must vouchsafe that I cannot determine with certainty the reasoning by which the Court concludes that these further requirements are now imperative. The Court begins from the premise, to which it gives force at several points, that juvenile courts need not satisfy "all of the requirements of a criminal trial." It therefore scarcely suffices to explain the selection of these particular procedural requirements for the Court to declare that juvenile court proceedings are essentially criminal, and thereupon to recall that these are requisites for a criminal trial. Nor does the Court's voucher of "authoritative opinion," which consists of four extraordinary juvenile cases, contribute materially to the solution of these issues. The Court has, even under its own premises, asked the wrong questions: the problem here is to determine what forms of procedural protection are necessary to guarantee the fundamental fairness of juvenile proceedings, and not which of the procedures now employed in criminal trials should be transplanted intact to proceedings in these specialized courts.

In my view, the Court should approach this question in terms of the criteria, described above, which emerge from the history of due process adjudication. Measured by them, there are compelling reasons at least to defer imposition of these additional requirements. First, quite unlike notice, counsel, and a record, these requirements might radically alter the character of juvenile court proceedings. The evidence from which the Court reasons that they would not is inconclusive,[11] and other available evidence suggests that they very likely would.[12] At the least, it is plain that these additional requirements would contribute materially to the creation in these proceedings of the atmosphere of an ordinary criminal trial, and would,

11. Indeed, my Brother Black candidly recognizes that such is apt to be the effect of today's decision. * * * The Court itself is content merely to rely upon inapposite language from the recommendations of the Children's Bureau, plus the terms of a single statute.

12. The most cogent evidence of course consists of the steady rejection of these requirements by state legislatures and courts. The wide disagreement and uncertainty upon this question are also reflected in Paulsen, Kent v. United States: The Constitutional Context of Juvenile Cases, 1966 Sup.Ct.Rev. 167, 186, 191. See also Paulsen, Fairness to the Juvenile Offender, 41 Minn.L.Rev. 547, 561-562; McLean,

even if they do no more, thereby largely frustrate a central purpose of these specialized courts. Further, these are restrictions intended to conform to the demands of an intensely adversary system of criminal justice; the broad purposes which they represent might be served in juvenile courts with equal effectiveness by procedural devices more consistent with the premises of proceedings in those courts. As the Court apparently acknowledges, the hazards of self-accusation, for example, might be avoided in juvenile proceedings without the imposition of all the requirements and limitations which surround the privilege against self-incrimination. The guarantee of adequate notice, counsel, and a record would create conditions in which suitable alternative procedures could be devised; but, unfortunately, the Court's haste to impose restrictions taken intact from criminal procedure may well seriously hamper the development of such alternatives. Surely this illustrates that prudence and the principles of the Fourteenth Amendment alike require that the Court should now impose no more procedural restrictions than are imperative to assure fundamental fairness, and that the States should instead be permitted additional opportunities to develop without unnecessary hindrance their systems of juvenile courts.

I find confirmation for these views in two ancillary considerations. First, it is clear that an uncertain, but very substantial number of the cases brought to juvenile courts involve children who are not in any sense guilty of criminal misconduct. Many of these children have simply the misfortune to be in some manner distressed; others have engaged in conduct, such as truancy, which is plainly not criminal.[13] Efforts are now being made to develop effective, and entirely noncriminal, methods of treatment for these children. In such cases, the state authorities are in the most literal sense acting *in loco paren-*

An Answer to the Challenge of Kent, 53 A.B.A.J. 456, 457; Alexander, Constitutional Rights in Juvenile Court, 46 A.B.A.J. 1206; Shears, Legal Problems Peculiar to Children's Courts, 48 A.B.A.J. 719; Siler, The Need for Defense Counsel in the Juvenile Court, 11 Crime & Delin. 45, 57-58. Compare Handler, The Juvenile Court and the Adversary System: Problems of Function and Form, 1965 Wis.L.Rev. 7, 32.

13. Estimates of the number of children in this situation brought before juvenile courts range from 26% to some 48%; variation seems chiefly a product both of the inadequacy of records and of the difficulty of categorizing precisely the conduct with which juveniles are charged. See generally Sheridan, Juveniles Who Commit Noncriminal Acts: Why Treat in a Correctional System? 31 Fed.Probation 26, 27. By any standard, the number of juveniles involved is "considerable." Ibid.

tis; they are, by any standard, concerned with the child's protection, and not with his punishment. I do not question that the methods employed in such cases must be consistent with the constitutional obligation to act in accordance with due process, but certainly the Fourteenth Amendment does not demand that they be constricted by the procedural guarantees devised for ordinary criminal prosecutions. Cf. State of Minnesota ex rel. Pearson v. Probate Court, 309 U.S. 270, 60 S.Ct. 523, 84 L.Ed. 744. It must be remembered that the various classifications of juvenile court proceedings are, as the vagaries of the available statistics illustrate, often arbitrary or ambiguous; it would therefore be imprudent, at the least, to build upon these classifications rigid systems of procedural requirements which would be applicable, or not, in accordance with the descriptive label given to the particular proceeding. It is better, it seems to me, to begin by now requiring the essential elements of fundamental fairness in juvenile courts, whatever the label given by the State to the proceeding; in this way the Court could avoid imposing unnecessarily rigid restrictions, and yet escape dependence upon classifications which may often prove to be illusory. Further, the provision of notice, counsel, and a record would permit orderly efforts to determine later whether more satisfactory classifications can be devised, and if they can, whether additional procedural requirements are necessary for them under the Fourteenth Amendment.

Second, it should not be forgotten that juvenile crime and juvenile courts are both now under earnest study throughout the country. I very much fear that this Court, by imposing these rigid procedural requirements, may inadvertently have served to discourage these efforts to find more satisfactory solutions for the problems of juvenile crime, and may thus now hamper enlightened development of the systems of juvenile courts. It is appropriate to recall that the Fourteenth Amendment does not compel the law to remain passive in the midst of change; to demand otherwise denies "every quality of the law but its age." Hurtado v. People of State of California, 110 U.S. 516, 529, 4 S.Ct. 111, 117, 28 L.Ed. 232.

III.

Finally, I turn to assess the validity of this juvenile court proceeding under the criteria discussed in this opinion. Measured by them, the judgment below must, in my opinion, fall. Gerald Gault and his parents were not provided adequate notice of the terms and purposes of the proceedings in which he was adjudged delinquent; they were not advised of their rights to be represented by counsel; and no record in any form was maintained of the proceedings. It follows, for the reasons given in this opinion, that Gerald Gault was deprived of his liberty without due process of law, and I therefore concur in the judgment of the Court.

Mr. Justice Stewart, dissenting.

The Court today uses an obscure Arizona case as a vehicle to impose upon thousands of juvenile courts throughout the Nation restrictions that the Constitution made applicable to adversary criminal trials. I believe the Court's decision is wholly unsound as a matter of constitutional law, and sadly unwise as a matter of judicial policy.

Juvenile proceedings are not criminal trials. They are not civil trials. They are simply not adversary proceedings. Whether treating with a delinquent child, a neglected child, a defective child, or a dependent child, a juvenile proceeding's whole purpose and mission is the very opposite of the mission and purpose of a prosecution in a criminal court. The object of the one is correction of a condition. The object of the other is conviction and punishment for a criminal act.

In the last 70 years many dedicated men and women have devoted their professional lives to the enlightened task of bringing us out of the dark world of Charles Dickens in meeting our responsibilities to the child in our society. The result has been the creation in this century of a system of juvenile and family courts in each of the 50 States. There can be no denying that in many areas the performance of these agencies has fallen disappointingly short of the hopes and dreams of the courageous pioneers who first conceived them. For a variety of reasons, the reality has sometimes not even approached the ideal, and much remains to be accomplished in the administration of public juvenile and family agencies—in personnel, in planning, in financing, perhaps in the formulation of wholly new approaches.

I possess neither the specialized experience nor the expert knowledge to predict with any certainty where may lie the brightest hope for progress in dealing with the serious problems of juvenile delinquency. But I am certain that the answer does not lie in the Court's opinion in this case, which serves to convert a juvenile proceeding into a criminal prosecution.

The inflexible restrictions that the Constitution so wisely made applicable to adversary criminal trials have no inevitable place in the proceedings of those public social agencies known as juvenile or family courts. And to impose the Court's long catalog of requirements upon juvenile proceedings in every area of the country is to invite a long step backwards into the nineteenth century. In that era there were no juvenile proceedings, and a child was tried in a conventional criminal court with all the trappings of a conventional criminal trial. So it was that a 12-year-old boy named James Guild was tried in New Jersey for killing Catharine Beakes. A jury found him guilty of murder, and he was sentenced to death by hanging. The sentence was executed. It was all very constitutional.[14]

A State in all its dealings must, of course, accord every person due process of law. And due process may require that some of the same restrictions which the Constitution has placed upon criminal trials must be imposed upon juvenile proceedings. For example, I suppose that all would agree that a brutally coerced confession could not constitutionally be considered in a juvenile court hearing. But it surely does not follow that the testimonial privilege against self-incrimination is applicable in all juvenile proceedings.[15] Similarly, due process clearly requires timely notice of the purpose and scope

14. State v. Guild, 5 Halst, 163, 10 N. J.L. 163, 18 Am.Dec. 404.
"Thus, also, in very modern times, a boy of ten years old was convicted on his own confession of murdering his bedfellow, there appearing in his whole behavior plain tokens of a mischievous discretion; and as the sparing this boy merely on account of his tender years might be of dangerous consequence to the public, by propagating a notion that children might commit such atrocious crimes with impunity, it was unanimously agreed by all the judges that he was a proper subject of capital punishment." 4 Blackstone, Commentaries 23 (Wendell ed. 1847).

15. Until June 13, 1966, it was clear that the Fourteenth Amendment's ban upon the use of a coerced confession is constitutionally quite different from the Fifth Amendment's testimonial privilege against self-incrimination. See, for example, the Court's unanimous opinion in Brown v. State of Mississippi, 297 U.S. 278, at 285-286, 56 S.Ct. 461, 464-465, 80 L.Ed. 682, written by Chief Justice Hughes and joined by such distinguished members of this Court as Mr. Justice Brandeis, Mr. Justice Stone, and Mr. Justice Cardozo. See also Tehan v. United States ex rel. Shott, 382 U.S. 406, 86 S.Ct. 459, 15 L.Ed.2d 453, decided January 19, 1966, where the Court emphasized the "contrast" between "the wrongful use of a coerced confession" and "the Fifth Amendment's privilege against self-incrimination." 382 U.S., at 416, 86 S.Ct.; at 465. The complete confusion of these separate constitutional doctrines in Part V of the Court's opinion today stems, no doubt, from Miranda v. State of Arizona, 384 U.S. 436, 86 S.Ct. 1602, a decision which we continue to believe was constitutionally erroneous.

of any proceedings affecting the relationship of parent and child. Armstrong v. Manzo, 380 U.S. 545, 85 S.Ct. 1187, 14 L.Ed. 2d 62. But it certainly does not follow that notice of a juvenile hearing must be framed with all the technical niceties of a criminal indictment. See Russell v. United States, 369 U.S. 749, 82 S.Ct. 1038, 8 L.Ed.2d 240.

In any event, there is no reason to deal with issues such as these in the present case. The Supreme Court of Arizona found that the parents of Gerald Gault "knew of their right to counsel, to subpoena and cross examine witnesses, of the right to confront the witnesses against Gerald and the possible consequences of a finding of delinquency." 99 Ariz. 181, 185, 407 P.2d 760, 763. It further found that "Mrs. Gault knew the exact nature of the charge against Gerald from the day he was taken to the detention home." 99 Ariz., at 193, 407 P.2d, at 768. And, as Mr. Justice White correctly points out, p. 1463, ante, no issue of compulsory self-incrimination is presented by this case.

I would dismiss the appeal.

C The Kent Decision

KENT v. UNITED STATES

Supreme Court of the United States, 1966.
383 U.S. 541, 86 S.Ct. 1045, 16 L.Ed.2d 84.

Mr. Justice Fortas delivered the opinion of the Court.

This case is here on certiorari to the United States Court of Appeals for the District of Columbia Circuit. The facts and the contentions of counsel raise a number of disturbing questions concerning the administration by the police and the Juvenile Court authorities of the District of Columbia laws relating to juveniles. Apart from raising questions as to the adequacy of custodial and treatment facilities and policies, some of which are not within judicial competence, the case presents important challenges to the procedure of the police and Juvenile Court officials upon apprehension of a juvenile suspected of serious offenses. Because we conclude that the Juvenile Court's order waiving jurisdiction of petitioner was entered without compliance with required procedures, we remand the case to the trial court.

Morris A. Kent, Jr., first came under the authority of the Juvenile Court of the District of Columbia in 1959. He was then aged 14. He was apprehended as a result of several housebreakings and an attempted purse snatching. He was placed on probation, in the custody of his mother who had been separated from her husband since Kent was two years old. Juvenile Court officials interviewed Kent from time to time during the probation period and accumulated a "Social Service" file.

On September 2, 1961, an intruder entered the apartment of a woman in the District of Columbia. He took her wallet. He raped her. The police found in the apartment latent fingerprints. They were developed and processed. They matched the fingerprints of Morris Kent, taken when he was 14 years old and under the jurisdiction of the Juvenile Court. At about 3 p. m. on September 5, 1961, Kent was taken into custody by the police. Kent was then 16 and therefore subject to the "exclusive jurisdiction" of the Juvenile Court. D.C.Code § 11—907 (1961), now § 11—1551 (Supp. IV, 1965). He was still on probation to that court as a result of the 1959 proceedings.

Upon being apprehended, Kent was taken to police head-quarters where he was interrogated by police officers. It appears that he admitted his involvement in the offense which led to his appre-hension and volunteered information as to similar offenses involving housebreaking, robbery, and rape. His interrogation proceeded from about 3 p. m. to 10 p. m. the same evening.[1]

Some time after 10 p. m. petitioner was taken to the Receiving Home for Children. The next morning he was released to the police for further interrogation at police headquarters, which lasted until 5 p. m.[2]

The record does not show when his mother became aware that the boy was in custody but shortly after 2 p. m. on September 6, 1961, the day following petitioner's apprehension, she retained counsel.

Counsel, together with petitioner's mother, promptly conferred with the Social Service Director of the Juvenile Court. In a brief in-terview, they discussed the possibility that the Juvenile Court might waive jurisdiction under D.C.Code § 11—914 (1961), now § 11—1553 (Supp. IV, 1965) and remit Kent to trial by the District Court. Counsel made known his intention to oppose waiver.

Petitioner was detained at the Receiving Home for almost a week. There was no arraignment during this time, no determination

1. There is no indication in the file that the police complied with the requirement of the District Code that a child taken into custody, unless released to his parent, guar-dian or custodian, "shall be placed in the custody of a probation officer or other person designated by the court, or taken immediately to the court or to a place of detention provided by the Board of Public Welfare, and the officer taking him shall immediately notify the court and shall file a petition when directed to do so by the court." D.C.Code § 11—912 (1961), now § 16—2306 (Supp. IV, 1965).

2. The elicited statements were not used in the subsequent trial before the United States District Court. Since the statements were made while petitioner was subject to the jurisdiction of the Juvenile Court, they were inadmissible in a subsequent criminal prosecution under the rule of Harling v. United States, 111 U.S.App.D.C. 174, 295 F.2d 161 (1961).

by a judicial officer of probable cause for petitioner's apprehension.[3]

During this period of detention and interrogation, petitioner's counsel arranged for examination of petitioner by two psychiatrists and a psychologist. He thereafter filed with the Juvenile Court a motion for a hearing on the question of waiver of Juvenile Court jurisdiction, together with an affidavit of a psychiatrist certifying that petitioner "is a victim of severe psychopathology" and recommending hospitalization for psychiatric observation. Petitioner's counsel, in support of his motion to the effect that the Juvenile Court should retain jurisdiction of petitioner, offered to prove that if petitioner were given adequate treatment in a hospital under the aegis of the Juvenile Court, he would be a suitable subject for rehabilitation.

At the same time, petitioner's counsel moved that the Juvenile Court should give him access to the Social Service file relating to petitioner which had been accumulated by the staff of the Juvenile Court during petitioner's probation period, and which would be available to the Juvenile Court judge in considering the question whether it should retain or waive jurisdiction. Petitioner's counsel represented that access to this file was essential to his providing petitioner with effective assistance of counsel.

The Juvenile Court judge did not rule on these motions. He held no hearing. He did not confer with petitioner or petitioner's parents

3. In the case of adults, arraignment before a magistrate for determination of probable cause and advice to the arrested person as to his rights, etc., are provided by law and are regarded as fundamental. Cf. Fed.Rules Crim. Proc. 5(a), (b); Mallory v. United States, 354 U.S. 449, 77 S.Ct. 1356, 1 L.Ed.2d 1479. In Harling v. United States, supra, the Court of Appeals for the District of Columbia has stated the basis for this distinction between juveniles and adults as follows:

"It is, of course, because children are, generally speaking, exempt from criminal penalties that safeguards of the criminal law, such as Rule 5 and the exclusionary Mallory rule, have no general application in juvenile proceedings." 111 U.S.App.D.C., at 176, 295 F.2d, at 163.

In Edwards v. United States, 117 U.S.App.D.C. 383, 384, 330 F.2d 849, 850 (1964) it was said that: "* * * special practices * * * follow the apprehension of a juvenile. He may be held in custody by the juvenile authorities—and is available to investigating officers—for five days before any formal action need be taken. There is no duty to take him before a magistrate, and no responsibility to inform him of his rights. He is not booked. The statutory intent is to establish a non-punitive, non-criminal atmosphere."

We indicate no view as to the legality of these practices. Cf. Harling v. United States, supra, 111 U.S.App.D.C., at 176, 295 F.2d, at 163, n. 12.

or petitioner's counsel. He entered an order reciting that after "full investigation, I do hereby waive" jurisdiction of petitioner and directing that he be "held for trial for [the alleged] offenses under the regular procedure of the U.S. District Court for the District of Columbia." He made no findings. He did not recite any reason for the waiver.[4] He made no reference to the motions filed by petitioner's counsel. We must assume that he denied, *sub silentio,* the motions for a hearing, the recommendation for hospitalization for psychiatric observation, the request for access to the Social Service file, and the offer to prove that petitioner was a fit subject for rehabilitation under the Juvenile Court's jurisdiction.[5]

Presumably, prior to entry of his order, the Juvenile Court judge received and considered recommendations of the Juvenile Court staff, the Social Service file relating to petitioner, and a report dated September 8, 1961 (three days following petitioner's apprehension), submitted to him by the Juvenile Probation Section. The Social Service file and the September 8 report were later sent to the District Court and it appears that both of them referred to petitioner's mental condition. The September 8 report spoke of "a rapid deterioration of [petitioner's] personality structure and the possibility of mental illness." As stated, neither this report nor the Social Service file was made available to petitioner's counsel.

The provision of the Juvenile Court Act governing waiver expressly provides only for "full investigation." It states the circumstances in which jurisdiction may be waived and the child held

4. At the time of these events, there was in effect Policy Memorandum No. 7 of November 30, 1959, promulgated by the judge of the Juvenile Court to set forth the criteria to govern disposition of waiver requests. It is set forth in the Appendix. This Memorandum has since been rescinded. See United States v. Caviness, 239 F.Supp. 545, 550 (D.C.D.C.1965).

5. It should be noted that at this time the statute provided for only one Juvenile Court judge. Congressional hearings and reports attest the impossibility of the burden which he was supposed to carry. See Amending the Juvenile Court Act of the District of Columbia, Hearings before Subcommittee No. 3 of the House Committee on the District of Columbia, 87th Cong., 1st Sess. (1961); Juvenile Delinquency, Hearings before the Subcommittee to Investigate Juvenile Delinquency of the Senate Committee on the Judiciary, 86th Cong., 1st Sess. (1959-1960); Additional Judges for Juvenile Court, Hearing before the House Committee on the District of Columbia, 86th Cong., 1st Sess. (1959); H.R.Rep.No.1041, 87th Cong., 1st Sess. (1961); S.Rep.No.841, 87th Cong., 1st Sess. (1961); S.Rep.No.116, 86th Cong., 1st Sess. (1959). The statute was amended in 1962 to provide for three judges for the court. 76 Stat. 21; D.C.Code § 11—1502 (Supp. IV, 1965).

for trial under adult procedures, but it does not state standards to govern the Juvenile Court's decision as to waiver. The provision reads as follows:

> "If a child sixteen years of age or older is charged with an offense which would amount to a felony in the case of an adult, or any child charged with an offense which if committed by an adult is punishable by death or life imprisonment, the judge may, after full investigation, waive jurisdiction and order such child held for trial under the regular procedure of the court which would have jurisdiction of such offense if committed by an adult; or such other court may exercise the powers conferred upon the juvenile court in this subchapter in conducting and disposing of such cases."[6]

Petitioner appealed from the Juvenile Court's waiver order to the Municipal Court of Appeals, which affirmed, and also applied to the United States District Court for a writ of habeas corpus, which was denied. On appeal from these judgments, the United States Court of Appeals held on January 22, 1963, that neither appeal to the Municipal Court of Appeals nor habeas corpus was available. In the Court of Appeals' view, the exclusive method of reviewing the Juvenile Court's waiver order was a motion to dismiss the indictment in the District Court. Kent v. Reid, 114 U.S.App. D.C. 330, 316 F.2d 331 (1963).

Meanwhile, on September 25, 1961, shortly after the Juvenile Court order waiving its jurisdiction, petitioner was indicted by a grand jury of the United States District Court for the District of Columbia. The indictment contained eight counts alleging two instances of housebreaking, robbery, and rape, and one of housebreaking and robbery. On November 16, 1961, petitioner moved the District Court to dismiss the indictment on the grounds that the waiver was invalid. He also moved the District Court to constitute itself a Juvenile Court as authorized by D.C.Code § 11—914 (1961), now § 11—1553 (Supp. IV, 1965). After substantial delay occasioned by petitioner's appeal and habeas corpus proceedings, the District Court addressed itself to the motion to dismiss on February 8, 1963.[7]

6. D.C.Code § 11—914 (1961), now § 11 1553 (Supp. IV, 1965).
7. On February 5, 1963, the motion to the District Court to constitute itself a Juvenile Court was denied. The motion was renewed orally and denied on February 8, 1963, after the District Court's decision that the indictment should not be dismissed.

The District Court denied the motion to dismiss the indictment. The District Court ruled that it would not "go behind" the Juvenile Court judge's recital that his order was entered "after full investigation." It held that "The only matter before me is as to whether or not the statutory provisions were complied with and the Courts have held * * * with reference to full investigation, that that does not mean a quasi judicial or judicial hearing. No hearing is required."

On March 7, 1963, the District Court held a hearing on petitioner's motion to determine his competency to stand trial. The court determined that petitioner was competent.[8]

At trial, petitioner's defense was wholly directed toward proving that he was not criminally responsible because "his unlawful act was the product of mental disease or mental defect." Durham v. United States, 94 U.S.App.D.C. 228, 241, 214 F.2d 862, 875, 45 A.L.R.2d 1430 (1954). Extensive evidence, including expert testimony, was presented to support this defense. The jury found as to the counts alleging rape that petitioner was "not guilty by reason of insanity." Under District of Columbia law, this made it mandatory that petitioner be transferred to St. Elizabeths Hospital, a mental institution, until his sanity is restored.[9] On the six counts of

8. The District Court had before it extensive information as to petitioner's mental condition, bearing upon both competence to stand trial and the defense of insanity. The court had obtained the "Social Service" file from the Juvenile Court and had made it available to petitioner's counsel. On October 13, 1961, the District Court had granted petitioner's motion of October 6 for commitment to the Psychiatric Division of the General Hospital for 60 days. On December 20, 1961, the hospital reported that "It is the concensus [sic] of the staff that Morris is emotionally ill and severely so * * * we feel that he is incompetent to stand trial and to participate in a mature way in his own defense. His illness has interfered with his judgment and reasoning ability * * *." The prosecutor opposed a finding of incompetence to stand trial, and at the prosecutor's request, the District Court referred petitioner to St. Elizabeths Hospital for psychiatric observation. According to a letter from the Superintendent of St. Elizabeths of April 5, 1962, the hospital's staff found that petitioner was "suffering from mental disease at the present time, Schizophrenic Reaction, Chronic Undifferentiated Type," that he had been suffering from this disease at the time of the charged offenses, and that "if committed by him [those criminal acts] were the product of this disease." They stated, however, that petitioner was "mentally competent to understand the nature of the proceedings against him and to consult properly with counsel in his own defense."
9. D.C.Code § 24—301 (1961).

housebreaking and robbery, the jury found that petitioner was guilty.[10]

Kent was sentenced to serve five to 15 years on each count as to which he was found guilty, or a total of 30 to 90 years in prison. The District Court ordered that the time to be spent at St. Elizabeths on the mandatory commitment after the insanity acquittal be counted as part of the 30- to 90-year sentence. Petitioner appealed to the United States Court of Appeals for the District of Columbia Circuit. That court affirmed. 119 U.S.App.D.C. 378, 343 F.2d 247 (1964).[11]

Before the Court of Appeals and in this Court, petitioner's counsel has urged a number of grounds for reversal. He argues that petitioner's detention and interrogation, described above, were unlawful. He contends that the police failed to follow the procedure prescribed by the Juvenile Court Act in that they failed to notify the parents of the child and the Juvenile Court itself, note 1, supra; that petitioner was deprived of his liberty for about a week without a determination of probable cause which would have been required in the case of an adult, see note 3, supra; that he was interrogated by the police in the absence of counsel or a parent, cf. Harling v. United States, 111 U.S.App.D.C. 174, 176, 295 F.2d 161, 163, n. 12 (1961), without warning of his right to remain silent or advice as to his right to counsel, in asserted violation of the Juvenile Court Act and in violation of rights that he would have if he were an adult; and that petitioner was fingerprinted in violation of the asserted intent of the Juvenile Court Act and while unlawfully detained and that the fingerprints were unlawfully used in the District Court proceeding.[12]

10. The basis for this distinction—that petitioner was "sane" for purposes of the housebreaking and robbery but "insane" for the purposes of the rape—apparently was the hypothesis, for which there is some support in the record, that the jury might find that the robberies had anteceded the rapes, and in that event, it might conclude that the housebreakings and robberies were not the products of his mental disease or defect, while the rapes were produced thereby.
11. Petitioner filed a petition for rehearing *en banc*, but subsequently moved to withdraw the petition in order to prosecute his petition for certiorari to this Court. The Court of Appeals permitted withdrawal. Chief Judge Bazelon filed a dissenting opinion in which Circuit Judge Wright joined. 119 U.S.App.D.C., at 395, 343 F.2d, at 264 (1964).
12. Cf. Harling v. United States, 111 U.S.App.D.C. 174, 295 F.2d 161 (1961); Bynum v. United States, 104 U.S.App.D.C. 368, 262 F.2d 465 (1958). It is not clear from the record whether the fingerprints used were taken during the detention period or were those taken while petitioner was in custody in 1959, nor is it clear that petitioner's counsel objected to the use of the fingerprints.

These contentions raise problems of substantial concern as to the construction of and compliance with the Juvenile Court Act. They also suggest basic issues as to the justifiability of affording a juvenile less protection than is accorded to adults suspected of criminal offenses, particularly where, as here, there is an absence of any indication that the denial of rights available to adults was offset, mitigated or explained by action of the Government, as *parens patriae,* evidencing the special solicitude for juveniles commanded by the Juvenile Court Act. However, because we remand the case on account of the procedural error with respect to waiver of jurisdiction, we do not pass upon these questions.[13]

It is to petitioner's arguments as to the infirmity of the proceedings by which the Juvenile Court waived its otherwise exclusive jurisdiction that we address our attention. Petitioner attacks the waiver of jurisdiction on a number of statutory and constitutional grounds. He contends that the waiver is defective because no hearing was held; because no findings were made by the Juvenile Court; because the Juvenile Court stated no reasons for waiver; and because counsel was denied access to the Social Service file which presumably was considered by the Juvenile Court in determining to waive jurisdiction.

We agree that the order of the Juvenile Court waiving its jurisdiction and transferring petitioner for trial in the United States District Court for the District of Columbia was invalid. There is no question that the order is reviewable on motion to dismiss the indictment in the District Court, as specified by the Court of Appeals in this case. Kent v. Reid, supra. The issue is the standards to be applied upon such review.

We agree with the Court of Appeals that the statute contemplates that the Juvenile Court should have considerable latitude within which to determine whether it should retain jurisdiction over

---

13. Petitioner also urges that the District Court erred in the following respects:

(1) It gave the jury a version of the "Allen" charge. See Allen v. United States, 164 U.S. 492, 17 S.Ct. 154, 41 L.Ed. 528.

(2) It failed to give an adequate and fair competency hearing.

(3) It denied the motion to constitute itself a juvenile court pursuant to D.C.Code § 11—914 (1961), now § 11—1553. (Supp. IV, 1965.)

(4) It should have granted petitioner's motion for acquittal on all counts, *n. o. v.* on the grounds of insanity.

We decide none of these claims.

a child or—subject to the statutory delimitation[14]—should waive jurisdiction. But this latitude is not complete. At the outset, it assumes procedural regularity sufficient in the particular circumstances to satisfy the basic requirements of due process and fairness, as well as compliance with the statutory requirement of a "full investigation." Green v. United States, 113 U.S.App.D.C. 348, 308 F.2d 303 (1962).[15] The statute gives the Juvenile Court a substantial degree of discretion as to the factual considerations to be evaluated, the weight to be given them and the conclusion to be reached. It does not confer upon the Juvenile Court a license for arbitrary procedure. The statute does not permit the Juvenile Court to determine in isolation and without the participation or any representation of the child the "critically important" question whether a child will be deprived of the special protections and provisions of the Juvenile Court Act.[16] It does not authorize the Juvenile Court, in total disregard of a motion for hearing filed by counsel, and without any hearing or statement or reasons, to decide—as in this case—that the child will be taken from the Receiving Home for Children and transferred to jail along with adults, and that he will be exposed to the possibility of a death sentence[17] instead of treatment for a maximum, in Kent's case, of five years, until he is 21.[18]

We do not consider whether, on the merits, Kent should have been transferred; but there is no place in our system of law for reaching a result of such tremendous consequences without ceremony—without hearing, without effective assistance of counsel,

14. The statute is set out at p. 1050, supra.

15. "What is required before a waiver is, as we have said, 'full investigation.' * * * It prevents the waiver of jurisdiction as a matter of routine for the purpose of easing the docket. It prevents routine waiver in certain classes of alleged crimes. It requires a judgment in each case based on 'an inquiry not only into the facts of the alleged offense but also into the question whether the *parens patriae* plan of procedure is desirable and proper in the particular case.' Pee v. United States, 107 U.S.App.D.C. 47, 50, 274 F.2d 556, 559 (1959)." Green v. United States, supra, at 350, 308 F.2d, at 305.

16. See Watkins v. United States, 119 U.S.App.D.C. 409, 413, 343 F.2d 278, 282 (1964); Black v. United States, 122 U.S.App.D.C. 393, 355 F.2d 104 (1965).

17. D.C.Code § 22—2801 (1961) fixes the punishment for rape at 30 years, or death if the jury so provides in its verdict. The maximum punishment for housebreaking is 15 years, D.C.Code § 22—1801 (1961); for robbery it is also 15 years, D.C.Code § 22—2901 (1961).

18. The jurisdiction of the Juvenile Court over a child ceases when he becomes 21. D.C.Code § 11—907 (1961), now § 11—1551 (Supp. IV, 1965).

without a statement of reasons. It is inconceivable that a court of justice dealing with adults, with respect to a similar issue, would proceed in this manner. It would be extraordinary if society's special concern for children, as reflected in the District of Columbia's Juvenile Court Act, permitted this procedure. We hold that it does not.

1. The theory of the District's Juvenile Court Act, like that of other jurisdictions,[19] is rooted in social welfare philosophy rather than in the *corpus juris.* Its proceedings are designated as civil rather than criminal. The Juvenile Court is theoretically engaged in determining the needs of the child and of society rather than adjudicating criminal conduct. The objectives are to provide measures of guidance and rehabilitation for the child and protection for society, not to fix criminal responsibility, guilt and punishment. The State is *parens patriae* rather than prosecuting attorney and judge.[20] But the admonition to function in a "parental" relationship is not an invitation to procedural arbitrariness.

2. Because the State is supposed to proceed in respect of the child as *parens patriae* and not as adversary, courts have relied on the premise that the proceedings are "civil" in nature and not criminal, and have asserted that the child cannot complain of the deprivation of important rights available in criminal cases. It has been asserted that he can claim only the fundamental due process right to fair treatment.[21] For example, it has been held that he is not entitled to bail; to indictment by grand jury; to a speedy and public trial; to trial by jury; to immunity against self-incrimination; to confrontation of his accusers; and in some jurisdictions (but not in the District of Columbia, see Shioutakon v. District of Columbia, 98 U.S.App.D.C. 371, 236 F.2d 666 (1956), and Black v. United States, supra) that he is not entitled to counsel.[22]

While there can be no doubt of the original laudable purpose of juvenile courts, studies and critiques in recent years raise serious

19. All States have juvenile court systems. A study of the actual operation of these systems is contained in Note, Juvenile Delinquents: The Police, State Courts, and Individualized Justice, 79 Harv.L.Rev. 775 (1966).

20. See Handler, The Juvenile Court and the Adversary System: Problems of Function and Form, 1965 Wis.L.Rev. 7.

21. Pee v. United States, 107 U.S.App.D.C. 47, 274 F.2d 556 (1959).

22. See Pee v. United States, supra, at 54, 274 F.2d, at 563; Paulsen, Fairness to the Juvenile Offender, 41 Minn.L.Rev. 547 (1957).

questions as to whether actual performance measures well enough against theoretical purpose to make tolerable the immunity of the process from the reach of constitutional guaranties applicable to adults.[23] There is much evidence that some juvenile courts, including that of the District of Columbia, lack the personnel, facilities and techniques to perform adequately as representatives of the State in a *parens patriae* capacity, at least with respect to children charged with law violation. There is evidence, in fact, that there may be grounds for concern that the child receives the worst of both worlds: that he gets neither the protections accorded to adults nor the solicitous care and regenerative treatment postulated for children.[24]

This concern, however, does not induce us in this case to accept the invitation[25] to rule that constitutional guaranties which would be applicable to adults charged with the serious offenses for which Kent was tried must be applied in juvenile court proceedings concerned with allegations of law violation. The Juvenile Court Act and the decisions of the United States Court of Appeals for the District of Columbia Circuit provide an adequate basis for decision of this case, and we go no further.

3. It is clear beyond dispute that the waiver of jurisdiction is a "critically important" action determining vitally important statutory rights of the juvenile. The Court of Appeals for the District of Columbia Circuit has so held. See Black v. United States, supra; Watkins v. United States, 119 U.S.App.D.C. 409, 343 F.2d 278 (1964). The statutory scheme makes this plain. The Juvenile Court is vested with "original and exclusive jurisdiction" of the child. This jurisdiction confers special rights and immunities. He is, as specified by the statute, shielded from publicity. He may be confined, but with rare exceptions he may not be jailed along with adults. He may be detained, but only until he is 21 years of age. The court is admonished by the statute to give preference to retaining the child in the custody of his parents "unless his welfare and the safety and protection of the public can not be adequately safeguarded without * * * removal." The child is protected against consequences of adult conviction such as the loss of civil rights, the use of adjudica-

23. Cf. Harling v. United States, 111 U.S.App.D.C. 174, 177, 295 F.2d 161, 164 (1961).
24. See Handler, op. cit. supra, note 20; Note, supra, note 19; materials cited in note 5, supra.
25. See brief of *amicus curiae*. 16—2313, 11—1586 (Supp. IV, 1965).

tion against him in subsequent proceedings, and disqualification for public employment. D.C.Code § § 11-907, 11—915, 11—927, 11—929 (1961).[26]

The net, therefore, is that petitioner—then a boy of 16—was by statute entitled to certain procedures and benefits as a consequence of his statutory right to the "exclusive" jurisdiction of the Juvenile Court. In these circumstances, considering particularly that decision as to waiver of jurisdiction and transfer of the matter to the District Court was potentially as important to petitioner as the difference between five years' confinement and a death sentence, we conclude that, as a condition to a valid waiver order, petitioner was entitled to a hearing, including access by his counsel to the social records and probation or similar reports which presumably are considered by the court, and to a statement of reasons for the Juvenile Court's decision. We believe that this result is required by the statute read in the context of constitutional principles relating to due process and the assistance of counsel.[27]

The Court of Appeals in this case relied upon Wilhite v. United States, 108 U.S.App.D.C. 279, 281 F.2d 642 (1960). In that case, the Court of Appeals held, for purposes of a determination as to waiver of jurisdiction, that no formal hearing is required and that the "full investigation" required of the Juvenile Court need only be such "as is needed to satisfy *that* court * * * on the question of waiver."[28] (Emphasis supplied.) The authority of Wilhite, however, is substantially undermined by other, more recent, decisions of the Court of Appeals.

In Black v. United States, decided by the Court of Appeals on December 8, 1965, the court[29] held that assistance of counsel in the

26. These are now, without substantial changes, § § 11—1551, 16—2307, 16—2308, 16—2313, 11—1586 (Supp. IV, 1965).

27. While we "will not ordinarily review decisions of the United States Court of Appeals [for the District of Columbia Circuit], which are based upon statutes * * * limited [to the District] * * *," Del Vecchio v. Bowers, 296 U.S. 280, 285, 56 S.Ct. 190, 192, 80 L.Ed. 229, the position of that court, as we discuss infra, is self-contradictory. Nor have we deferred to decisions on local law where to do so would require adjudication of difficult constitutional questions. See District of Columbia v. Little, 339 U.S. 1, 70 S.Ct. 468, 94 L.Ed. 599.

28. The panel was composed of Circuit Judges Miller, Fahy and Burger. Judge Fahy concurred in the result. It appears that the attack on the regularity of the waiver of jurisdiction was made 17 years after the event, and that no objection to waiver had been made in the District Court.

29. Bazelon, C.J., and Fahy and Leventhal, J.J.

"critically important" determination of waiver is essential to the proper administration of juvenile proceedings. Because the juvenile was not advised of his right to retained or appointed counsel, the judgment of the District Court, following waiver of jurisdiction by the Juvenile Court, was reversed. The court relied upon its decision in Shioutakon v. District of Columbia, 98 U.S.App.D.C. 371, 236 F.2d 666 (1956), in which it had held that effective assistance of counsel in juvenile court proceedings is essential. See also McDaniel v. Shea, 108 U.S.App.D.C. 15, 278 F.2d 460 (1960). In Black, the court referred to the Criminal Justice Act, enacted four years after Shioutakon, in which Congress provided for the assistance of counsel "in proceedings before the juvenile court of the District of Columbia." D.C.Code § 2—2202 (1961). The court held that "The need is even greater in the adjudication of waiver [than in a case like Shioutakon] since it contemplates the imposition of criminal sanctions." 122 U.S.App.D.C., at 395, 355 F.2d, at 106.

In Watkins v. United States, 119 U.S.App.D.C. 409, 343 F.2d 278 (1964), decided in November 1964, the Juvenile Court had waived jurisdiction of appellant who was charged with housebreaking and larceny. In the District Court, appellant sought disclosure of the social record in order to attack the validity of the waiver. The Court of Appeals held that in a waiver proceeding a juvenile's attorney is entitled to access to such records. The court observed that

> "All of the social records concerning the child are usually relevant to waiver since the Juvenile Court must be deemed to consider the entire history of the child in determining waiver. The relevance of particular items must be construed generously. Since an attorney has no certain knowledge of what the social records contain, he cannot be expected to demonstrate the relevance of particular items in his request.
>
> "The child's attorney must be advised of the information upon which the Juvenile Court relied in order to assist effectively in the determination of the waiver question, by insisting upon the statutory command that waiver can be ordered only after 'full investigation,' and by guarding against action of the Juvenile Court beyond its discretionary authority." 119 U.S.App.D.C., at 413, 343 F.2d, at 282.

The court remanded the record to the District Court for a determination of the extent to which the records should be disclosed.

The Court of Appeals' decision in the present case was handed down on October 26, 1964, prior to its decisions in Black and

Watkins. The Court of Appeals assumed that since petitioner had been a probationer of the Juvenile Court for two years, that court had before it sufficient evidence to make an informed judgment. It therefore concluded that the statutory requirement of a "full investigation" had been met. It noted the absence of "a specification by the Juvenile Court Judge of precisely why he concluded to waive jurisdiction." 119 U.S.App.D.C., at 384, 343 F.2d at 253. While it indicated that "in some cases at least" a useful purpose might be served "by a discussion of the reasons motivating the determination," id., at 384, 343 F.2d, at 253, n. 6, it did not conclude that the absence thereof invalidated the waiver.

As to the denial of access to the social records, the Court of Appeals stated that "the statute is ambiguous." It said that petitioner's claim, in essence, is "that counsel should have the opportunity to challenge them, presumably in a manner akin to cross-examination." Id., at 389, 343 F.2d, at 258. It held, however, that this is "the kind of adversarial tactics which the system is designed to avoid."

It characterized counsel's proper function as being merely that of bringing forward affirmative information which might help the court. His function, the Court of Appeals said, "is not to denigrate the staff's submissions and recommendations." Ibid. Accordingly, it held that the Juvenile Court had not abused its discretion in denying access to the social records.

We are of the opinion that the Court of Appeals misconceived the basic issue and the underlying values in this case. It did note, as another panel of the same court did a few months later in Black and Watkins, that the determination of whether to transfer a child from the statutory structure of the Juvenile Court to the criminal processes of the District Court is "critically important." We hold that it is, indeed, a "critically important" proceeding. The Juvenile Court Act confers upon the child a right to avail himself of that court's "exclusive" jurisdiction. As the Court of Appeals has said, "[I]t is implicit in [the Juvenile Court] scheme that noncriminal treatment is to be the rule—and the adult criminal treatment, the exception which must be governed by the particular factors of individual cases." Harling v. United States, 111 U.S.App.D.C. 174, 177—178, 295 F.2d 161, 164—165 (1961).

Meaningful review requires that the reviewing court should review. It should not be remitted to assumptions. It must have before it a statement of the reasons motivating the waiver including, of course, a statement of the relevant facts. It may not "assume" that there are adequate reasons, nor may it merely assume that "full investigation" has been made. Accordingly, we hold that it is incumbent upon the Juvenile Court to accompany its waiver order with a statement of the reasons or considerations therefor. We do not read the statute as requiring that this statement must be formal or that it should necessarily include conventional findings of fact. But the statement should be sufficient to demonstrate that the statutory requirement of "full investigation" has been met; and that the question has received the careful consideration of the Juvenile Court; and it must set forth the basis for the order with sufficient specificity to permit meaningful review.

Correspondingly, we conclude that an opportunity for a hearing which may be informal, must be given the child prior to entry of a waiver order. Under Black, the child is entitled to counsel in connection with a waiver proceeding, and under Watkins, counsel is entitled to see the child's social records. These rights are meaningless—an illusion, a mockery—unless counsel is given an opportunity to function.

The right to representation by counsel is not a formality. It is not a grudging gesture to a ritualistic requirement. It is of the essence of justice. Appointment of counsel without affording an opportunity for hearing on a "critically important" decision is tantamount to denial of counsel. There is no justification for the failure of the Juvenile Court to rule on the motion for hearing filed by petitioner's counsel, and it was error to fail to grant a hearing.

We do not mean by this to indicate that the hearing to be held must conform with all of the requirements of a criminal trial or even of the usual administrative hearing; but we do hold that the hearing must measure up to the essentials of due process and fair treatment.

With respect to access by the child's counsel to the social records of the child, we deem it obvious that since these are to be considered by the Juvenile Court in making its decision to waive, they must be made available to the child's counsel. This is what the Court of Appeals itself held in Watkins. There is no doubt as to the statutory basis for this conclusion, as the Court of Appeals pointed out in Watkins. We cannot agree with the Court of Appeals in the present case that the statute is "ambiguous." The statute expressly provides that the record shall be withheld from "indiscriminate" public inspection, "except that such records or parts thereof *shall* be made available by rule of court or special order of court to such persons * * * as have a *legitimate interest* in the protection * * * of the child * * *." D.C.Code § 11—929(b) (1961), now § 11—1586(b) (Supp. IV, 1965). (Emphasis supplied.)[30] The Court of Appeals has held in Black, and we agree, that counsel must be afforded to the child in waiver proceedings. Counsel, therefore, have a "legitimate interest" in the protection of the child, and must be afforded access to these records.[31]

We do not agree with the Court of Appeals' statement, attempting to justify denial of access to these records, that counsel's role is limited to presenting "to the court anything on behalf of the child which might help the court in arriving at a decision; it is not to denigrate the staff's submissions and recommendations." On the contrary, if the staff's submissions include materials which are susceptible to challenge or impeachment, it is precisely the role of counsel to "denigrate" such matter. There is no irrebuttable presumption of accuracy attached to staff reports. If a decision on waiver is "critically important" it is equally of "critical importance" that the material submitted to the judge—which is protected by the statute only against "indiscriminate" inspection—be subjected, within reasonable limits having regard to the theory of the Juvenile Court Act, to examination, criticism and refutation. While the Juvenile Court judge may, of course, receive *ex parte* analyses and recommendations from his staff, he may not, for purposes of a decision on waiver, receive and rely upon secret information, whether emanating from his staff or otherwise. The Juvenile Court is governed in this respect by the established principles which control courts and quasi-judicial agencies of the Government.

For the reasons stated, we conclude that the Court of Appeals and the District Court erred in sustaining the validity of the waiver by the Juvenile Court. The Government urges that any error com-

30. Under the statute, the Juvenile Court has power by rule or order, to subject the examination of the social records to conditions which will prevent misuse of the information. Violation of any such rule or order, or disclosure of the information "except for purposes for which * * * released," is a misdemeanor. D.C.Code § 11—929 (1961), now, without substantial change, § 11—1586 (Supp. IV, 1965).
31. In Watkins, the Court of Appeals seems to have permitted withholding of some portions of the social record from examination by petitioner's counsel. To the extent that Watkins is inconsistent with the standard which we state, it cannot be considered as controlling.

mitted by the Juvenile Court was cured by the proceedings before the District Court. It is true that the District Court considered and denied a motion to dismiss on the grounds of the invalidity of the waiver order of the Juvenile Court, and that it considered and denied a motion that it should itself, as authorized by statute, proceed in this case to "exercise the powers conferred upon the juvenile court." D.C.Code § 11—914 (1961), now § 11—1553 (Supp. IV, 1965). But we agree with the Court of Appeals in Black, that "the waiver question was primarily and initially one for the Juvenile Court to decide and its failure to do so in a valid manner cannot be said to be harmless error. It is the Juvenile Court, not the District Court, which has the facilities, personnel and expertise for a proper determination of the waiver issue." 122 U.S.App.D.C., at 396, 355 F.2d, at 107.[32]

Ordinarily we would reverse the Court of Appeals and direct the District Court to remand the case to the Juvenile Court for a new determination of waiver. If on remand the decision were against waiver, the indictment in the District Court would be dismissed. See Black v. United States, supra. However, petitioner has now passed the age of 21 and the Juvenile Court can no longer exercise jurisdiction over him. In view of the unavailability of a redetermination of the waiver question by the Juvenile Court, it is urged by petitioner that the conviction should be vacated and the indictment dismissed. In the circumstances of this case, and in light of the remedy which the Court of Appeals fashioned in Black, supra, we do not consider it appropriate to grant this drastic relief.   Accordingly, we vacate the order of the Court of Appeals and the judgment of the District Court and remand the case to the District Court for a hearing *de novo* on waiver, consistent with this opinion.   If that court finds that waiver was inappropriate, petitioner's conviction must be vacated. If, however, it finds that the waiver order was proper when originally made, the District Court may proceed, after consideration of such motions as counsel may make and such further proceedings, if any, as may be warranted, to enter an appropriate judgment. Cf. Black v. United States, supra.

Reversed and remanded.

---

32. It also appears that the District Court requested and obtained the Social Service file and the probation staff's report of September 8, 1961, and that these were made available to petitioner's counsel. This did not cure the error of the Juvenile Court. Perhaps the point of it is that it again illustrates the maxim that while nondisclosure may contribute to the comfort of the staff, disclosure does not cause heaven to fall.

D | The Winship Decision

IN RE WINSHIP

Supreme Court of the United States, 1970.
397 U.S. 358, 90 S.Ct. 1068, 25 L.Ed.2d 368.

Mr. Justice Brennan delivered the opinion of the Court.

Constitutional questions decided by this Court concerning the juvenile process have centered on the adjudicatory stage at "which a determination is made as to whether a juvenile is a 'delinquent' as a result of alleged misconduct on his part, with the consequence that he may be committed to a state institution." In re Gault, 387 U.S. 1, 13, 87 S.Ct. 1428, 1436, 18 L.Ed.2d 527 (1967). *Gault* decided that, although the Fourteenth Amendment does not require that the hearing at this stage conform with all the requirements of a criminal trial or even of the usual administrative proceeding, the Due Process Clause does require application during the adjudicatory hearing of "the essentials of due process and fair treatment." * * * This case presents the single, narrow question whether proof beyond a reasonable doubt is among the "essentials of due process and fair treatment" required during the adjudicatory stage when a juvenile is charged with an act which would constitute a crime if committed by an adult.[16]

16. Thus, we do not see how it can be said in dissent that this opinion "rests entirely on the assumption that all juvenile proceedings are 'criminal prosecutions,' hence subject to constitutional limitations." As in *Gault*, "we are not here concerned with * * * the pre-judicial stages of the juvenile process, nor do we direct our attention to the post-adjudicative or dispositional process." * * * In New York, the adjudicatory stage of a delinquency proceeding is clearly distinct from both the preliminary phase of the juvenile process and from its dispositional stage. * * * Similarly, we intimate no view concerning the constitutionality of the New York Procedures governing children "in need of supervision." * * * Nor do we consider whether there are other "elements of due process and fair treatment" required during the adjudicatory hearing of a delinquency proceeding. Finally, we have no occasion to consider appellant's argument that § 744(b) is a violation of the Equal Protection Clause, as well as a denial of due process.

Section 712 of the New York Family Court Act defines a juvenile delinquent as "a person over seven and less than sixteen years of age who does any act which, if done by an adult, would constitute a crime." During a 1967 adjudicatory hearing, conducted pursuant to § 742 of the Act, a judge in New York Family Court found that appellant, then a 12-year-old boy, had entered a locker and stolen $112 from a woman's pocketbook. The petition which charged appellant with delinquency alleged that his act, "if done by an adult, would constitute the crime or crimes of Larceny." The judge acknowledged that the proof might not establish guilt beyond a reasonable doubt, but rejected appellant's contention that such proof was required by the Fourteenth Amendment. The judge relied instead on § 744(b) of the New York Family Court Act which provides that "[a]ny determination at the conclusion of [an adjudicatory] hearing that a [juvenile] did an act or acts must be based on a preponderance of the evidence."[17] During a subsequent dispositional hearing, appellant was ordered placed in a training school for an initial period of 18 months, subject to annual extensions of his commitment until his 18th birthday—six years in appellant's case. The Appellate Division of the New York Supreme Court, First Judicial District, affirmed without opinion * * * The New York Court of Appeals then affirmed by a four-to-three vote, expressly sustaining the constitutionality of § 744(b), 24 N.Y.2d 196, 299 N.Y.S.2d 414, 247 N.E.2d 253 (1969). We noted probable jurisdiction. * * * We reverse.

[In the portion of the opinion omitted here, the Court concluded that the "proof beyond a reasonable doubt" standard was constitutionally mandated in criminal cases.]

---

17. The ruling appears in the following portion of the hearing transcript:

Counsel: "Your Honor is making a finding by the preponderance of the evidence."

Court: "Well, it convinces me."

Counsel: "It's not beyond a reasonable doubt, Your Honor."

Court: "That is true * * * Our statute says a preponderance and a preponderance it is."

II.

We turn to the question of whether juveniles, like adults, are constitutionally entitled to proof beyond a reasonable doubt when they are charged with violation of a criminal law. The same considerations which demand extreme caution in factfinding to protect the innocent adult apply as well to the innocent child. We do not find convincing the contrary arguments of the New York Court of Appeals; *Gault* rendered untenable much of the reasoning relied upon by that court to sustain the constitutionality of § 744(b). The Court of Appeals indicated that a delinquency adjudication "is not a 'conviction' (§ 781); that it affects no right or privilege, including the right to hold public office or to obtain a license (§ 782); and a cloak of protective confidentiality is thrown around all the proceedings (§ § 783–784)." * * * The court said further: "The delinquency status is not made a crime; and the proceedings are not criminal. There is, hence, no deprivation of due process in the statutory provision [challenged by appellant] * * *," * * * In effect the Court of Appeals distinguished the proceedings in question here from a criminal prosecution by use of what *Gault* called the " 'civil' label-of-convenience which has been attached to juvenile proceedings." * * * But *Gault* expressly rejected that distinction as a reason for holding the Due Process Clause inapplicable to a juvenile proceeding. * * * The Court of Appeals also attempted to justify the preponderance standard on the related ground that juvenile proceedings are designed "not to punish, but to save the child." * * * Again, however, *Gault* expressly rejected this justification. * * * We made clear in that decision that civil labels and good intentions do not themselves obviate the need for criminal due process safeguards in juvenile courts, for "[a] proceeding where the issue is whether the child will be found to be 'delinquent' and subjected to the loss of his liberty for years is comparable in seriousness to a felony prosecution."* * *

Nor do we perceive any merit in the argument that to afford juveniles the protection of proof beyond a reasonable doubt would risk destruction of beneficial aspects of the juvenile process. Use of the reasonable-doubt standard during the adjudicatory hearing will not disturb New York's policies that a finding that a child has violated a criminal law does not constitute a criminal conviction, that such a finding does not deprive the child of his civil rights, and that juvenile proceedings are confidential. Nor will there be any effect on the informality, flexibility, or speed of the hearing at which the fact-finding takes place. And the opportunity during the post-adjudicatory or dispositional hearing for a wide-ranging review of the child's social history and for his individualized treatment will remain unimpaired. Similarly, there will be no effect on the procedures distinctive to juvenile proceedings which are employed prior to the adjudicatory hearing.

The Court of Appeals observed that "a child's best interest is not necessarily, or even probably, promoted if he wins in the particular inquiry which may bring him to the juvenile court." * * * It is true, of course, that the juvenile may be engaging in a general course of conduct inimical to his welfare which calls for judicial intervention. But that intervention cannot take the form of subjecting the child to the stigma of a finding that he violated a criminal law[18] and to the possibility of institutional confinement on proof insufficient to convict him were he an adult.

We conclude, as we concluded regarding the essential due process safeguards applied in *Gault,* that the observance of the standard of proof beyond a reasonable doubt "will not compel the States to abandon or displace any of the substantive benefits of the juvenile process." Finally, we reject the Court of Appeals' suggestion that there is, in any event, only a "tenuous difference" between the reasonable-doubt and preponderance standards. The suggestion is singularly unpersuasive. In this very case, the trial judge's ability to distinguish between the two standards enabled him to make a finding of guilt which he conceded he might not have made under the standard of proof beyond a reasonable doubt. Indeed, the trial judge's action evidences the accuracy of the observation of commentators that "the preponderance test is susceptible to the misinterpretation that it calls on the trier of fact merely to perform an abstract weighing of the evidence in order to determine which side has produced the greater quantum, without regard to its effect in convincing his mind of the truth of the proposition asserted." * * *

---

18. The more comprehensive and effective the procedures used to prevent public disclosure of the finding, the less the danger of stigma. As we indicated in *Gault,* however, often the "claim of secrecy * * * is more rhetoric than reality."

III.

In sum, the constitutional safeguard of proof beyond a reasonable doubt is as much required during the adjudicatory stage of a delinquency proceeding as are those constitutional safeguards applied in *Gault*—notice of charges, right to counsel, the rights of confrontation and examination, and the privilege against self-incrimination. We therefore hold, in agreement with Chief Judge Fuld in dissent in the Court of Appeals, "that, where a 12-year-old child is charged with an act of stealing which renders him liable to confinement for as long as six years, then, as a matter of due process * * * the case against him must be proved beyond a reasonable doubt." * * *

Reversed.

Mr. Justice Harlan, concurring.

No one, I daresay, would contend that state juvenile court trials are subject to *no* federal constitutional limitations. Differences have existed, however, among the members of this Court as to *what* constitutional protections do apply. * * *

The present case draws in question the validity of a New York statute which permits a determination of juvenile delinquency, founded on a charge of criminal conduct, to be made on a standard of proof which is less rigorous than that which would obtain had the accused been tried for the same conduct in an ordinary criminal case. While I am in full agreement that this statutory provision offends the requirement of fundamental fairness embodied in the Due Process Clause oɩ the Fourteenth Amendment, I am constrained to add something to what my Brother Brennan has written for the Court, lest the true nature of the constitutional problem presented become obscured or the impact on state juvenile court systems of what the Court holds today be exaggerated.

I.

Professor Wigmore, in discussing the various attempts by courts to define how convinced one must be to be convinced beyond a reasonable doubt, wryly observed: "The truth is that no one has yet invented or discovered a mode of measurement for the intensity of human belief. Hence there can be yet no successful method of communicating intelligently * * * a sound method of self-analysis for one's beliefs," 9 Wigmore, Evidence 325 (1940).

Notwithstanding Professor Wigmore's skepticism, we have before us a case where the choice of the standard of proof has made a difference: the juvenile judge below forthrightly acknowledged that he believed by a preponderance of the evidence, but was not convinced beyond a reasonable doubt, that appellant stole $112 from the complainant's pocketbook. Moreover, even though the labels used for alternative standards of proof are vague and not a very sure guide to decisionmaking, the choice of the standard for a particular variety of adjudication does, I think, reflect a very fundamental assessment of the comparative social costs of erroneous factual determinations.

To explain why I think this so, I begin by stating two propositions, neither of which I believe can be fairly disputed. First, in a judicial proceeding in which there is a dispute about the facts of some earlier event, the factfinder cannot acquire unassailably accurate knowledge of what happened. Instead, all the factfinder can acquire is a belief of what *probably* happened. The intensity of this belief—the degree to which a factfinder is convinced that a given act actually occurred—can, of course, vary. In this regard, a standard of proof represents an attempt to instruct the factfinder concerning the degree of confidence our society thinks he should have in the correctness of factual conclusions for a particular type of adjudication. Although the phrases "preponderance of the evidence" and "proof beyond a reasonable doubt" are quantitatively imprecise, they do communicate to the finder of fact different notions concerning the degree of confidence he is expected to have in the correctness of his factual conclusions.

A second proposition, which is really nothing more than a corollary of the first, is that the trier of fact will sometimes, despite his best efforts, be wrong in his factual conclusions. In a lawsuit between two parties, a factual error can make a difference in one of two ways. First, it can result in a judgment in favor of the plaintiff when the true facts warrant a judgment for the defendant. The analogue in a criminal case would be the conviction of an innocent man. On the other hand, an erroneous factual determination can result in a judgment for the defendant when the true facts justify a judgment in plaintiff's favor. The criminal analogue would be the acquittal of a guilty man.

The standard of proof influences the relative frequency of these two types of erroneous outcomes. If, for example, the standard of proof for a criminal trial were a preponderance of the evidence rather than proof beyond a reasonable doubt, there would be a smaller risk of factual errors that result in freeing guilty persons, but a far greater risk of factual errors that result in convicting the innocent. Because the standard of proof affects the comparative frequency of these two types of erroneous outcomes, the choice of the standard to be applied in a particular kind of litigation should, in a rational world, reflect an assessment of the comparative social disutility of each.

When one makes such an assessment, the reason for different standards of proof in civil as opposed to criminal litigation becomes apparent. In a civil suit between two private parties for money damages, for example, we view it as no more serious in general for there to be an erroneous verdict in the defendant's favor than for there to be an erroneous verdict in the plaintiff's favor. A preponderance of the evidence standard therefore seems peculiarly appropriate for, as explained most sensibly, it simply requires the trier of fact "to believe that the existence of a fact is more probable than its nonexistence before [he] may find in favor of the party who has the burden to persuade the [judge] of the fact's existence."

In a criminal case, on the other hand, we do not view the social disutility of convicting an innocent man as equivalent to the disutility of acquitting someone who is guilty. As Mr. Justice Brennan wrote for the Court in Speiser v. Randall, 357 U.S. 513, 525—526, 78 S.Ct. 1332, 1341—1342, 2 L.Ed.2d 1460:

> *"There is always in litigation a margin of error, representing error in fact-finding, which both parties must take into account. Where one party has at stake an interest of transcending value—as a criminal defendant his liberty—this margin of error is reduced as to him by the process of placing on the other party the burden * * * of persuading the fact-finder at the conclusion of the trial of his guilt beyond a reasonable doubt."*

In this context, I view the requirement of proof beyond a reasonable doubt in a criminal case as bottomed on a fundamental value determination of our society that it is far worse to convict an innocent man than to let a guilty man go free. It is only because of the nearly complete and long-standing acceptance of the reasonable-doubt standard by the States in criminal trials that the Court has not before today had to hold explicitly that due process, as an expression of fundamental procedural fairness, requires a more stringent standard for criminal trials than for ordinary civil litigation.

II.

When one assesses the consequences of an erroneous factual determination in a juvenile delinquency proceeding in which a youth is accused of a crime, I think it must be concluded that, while the consequences are not identical to those in a criminal case, the differences will not support a distinction in the standard of proof. First, and of paramount importance, a factual error here, as in a criminal case, exposes the accused to a complete loss of his personal liberty through a state-imposed confinement away from his home, family, and friends. And, second, a delinquency determination, to some extent at least, stigmatizes a youth in that it is by definition bottomed on a finding that the accused committed a crime.[19] Although there are no doubt costs to society (and possibly even to the youth himself) in letting a guilty youth go free, I think here, as in a criminal case, it is far worse to declare an innocent youth a delinquent. I therefore agree that a juvenile court judge should be no less convinced of the factual conclusion that the accused committed the criminal act with which he is charged than would be required in a criminal trial.

---

19. The New York statute was amended to distinguish between a "juvenile delinquent"—*i.e.,* a youth "who does any act which, if done by an adult, would constitute a crime," N.Y.Family Ct.Act § 712 (1963), and a "[p]erson in need of supervision" [PINS] who is a person "who is an habitual truant or who is incorrigible, ungovernable or habitually disobedient and beyond the lawful control of parent or other lawful authority." The PINS category was established in order to avoid the stigma of finding someone to be a "juvenile delinquent," unless he committed a criminal act. The Legislative Committee report stated: " 'Juvenile delinquent' is now a term of disapproval. The judges of the Children's Court and the Domestic Relations Court of course are aware of this and also aware that government officials and private employers often learn of an adjudication of delinquency." N.Y.Jt. Legislative Committee on Court Reorganization, The Family Court Act, Pt. 2, at 7 (1962). Moreover, the powers of the police and courts differ in these two categories of cases. See *id.,* at 7—9. Thus, in a PINS type case, the consequences of an erroneous factual determination are by no means identical to those involved here.

III.

I wish to emphasize, as I did in my separate opinion in *Gault,* 387 U.S. 1, 65, 87 S.Ct. 1428, 1463, that there is no automatic congruence between the procedural requirements imposed by due process in a criminal case, and those imposed by due process in juvenile cases.[20] It is of great importance, in my view, that procedural strictures not be constitutionally imposed that jeopardize "the essential elements of the State's purpose" in creating juvenile courts, *id.,* at 72, 87 S.Ct. at 1467. In this regard, I think it worth emphasizing that the requirement of proof beyond a reasonable doubt that a juvenile committed a criminal act before he is found to be a delinquent does not (1) interfere with the worthy goal of rehabilitating the juvenile, (2) make any significant difference in the extent to which a youth is stigmatized as a "criminal" because he has been found to be a delinquent, or (3) burden the juvenile courts with a procedural requirement which will make juvenile adjudications significantly more time consuming, or rigid. Today's decision simply requires a juvenile judge to be more confident in his belief that the youth did the act with which he has been charged.

With these observations, I join the Court's opinion, subject only to the constitutional reservations expressed in my opinion in *Gault.*

Mr. Chief Justice Burger, with whom Mr. Justice Stewart joins, dissenting.

The Court's opinion today rests entirely on the assumption that all juvenile proceedings are "criminal prosecutions," hence subject to constitutional limitations. This derives from earlier holdings, which like today's holding, were steps eroding the differences between juvenile courts and traditional criminal courts. The original concept of the juvenile court system was to provide a benevolent and less formal means than criminal courts could provide for dealing

---

20. In Gault, for example, I agree with the majority that due process required (1) adequate notice of the "nature and terms" of the proceedings; (2) notice of the right to retain counsel, and an obligation on the State to provide counsel for indigents "in cases in which the child may be confined"; and (3) a written record "adequate to permit effective review." 387 U.S., at 72, 87 S.Ct., at 1467. Unlike the majority, however, I thought it unnecessary at the time of *Gault* to impose the additional requirements of the privilege against self-incrimination, confrontation, and cross-examination.

with the special and often sensitive problems of youthful offenders. Since I see no constitutional requirement of due process sufficient to overcome the legislative judgment of the States in this area, I dissent from further strait-jacketing of an already overly-restricted system. What the juvenile court systems need is not more but less of the trappings of legal procedure and judicial formalism; the juvenile system requires breathing room and flexibility in order to survive, if it can survive the repeated assaults from this Court.

Much of the judicial attitude manifested by the Court's opinion today and earlier holdings in this field is really a protest against inadequate juvenile court staffs and facilities; we "burn down the stable to get rid of the mice." The lack of support and the distressing growth of juvenile crime have combined to make for a literal breakdown in many if not most juvenile courts. Constitutional problems were not seen while those courts functioned in an atmosphere where juvenile judges were not crushed with an avalanche of cases.

My hope is that today's decision will not spell the end of a generously conceived program of compassionate treatment intended to mitigate the rigors and trauma of exposing youthful offenders to a traditional criminal court; each step we take turns the clock back to the pre-juvenile court era. I cannot regard it as a manifestation of progress to transform juvenile courts into criminal courts, which is what we are well on the way to accomplishing. We can only hope the legislative response will not reflect our own by having these courts abolished.

Mr. Justice Black, dissenting [omitted].

Index

DATE DUE
REMINDER

MAR 0 9 2007

MAY 0 7 2008

MAY 1 3 2010

**Please do not remove
this date due slip.**